Narrating Rape

Narrating Rape

*Shifting Perspectives in Biblical Literature
and Popular Culture*

Edited by

L. Juliana Claassens,
Rhiannon Graybill,
and Christl M. Maier

© Editors and Contributors 2024
Published in 2024 by SCM Press
Editorial office
3rd Floor, Invicta House,
110 Golden Lane,
London EC1Y 0TG, UK
www.scmpress.co.uk

SCM Press is an imprint of Hymns Ancient & Modern Ltd
(a registered charity)

Hymns Ancient & Modern® is a registered trademark of
Hymns Ancient & Modern Ltd
13A Hellesdon Park Road, Norwich,
Norfolk NR6 5DR, UK

All rights reserved. No part of this publication may be reproduced,
stored in a retrieval system, or transmitted,
in any form or by any means, electronic, mechanical,
photocopying or otherwise, without the prior permission of
the publisher, SCM Press.

The editors and contributors have asserted their right under the Copyright,
Designs and Patents Act 1988 to be identified as the Authors of this Work

Scripture quotations marked NRSVUE are taken from the New Revised Standard Version Updated Edition. Copyright © 2021 National Council of Churches of Christ in the United States of America. Used by permission. All rights reserved worldwide.

Scripture quotations marked NIV UK are taken from The Holy Bible, New International Version (Anglicised edition) copyright © 1979, 1984, 2011 by Biblica (formerly International Bible Society). Used by permission of Hodder & Stoughton Publishers, an Hachette UK company. All rights reserved.

British Library Cataloguing in Publication data
A catalogue record for this book is available
from the British Library

ISBN: 978-0-334-06625-5

Typeset by Regent Typesetting

Contents

Contributors vii
Acknowledgements ix

Introduction: On Narrating Rape 1
L. Juliana Claassens, Rhiannon Graybill and Christl M. Maier

Part 1: Stories of Rape in the Bible and Popular Culture

1 Recovering from Rape? *Lacuna* (Fiona Snyckers) in
  Conversation with Daughter Zion in Isaiah 51.17—52.2 15
  L. Juliana Claassens

2 'Long Since Murdered': Cozbi, *The Kreutzer Sonata*,
  and the Limits of Narrating Sexual Violence 29
  Rhiannon Graybill

3 Consensual Sex or Rape? Bathsheba Encircled by
  Hegemonic Masculinity 48
  Christl M. Maier

4 *Women Talking* and Women Not Talking: Speaking *for* (?)
  in Fiction and Judges 21 63
  Alexiana Fry

5 Filling in the Gaps: Reading Hosea 1—3 with Francine
  Rivers's *Redeeming Love* 83
  Kirsi Cobb

6 Will You Accept This Rose? The Magic Circle in the
  Book of Esther 101
  Steed V. Davidson

7 Rape Jokes, Sexual Violence and Empire in Revelation and
   This Is the End   121
   Meredith J. C. Warren

Part 2: Rape and Sexual Violence in Ancient and Contemporary Contexts

8 Resistance, Rage and Re-enactment: Trauma Responses
   in the Sumerian Rape Narratives   141
   Renate Marian van Dijk-Coombes

9 Things Too Indecent to be Recorded: The Soldiers Mocking
   the Death of Herod Agrippa   157
   David Tombs

10 'Slaves of Christ': Rape Culture in the New Testament   173
   Jeremy Punt

11 'Madoda Sabelani' and Matthew 2.18: Lamenting
   Hegemonic Masculinity   192
   Dewald Jacobs

12 The Poetics of Redacted Absence as Presence: Kin Eyes
   Hearing Tamar (2 Samuel 13)   208
   Gerald O. West

13 Under Rug Swept: Creating Space to Engage the Reality
   of Homophobic Hate Crimes in the South African Faith
   Landscape   225
   Charlene van der Walt

Index of Scriptures and Other Ancient Sources   243
Index of Names and Subjects   249

Contributors

L. Juliana Claassens, Professor of Old Testament and Head of Gender Unit, Faculty of Theology, Stellenbosch University, South Africa.

Kirsi Cobb, Lecturer in Biblical Studies, Cliff College, Hope Valley, United Kingdom.

Steed V. Davidson, Executive Director Society of Biblical Literature; Extraordinary Visiting Professor, Old Testament, Department of Old and New Testament, Stellenbosch University, South Africa.

Alexiana Fry, Postdoctoral Researcher, 'Divergent Views of Diaspora in Ancient Judaism', Faculty of Theology, University of Copenhagen, Denmark.

Rhiannon Graybill, Marcus M. and Carole M. Weinstein & Gilbert M. and Fannie S. Rosenthal Chair of Jewish Studies; Professor of Religious Studies, University of Richmond, Richmond, VA, United States.

Dewald Jacobs, PhD student in New Testament, Faculty of Theology, Stellenbosch University, South Africa.

Christl M. Maier, Professor of Old Testament, Philipps-Universität Marburg, Germany; Extraordinary Professor at the Department of Old and New Testament, Faculty of Theology, Stellenbosch University.

Jeremy Punt, Professor of New Testament, Faculty of Theology, Stellenbosch University, South Africa.

David Tombs, Professor of Theology and Public Issues, University of Otago, Aotearoa New Zealand.

CONTRIBUTORS

Charlene van der Walt, Honorary Associate Professor Gender and Religion, University of KwaZulu-Natal, South Africa.

Renate Marian van Dijk-Coombes, Mellon Foundation-funded Postdoctoral Research Fellow, Department of Ancient and Modern Languages and Cultures, University of Pretoria, South Africa.

Meredith J. C. Warren, Director, Sheffield Centre for Interdisciplinary Biblical Studies; Senior Lecturer, Biblical and Religious Studies, School of English, University of Sheffield, United Kingdom.

Gerald O. West, Emeritus Professor of Old Testament, Ujamaa Centre, School of Religion, Philosophy and Classics, University of KwaZulu-Natal, South Africa.

Acknowledgements

A project such as *Narrating Rape* is truly a labour of love. Not only does it reflect the vision of three Hebrew Bible colleagues from different parts of the world, connected by shared passions and research interests which evolved into friendship, but also of a group of scholars, students, church leaders and societal partners from around the world who increasingly are drawn to the task of finding other ways of reading: reading biblical literature in conjunction with other texts, and reading in the hope of bringing about change.

As editors, we would like to thank several people who played a pivotal role in shepherding this collection of essays from the original Gender Unit conference, hosted at the Faculty of Stellenbosch in March 2023, to publication.

We are grateful for the ongoing support of Stellenbosch University and, in particular, the Faculty of Theology for the work we do in the Gender Unit which seeks to create spaces for thought-provoking interdisciplinary research that explores the intersections between gender, race, class and sexual identity. This research not only advances knowledge in these crucial areas, but also empowers students and members of the community to assume the role of thought leaders and change agents in a wide variety of communities within South Africa and beyond.

We want to recognize Estelle Muller, Melicia Adams, Simba Pondani, Tannie Minnie Philander, Joseph Fillies, Kara Hutten and Zandré Marais, who provided invaluable administrative assistance before and during the conference, and Alexandra Banks for compiling the indexes for this volume.

We want to thank SCM Press, Rachel Geddes, Linda Carroll, Kate Hughes, and especially David Shervington, for their dedication to bringing our rich conversations during the Narrating Rape Gender Unit conference to a global audience (cf. also the 2022 Gender Unit conference *Queering the Prophet* which was also published by SCM Press in 2023). We are looking forward to seeing how these conversations continue to unfold.

ACKNOWLEDGEMENTS

We are grateful that many women and men found the courage to speak out about toxic individuals and systems that have violated the bodies and souls of so many women and men. This is exemplified in the 2022 film *She Said*, which documents the persistence of two journalists in creating safe spaces for women to share their experiences of abuse at the hands of a powerful movie executive (cf. Christl Maier's engagement with this film in her contribution to this volume). However, we also know that for every woman who finds the courage to speak, hundreds and thousands are still silenced and their stories are not told or told in ways that do more harm than good. We dedicate this book to ongoing efforts to narrate rape in a way that makes the world safer for our daughters, our students, and our nieces and nephews to come.

Juliana Claassens
Rhiannon Graybill
Christl Maier

Stellenbosch / Richmond / Marburg
23 July 2024

Introduction: On Narrating Rape

L. JULIANA CLAASSENS, RHIANNON GRAYBILL AND CHRISTL M. MAIER

Why is it that so many stories of rape avoid or speak around the very topic they set forth to address? One name that is given to such absences in narrative is *lacuna*. A lacuna is a gap, a hiatus, an absence. The word in English comes from Latin, where it has the meaning of a hole or pit and is related to the word *lacus*, lake. And like the glassy surface of a calm summer lake, this lacuna often hides something in its seeming absence.

Lacuna is also the title of Fiona Snyckers's feminist rewriting (2022) of J. M. Coetzee's acclaimed (though contested) novel *Disgrace* (2017, original publication 1999). *Disgrace*, which won the Booker Prize in 1999 (with the Nobel following for Coetzee four years later), tells the story of David Lurie, a white professor at the fictional Constantia University in Cape Town, South Africa. After a disastrous affair with a student (which well might amount to rape) and the subsequent administrative proceedings, Lurie is fired and goes to stay with his daughter Lucy at her farmhouse on the Eastern Cape. While Lurie is present, Lucy is raped by a group of strangers, who also attempt to kill her father by setting fire to him. Though crucial to the plot, Lucy Lurie's rape is a lacuna in the narrative – an event that defines the plot, but one that is never narrated. Coetzee is less interested in Lucy's rape as a rape than as a symbol, one that captures the trauma associated with geopolitical upheaval in post-apartheid South Africa. Insofar as the novel narrates rape, it is a political symbol, even as a real raped body lies at the novel's centre.

In *Lacuna*, Snyckers's protagonist is also named Lucy Lurie. This Lucy is at once the same Lucy as in Coetzee's novel, but also someone very different. Snyckers's novel explores the possibilities for Lucy to talk back and reclaim her own story, critiquing the narrative portrayal of what she describes as Fictional Lucy and the many (mis)perceptions regarding rape and its aftermath that find expression in *Disgrace*. In an intriguing dialogue between Lucy (here imagined to be Coetzee's junior colleague) and Essie September, a senior professor in Women's Studies in Literature, Professor September reflects on 'why it is okay that [Lucy's] rape is the one part in Coetzee's book that goes undescribed':

> 'It's a lacuna, Lucy. You remember what that means?'
> 'An unfilled space. A gap.' Ever the good student, I parrot the definition.
> 'Then you know the power of the lacuna in literary fiction. The absence of something can be more powerful than its presence.' (Snyckers, 2022, pp. 71–2)

And yet, as the two women continue to reflect on the meaning of this lacuna in narrating rape, it soon becomes evident that there are multiple perspectives associated with how the story of Lucy Lurie's rape is told, and to what purpose. Professor September contends that:

> By omitting the actual assault, Coetzee creates a performative situation in which his text mimics the very tendency of Western society to turn a blind eye towards rape. It is a powerful critique of exactly what concerns you. (Snyckers, 2022, p. 72)

When pushed, Professor September further suggests that Coetzee did not narrate the rape as he 'chose to spare you that. He didn't allow your assault to become a spectacle.' To this, Lucy retorts:

> It occurs to me that she can't have it both ways. Either he was trying to make the violence of the rape extra powerful by turning it into a kind of howling black hole in the middle of the text, or he was being sensitive and sparing my feelings by toning the whole thing down. (Snyckers, 2022, p. 72)

This imaginative engagement raises several intriguing questions regarding the possibility or inability to recount the violence of rape and, in particular, what is at stake in narrating rape.

Just as Snyckers's Lucy challenges 'J. M. Coetzee' (the character, the real-life inspiration, and the patriarchal academic power structures he represents), so too have feminist scholars challenged the ways that rape is narrated in the Bible, and in biblical scholarship (see, among others, Trible, 1984; Exum, 1993; Weems, 1995; Schüssler Fiorenza, 2001; Scholz, 2010). Often, these feminist challenges have begun by noticing, and seeking to fill in, the lacunas that surround biblical rape stories. The

INTRODUCTION

chapters included in this volume continue this work, participating in a larger project of feminist and activist responses to biblical and biblically informed sexual violence.

Sexual violence in and around the Bible

Rape and sexual violence are pervasive in the Hebrew Bible (Scholz, 2010; Graybill, 2021). Perhaps the most famous stories of rape are the rape of Dinah (Gen. 34) and of Tamar (2 Sam. 13), as well as the collective rape and murder of the nameless woman known as the Levite's concubine (Judg. 19—21). But these are far from the only victims, or the only rape stories. Genesis alone contains a number of stories of rape, sexual violence and sexualized harm beyond Dinah's rape: the violation or rape of Noah by Ham (Gen. 9), the rape threats against the divine messengers in Sodom (Gen. 19), the rape of Lot by his daughters (or perhaps of his daughters by Lot, Gen. 19.30–38), the threat of sexual exploitation against Sarah in Egypt (Gen. 12), the sexual abuse of enslaved women (Gen. 16; 30—31), the sexual deception of Judah by Tamar (Gen. 38), the accusation of rape against Joseph by Potiphar's wife (Gen. 39). Nor does the sexual violence come to an end with Genesis. The so-called David story, which includes the rape of David's daughter Tamar (2 Sam. 13; see also West, Chapter 12 in this volume), also gives us the rape or exploitation of Bathsheba at David's hands (2 Sam. 11; see also Maier, Chapter 3 in this volume), as well as Absalom's public raping of David's concubines (2 Sam. 16.20–23). Sexual violence against defeated and detained persons is a key feature of biblical warfare (not unlike modern warfare); the biblical text even includes laws regulating how long before it is permissible to have sex with a female war captive (Deut. 21.10–13). The kidnapping of women for forced marriage and mass rape is attested in Judges 20—21 and alluded to elsewhere in the texts (see also Fry, Chapter 4 in this volume). The prophetic books, meanwhile, imagine sexual violence, including stripping, exposure and assault, as forms of punishment against metaphorical women, whose bodies represent cities and nations (Jerusalem in Jer. 13.20-27; Ezek. 16.36-42; 23.9–29; Nineveh in Nahum 3.5–7; Babylon in Isa. 47.3; Jer. 50.41–46; Israel in Hos. 2.10). Daughter Zion, a personified representation of the people in the form of a woman, is likewise figured as a rape victim in the book of Lamentations (see Claassens, Chapter 1 in this volume).

Biblical representations of sexual violence are informed by the text's larger ideas about gender, sex and sexuality. In the world of the Hebrew

Bible, women are not understood to be agents or subjects with control over their own sexuality. Instead, female sexuality 'belongs' to a man, either a father, brother or husband. In the case of a woman's rape, the 'victim' is not the woman, but rather the responsible male. Biblical laws also set out basic understandings about which sorts of sex constitute sex crimes: sex between a man and a married woman, regardless of her consent, is regarded as adultery and both parties are punished with death (Deut. 22.22). The only exception is when the sexual encounter occurs in a field, where a woman would be unable to be heard if she cried for help; in this case, she is considered innocent and not punished (Deut. 22.25–27). Sex between a man and an unmarried woman, in contrast, results only in a fine and the expectation that the man marries the woman (Deut. 22.28–29). A woman accused of adultery may also be subjected to the Sotah ritual (Num. 5.11–31), forced to drink a potion that will radically transform and deform her body – in sexual ways – if she is judged 'guilty'.

As the above summary suggests, most of the sexual violence in the Hebrew Bible is perpetrated by men against women (or, in the case of the marriage metaphor, by a male god against a feminized Israel or foreign nation). There are, however, occasional references to sexual violence against men (Greenough, 2021). The fear of male rape by other men motivates the violence at Sodom (Gen. 19), as well as in the story of the Levite's concubine (Judg. 19; cf. Harding, 2016). Sexual humiliation and violation are tactics used against male captives in warfare, as attested by both biblical texts and evidence from material culture (e.g. Kelle, 2008; Smith-Christopher, 2004; Magdalene, 1995). Very occasionally in the text, men may be the object of sexual violence by women; this is one possible reading of Lot and his daughters (Gen. 19.30–38; cf. Lehmann, 2024).

Like the Hebrew Bible, the New Testament is also filled with sexual violence. Perhaps most egregious is the book of Revelation (see also Warren, Chapter 7 in this volume), which adopts and amplifies some of the most sexually violent images from the Hebrew prophets. The Whore of Babylon is subjected to outrageous violence, including sexualized violence, before being murdered (Rev. 17—18). Nor is this violence limited to metaphorical or symbolic entities: John of Patmos, Revelation's narrator and purported author, also threatens sexual violence against a rival religious leader, a woman he calls only 'Jezebel' (Rev. 2.19–24). By threatening to throw Jezebel on a bed (Rev. 2.22), John, in effect, threatens to rape her.

Sexual violence in the New Testament is not limited to Revelation. Paul makes use of vice lists and other sexually charged rhetoric across his epistles (cf. Rom. 1.18–32; 1 Cor. 6.9–10), mobilizing rhetorical sexual violence in the service of theology. The Gospels, meanwhile, also include suggestions of sexual violence, such as in the representation of the woman accused of adultery (John 8.1–11; cf. Knust, 2017), and in the violence of the crucifixion scene (Tombs, 2021). It has sometimes been suggested that Mary, Jesus' mother, is a victim of sexual exploitation or rape (Schaberg, 2006, p. 58; Daly, 1990, p. 85; see also the discussion in Jacob, 2015, pp. 76–89). More recent scholarship has also attended to Jesus, suggesting that he may have been a victim of sexual violence, both in the Praetorium and on the cross. David Tombs, who has contributed Chapter 9 in this volume, is at the forefront of this work (see, for example, Reaves, Tombs and Figueroa, 2021). The world of the New Testament – Roman-occupied Palestine – was also a world in which sexual violence was pervasive, as numerous scholars have shown (including Punt in this volume). It is thus not surprising that early Christian literature is full of narratives of sexual violence and rape (Cobb and Vanden Eykel, 2022).

Rape culture and narrating rape

This prevalence of sexual violence in the Hebrew Bible and its ancient Near Eastern context, the New Testament and other early Christian literature has led scholars to suggest that one can speak of a 'rape culture' (Washington, 1997, p. 352). In our contemporary context, the term 'rape culture' has become an increasingly popular way to explain why heteronormative violence against women seems to have been normalized. Alisa Kessel (2022) helpfully outlines how this term emerged in the mid-1970s, became more mainstream in the 1990s, and exploded after 2010. Traditionally, rape culture helped to move the conversation beyond individual acts of gender-based violence to a 'culture that fosters discourses and practices beyond rape itself (such as street harassment, romanticization of manipulation and violence, and normalization of "appropriate" styles of dress) that reinforce the ubiquitous threat of rape and regulate the behavior of women' (Kessel, 2022, p. 131; cf. also Sheffield, 2020, p. 192). However, in terms of an intersectional understanding of gender, there has been a widespread call to expand the meaning of rape culture to not only include violence against women that is inflicted by men. With this in mind, Kessel (2022, p. 132) defines a 'rape culture' to include a 'set of intersubjective and collectively reproduced myths, discourses, and practices ... that normalizes rape and other sexual violence as an effective ... way to reinforce relations of subordination ... to *any* group that threatens' the control by 'white heteropatriarchy'.

Particularly relevant for this project, 'these myths, discourses, and practices of a rape culture' are, according to Kessel (2022, p. 132), 'represented in film and television; ... literature; music; and memes, tweets, and other digital media'. The chapters in *Narrating Rape* contemplate how the very retellings of the respective rape stories contribute to the formation of rape culture. As evident in the previous section, in the numerous stories of rape in the Bible and its world, the stories one tells regarding sexual violence from time immemorial, as well as in contemporary forms of literature as evident in literature, film, poetry and reality TV, individually and collectively contribute to the shaping of a world in which rape is normalized.

Central to this project is the call to challenge rape culture in contemporary culture, by identifying it in rape narratives from antiquity, to, as Kessel (2022, p. 132) proposes, 'expose the ways that cultural mythologies and discourses about rape are reproduced through everyday practices to sustain a culture in which sexual violence is a persistent mode of domination'. The chapters in *Narrating Rape* similarly reflect the way stories regarding rape shape culture – in antiquity, but also in the various communities in which we live and work, and for whom we write. In particular, the engagement between the Bible and various forms of popular culture helps many of the authors to reflect on the various ways in which stories of rape are told across time and space. These chapters are united in the understanding that these narrative and poetic accounts in both the ancient literature, as well as in contemporary examples of literature, film, poetry and reality TV, are shaped by the respective cultures they represent, but also how these stories narrating sexual violence in turn contribute to the shaping of a rape culture in which violence against women and other vulnerable entities is tolerated.

Finally, important to note for the purpose of this book, as well as for future work that might be done in this area, is Kessel's emphasis on expanding the meaning and significance of rape culture to include all forms of subjugation that also include attention to the role of class, ethnicity and sexual orientation in terms of the way gender-based violence is inflicted and narrated. In this volume, especially the chapters by Davidson, West, Jacobs, and van der Walt move in this direction. However, one can imagine that further work exploring the intersections of gender, race, class, sexual orientation and social location is necessary, and pressing.

INTRODUCTION

About the chapters

The contributors in this volume hail from a variety of nationalities, four continents, and include emerging scholars as well as leading voices in the field. They engage with a wide range of biblical texts and an even wider range of works in popular culture. What unites the chapters in *Narrating Rape*, beyond their focus on sexual violence in biblical texts, is a shared commitment to finding new ways of reading, processing and pushing back against rape and rape culture in biblical texts – and against their histories of interpretation and reception. Like Snyckers's Lucy Lurie, they name and challenge the *lacuna*.

The following chapters are divided into two parts. Part 1 focuses on 'Stories of Rape in the Bible and Popular Culture'. The seven chapters in this section all use literature (in the case of Claassens, Graybill, Fry, Maier and Cobb), film (Fry, Maier, Cobb and Warren) and television (Davidson) as hermeneutic lenses to approach biblical rape stories. In 'Recovering from Rape? *Lacuna* (Fiona Snyckers) in Conversation with Daughter Zion in Isaiah 51.17—52.2' (Chapter 1), Juliana Claassens stages an in-depth conversation between Snyckers's novel and the rape of Daughter Zion, a personified woman/daughter/city found in the biblical books of Lamentations and Deutero-Isaiah. Claassens's focus is on the aftermath of rape, and how we might narrate stories of trauma and survival. Trauma (though without survival) is also the focus of Rhiannon Graybill's chapter, '"Long Since Murdered": Cozbi, *The Kreutzer Sonata*, and the Limits of Narrating Sexual Violence' (Chapter 2). Like Claassens, Graybill pairs a biblical text – here Numbers 25, the story of the sexualized murder of the Midianite woman Cozbi – with a literary work, here Lev Tolstoy's *The Kreutzer Sonata*. Both texts are stories of male jealousy and fatal violence, with devastating consequences for innocent women. Graybill constellates these two texts with a series of related writings, including a rival novella by Tolstoy's wife, Sofiya Andreevna Tolstaya, Tolstaya's diaries and memoir, and radical feminist Andrea Dworkin's influential reading of Tolstoy in *Intercourse*. By reading literary and para-literary texts together, Graybill helps us conceptualize the project of narrating rape, which lies at the heart of this book.

Christl Maier brings to the project of narrating rape a particular focus on masculinity and its role in sustaining sexual violence. And who in the Bible represents hegemonic masculinity better than King David? This is the focus of 'Consensual Sex or Rape? Bathsheba Encircled by Hegemonic Masculinity' (Chapter 3). Maier approaches David through the sociological theory of hegemonic masculinity (associated most closely with the work of Raewyn Connell) and through a persuasive contemporary parallel to the biblical king: disgraced Hollywood producer and kingmaker Harvey Weinstein. Drawing on the 2022 film *She Said* (director Maria Schrader) as well as Megan Twohey and Jodi Kantor's 2019 book of the same name, Maier shows how Weinstein's history of sexual misconduct casts new light on Bathsheba's story, as well as the assumptions about rape, gender and labour that underlie both ancient and modern contexts. A book and its film adaptation also lie at the centre of Alexiana Fry's contribution to this volume (Chapter 4), 'Women Talking and Women Not Talking: Speaking *for* (?) in Fiction and Judges 21'. *Women Talking*, Fry's contemporary intertext, is a 2018 novel by Miriam Toews that provides a fictional account of a real-life horror: the pervasive drugging and rape of women and girls in a remote Mennonite colony in Bolivia. In the book and the film, the 'women talking' debate three options: do nothing, stay and fight, or leave. Fry uses the novel and film to open an exploration into a biblical text of terror, the mass rape of the women of Jabesh-Gilead, and Shiloh in Judges 21. Fry asks, how can we fill gaps in these terrible stories, and imagine an *after* for victims and survivors, without doing epistemic or real violence? Fry finds one answer in the practice of 'critical fabulation'. A different sort of reimagining biblical narrative and filling in of gaps informs Kirsi Cobb's chapter (Chapter 5). 'Filling in the Gaps: Reading Hosea 1—3 with Francine Rivers's *Redeeming Love*' pairs one of the Hebrew Bible's most infamous prophetic texts, Hosea's version of the marriage metaphor, with a popular Christian romance novel that takes Hosea as its inspiration. Cobb interrogates the 'pre-conceived notions of Hosea, Gomer, and God as well as those of marriage, agency, and trauma' that inform River's novel, reflecting on the question of whether *Redeeming Love*'s retelling of the book Hosea 'offers in fact a love story of redemption or a tale of dysfunction' (p. 83).

The final two chapters in Part 1 of *Narrating Rape* are focused on popular culture, with a critical eye to its points of contact with biblical rape stories and rape culture. Steed Davidson's 'Will You Accept This Rose? The Magic Circle in the Book of Esther' (Chapter 6) brings together the popular television franchise *The Bachelor* with the book of Esther, and in particular the competition between women that the King arranges and in which Esther ultimately emerges victorious. Contemplating questions of sexual consent, Davidson proposes that the story of 'Esther pairs well with the best romantic movies and the myth of reality dating shows' (p. 101). The framework of rape culture also undergirds Meredith Warren's chapter, 'Rape Jokes, Sexual Violence and Empire in Revelation and *This Is the End*' (Chapter 7). Warren reads the book of Revelation with and through the 2013 comedy/horror film *This Is the End* (directors Seth Rogen and Evan Goldberg), focusing on the rape jokes that aim at empowering those individuals and groups who are feeling disempowered. In Warren's chapter, sexual violence is used to rhetorical effect to empower those who have been subjugated by the Empire (pp. 133–4). Yet at the same time she demonstrates how these rape jokes ultimately reinforce rather than critique rape culture.

Part 2 of *Narrating Rape* turns to 'Rape and Sexual Violence in Ancient and Contemporary Contexts'. In Chapter 8 in Part 2, 'Resistance, Rage and Re-enactment: Trauma Responses in the Sumerian Rape Narratives', Renate Marian van Dijk-Coombes introduces us to three Sumerian rape stories: the three mythological narratives of Enlil and Ninlil, in which the goddess Ninlil is raped by the god Enlil; Enki and Ninḫursaĝa, in which the goddess Uttu is raped by the god Enki; and Inana and Šukaletuda, in which the goddess Inana is raped by the mortal gardener Šukaletuda. Chapter 8 explores how the female experience of rape and its aftermath is portrayed in these three narratives to determine differences and similarities with the modern experience. By attending to rape stories in ancient Sumer, van Dijk-Coombes's work breaks new ground in studies of sexual violence in the ancient Near East while also offering a richer background for understanding sexual violence in the Hebrew Bible. The next chapter in Part 2 also provides helpful extra-biblical context. David Tombs' essay, 'Things Too Indecent to be Recorded: The Soldiers Mocking the Death of Herod Agrippa' (Chapter 9), offers a rich historical exploration of the hostility and sexualized mockery that emerged in celebrations of the death of Herod Agrippa (AD 44). Tombs begins with the accounts in Josephus' *Antiquities of the Jews* but quickly broadens his scope to include other ancient historical sources. The lacuna in Josephus – 'things too indecent to be recorded' – surfaces two additional lacunae in New Testament studies: the first involving Agrippa's mockery, the second the mockery of Jesus. Tombs summons us to pay close and careful attention to the ways that sexual violence against male victims is elided, silenced or ignored.

The next two chapters focus on New Testament texts. Like Tombs, Jeremy Punt is also invested in the practice of critiquing violence, though his focus is more on a thick description of the problem, rather than a cure. '"Slaves of Christ": Rape Culture in the New Testament' (Chapter 10) argues that the New Testament's metaphors of slavery are far from benign. Because slaves faced routine sexual abuse and rape, the language of 'slaves of Christ' is deeply infused with sexual violence. Pauline texts such as Romans 6 and 1 Corinthians 7 thus represent troubling examples of New Testament rape culture. Masculinity and violence are also a concern for Dewald Jacobs. In '"Madoda Sabelani" and Matthew 2.18: Lamenting Hegemonic Masculinity' (Chapter 11), Jacobs uses a contemporary South African song, and broader South African discussions over hegemonic masculinity and gender-based violence, to offer an innovative new reading of biblical lament. Centring the lament passage in Matthew 2.18 (which, in turn, draws on Jeremiah), Chapter 11 crafts a lament over gender-based violence. In addition to holding a space for grief, Jacobs also holds a space for the possibility of acting differently and critiquing violence.

The final two chapters of the book return to the Hebrew Bible. Gerald West's chapter, 'The Poetics of Redacted Absence as Presence: Kin Eyes Hearing Tamar (2 Samuel 13)' (Chapter 12), builds on the work of Phyllis Trible, arguing that the remarkable poetic voice of Tamar 'summons women (and many men) to hear and speak out' (p. 209). West draws our attention to 'the residual presence that remains of Tamar's voice, interrogating both its presence and absence'. For West, both Tamar's 'present elite voice and her sisters' absent subaltern voices' are preserved for us in the form of poetry in 2 Samuel 13 (p. 211).

Finally, Charlene van der Walt's chapter, 'Under Rug Swept: Creating Space to Engage the Reality of Homophobic Hate Crimes in the South African Faith Landscape' (Chapter 13), outlines two interventions developed by the Ujamaa Centre for Biblical and Theological Community Development and Research (University of KwaZulu-Natal, Pietermaritzburg, South Africa) that seek to counteract homophobic hate crimes in South Africa. These intentionally discomforting interventions include the annual Eudy Simelane Memorial Lecture that commemorates the brutal rape and murder of a young lesbian South African national soccer player, as well as a Contextual Bible Study on Joseph and his 'princess dress' in Genesis 37 which offer different ways of facilitating 'collective discussion, reflection, and critical engagement within South African faith communities when engaging LGBTIQA+ lived realities' (p. 229).

In these two final chapters in Part 2 of *Narrating Rape* we see how the engagement with stories that recount gender-based violence in the Hebrew Bible are creatively employed by socially engaged Bible scholars such as Gerald West and Charlene van der Walt – their contributions serving as creative interventions that seek to disrupt and challenge the scripts that have contributed to the formation of rape culture.

Fiona Snyckers's *Lacuna* ends with an interlocutor urging Lucy to write, at last, her own story in the form of a novel:

INTRODUCTION

'You have a problem with the way he framed your story, with the way he imagined your thoughts and reactions. So write your own novel. It will set up a tension between the two works. Your story will always exist in intertextual conversation with Coetzee's story.'

'But it will be female and angry and incoherent and messy and ugly and raw.'

'Then let it be so.' (Snyckers, 2022, p. 255)

Like the novel that hangs in the air at the end of *Lacuna*, and like *Lacuna* itself, the chapters gathered in *Narrating Rape* all exist in intertextual conversation with the Bible's rape stories. The act of retelling is an act of reframing. It is also an act of tension. Sometimes, the results are poetic, illuminating, clear; at other points, they are angry, ugly, raw. But in the retelling, and in the reimagining of how to (re)tell silent and silenced stories, vital feminist work occurs. Let it be so.

Bibliography

Cobb, Christy, and Eric Vanden Eykel (eds), 2022, *Sex, Violence, and Early Christian Texts*, Lanham, MD: Lexington Books.
Coetzee, J. M., 2017, *Disgrace*, New York: Penguin Books.
Daly, Mary, 1990, *Gyn/Ecology: The Metaethics of Radical Feminism*, Boston, MA: Beacon Press.
Exum, J. Cheryl, 1993, *Fragmented Women: Feminist (Sub)Versions of Biblical Narratives*, JSOTSup 163, Sheffield: JSOT Press.
Graybill, Rhiannon, 2021, *Texts after Terror: Rape, Sexual Violence, and the Hebrew Bible*, New York: Oxford University Press.
Greenough, Chris, 2021, *The Bible and Sexual Violence Against Men*, Rape Culture, Religion and the Bible, New York: Routledge.
Harding, James, 2016, 'Homophobia and Masculine Domination in Judges 19–21', *The Bible and Critical Theory* 12/2, pp. 41–74.
Jacob, Sharon, 2015, *Reading Mary Alongside Indian Surrogate Mothers: Violent Love, Oppressive Liberation, and Infancy Narratives*, The Bible and Cultural Studies, New York: Palgrave Macmillan.
Kelle, Brad E., 2008, 'Wartime Rhetoric: Prophetic Metaphorization of Cities as Female' in Brad E. Kelle and Frank R. Ames (eds), *Writing and Reading War: Rhetoric, Gender, and Ethics in Biblical and Modern Contexts*, Atlanta, GA: SBL Press, pp. 95–111.
Kessel, Alisa, 2022, 'Rethinking Rape Culture: Revelations of Intersectional Analysis', *The American Political Science Review* 116/1, pp. 131–43.
Knust, Jennifer, 2017, 'Can an Adulteress Save Jesus? The Pericope Adulterae, Feminist Interpretation, and the Limits of Narrative Agency' in Yvonne Sherwood with the assistance of Anna Fisk (eds), *The Bible and Feminism: Remapping the Field*, New York: Oxford University Press, pp. 402–31.

Lehmann, Jennifer, 2024, 'What Is This You Have Done to Me? Male Victims of Sexual Violence in Genesis', PhD Dissertation, Graduate Theological Union, Berkeley, CA, USA.

Magdalene, F. Rachel, 1995, 'Ancient Near Eastern Treaty-Curses and the Ultimate Texts of Terror: A Study of the Language of Divine Sexual Abuse in the Prophetic Corpus' in Athalya Brenner (ed.), *A Feminist Companion to the Latter Prophets*, The Feminist Companion to the Bible 8, Sheffield: Sheffield Academic Press, pp. 326–52.

Reaves, Jayme R., David Tombs and Rocio Figueroa (eds), 2021, *When Did We See You Naked? Jesus as a Victim of Sexual Abuse*, London: SCM Press.

Schaberg, Jane, 2006, *The Illegitimacy of Jesus: A Feminist Theological Interpretation of the Infancy Narratives*, expanded 20th anniversary edn, Sheffield: Sheffield Phoenix Press.

Scholz, Susanne, 2010, *Sacred Witness: Rape in the Hebrew Bible*, Minneapolis, MN: Fortress Press.

Schüssler Fiorenza, Elisabeth, 2001, *Sharing Her Word: Feminist Biblical Interpretation in Context*, Edinburgh: T&T Clark.

Sheffield, Carole J., 2020, 'Sexual Terrorism in the Twenty-First Century' in Laura L. O'Toole, Jessica R. Schiffman and Margie L. Kiter Edwards (eds), *Gender Violence: Interdisciplinary Perspectives*, 3rd edn, New York: New York University Press, pp. 190–211.

Smith-Christopher, Daniel L., 2004, 'Ezekiel in Abu Ghraib: Rereading Ezekiel 16:37-39 in the Context of Imperial Conquest' in Stephen L. Cook and Corrine L. Patton (eds), *Ezekiel's Hierarchical World: Wrestling with a Tiered Reality*, Atlanta, GA: SBL Press, pp. 141–58.

Snyckers, Fiona, 2022, *Lacuna*, New York: Europa Editions (original publication 2019 by Pan Macmillan South Africa).

Tombs, David, 2021, 'Crucifixion and Sexual Abuse' in Jayme R. Reaves, David Tombs and Rocio Figueroa (eds), *When Did We See You Naked? Jesus as a Victim of Sexual Abuse*, London: SCM Press, pp. 15–27.

Trible, Phyllis, 1984, *Texts of Terror: Literary-Feminist Readings of Biblical Narratives*, Minneapolis, MN: Fortress Press.

Washington, Harold C., 1997, 'Violence and the Construction of Gender in the Hebrew Bible: A New Historicist Approach', *Biblical Interpretation* 5/4, pp. 324–63.

Weems, Renita J., 1995, *Battered Love: Marriage, Sex, and Violence in the Hebrew Prophets*, Minneapolis, MN: Fortress Press.

PART I

Stories of Rape in the Bible and Popular Culture

I

Recovering from Rape?
Lacuna (Fiona Snyckers) in Conversation with Daughter Zion in Isaiah 51.17—52.2

L. JULIANA CLAASSENS

Introduction

What happens *after* the rape? This is the question with which Rhiannon Graybill (2021, p. 113) starts her chapter on 'Daughter Zion in Lamentations and the Archive of Rape Stories'. The question of 'what happens *after* rape' is particularly pertinent for our reflection on the chapters in *Narrating Rape* on whether one is able, or perhaps also *not* able, to tell the story of rape or sexual violation. And what's more, whether one is able to narrate rape in a way that does not succumb to all those rape scripts circulating in any given society.

This question is also at the heart of this current chapter that brings into conversation two stories, one a contemporary novel and one a biblical text from long ago; both give narrative shape to the trauma and recovery associated with rape in interesting ways – that is, if one ever truly can be said to recover from rape. We will see in this chapter that there are no simple answers to the manifold complicated questions generated by rape and its aftermath, neither in literature nor in life. As Graybill (2021, p. 121) has suggested, recovery from rape, like rape itself, is fuzzier, messier, or 'grittier', as evident in the case of her reflection on a 'Grittier Daughter Zion'.

In my 2020 monograph *Writing and Reading to Survive*, a book that forges creative conversations between biblical and contemporary trauma narratives, I show in one of my chapters how both in the book of Lamentations as well as in the book *Disgrace* by J. M. Coetzee, the rape of a young woman (Daughter Zion in Lamentations and Lucy Lurie in *Disgrace*) serves as a narrative device to symbolize the violation the community experienced on a collective level (Claassens, 2020, pp. 127–52).

As I was contemplating a new topic for the 2023 Gender Unit conference (hosted yearly by the Faculty of Theology, Stellenbosch University), something slightly less controversial than the Queering the Prophet conference of 2022,[1] I came across Fiona Snyckers's fascinating novel *Lacuna* (2022, original publication 2019), which has been described as a feminist-inspired reworking of *Disgrace*. *Lacuna* provides Lucy Lurie with an alternative story that captures her tentative and complicated attempts to carve out a life for herself in the wake of the assault. Offering a very different literary portrayal than Disgrace's 'Fictional Lucy',[2] Lucy Lurie in *Lacuna* is a powerful example of talking back to a male author, challenging how John Coetzee, the imagined author of *Disgrace* in *Lacuna*, has narrativized her rape to great literary and monetary success. Lucy rants when she goes to confront John Coetzee in his house in the Bo-Kaap: 'He turned my rape into a spectacle and me into a public figure. I will never be at peace with it.' And as she unequivocally states upon knocking on his door: 'There. I will not be ignored. I have come to state my case. I am nobody's lacuna' (Snyckers, 2022, p. 43).

Lucy Lurie's complicated journey towards recovery as she seeks to wrest back the life that had been robbed from her can be brought into conversation with the afterlife imagined for Daughter Zion in the post-exilic book of Deutero-Isaiah. Deutero-Isaiah, and for this chapter, specifically Isaiah 51.17—52.2, has long since been shown to offer a response to Lamentations in which Daughter Zion, in the words of Carleen Mandolfo (2007, pp. 110–15), talks back to the Prophets, as a way to describe the process of hearing Daughter Zion's counter story into speech.

I chose this text from Deutero-Isaiah because of its intricate blending of themes concerning the traumatic memories of rape and the complex portrayal of recovery. Framed with the repeated call to Zion to rise up, to 'rouse yourself', to wake up, Isaiah 51.17—52.2 implores Daughter Zion to be free, to regain her strength. However, amid the narrative description of Daughter Zion's convoluted journey towards recovery that forms part of Deutero-Isaiah's emphasis on restoration and the healing of the traumatized community, one also finds that the story of Daughter Zion's violation is told once more.

These two atypical stories of rape and recovery will create the space for us in this chapter to consider the complexities associated with narrating the trauma of rape and the possibilities regarding narrating recovery.[3] What do these ancient and contemporary stories have to say about the ambiguous nature of female agency in the aftermath of rape and how victims/survivors are able/unable to take control of their story? And in the concluding section, we will reflect on how at the heart of these stories that give narrative shape to rape and its aftermath is ultimately the quest to generate hope – not only for the literary characters but also for the countless real victims of gender-based violence who all too often get lost amid the narratives constructed about them.

Narrating rape

> Rape is the gift that keeps on giving. I was raped many times that evening at the farmhouse. Too many times to count. You'd think that would be something you would never lose track of. But I did – and I have also lost count of how many times I have been raped in my dreams. (Snyckers, 2022, p. 34)

Lucy Lurie's words in *Lacuna* poignantly capture the haunting after-effects of rape that last long after the initial act of violation in the form of flashbacks and dreams, which she admits she does not always remember. However, whenever she awakes 'with tears on [her] cheeks and pain between [her] legs, she deduces that 'it has happened again' (Snyckers, 2022, p. 34). In graphic detail, the all too vivid memory of rape is narrated by Lucy on the very first page of the novel:

> My vagina is a lacuna that my attackers filled with their penises. They saw the lack in me and chose to supply what I couldn't. Their penises were rough and dry and scraped my lacuna raw, bruising my cervix, and tearing my perineum. (Snyckers, 2022, p. 15)

In a classic case of disassociation, she imagines herself in another room, 'the soundtrack on the other side of the wall lets me know how far they have progressed. Now they are taking a break. Now they have got their second wind and are starting again' (Snyckers, 2022, p. 15). A classic protective measure, Lucy states, 'It is less harrowing than being in that room myself. Experiencing something at one remove is a pale shadow of the real thing' (Snyckers, 2022, p. 15).

With these detailed – almost too detailed – descriptions of Lucy's experience of rape, which she acknowledges constitutes 'stomach turning violence' that people surely do not want to have to watch, *Lacuna* seeks to remedy John Coetzee's (intentional) lacuna in divulging any details regarding Lucy's rape. As Kim Middleton and Julie Townsend (2009, p. 123) argue, shortly after the attack in *Disgrace* 'neither David nor Lucy has verbalized the word "rape" yet; it will be many pages, many weeks in narrative time before David does' (cf. also Claassens, 2020, p. 139 for further reflection on this silence surrounding Lucy's rape).

In a world away, we find another example of the ongoing effects of rape in the form of flashbacks in Isaiah 51.17—52.2's account that offers a direct response to the book of Lamentations. As in Lamentations 1.21 (cf. the Piel form of '-n-h), the language of rape is used in Isaiah 51.21 (adjective feminine singular of '-n-h) to express the traumatic memory of the City's walls being breached and her sanctuaries penetrated.[4] As Ruth Poser (2021, p. 342) argues, in antiquity, 'in siege warfare, real violence against a city as metaphorical woman merged into real violence against real women living in the city' (see, for example, Maier, 2008, pp. 146–7; Guest, 1999, pp. 417–18; Kelle, 2008, pp. 95–112).

In the aftermath of the violation as envisioned here in Isaiah 51.17—52.2, the City, personified as a victim of gender-based violence, is a shadow of her former self. Daughter Zion is the victim of imperial violence, as evident in the adjectives 'devastation' (*shod*) and destruction (cf. the root *sh-b-r* that denotes brokenness) to describe the devastating effects of 'famine and sword' (Isa. 51.19) that elsewhere in the Prophets feature as a metonym for war and its aftermath (see for example, the Jeremianic triad of 'sword, famine, and pestilence' in Jer. 14.12; 24.10; 29.18). Her children, an extension of herself, are fainting away, their life ebbing away as they are as vulnerable as a deer caught in a trap (Isa. 51.20). In Isaiah 51.23, Daughter Zion's ultimate humiliation is vividly depicted in the description of the violated young woman whom her tormentors command: 'Bow down, that we may walk on you', lying on her back with her violators trampling over her as if she is a 'street for them to walk on.'

In Isaiah 51.18–19, Daughter Zion is acknowledged to be alone. As she repeatedly stated in Lamentations, she has no one to comfort her. This language of profound loneliness felt by a victim/survivor of rape, nobody being able to share her plight or understand the depths of her despair, is elsewhere in Deutero-Isaiah (Isa. 54.1) captured in the adjective *shomemah*, 'utterly destroyed' – a description that is also used to describe the desolation experienced by Tamar in 2 Samuel 13.20; these are the only instances in the Hebrew Bible where this term is used for a woman (Adelman, 2021, p. 96; Maier, 2008, p. 149).

These two stories reveal the complexity of putting the damaging effects of rape into narrative form. For one, when Lucy Lurie is invited to speak on a panel of what is described as the 'Well-meaning people of RASA' (Rape Awareness South Africa), the story she tells about her rape falls short in her own mind and also in that of others. Despite the wordiness associated with Lucy's memories of rape that present the reader with quite a bit of (graphic) detail, at the beginning of *Lacuna*, when she is called to speak on the panel, Lucy recounts the devastating events in a mere ten words: 'Six men broke into my father's farmhouse and raped me' (Snyckers, 2022, p. 51). Acknowledging that she did not have her co-panellist Marion's gift of storytelling, and even fell short of 'Fictional Lucy' who is a better survivor than she, Lucy grades herself, giving her a D- in contrast to the other speakers' A+ rape trauma narratives.

In contrast to Lamentations 1, in which Daughter Zion in the first person shares her anguish, even though channelled through a male author, in the third-person account in Isaiah 51.17—52.2 we do not hear Daughter Zion's voice at all. It is the narrator telling her story – Daughter Zion is not even invited to the panel! Instead, the audience joins the narrator in observing the aftermath of the violation – the flashbacks to her suffering as debilitating as the debilitating nightly dreams in *Lacuna*.

This makes *Lacuna* such a compelling conversation partner. We are given unfettered access to Lucy Lurie's imagined thoughts and feelings, even though told in terms of an unreliable narrator – as Lucy herself admits after presenting the reader with a report from her therapist in which Ms Lurie's delusional fixation on John Coetzee is outlined:

That's not real.
I wrote it.
I am untrustworthy. But I'm the only access you have to this story. My lens is the only one through which you are permitted to peek. (Snyckers, 2022, p. 26)

This narrative device of the unreliable narrator captures the complexity and ambiguity associated with the aftermath of rape, particularly the question of whether women are believed. As Lucy tells the reader, her 'worst fear is that [she] will not be believed'. Despite 'all the medical evidence supporting her claim', she still feels like she is 'the unreliable witness' and 'the inherently untruthful complainant' (Snyckers, 2022, p. 27).

This again is where Isaiah 51.17—52.2 offers a valuable perspective in this conversation on how rape victims/survivors' stories are received. The trauma narrative narrated in Isaiah 51.17—52.2 affirms, or corroborates, what Daughter Zion has said all along in Lamentations 1—2 regarding her experience of being utterly alone. In Isaiah 51.18, there is no one to guide her or take her by the hand. In the context of her devastation and destruction the narrator in Isaiah 51.19 (NRSVUE) asks: 'Who will grieve with you? ... Who will comfort you?' Despite numerous attempts to 'comfort' Zion (Isa. 49.13; 51.12), Daughter Zion has not received the comfort she so desperately desires (Isa. 54.7–8). Moreover, by revisiting the memories of violation captured in terms of the language of rape, Isaiah 51.17—52.2 does not shy away from acknowledging the depths of traumatic memories associated with the aftermath of rape, which, as will be evident in the next section, continue to impede the recovery of Daughter Zion and the people she represents.

Narrating recovery

In both *Lacuna* and Isaiah 51.17—52.2, the difficulty in – or perhaps even the impossibility of – recovering from trauma is showcased. One finds this, for instance, in Lucy's inability to finish revisions to her thesis that amount to a couple of hundred words; or being unable to forge meaningful connections that, according to Judith Herman (1997, pp. 3, 155), is an essential step in moving from trauma to recovery.[5] As Lucy laments:

> They say old age turns you into a caricature of yourself. This is what rape has done to me. It has stripped me of my youthful ability to tolerate people and things. I am no longer adaptable. I can't take life as it comes. I struggle to walk and talk at the same time. I need plenty of warning if something is going to happen. I hate spontaneity. I find refuge in routine. (Snyckers, 2022, p. 61)

And in Isaiah 51.17—52.2, it is ironic that in a book that traditionally emphasizes hope and healing, images of restoration and new life – references to a well-watered garden in the wilderness (Isa. 44.3–4; 51.3), a highway through the wilderness (Isa. 40.3–4), and the joyful return of Zion's children (Isa. 54.1–3; 55.12) – are interspersed with flashbacks to violence and humiliation, as was outlined in the previous section.

In both *Lacuna* and Isaiah 51.17—52.2, a central motif regards the propensity of clothes to signal the convoluted process of narrating the trauma and recovery of rape. For instance, in Isaiah 52.1 Zion is called upon to arise and put on beautiful garments that are equated with clothing herself in strength. She is to take off the mourning clothes she had been wearing (cf. shaking off the dust) and remove the yoke around her neck. She is a captive no longer but instead adorned in the clothes of a queen (Adelman, 2021, p. 100). Mandolfo (2007, p. 116) argues that this command to Daughter Zion to dress herself in clothes fit for royalty reverses the harsh imagery used elsewhere in the prophetic literature of being stripped naked (see, for example, Hos. 2.5; Jer. 13.26; Ezek. 16.37). The imperatives to captive Daughter Zion in Isaiah 52.2 ('Shake yourself from the dust; rise up ... loose the bonds from your neck') talk back to the portrayal of Daughter Zion in Lamentations 1—2 as evident in references to Yhwh's yoke weighing heavy on her (Lam. 1.14), and how her elders are sitting with dust on their heads (Lam. 2.10). Indeed, Isaiah 51.17—52.2 triumphantly announces Daughter Zion's salvation: 'the time has come to rise from the dust, to reassume a position of honor, to no longer be bound like a servant' (Mandolfo, 2007, p. 114).

This text that speaks of Zion's restoration, moreover, offers an interesting counterpart to the quintessential rape story of Tamar in 2 Samuel 13.18-19, who tears her long-sleeved robe (*ketonet passim*) as an act of profound grief due to the violation she experienced by the hand of Amnon. The torn robe serves as a visual, very public, sign of Tamar's desolation which, as Adelman (2021, p. 95) has argued, 'foreshadows the rending of the fabric of the kingdom'. In contrast, the new robe that Daughter Zion is called to put on signals the emergence of a new self, albeit juxtaposed with flashbacks of the traumatic memories associated with her violation, so emphasizing the convoluted, drawn-out process towards recovery. Similarly, in *Lacuna*, clothes serve as a vital measure of whether Lucy can be said to recover or not. In one particularly hopeful vignette, Lucy's friend Moira helps her, in the words of Isaiah 52.2, to 'shake [her]self from the dust, [to] rise up ... [and to] loose the bonds from [her] neck'. Moira encourages her to clean up the chaos in her apartment, redecorate, and eat right: 'magical foods' and 'magical water that cleans me from the inside out' (Snyckers, 2022, p. 56). Lucy puts on a new outfit, specifically fitness clothes ('tight, bright Lululemon gym-wear' (Snyckers, 2022, p. 56) instead of the baggy outfits she used to wear. Her 'outfit metamorphosis' signals a renewed commitment to health and vitality. What's more, her new exercise regime, along with her healthy salads and smoothies, leads to a new lease of life with Lucy landing a (corporate) job that involves yet another change of outfit, now putting on the 'beautiful garments' associated with corporate dress. What follows is meeting a new fellow, getting married, becoming pregnant, and going to live in the suburbs. As Lucy states at the end of chapter 5, 'That's how you get over rape' (Snyckers, 2022, p. 57).

However, the reader then hears at the beginning of chapter 6: no, this did not happen. Once again, the unreliable narrator in *Lacuna* lured readers into believing that Lucy might, after all, be recovering from the aftermath of rape. This portrayal played on readers' sincere hope that Lucy will not succumb to rape's cruel after-effects, cheering her on to a similar call to Daughter Zion in Isaiah 51.17 and 52.1 to 'rise up', 'to wake up', 'to put on your strength'.

Instead, Lucy is said to wear dowdy clothes, which captures the less glamorous, ugly reality of the aftermath of her violation:

> I put on my full-length knickers, my American tan tights, my bra and girdle, my long, thick skirt, the blouse that buttons all the way up to my chin, my cardigan. I lace my feet into flat leather shoes. I put on spectacles to shield my face.
>
> I know what I am doing. I am making myself less rape-able. I'm falling for the old lie – that women are raped because of what they are wearing. But I can't help myself. It feels as though I am going into battle fully prepared. (Snyckers, 2022, p. 61)

The truth is that Lucy's clothes serve as a way to hide herself. She no longer regards herself as a sensual being – that part of her had been destroyed, robbed from her by her violators.

Graybill's argument regarding the complexity of the healing process in the aftermath of the trauma of rape is helpful. Citing the work of Leah Lakshmi Piepzna-Samarasinha's *Care Work: Dreaming Disability Justice* (2018), Graybill (2021, p. 121) argues that it is only natural that one wants the pain to stop. However, very much relevant to Lucy in *Lacuna* and Daughter Zion in Isaiah 51.17—52.2, the recovery process is far messier and fraught with ambiguity. 'It is not always over, not always healed', writes Graybill (2021, p. 137). Instead, in terms of her engagement with Daughter Zion in Lamentations and a selection of novels that tell the story of rape in unconventional ways, Graybill (2021, p. 137) contemplates 'the possibility of survival outside of repair', imagining a future in the aftermath of rape in which one, in the words of Piepzna-Samarasinha (2018, p. 232), is 'thriving but not cured'.

Graybill (2021, p. 138) is thus not convinced of intertextual readings that seek to 'heal' Daughter Zion. Isaiah 51.17—52.2 is a case in point, as in the 'more "hopeful" texts in Deutero-Isaiah', one nevertheless sees evidence of Daughter Zion's silence in response to the narrator's call to pick herself up, in addition to the traumatic memories of loneliness, profound grief and the lack of a comforter. In Isaiah 51.17—52.2, as also in *Lacuna*, survival and healing are much more ambivalent and convoluted, opening up the possibility that even in a text intent on getting Daughter

Zion to arise and be alive again, 'she may never thrive' (Graybill, 2021, p. 138).

A second aspect of narrating recovery is the convoluted process of meaning-making associated with the aftermath of events surrounding rape. What is the story that is told? And who is blamed in a particular construction of such a narrative? In Isaiah 51.17—52.2, it is significant that God is taking responsibility as God is said to admit that it is because of God's great anger that the violation occurred (cf. Isa. 51.17 that states that Daughter Zion was forced to drink from the cup of wrath as well as the reversal in Isa. 51.22). Actually, in Lamentations 1, Daughter Zion and the narrator repeatedly accused God that it is God's burning anger that is responsible for Daughter Zion/ the City of Jerusalem being entered by the enemy soldiers and completely and utterly destroyed (Lam. 1.6; 2.1, 4, 8, 10, 13; 4.22) (Adelman, 2021, p. 97). It is significant that in Deutero-Isaiah's response to this narrative, God claims responsibility, so corroborating Daughter Zion's version of events (Mandolfo, 2007, p. 116).

According to Christl Maier (2008, p. 150), the argument that it is *God* and not the Babylonians responsible for the violation is a good example of cultural trauma – that is, a counter-imperial narrative constructed in which blame is assigned to the people of Judah's Deity. This narrative rendition offers in some sense a healthy, or at least less harmful, move away from self-blame, as well as the typical blaming-the-victim explanations that permeate the discourse elsewhere in the Hebrew Bible prophets (cf. O'Connor, 2014, p. 217; Frechette, 2015, p. 33).

Lacuna takes this question of who is to blame even further. In what constitutes a serious spoiler alert, to the great shock of Lucy (and the readers) it turns out to be Lucy's father who, in an elaborate foil to get insurance money, feigned the burning down of the farmhouse and its imagined valuable furniture – in the process using the rape of his daughter to make the attack look authentic (Snyckers, 2022, pp. 142-4). This shocking narrative development in *Lacuna* offers a very different ending to *Disgrace*'s original story – and not one that the reader or Lucy of *Lacuna* saw coming. Instead, Lucy's initial recollection of her father's role in the aftermath of the rape is that he looked at her with pity, covering her with a blanket. However, what Lucy in *Lacuna* initially thought was the reason for her father not looking her solidly in the eye – '[her] shame hangs between us' – was instead some semblance of shame regarding his culpability in his daughter's rape. She bemoans the fact that her father may even have 'found it exciting to engineer [her] rape':

> For years, I believed it was shock and grief I saw on his face as he watched me being raped, but a part of me always recognised it as excitement. It was thrilling for him to witness my violation. I don't think he knew himself how he would react until it happened. He is not a good man. My mother was a good woman, but my father is not a good man. (Snyckers, 2022, p. 243)

What does it do to Lucy Lurie to know that her father is responsible for her rape? And what does it do to the people represented by Zion, past and present, that God, the Father/Warrior/Patriarch par excellence, admits responsibility for the city's ruin? In both these trauma narratives that talk back to the rape scripts that perpetuate harmful coping strategies such as self-blame, an alternative narrative is forged, which in interesting ways narrativizes the culpability of patriarchy in which men, directly and indirectly, are implicated in gender-based violence. According to Rachel Adelman (2021, p. 89), the stories of Tamar, the King's daughter, and Bat Tzion, the 'daughter' of the Divine, 'articulate and embody a critique of the father's rule'. And role. In the narrative of Tamar's violation (2 Sam. 13), King David is implicated in the violation of his daughter – with Dinah 'set up by her father, raped by one brother, and silenced by another' (Adelman, 2021, p. 99).[6]

Moreover, in Isaiah 51.17—52.2 in which we see a turn towards God's acknowledgment of his rash anger (Isa. 51.17, 10, 22; 54.8):

> The deflection away from the principle of divine retribution, and the turn toward God's acknowledgment of his rash anger – 'in an outburst of anger I hid my face from you a while' (Isa. 54.8) – presents an alternative theodicy. Ultimately, the daughters' debasement (both literal and figurative) implicates the fathers (and 'the Father'). (Adelman, 2021, p. 101)

For Adelman (p. 102), these stories are significant as we hear in Tamar's voice a resounding, insistent 'Don't', which not only pertains to her rapist, Amnon, but also to her father and his entire kingdom. And Bat Tzion's presence in the book of Lamentations and Deutero-Isaiah continues this challenge, 'exposing the patriarchal assumptions embedded in the text and inviting the women to speak from between the lines of the narrative'. In this way, Tamar, Daughter Zion – and one could also say Lucy Lurie in *Lacuna* – may be transformed, as Adelman (2021, p. 102) puts it, 'from an object of male abuse into a subject of feminist critique'.[7]

Narrating hope

When the final programme for the Gender Unit conference that would result in this current collection of chapters was sent out, in what could well be taken as a Freudian slip, it was sent out under the subject line of *Narrating Hope*. There is much substance to this error that is central to why we, as feminist scholars, keep on writing about these troubling topics. We are writing to survive, writing our way through trauma, writing the wrongs of the world. But we also write because we have not given up hope. Ultimately, we want to, in the process of narrating rape and narrating recovery, also find ways to narrate hope. To speak in nuanced terms about healing, recovery and restoration, which involves the ability to live again, to experience pleasure and even joy again.

Through stories such as *Lacuna* and Isaiah 51.17—52.2, one is presented with examples of authors and narrators, even and especially unreliable ones, showcasing the diversity of experiences associated with the aftermath of rape in terms of the narratives they tell. In *Lacuna* and Isaiah 51.17—52.2, we have seen spaces being cultivated for the characters and their readers to engage in the process of recovery, which is to occur at their own pace. In this chapter, we have seen through the examples of the imagined aftermath of Daughter Zion and Lucy Lurie's rape, representing the too many real victims of gender-based violence, that any reference to healing should not be prescriptive. Victims/survivors ought to be granted the essential commodities, time and space, to deal with what has happened to them.

Moreover, there is something profoundly hopeful in that these stories provide examples of victims of violence who resist getting lost in the stories told about them. In this regard, Mandolfo (2007, p. 81) writes that in a context in which 'stories are circulating about us', our first inclination is 'to retell the story, filling in those ingredients that the original story failed to furnish'. Stories like that of *Lacuna* (in conversation with *Disgrace*), and Isaiah 51.17—52.2 (in conversation with Lamentations), are examples of constructing a counter-story, respectively for Lucy Lurie and Daughter Zion, that does justice to the inherent complexities of narrating the aftermath of rape. These stories that so eloquently narrate rape and recovery are particularly successful because they hold multiple endings in tension as the main characters simultaneously are shown to be restored and not restored, healed and not healed.

Bibliography

Adelman, Rachel, 2021, 'The Rape of Tamar as a Prefiguration for the Fate of Fair Zion', *Journal of Feminist Studies in Religion* 37/1, pp. 87–102.

Claassens, L. Juliana, 2014, 'Transforming God-Language: The Metaphor of God as Abusive Spouse (Ezekiel 16) in Conversation with the Portrayal of God in *The Color Purple*', *Scriptura* 113, pp. 1–11.

Claassens, L. Juliana, 2016, 'Trauma and Recovery: A New Hermeneutical Framework for the Rape of Tamar (2 Samuel 13)' in Elizabeth Boase and Christopher G. Frechette (eds), *Bible Through the Lens of Trauma*, Semeia Studies 86, Atlanta, GA: SBL Press, pp. 177–92.

Claassens, L. Juliana, 2020, *Writing and Reading to Survive: Biblical and Contemporary Trauma Narratives in Conversation*, Sheffield: Sheffield Phoenix Press.

Claassens, L. Juliana, forthcoming, '"History Does Not Repeat Itself, But It Rhymes": Exploring Literary Representations of Violence in Bible in/and Literature' in Chris Greenough et al. (eds), *The Bible and Violence*, London: Bloomsbury T&T Clark.

Claassens, L. Juliana et al. (eds), 2023, *Queering the Prophet: On Jonah, and Other Activists*, London: SCM Press.

Coetzee, J. M., 1999, *Disgrace*, New York: Viking.

Day, Linda, 2000, 'Rhetoric and Domestic Violence in Ezekiel 16', *Biblical Interpretation* 8, pp. 205–29.

Frechette, Christopher G., 2015, 'The Old Testament as Controlled Substance: How Insights from Trauma Studies Reveal Healing Capacities in Potentially Harmful Texts', *Interpretation* 69, pp. 20–34.

Gordon, Pamela, and Harold C. Washington, 1995, 'Rape as Military Metaphor in the Hebrew Bible' in Athalya Brenner (ed.), *A Feminist Companion to the Latter Prophets*, Sheffield: Sheffield Academic Press, pp. 308–25.

Graybill, Rhiannon, 2021, *Texts after Terror: Rape, Sexual Violence, and the Hebrew Bible*, New York: Oxford University Press.

Guest, Deryn, 1999, 'Hiding Behind the Naked Women in Lamentations: A Recriminative Response', *Biblical Interpretation* 7/4, pp. 413–48.

Herman, Judith, 1997, *Trauma and Recovery: The Aftermath of Violence – from Domestic Abuse to Political Terror*, New York: Basic Books.

Herman, Judith, 2023, *Truth and Repair: How Trauma Survivors Envision Justice*, New York: Basic Books.

Kelle, Brad E., 2008, 'Wartime Rhetoric: Prophetic Metaphorization of Cities as Female' in Brad E. Kelle and Frank R. Ames (eds), *Writing and Reading War: Rhetoric, Gender and Ethics in Biblical and Modern Contexts*, Atlanta, GA: SBL Press, pp. 95–112.

Maier, Christl M., 2008, *Daughter Zion, Mother Zion: Gender, Space, and the Sacred in Ancient Israel*, Minneapolis, MN: Fortress Press.

Mandolfo, Carleen, 2007, *Daughter Zion Talks Back to the Prophets: A Dialogic Theology of the Book of Lamentations*, Atlanta, GA: SBL Press.

Middleton, Kim, and Julie Townsend, 2009, 'Tenuous Arrangements: The Ethics of Rape in *Disgrace*' in Bill McDonald (ed.), *Encountering Disgrace: Reading and Teaching Coetzee's Novel*, Rochester, NY: Camden House, pp. 118–35.

O'Brien, Julia M., 2008, *Challenging Prophetic Metaphor: Theology and Ideology in the Prophets*, Louisville, KY: Westminster John Knox.
O'Connor, Kathleen M., 2014, 'How Trauma Studies Can Contribute to Old Testament Studies' in Eve-Marie Becker et al. (eds), *Trauma and Traumatization in Individual and Collective Dimensions: Insights from Biblical Studies and Beyond*, Göttingen: Vandenhoeck & Ruprecht, pp. 210–22.
Piepzna-Samarasinha, Leah Lakshmi, 2018, *Care Work: Dreaming Disability Justice*, Vancouver: Arsenal Pulp Press.
Poser, Ruth, 2021, 'Embodied Memories: Gender Specific Aspects of Prophecy as Trauma Literature' in L. Juliana Claassens and Irmtraud Fischer (eds), *Prophecy and Gender in the Hebrew Bible*, The Bible and Women 1.2, Atlanta, GA: SBL Press, pp. 333–58.
Snyckers, Fiona, 2022, *Lacuna*, New York: Europa Editions (original publication 2019 by Pan Macmillan South Africa).

Notes

1 There was quite a bit of controversy surrounding this conference, with angry letters in the newspapers and on social media, and even a couple of protestors outside the Faculty of Theology protesting about what they called 'Toxic Theology'. Nevertheless, the conference went well, and a collection of essays was published by SCM Press in 2023 with the title *Queering the Prophet: On Jonah, and Other Activists* (L. Juliana Claassens et al. (eds)).

2 J. M. Coetzee imagines Lucy in *Disgrace* as keeping the baby that resulted from being raped, and marrying her neighbour Petrus. Snyckers (2022, p. 123) imagines 'Fiction-Lucy': 'She is coming in from the fields, walking shoulder-to-shoulder with her rapist. Her child is strapped to her back with two blankets tied at the corners. I can't tell if it's a boy or a girl. It is not an option for her to hand her child to a babysitter. She and the women who work here take it in turns to watch each other's children. She has no special status. She is not the madam. Her privilege has been stripped away, leaving behind a woman like any other – one who must work for her place in the world while raising her child ... Lucy and Petrus parent the child together. It is not important whether Petrus, who was not one of the rapists, is literally the father of the boy. It is not necessary for him to share DNA with the child to be its father. The boy is the child of everyone who participated in the rape, and their associates, and as such, he belongs to all of them.' See my discussion of this ambiguous portrayal of Lucy's resistance by Coetzee who, on the one hand, talks back to her father, who questions her decisions, but on the other hand presents a rather romanticized vision of recovery from rape which involves 'dedicate[ing] herself to cultivating flowers and caring for animals' (Claassens, 2020, p. 149). See also Middleton and Townsend, 2009, p. 129, for an insightful feminist analysis regarding questions of Lucy's agency and recovery from rape in *Disgrace*, which aligns with some of the alternative narrative choices presented in *Lacuna*.

3 For more on the methodological presuppositions involved when contemplating the way in which the Bible is represented *in* Literature as well as the Bible *and* Literature, see my forthcoming essay '"History Does Not Repeat Itself But It Rhymes": Exploring Literary Representations of Violence in Bible in/and Literature', in the encyclopaedic volume *The Bible and Violence*, edited by Chris

Greenough et al. (Claassens, forthcoming). This current chapter brings together biblical and contemporary texts that at first glance do not seem to be connected, but which generate new meaning when texts are read together. As Graybill (2021, p. 25), who follows a similar approach, argues: 'Texts crack open when they are made to talk to other texts.'

4 In Lamentations 1.21, the technical term for rape, the Piel form of '-n-h, is used to capture the subjugation and violation of cities in the ancient Near East. See also the reference to Daughter Zion being pursued and taken in a confined space (cf. the translation 'narrow places' for *ben ha-metsarim* in Lam. 1.3) that has been argued is suggestive of the context of rape (cf. also Gordon and Washington, 1995, p. 313; Claassens, 2020, p. 137).

5 Judith Herman (1997, pp. 3, 155) outlines three stages in the process of recovering from a traumatic event: (1) Establishing safety; (2) Remembering and mourning the traumatic event; (3) Reconnecting with ordinary life (Claassens, 2016, p. 182). I have found these stages of recovery helpful in contemplating Tamar's potential recovery in the aftermath of being raped by Amnon in 2 Samuel 13 (Claassens, 2016, pp. 182–90).

6 Given that it most often is not strangers who are responsible for gender-based violence, but rather individuals known to the victim (e.g. intimate partners and other members inside the house), the fact that in both *Lacuna* and in the case of Daughter Zion it is father-figures who are responsible for harm is significant.

7 Feminist scholars over the years have offered numerous examples and strategies for challenging gender-based violence in the prophetic traditions. See, for example, Julia O'Brien's book *Challenging Prophetic Metaphor* (2008) which reflects on 'challenging' divine metaphors such as God as (Abusing) Husband and God as (Authoritarian Father), unpacking the complex power dynamics underlying these metaphors in their respective socio-cultural contexts. See also Day, 2000; Guest, 1999; Claassens, 2014.

2

'Long Since Murdered': Cozbi, *The Kreutzer Sonata*, and the Limits of Narrating Sexual Violence

RHIANNON GRAYBILL

Introduction

This chapter begins with a silhouette and a thread. First, the silhouette: William Faulkner famously described his novel *The Sound and the Fury* as beginning with an image: a little girl in muddy underwear climbing a tree (Stein, 1956, pp. 413–14). Similarly, this chapter also begins with an image, really little more than a silhouette: a man and woman embracing; another man off to the side, a weapon raised, threatening. And, a moment later, the man attacking the couple, a fatal assault. This tableau lies at the heart of the story of Cozbi, found in the book of Numbers in the Hebrew Bible. It is also the heart of Lev Nikolaevich Tolstoy's novella *The Kreutzer Sonata*, written more than two millennia later. Tolstoy is a famously complicated religious writer, and *The Kreutzer Sonata* has its share of biblical references (though never to Cozbi). And yet the climaxes of both stories are striking, and striking in their similarity.

Consider the biblical story referenced here. Numbers 25 begins with the Israelites in Shittim. Typically for the wilderness narrative, they are up to no good: they have begun having sex with Moabite women, offering sacrifices to their gods, and worshipping Baal of Peor (Num. 25.1–3). This enrages Yahweh, who commands Moses to execute their leaders; Moses parries and instead instructs the leaders to kill the people who have transgressed (Num. 25.4–5). Then, suddenly, the narrative shifts:

> Just then a man from the Israelites came and brought a Midianite woman to his brothers, in the eyes of Moses and the eyes of all the Israelites, who were weeping at the entrance to the tent of meeting. Phinehas the son of Eleazar, the son of Aaron the priest, saw. He got

up from the midst of the congregation and took a spear in his hand. He came after the Israelite man into the tent and pierced the two of them, the Israelite man and the woman in the belly. And the plague was brought to an end among the Israelites. There were 24,000 people who died from the plague. (Num. 25.6–9)[1]

From a story of transgression that begins with Moabite women, we now have a single Midianite woman – who enters the story only to die. Her killer, the priest Phinehas, is praised for his actions, as well as rewarded by Yahweh with 'a covenant of perpetual priesthood' (Num. 25.13). It is several verses later that we learn the woman's name, her history, and the name of her partner:

The name of the Israelite man who was slain with the slain Midianite woman was Zimri, son of Salu, head of the ancestral house (*beyt-'av*) of the Simeonites. The name of the slain woman was Cozbi, daughter of Zur, head of a clan, an ancestral house in Midian. (Num. 25.14–15)

The second story I have referenced is *The Kreutzer Sonata*. First published in 1889, it was promptly censored by Russian authorities (though this only increased its appeal).[2] Tolstoy intended the work to be an indictment of carnal love and an argument for chastity (Tolstoy, 2014b, pp. 297–9). It is most notable, however, for its misogynistic violence.[3] Like Numbers 25, the story begins in the midst of a long journey (here, by train); several characters fall into conversation together and begin debating love and marriage. Eventually, a man named Pozdnyshev begins sharing his story with the narrator. Pozdnyshev, it is quickly revealed, murdered his wife in a fit of sexual jealousy. As he recounts, he became consumed with jealousy when his wife made the acquaintance of a violin player and began to spend time with him. In response, he began to imagine her infidelity – and to plot a deadly punishment. Upon returning home from a business trip, he attempts a double murder: first strangling his wife and then stabbing her, and also stabbing the violinist.[4] The other man escapes and survives; the wife does not. Pozdnyshev is acquitted of her murder on the grounds of (assumed) spousal adultery.

Both stories share the same murderous tableau: two men, one woman, a phallic weapon, a shocking dénouement. The similarities do not end here. The murders themselves are a swirling mess of sexual desire, sex and misogynistic rage. Cozbi is stabbed through the *qevah*, her womb, uterus or vagina (Num. 25.8).[5] Pozdnyshev aims his weapon similarly. As he describes:

I knew that I was stabbing her below the ribs and that the dagger would penetrate ... I heard and recall the momentary resistance of her corset and of something else, then the penetration of the knife into something soft. She grabbed the dagger with her hands, cut them, but didn't let go. (Tolstoy, 2014b, p. 66)

The violence is amplified by the sexual charge of the image, which clearly plays on the multiple forms of penetration and their gendered significance. In both texts, murder becomes rape becomes murder. Furthermore, both murders are carried out by an aggrieved zealot against a man and a woman who are likely innocent of all charges. Notably, the guilt of Pozdnyshev's wife (he suspects her of adultery) is never established, and indeed there are some suggestions of her innocence. The same is true, of course, of Cozbi who, despite the efforts of a certain subset of commentators to prove otherwise, does nothing wrong.[6] Zimri, too, seems an innocent man. But in spite of all this, the sympathies of both narratives clearly lie with the murderer. Pozdnyshev shares clear similarities with Tolstoy himself, including an increasingly obsessive vacillation between sexual revulsion and sexual obsession, an iconoclastic Christian faith (and interpretation of biblical texts), and a sweeping misogyny. Phinehas, for his part, is rewarded with an eternal covenant for his actions and functions as an object of praise, rather than censure.

But as feminist criticism has taught us, we do not have to read with the grain, or accept the author's own interpretation of a text. The author or authors of Numbers 25 should be viewed with suspicion; Tolstoy, too, may be wrong. Tolstoy's wife, Sofiya (Sonya) Andreevna Tolstaya, certainly thought he was wrong: upon reading an early draft of the novella, she pressured him to increase the ambiguity around the wife's guilt (Katz, 2014a, p. v). She also wrote her own response, which she entitled *Whose Fault? Apropos of the Kreutzer Sonata* (rejected titles included 'Is She Guilty?', 'Murdered', 'Long Since Murdered', and 'How Husbands Murder Their Wives' (Tolstaya, 2014d; Katz, 2014a, p. xvi)). And she wrote with frustration and sadness about *The Kreutzer Sonata* in her diaries, as well as her memoir (Tolstaya, 2014a; 2014b). Her interest was not simply literary: as many feminist critics have noted, there were many unhappy similarities between the novella and the Tolstoys' own marriage (though the latter did not end with murder). Sonya Tolstaya was not being paranoid when she expressed concern that readers would treat her husband's work as autobiographical, and associate Pozdnyshev's wife with her. It is also worth pausing to note the unhappy conditions of the Tolstoys' marriage: Lev, despite his commitments to chastity, also frequently forced himself on his wife, and Sonya endured 16 pregnancies and gave birth to 13 children, eight of whom survived to adulthood.

Sonya Tolstaya's responses to *The Kreutzer Sonata* are the first knot on the thread that I have alluded to before, a thread connecting Tolstoy's text to the circumstances of its composition and its history of reception. There are others. There is the son Lev Lvovich Tolstoy (2014), who wrote his own critical response to his father's work: a knot on the thread. There is Gustav Mahler, another jealous husband, who presented his wife Alma with a copy of *The Kreutzer Sonata*, warned her lest she end up like the wife in the novella, and raped her: a knot on the thread (Dworkin, 2007, pp. 3–4).[7] There is Andrea Dworkin, radical feminist, who opened her monumental feminist work *Intercourse*, first published in 1987, with a chapter on *The Kreutzer Sonata*, and with Mahler's violent repurposing of the novella against his wife: another knot on the thread (Dworkin, 2007, pp. 3–24). There is the complicated legacy of Dworkin's work (Fateman, 2019, pp. 3–43), which gives us the language to describe and understand extreme misogynistic violence – like Tolstoy's, like Phinehas' – but which has also been critiqued by later feminists for its singular focus on gender: another knot on the thread. There is the messiness of Dworkin's own life and writing, including her experiences of rape and of being disbelieved about her rape, and the attempts by other feminists to reckon with this legacy, to claim Dworkin or repudiate her. There is Beethoven's original *Kreutzer Sonata*, which lies before Tolstoy's text, and René-Xavier Prinet's famous painting 'The Kreutzer Sonata', which comes after. There are the novella's many literary and film adaptations, as well as literary and cinematic retellings of the Tolstoys' lives and marriage that constitute more knots.

We have strayed far from Cozbi. Or, perhaps, not far at all – as I hope to show, we can use this body of work to experiment with filling the gaps in the biblical account of Cozbi. I am interested in how reading literary and adjacent texts together, especially across time, helps us to conceptualize the project of narrating rape. I will highlight four themes and their significance for narrating rape stories: misogyny, masculinity, purity and the outfolding trauma. I will then turn to *The Kreutzer Sonata* to consider how the texts and textual ephemera that surround Tolstoy's novella might help us sketch a richer understanding of Cozbi's violation, without falling into the trap of *speaking for her*. The end goal is a more nuanced and complex account of narrating sexual violence both in and beyond the Hebrew Bible.

Misogyny

While perhaps obvious, it bears repeating: both Numbers 25 and *The Kreutzer Sonata* are texts riddled with misogyny. In using this specific term, I am guided by feminist philosopher Kate Manne and her work *Down Girl: The Logic of Misogyny*. As Manne argues, we misunderstand and dangerously underestimate misogyny when we treat it as an individual attitude or behaviour. Misogyny is not a personal attitude or a few (or more than a few) bad men. Instead, it is a system that is built on a set of enduring assumptions about how relations between men and women ought to be organized: specifically, women ought to occupy subordinate, functional and relational roles that are directed towards men (Manne, 2019, pp. xxi, 57). Under this system, men maintain certain 'masculine-coded perks and privileges' which include 'power, prestige, public recognition, rank, reputation, honor, "face," respect, money and other forms of wealth, hierarchical status, upward mobility, and the status conferred by having a high-ranking women's loyalty, love, devotion' (Manne, 2019, p. 130). They likewise assert entitlement to 'feminine-coded goods', including attention, affection, sympathy, sex, children, home, security and comfort (Manne, 2019, p. 120).

Misogyny is sustained by *himpathy* and *testimonial injustice*. Himpathy describes the special sympathy extended to men (especially powerful men) but withheld from women. Powerful men are more likely to be believed, especially when the alleged wrongdoing involves a woman; when such wrongdoing is definitively established, they are more likely to receive sympathy. Manne coins the term 'himpathy' to describe this process (see the discussion in Manne, 2019, pp. 195–205). The flipside of himpathy is the corresponding hostility, disbelief and withholding of empathy that women face when they claim to be victims of misogyny.[8] Seeking to understand this response, Manne introduces the notion of 'testimonial injustice', adopted from fellow philosopher Miranda Fricker, which seeks to understand why some subjects' testimony is taken as trustworthy (i.e. men's) and others' is not (i.e. the testimony of women) (Manne, 2019, p. 186; Fricker, 2007, *passim*). The 'credibility deficit' that women face works like other structures of testimonial injustice (e.g. that faced by Black, Latinx and Native Americans in the US justice system): to uphold existing structures of inequality.

These terms – misogyny, himpathy, testimonial injustice – give us some useful language to describe the narrative strategies of both *The Kreutzer Sonata* and Numbers 25. Both Pozdnyshev and Phinehas are clear beneficiaries of himpathy; their respective stories treat them with favour, over and against the women they murder. In Numbers 25, I would suggest, himpathy extends to two other male characters as well: first, Cozbi's Israelite husband, Zimri, who brings her into the Israelite assembly without consent and under somewhat suspicious conditions and, second, the Hebrew god Yahweh, whose rivalry with 'Baal of Peor', the Moabites' god, is specifically a rivalry over masculine entitlement to goods and services. Both stories likewise show us testimonial injustice: Pozdnyshev is acquitted of his wife's murder on the grounds of spousal adultery (of course, she is dead at the time of the trial and cannot speak). And Cozbi's name literally means 'lie'. Fricker describes the harm of testimonial injustice that also harms the subject who is not believed as follows: 'The subject is wronged in her capacity as a knower. To be wronged in one's capacity as a knower is to be wronged in a capacity essential to human value' (Fricker, 2007, p. 44). Both Cozbi and Pozdnyshev's wives are wronged in this way – and the consequences are deadly.

Masculinity

Misogyny is intertwined with masculinity. Here, relations of power and domination are central. These relations are chiefly negotiated between men: women and women's bodies function as objects. In the Hebrew Bible, the text allows for spaces of remarkable male intimacy, such as David's relationship with Jonathan, Saul's pursuit of David, the homosocial intimacies of Elijah and Elisha, the configurations of warriors and armies in Judges, and of course Yahweh's relations with the prophets. Meanwhile, relations between men are negotiated through the bodies of women – and not infrequently, this negotiation takes the form of extreme violence. For instance, in Judges 19—21, the rape threat against the male Levite by the men of Gibeah is 'resolved' through the rape and murder of the Levite's concubine, the subsequent war on Benjamin, and the mass rapes of women from Jabesh-Gilead and Shiloh (on masculinity in this story, see Harding, 2018, pp. 159–78).

We see a similar logic in Numbers 25. The threat to masculinity is worked out through extreme violence against the female body. Here the male that is threatened is Yahweh: the Israelites' interactions with the Moabites represent a 'betrayal' of the 'marriage'/exclusive (sexual) contract between the male Israelite deity and the feminized national body of Israel. Violence – enacted by the representative male agent, Phinehas – restores masculinity to its privileged position. That Cozbi, who bears the brunt of the violence, is not actually involved in the events that precipitate it does not matter. Dworkin's analysis is fitting:

> Any woman who acts on a man's sensuality by provoking it – which she does just by being a sexual object in looks and behavior – makes him intoxicated, deranged, stupified; he wants to call a policeman and have her put away. She is this danger, has this power, dominates him, directly as a consequence of her inequality, the meaning of which is in her reduction to a sexual object ... This anguish ended only with killing her, because only in death was she incapable of defying him. (Dworkin, 2007, pp. 19, 22)

Dworkin is in fact writing about *The Kreutzer Sonata*, but her description resonates closely with the biblical story. Cozbi 'acts on Yhwh's/[Phinehas]'s sensuality' in the way that so many victims of misogynistic rage do – simply by existing, by seeming to be a sexual subject. That Cozbi is with Zimri does not matter; that Zimri is an Israelite – and a high-ranking one at that – does not matter. In fact, it does not even matter to Phinehas whether Cozbi has been brought into the Israelite assembly against her will. All that matters is that she has provoked a man.

As the applicability of this quote to Numbers 25 suggests, in Tolstoy's novella we find a similar pattern. In *The Kreutzer Sonata*, however, the problem is not masculinity in general, but sexual desire in particular. The novella's representations of masculinity are inextricable from the fantasy of violence against the female body, and against the feminine. It is only in death that Pozdnyshev's wife becomes, at last, human: that is, when her husband's masculinity is finally secured.[9]

Purity

Equally relevant in both of these stories is the preoccupation with purity. In analysing purity as a structuring principle of sexual violence in Numbers 25, I am in conversation with other scholars who have analysed purity, sex and contagion. In her classic study *Purity and Danger*, Mary Douglas analyses the relationship between the individual body and the social body, suggesting that we are especially concerned with the boundaries of the individual body (and entry points such as the mouth, eyes and genitals) because the individual body metonymically represents the social body (Douglas, 2013). M. Cooper Minister (2018) argues that Douglas's analysis of purity and the boundaries of the body helps us to understand the treatment of victims and survivors of sexual violence. Rape or other sexual violence is a violation not just of the individual body, but of the social body. Furthermore, victims and survivors are often censored or punished because they function as a reminder that the purity of the community has been breached. In particular, we find that sexual violence transforms the victim's body into a contagious, threatening body:[10]

> Because the physical and social bodies are related, the threat of individual, bodily pollution threatens the social order ... Sexual purity, in this sense, is not merely something that happens on an individual level but becomes a social issue. (Minister, 2018, pp. 5, 7)

Numbers 25 thematizes this concern for purity (sexual and social) and anxiety over contagion. In the opening verses, the Israelites transgress with the Moabite women both by sharing sexual intimacy and through eating. The conjoining of these two practices in the narrative highlights the anxiety over the openings and margins of the body, represented by both mouths and genitals.[11] Such sexual and culinary 'bodily pollution' thus 'threatens the social order' of Yahwistic Israelite practice. The contagious touch of the Moabite women unfolds across the first three verses: first sex, then sacrifices, then food, then the pledging of loyalty to Baal of Peor. One thing leads to another – yet another vision of forbidden sex ending in impurity and disaster.

Purity and contagion also animate the Cozbi episode. Though Cozbi is Midianite, not Moabite, Zimri's physical touch, which occurs before 'the eyes of all the Israelites' (Num. 25.6), represents the threat to this order. Phinehas' violent act undertakes the restoration of the social order by brutally punishing this violation of the physical/social integrity of the body (the sexually opened Cozbi doubles for the sexually open Moabites). This suggests, as well, another significance to Phinehas' use of the spear: it is not simply a phallic signifier, but also a protection against touch. Phinehas penetrates with the spear so that he does not have to touch with his body. Thus, the act is purifying, while also protecting the actor, Phinehas, from self-contamination. The plague at Peor, mentioned twice in passing (in Num. 25.12, 18) represents a second attempt to secure purity in the text, through a wave of deaths that washes the slate clean.

In *The Kreutzer Sonata*, purity plays out in other ways.[12] Pozdnyshev is clearly obsessed with sexual purity, even as he finds such purity impossible. But I would suggest that the literary structure of the work also reflects, more obliquely, concerns with purity. The act of striking violence, horrific and unforgettable, is carefully insulated in multiple narrative layers – we encounter it only through Pozdnyshev's memories, recounted after the fact, on a train, to a sympathetic listener. But even that is not the end of the insulating – this train conversation is itself nested within a frame narrative involving other passengers on the train and their political and ethical debates. This nesting functions as a literary technique of purity, not unlike the positioning of the violence against Cozbi within the only tangentially related frame narrative of Moabite women.

A focus on purity also helps us understand the reception of the novella, and the responses it inspired. The work was quickly censored, only increasing its appeal – this is not surprising. Instead, I am interested in how purity, and a desire to protect the purity of his ideas, helps us to understand Tolstoy's own response to his work: faced with criticism, he published a 'purified' second iteration of the work that stripped away the narrative in favour of strict ideology (Tolstoy, 2014a, pp. 297–308). Even fiction, it seems, risks becoming a distraction from ideological purity.

Replication, re-narration and trauma

All this leads to the fourth theme I want to discuss, with which I want to linger a bit longer: the transmission and replication of trauma across narrative and extra-narrative moments in both texts. Trauma is almost never limited to a single, self-contained event; this is certainly true of sexual trauma.[13] Though Phinehas, Yahweh and Moses all seek, variously, to contain the events at Shittim through violence, the trauma is never fully contained. The first sign of this failure comes in the reference to Cozbi's name and family (and, indeed, to Zimri's) in Numbers 25.14–15. *These dead among us are not nameless*, the text concedes. *They had names, families*. As Dworkin observes, Pozdnyshev's murdered wife becomes human in his eyes only after he has killed her: 'When she is dead, bruised, disfigured, inert, a cadaver, he calls her human. The cost of the recognition is death' (Dworkin, 2007, p. 23). But also, it seems, death does not merely erase – recognition comes, even if in mourning.

The stickiness of trauma, the ways that one experience or moment unfolds or touches or alters others, helps explain what holds together the two distinct threads of Numbers 25, the Moabite women thread and the Cozbi thread.[14] Both are stories (or partial stories) of violence caused by and carried out against the female body. Neither story, on its own, is complete, despite the efforts of the final verse of the chapter to knit the two together by redescribing the Moabites as Midianites and Cozbi as their 'sister' (Num. 25.18). But what they do show is how narratives of trauma resemble, reflect and refract one another.[15] The sexual traumas narrated in Numbers 25 unfold backwards and forwards to other scenes of sexual violence in the Israelite encounter with Midianites and Moabites alike. The events at Peor are not separable from the Moabites' origins in Lot's drunken sexual acts with his daughters (Gen. 19.31–36). These Moabite women are the nameless daughter's nameless daughters' daughters. And, of course, the Midianites are threatened with genocide via Yahweh's promise of the land to Abraham (Gen. 17.6–8) – a promise that hangs proleptically over the encounter in the wilderness here. And there is the more proximate violence, explicitly linked to the events of Baal of Peor, which follow in Numbers 31, when Moses demands the murder of every man and non-virgin woman, while 'every female child who has not slept with a male, keep alive for yourselves' (Gen. 31.15–18).

We could treat *The Kreutzer Sonata* and its reception and afterlives as another example of such cross-contaminating narratives of trauma. I am especially interested in how Sonya Tolstaya's writings help us deepen our understanding of this problem. Tolstaya was deeply unsettled and unhappy about Tolstoy's novella; she told him so, and, moreover, wrote about it at multiple points in her diary. And yet when the novella was censored, she visited the Tsar and pleaded to allow its publication with Tolstoy's complete works; the Tsar eventually obliged (Katz, 2014a, p. xii). But Tolstaya's entanglement with the work did not end here: she also wrote two novellas of her own in response, 'Whose Fault?' (2014d) and 'Song Without Words' (2014c). But, like the words of Cozbi, both remained unheard (on her family's wishes) – until they were finally published almost a century after their composition.

'Whose Fault?', in particular, rewrites *The Kreutzer Sonata* from the perspective of the wife. Here, she is named Anna; she falls in love but, after marriage, she suffers. Tolstaya's rewriting of the death scene is especially important. While the original novella describes the wife as looking like a furious cornered rat (Tolstoy, 2014b, p. 65) while granting psychic interiority only to her husband, Tolstaya centres Anna. Picking up on a detail in the original, she also emphasizes the presence of the children in the scene (Tolstaya, 2014d, pp. 161–3). The oldest daughter becomes a female witness, suggesting a slim, if possible, space of solidarity.[16]

There are other changes in Tolstaya's work as well. The murder weapon is no longer a dagger but, instead, a paperweight (Tolstaya, 2014d, p. 160). The exotic weapon is replaced by a humble domestic object – but the consequences are no less deadly. This is fitting: gender violence and sexual violence are not shocking interruptions; they are, as rape culture teaches us, part of everyday culture. And, of course, the cruellest forms of torture rely not on elaborate devices but on the repurposing of the everyday, as Elaine Scarry (1987, p. 41) has shown. In keeping with the recentring of the narrative on the wife, she is given the opportunity to speak in the death scene, an opportunity she uses to condemn her murderer. And the story ends not with the violence, but with her burial – forcing us to consider the violence we have witnessed. And the icky voyeurism of Tolstoy's original is gone, replaced with a more familiar – to me, at least – mix of anger and sadness.

I wish that I could tell you that 'Whose Fault?' is a brilliant novella. I wish that I could report that it brilliantly deconstructs every move of Tolstoy's original. I wish that I could tell you that I loved it – as I would say about many feminist rewritings, from Virginia Woolf's famous account of 'Shakespeare's Sister' to Fiona Snyckers in *Lacuna* giving voice to Lucy Lurie from J. M. Coetzee's *Disgrace* (see also Claassens's Chapter 1 in this volume). But 'Whose Fault?' is not brilliant. It is a fine novella – mixed, but fine. Perhaps, it's most notable in its unremarkability. But also: perhaps we should not have to be brilliant in order to earn the right to repudiate misogyny.

I also want to linger with the complexity of Tolstaya's response, to see what we might learn from it to apply to Numbers 25. She hated her husband's novella – but also invested great personal effort in promoting it. She insisted on its literary value even as she hated it. She wrote her own response, seeking to deconstruct it and expose the workings of its misogyny, only to find her response silenced. She attracted more pity than respect. She also was not innocent of the power networks she participated in, including class exploitation. In Sonya Tolstaya, I see a precursor of the feminist biblical scholar and the dilemmas we face in interpreting a text filled with misogyny and sexual violence, working within a field that not infrequently replicates this misogyny. Reading Numbers 25, I find myself as Sonya's ambivalent heir.

Andrea Dworkin and *Intercourse*

There is one more knot in the thread I wish to untangle, or perhaps tangle more thoroughly: Andrea Dworkin's treatment of sexual violence, and of *The Kreutzer Sonata* in particular, in *Intercourse* (Dworkin, 2007). *Intercourse* is a brilliant, difficult book, by a brilliant, difficult thinker. In it, Dworkin set out to understand the act of intercourse – as sex, as domination, as defining feature of the relations between men and women. In her preface, written eight years after the book was first published, Dworkin describes the book as follows:

> *Intercourse* is a book that moves through the sexed world of dominance and submission. It moves in descending circles, not in a straight line, and as a vortex each spiral goes down deeper. Its formal model is Dante's *Inferno*; its lyrical ebb is to Rimbaud; the equality it envisions is rooted in the dreams of women, silent generations, pioneer voices, lone rebels, and masses who agitated, demanded, cried out, broke law, and even begged. The begging was a substitute for retaliatory violence: doing bodily harm back to those who use or injure you. I want women to be done with begging. (Dworkin, 2007, p. xxx)

In place of begging, she offers a rigorous philosophical exploration, equal parts harsh and dazzling, that seeks to 'convey the density, complexity, and political significance of the act of intercourse' (Dworkin, 2007, p. xxxiv). The starting point is not sex as such but literature, with a particular focus on the nineteenth-century (masculine) canon. Dworkin's readings come from a place of love but not of sympathy: 'I love the literature these men created; but I will not live my life as if they are real and I am not' (Dworkin, 2007, p. xxxii).

One of these men is Lev Tolstoy. In *Intercourse*, The Kreutzer Sonata is given the opening chapter, beating out works by Gustave Flaubert, D. H. Lawrence, Bram Stoker and others. In taking on *The Kreutzer Sonata*, Dworkin knew, of course, the outlines of Tolstoy's life, as well as Tolstaya's. She had access to the latter's memoirs and her diaries, though not to her fiction. And, of course, a voluminous scholarly literature on Tolstoy already existed, though Dworkin mostly concerns herself with a close literary and philosophical engagement with the text, rather than its academic reception.

Of special interest in Dworkin's reading of Tolstoy is just how seriously she takes him and his work. Dworkin is often reduced to a caricature by non-feminists and feminists alike. According to this caricature, she's the angry one, the one who hates sex, the one who hates men, the one who only wears overalls. She and other feminists like her are the reason that feminism is *not sexy* and *not fun*. She's widely taken to be a misandrist, famous for pronouncing 'all sex is rape' (even though she never actually said this).[17] But it is Andrea Dworkin – *this* Andrea Dworkin – who offers one of the most insightful readings of the achingly misogynistic, deeply troubling *The Kreutzer Sonata*, both as a work in its own right and as a reflection of larger cultural dimensions of misogyny.[18] Dworkin's reading proceeds methodically, showing us how Tolstoy's argument works, why it matters, and why we should care.

If Sonya Tolstaya offers a model of dismantling rape stories by refocalizing and telling them differently, Andrea Dworkin suggests another possibility: close reading of literary misogyny as a strategy of feminist critique. And Dworkin is a highly effective and insightful reader. Her literary readings open the text in new ways. Furthermore, and significantly, what she is modelling in her readings in *Intercourse* – and first and foremost in her reading of *The Kreutzer Sonata* – is precisely what 'traditional' biblical criticism demands: close literary reading, attention to historical contexts and the material conditions of a work's composition, an eye for detail. And, I would add, openness and even a posture of intellectual generosity towards the text – the better to understand it and dismantle it.

Often, feminist biblical interpreters who are interested in pushing back against misogyny and other structures of oppression in biblical texts are faced with a dilemma: *What can we do, really?* What avenues of response are available to us? In what ways can we respond? And what sort of stories is it possible to tell, anyway? In many ways, these are the same questions that surface when we delve into the problem of 'narrating rape', or of exploring ways to talk about – and talk back to – sexual violence. One possibility is a kind of creative response that tells a new story, or that tells the story from a different perspective. Sonya Tolstaya's work (2014c; 2014d) does this; so too does feminist midrash and similar practices of narrative retelling (to begin, see Buchmann and Spiegel, 2012; Ostriker, 1994; Plaskow, 2015). These are beautiful, fiery, life-giving feminist literary works. I love them. They are rich and valuable. But at the same time, literary fabulation and counter-narrations should not be the only possibilities available to us as feminist critics – nor are they. Dworkin suggests another path, a path of *criticism itself*, and close textual engagement, as a path of feminist critical undoing. We can be just as bold and as angry and as persuasive in our works of critique as our works of storytelling. There's more than one way to catch a misogynist in his literary tracks. Or, as Dworkin (2007, p. xxxii) writes, 'Habits of deference can be broken, and it is put to writers to break them. Submission can be refused; and I refuse it.'

All this leads us back to Numbers 25. I will not end by offering a literary retelling of the Cozbi story, one that invites us to imagine Cozbi as she enters the assembly, as she embraces Zimri, as she senses Phinehas raising his weapon, as she collapses. Others have done this work, and beautifully – particularly Yael Klangwisan in her imaginative essay

'Twelve Steps to the Tent of Zimri: An Imaginarium' (2018, pp. 103–15). As Klangwisan envisions:

> I see Zimri turn in surprise and place his body before hers. I see Cozbi grasp hold of his arm in fright. The shout as this prince of Simeon steps forward with hand outstretched. Phinehas, with his blanched face and sheen of sweat. The tremble in his hand. The stink of his cowardice and his murderous arousal. The spear that he thrusts past Zimri to stab Cozbi through the middle. He's aiming for her belly, her belly that would have carried Zimri's child. Zimri draws her behind him but the spear finds its target. How long they lie dying in this profane scene, skewered like pigs, cut down like beasts, with their life blood mingling, soaking through the mats of the tent. The observer is not permitted to know. I know because in the imaginarium I hopelessly hold my hands to Cozbi's side but can't stem the blood flow. It keeps seeping out, its tinny scent, sticky on my fingers. She whimpers, clasps my wrist and dies slowly, Zimri collapsed near her, arm across her. A bloodied Romeo. Was his death instantaneous or was it slow? It might be very slow, perhaps days. But I wonder, as I view the hidden scenes …
>
> A veil lies across these scenes (like the flap of a tent), yet they haunt the text. The miasma of horror seeps out of the print, and writhes. Like a fold or a *punctum*, in the narrative it waits.
> The beloved couple will die.
> The beloved couple will surely die.
> The beloved couple will die horribly.
> (Klangwisan, 2018, pp. 108, 109)

To Klangwisan's vision, to Cozbi's death, to Pozdnyshev's bleeding wife, to Tolstaya's tragic Anna, fatally wounded with a simple paperweight, I can add only a few critical remarks. First, texts illuminate one another, especially in their moments of perverse symmetry. Feminist criticism, and other criticism, can learn from reading such texts together. Thus, *The Kreutzer Sonata* and Numbers 25 offer mirror tableaux of violence, parallel sympathies for the male protagonist/murderer, and similar dynamics of himpathy. Women are treated as objects, their identities crudely sketched or erased (consider the name Cozbi, 'lie'). They are mostly interchangeable with one another; they exist as objects of masculine desire and violence. It is only in death that the female character is granted subjectivity – she can only become a subject when it is too late. Beyond their violence, *The Kreutzer Sonata* and Numbers 25 are also each intensely concerned with purity: purity from sexual contamination, purity of the body and its boundaries, purity of the community. This is neither accident nor distraction. Instead, violence and anxiety over purity are intertwined and mutually sustaining structures in the texts – with fatal consequences for their female victims. Similarly, sexual violence and sexual trauma are almost never singular events; they fold forwards and backwards into other traumas and scenes of violence.

It is not only in their shared details that texts can illuminate one another. Instead, the reception of a text, the literary, philosophical and other responses it engenders, can also aid in the practice of interpretation across texts and times. Much more is known about the composition and reception of Tolstoy's text than of Numbers 25. This can help us embark on a feminist project of imagining a richer world around the biblical text, which is partial and fragile. In particular, Sonya Tolstaya's complex response to her husband's violent novella – including her documented hatred of it, her public intervention to allow its circulation, her private concerns over it in her diary, and her own counter-novella – offer a clear example of the difficult, contradictory positions that we find ourselves in as we try to respond to powerful, troubling works of misogyny. As with *The Kreutzer Sonata*, so too with the Bible: Sonya Tolstaya is a proto-paradigm of the feminist biblical scholar struggling with the text and the Fathers of the field.[19] Similarly, Andrea Dworkin's reading of *The Kreutzer Sonata* in *Intercourse* points to another path of feminist possibility: close reading and other forms of 'traditional' criticism as tools of documenting – and perhaps dismantling – misogyny.

At the conclusion of her preface, Dworkin (2007, p. xxxiv) writes, 'I have always loved the writing that takes one down deep, no matter how strange or bitter or dirty the descent.' Our descent in this chapter has been strange, often bitter, sometimes dirty. Cozbi remains dead; Pozdnyshev's wife unavenged. And yet in going deep, my goal has not been to save, or even to salvage, but rather to illuminate a range of possibilities for feminist work. Sometimes, this work means restoring women's stories or revivifying victims of misogyny. But it can equally mean the work of tracing a parallel, of listening for an echo, of following a thread. A feminist practice of narrating violence, or narrating rape, is not always a happy ending. Instead, it is equally an exploration of the depths. Where else is feminist wisdom to be found?

Bibliography

Allen, Leah Claire, 2016, 'The Pleasures of Dangerous Criticism: Interpreting Andrea Dworkin as a Literary Critic', *Signs* 42/1, pp. 49–70.
Buchmann, Christina, and Celina Spiegel (eds), 2012, *Out of the Garden: Women Writers on the Bible*, New York: Ballantine Books.
Douglas, Mary, 2013, *Purity and Danger: An Analysis of Concepts of Pollution and Taboo*, New York: Routledge.
Dworkin, Andrea, 1976, *Woman Hating: A Radical Look at Sexuality*, New York: Dutton.
Dworkin, Andrea, 2007, *Intercourse*, 20th anniversary edn, New York: Basic Books.
Fateman, Johanna, 2019, 'Introduction' in Johanna Fateman and Amy Scholder (eds), *Last Days at Hot Slit: The Radical Feminism of Andrea Dworkin*, Semiotext(e) Native Agents, Semiotext(e).
Faulkner, William, 1973, 'An Introduction to "The Sound and the Fury"', *The Mississippi Quarterly* 26/3, pp. 410–15.
Felman, Shoshana, 1997, 'Forms of Judicial Blindness, or the Evidence of What Cannot Be Seen: Traumatic Narratives and Legal Repetitions in the OJ Simpson Case and in Tolstoy's "The Kreutzer Sonata"', *Critical Inquiry* 23/4, pp. 738–88.
Fleurant, Josebert, 2011, 'Phinehas Murdered Moses' Wife: An Analysis of Numbers 25', *Journal for the Study of the Old Testament* 35/3, pp. 285–94.
Fricker, Miranda, 2007, *Testimonial Injustice*, New York: Oxford University Press.
Graybill, Rhiannon, 2017, 'Critiquing the Discourse of Consent', *Journal of Feminist Studies in Religion* 33/1, pp. 175–6.
Graybill, Rhiannon, 2021, *Texts after Terror: Rape, Sexual Violence, and the Hebrew Bible*, New York: Oxford University Press.
Grossman, Jonathan, 2007, 'Divine Command and Human Initiative: A Literary View on Numbers 25–31', *Biblical Interpretation* 15/1, pp. 54–79.
Harding, James E., 2018, 'Homophobia and Rape Cultures in the Narratives of Early Israel' in Caroline Blyth, Emily Colgan and Katie B. Edwards (eds), *Rape Culture, Gender Violence, and Religion: Biblical Perspectives*, Religion and Radicalism, Palgrave Macmillan, pp. 159–78.
Katz, Michael R., 2014a, 'Introduction: The Tolstoy Family Story Contest' in Katz (2014b, pp. xi–xxi).
Katz, Michael R. (ed.), 2014b, *The Kreutzer Sonata Variations: Lev Tolstoy's Novella and Counterstories by Sofiya Tolstaya and Lev Lvovich Tolstoy*, New Haven, CT: Yale University Press.
Kelso, Julie, 2018, 'Andrea Dworkin on the Biblical Foundations of Violence against Women' in Caroline Blyth, Emily Colgan and Katie B. Edwards (eds), *Rape Culture, Gender Violence, and Religion: Biblical Perspectives*, Religion and Radicalism, Palgrave Macmillan, pp. 83–102.
Klangwisan, Yael, 2018, 'Twelve Steps to the Tent of Zimri: An Imaginarium' in Caroline Blyth, Emily Colgan and Katie B. Edwards (eds), *Rape Culture, Gender Violence, and Religion: Biblical Perspectives*, Religion and Radicalism, Palgrave Macmillan, pp. 103–15, available at https://link.springer.com/book/10.1007/978-3-319-72224-5 (accessed 8.12.2023).

Manne, Kate, 2019, *Down Girl: The Logic of Misogyny*, New York: Penguin Books.
Miller, Chanel, 2019, *Know My Name: A Memoir*, Viking.
Minister, M. Cooper, 2018, *Rape Culture on Campus*, Lanham; Boulder; New York; London: Lexington Books.
Monroe, Lauren A. S., 2012, 'Phinehas' Zeal and the Death of Cozbi: Unearthing a Human Scapegoat Tradition in Numbers 25:1-18', *Vetus Testamentum* 62/2, pp. 211-31.
Newman, Nancy, 2022, '#AlmaToo: The Art of Being Believed', *Journal of the American Musicological Society* 75/1, pp. 39-79.
Organ, Barbara E., 2001, 'Pursuing Phinehas: A Synchronic Reading', *The Catholic Biblical Quarterly* 63/2, pp. 203-18.
Ostriker, Alicia, 1994, *The Nakedness of the Fathers: Biblical Visions and Revisions*, New Brunswick, NJ: Rutgers University Press.
Plaskow, Judith, 2015, *The Coming of Lilith: Essays on Feminism, Judaism, and Sexual Ethics, 1972-2003*, Boston, MA: Beacon Press.
Reif, Stefan C., 1971, 'What Enraged Phinehas? A Study of Numbers 25:8', *Journal of Biblical Literature* 90/2, pp. 200-206.
Rowlett, Lori L., 2000, 'Disney's Pocahontas and Joshua's Rahab in Postcolonial Perspective' in George Aichele (ed.), *Culture, Entertainment, and the Bible*, JSOTSup 309, Sheffield: Sheffield Academic Press, pp. 66-75.
Scarry, Elaine, 1987, *The Body in Pain: The Making and Unmaking of the World*, New York: Oxford University Press.
Schulman, Sarah, 2016, *Conflict Is Not Abuse: Overstating Harm, Community Responsibility, and the Duty of Repair*, Vancouver: Arsenal Pulp Press.
Shectman, Sarah, 2009, *Women in the Pentateuch: A Feminist and Source-Critical Analysis*, Sheffield: Sheffield Phoenix Press.
Snyder, Rachel Louise, 2019, *No Visible Bruises: What We Don't Know About Domestic Violence Can Kill Us*, New York: Bloomsbury.
Stein, Jean, 1956, 'Interview with William Faulkner', *The Paris Review* IV, pp. 28-52.
Stoltenberg, John, 2020, 'Andrea Dworkin Was a Trans Ally', *Boston Review*, 8 April 2020, https://www.bostonreview.net/articles/john-stoltenberg-andrew-dworkin-was-trans-ally/ (accessed 8.12.2023).
Tolstoy, Lev Lvovich, 2014, 'Chopin's Prelude' in Katz (2014b, pp. 255-94).
Tolstoy, Lev Nikolaevich, 2014a, 'Epilogue to *The Kreutzer Sonata*' in Katz (2014b, pp. 297-308).
Tolstoy, Lev Nikolaevich, 2014b, 'The Kreutzer Sonata' in Katz (2014b, pp. 3-70).
Tolstoy, Lev Nikolaevich, 2014c, '"The Wife Murderer": A Fragment' in Katz (2014b, pp. 3-70).
Tolstaya, Akexandra Lvovna, 2014, 'Tolstoy: A Life of My Father (Excerpts)' in Katz (2014b, pp. 347-52).
Tolstaya, Sofiya Andreevna, 2014a, 'Diary Entries (Excerpts)' in Katz (2014b, pp. 321-28).
Tolstaya, Sofiya Andreevna, 2014b, '*My Life* (Excerpts)' in Katz (2014b, pp. 329-42).
Tolstaya, Sofiya Andreevna, 2014c, 'Song Without Words' in Katz (2014b, pp. 165-244).

Tolstaya, Sofiya Andreevna, 2014d, 'Whose Fault?' in Katz (2014b, pp. 71–164).
Washington, Harold C., 1997, 'Violence and the Construction of Gender in the Hebrew Bible: A New Historicist Approach 1', *Biblical Interpretation: A Journal of Contemporary Approaches* 5/4, pp. 324–63.
Williams, Cristan, 2016, 'Radical Inclusion: Recounting the Trans Inclusive History of Radical Feminism', *TSQ: Transgender Studies Quarterly* 3/1–2, pp. 254–8.
Wilson, Jennifer, 2016, 'The Revolution Will Not Be Consummated: The Politics of Tolstoyan Chastity in the West', *The Slavic and East European Journal* 60/3, pp. 494–511.

Notes

1 Translations from the Hebrew Bible are my own.

2 For an introduction to the novella and the contexts of its publication, see Katz, 2014.

3 In making this claim, I necessarily (and intentionally) flatten some of the ambiguity and richness of both the novella and its reception. Katz (2014a) provides a brief introduction and orientation to the major directions in the scholarship. My focus here is not on Tolstoy's novella as such, but instead how the text and its reception can help in the specific project of a feminist response to biblical sexual violence.

4 The detail of the strangling is significant, given recent work on strangling and misogyny. In situations of domestic violence, strangling is the final warning sign for murder. See Manne, 2019, pp. 1–4; Snyder, 2019, pp. 65–8.

5 The Hebrew word is used only here and in Deuteronomy 18.3, where it refers to a portion of the sacrificed animal's body to be given to the priests. It refers to a portion of the lower abdomen – translated, variously, as 'belly', 'stomach', 'womb' or 'sexual organs'. The sexual implications of this sort of penetration are clear. *Qevah* also plays on *qubbah*, the interior of the tent and the location where the murder takes place. See, further, Reif, 1971, pp. 200–6.

6 For example, Reif (1971, p. 205) associates Cozbi with 'some forbidden cultic activity', perhaps divination, and blames Zimri for bringing her into the Israelite camp; Organ (2001, p. 203) also suggests divination but notes as well the suggestion of an unspecified sexual offence. Grossman (2007, p. 60) charges that Zimri committed 'harlotry' with Cozbi, a suggestion also found in the Babylon Talmud, Sanhedrin 82a. Shectman (2009, p. 162), in contrast, blames Cozbi and Zimri for coming too close to the sanctuary. Monroe (2012, p. 211) reads the story as reflecting a 'human sacrifice tradition', with Cozbi as scapegoat. Fleurant (2011, pp. 285–94) suggests that Cozbi was in fact Zipporah.

7 For a more recent scholarly defence of Alma, see Newman, 2022, pp. 39–79.

8 Women who make such claims are typically met with suspicion; they are accused of seeking advantage, of misunderstanding or misinterpreting the situation, of being crazy, of holding a grudge. See Manne, 2019, pp. 217–18.

9 Here my analysis draws on Dworkin's reading in *Intercourse* (1987).

10 See also my analysis of the survivor as 'unhappy object' in Graybill, 2017, pp. 175–6.

11 Of course, sex does not always involve the genitals, though this is hardly reassuring for the biblical purity discourse.

12 See, more broadly, Wilson, 2016, pp. 494–511.

13 My thinking about harm in this section is especially informed by Sarah Schulman's *Conflict Is Not Abuse: Overstating Harm, Community Responsibility, and the Duty of Repair* (Schulman, 2016). Schulman offers a careful and thoughtful discussion of intergenerational trauma and its folding forwards and backwards. On traumatic repetition and *The Kreutzer Sonata*, see also Felman, 1997, pp. 738–88.

14 In using the language of 'stickiness', I intend an echo of Sara Ahmed's work on 'sticky' affects. See Ahmed, 2010, pp. 21–49, especially 40, 44 and 230, n. 1. On the relevance of this concept for rethinking biblical sexual violence, see Graybill, 2021, pp. 23–4.

15 For a contemporary perspective, see Miller, 2019. Another more cynical perspective is that the Israelite authors treat all non-Israelites as basically interchangeable, much as, for example, Europeans and white Americans treat Native American cultures as basically interchangeable. On this point as it applies to the Canaanites, and Rahab in particular, see Rowlett, 2000, pp. 66–75.

16 Given the role of the daughter in the novella, it is notable that Tolstaya's daughter Alexandra Lvovna Tolstaya (2014, pp. 347–52) vociferously rejected her mother, siding with her father and writing two memoirs about him.

17 For a nuanced take on Dworkin and her legacy, see Fateman, 2009, pp. 3–43. Given Dworkin's radical feminism, I also want to address the question of transphobia directly. On Dworkin's trans-inclusive politics, see Williams, 2016, pp. 254–8; Stoltenberg, 2020, n.p. From Dworkin's own works, chapter 9 of *Woman Hating*, entitled 'Androgyny: Androgyny, Fucking, and Community', is a good starting point. See Dworkin's *Woman Hating*, 1976.

18 On Dworkin as a literary critic, see also Allen, 2016.

19 There is of course more to be said about abusers in the field and Tolstoy as an abusive husband.

3

Consensual Sex or Rape? Bathsheba Encircled by Hegemonic Masculinity

CHRISTL M. MAIER

Introduction

In the narrative world of the books of Samuel and Kings, David is portrayed as a strong, virile and persuasive man, a paragon of masculinity. In the episode about his adulterous sexual intercourse with Bathsheba (2 Sam. 11), there are several lacunas with regard to the question as to whether Bathsheba is raped at all and how she experiences this event. When examining the power relations between the figures in this chapter, Bathsheba does not seem to have a choice. Yet, in her later rise to the rank of queen mother (1 Kings 1—2), she appears as strong-willed and active. In the age of the #MeToo movement, Bathsheba's life looks like the life of many (contemporary) career women, in which hegemonic masculinity turns toxic and the woman is caught in a dilemma, but always encircled by men who are complicit with her subordination.

In this chapter, I will address the characterization of King David using the concept of hegemonic masculinity as defined by the Australian sociologist Raewyn Connell. I will then continue to analyse the narrative of Bathsheba's rise to power. In the final part of this chapter, I will interpret Bathsheba's story against the background of the book and film *She Said*, which narrates the US American film mogul Harvey Weinstein's history of sexual misconduct, eventually led to his fall, and made the #MeToo movement go viral. My idea is that both stories help contemporary readers to realize when hegemonic masculinity becomes toxic and how to break its oppressive power structure.

King David as a paragon of hegemonic masculinity

The Australian sociologist Raewyn Connell is well known for her work on hegemonic masculinity that she developed based on biographical interviews with men of different classes and age groups as well as analyses of the power structures among them. In her monograph *Masculinities* (2005, p. 77) Connell defines hegemonic masculinity as a 'configuration of gender practice which embodies the currently accepted answer to the problem of the legitimacy of patriarchy, which guarantees (or is taken to guarantee) the dominant position of men and the subordination of women'.[1] Although only a few men might enact hegemonic masculinity, it is normative for the behaviour of most people in a given society in the sense that it comprises an ideal of masculine behaviour and privilege compared to other men and women and is stabilized by institutions, bureaucracies and the media. Connell argues (2005, p. 81), however, that hegemonic masculinity is not a fixed character type and may differ in various social settings. Moreover, hegemonic masculinity relates to other forms of masculinity – namely, subordinated, complicit and marginalized masculinity (Connell, 2005, pp. 78–81). All these patterns are subject to historical change. Connell's theory highly influenced the emerging fields of critical men's studies and masculinity studies. Although being criticized from different viewpoints, the concept has been widely used in cultural and literary studies, among them also biblical studies.[2]

With regard to hegemonic masculinity in the Hebrew Bible, David appears as the ideal king in ancient Israel's early monarchic period (cf. Clines, 1995). Chosen by the deity and anointed by Samuel (1 Sam. 16.13), David is portrayed as physically without blemish, handsome (1 Sam. 16.12), wise and persuasive in speech (1 Sam. 27.5–6). He emerges as a valiant warrior (1 Sam. 17.41–51; 18.7), diplomatically skilled and connected with leading families by marriage (1 Sam. 18.27; 27.3). David scores high in these regards as noted by a servant in 1 Samuel 16.18: 'I have observed a son of Jesse the Bethlehemite who is skilled in music; he is a stalwart fellow and a warrior, sensible in speech, and handsome in appearance, and the LORD is with him.'[3] Only with regard to God is David subordinated and succumbs to God's commands (2 Sam. 12.13–14; 24.10–15).

A close reading of the narrative, however, reveals ambivalent traits in the portrayal of David: he gathers a troop of marauding men around him with whom he begins to extort danegeld (1 Sam. 25). He even changes sides, joins the Philistines, and raids villages in the south (1 Sam. 27). When the Philistines strike the Israelite troops at Mount Gilboa, he does not intervene while Saul and his sons are killed in battle (1 Sam. 31).

Now the way to Saul's throne is free for David (2 Sam. 5.1–5). The rise of this nobody from a lowly background is paved with countless war dead, conspiracies and cruelties. Nevertheless, everyone loves this ruthless man: Saul (1 Sam. 16.21), Israel and Judah (1 Sam. 18.6–7, 16), Jonathan, the heir of Saul's throne (1 Sam. 18.1), and his sister Michal, whom David marries (1 Sam. 18.20). Yet in the narrative David is never the subject of the verb '-h-b, 'to love', and only once, in the dirge over Jonathan, does he admit that Jonathan's love was precious to him (2 Sam. 1.26). At the height of his career, David meets Bathsheba and this encounter leads to the murder of her husband and marks a turning point in David's career. Afterwards, David's reputation is in decline and his sons start fighting over the throne (cf. 2 Sam. 12.7–12). Although this narrative is highly fictitious, David's portrayal as king includes patterns of behaviour that are typical for a person of his standing and represent what Connell calls 'hegemonic masculinity'.

Bathsheba among powerful men

When Bathsheba[4] is mentioned first, she is called 'a woman', and subjected to the gaze of David, as 2 Samuel 11.2 reads: 'Late one afternoon, David rose from his couch and strolled on the roof of the royal palace; and from the roof he saw a woman bathing. The woman was very beautiful.' Here the narrator comments on David's male gaze and informs readers about the woman's beauty so that they may understand David's reaction. David does not know her and his inquiry discloses, 'She is Bathsheba daughter of Eliam and wife of Uriah the Hittite' (2 Sam. 11.3). As a daughter of Eliam, Bathsheba is a granddaughter of David's adviser Ahithophel (cf. 2 Sam. 23.34) and married to one of David's elite soldiers. This pedigree and marriage, even if both may be later additions (cf. Gardner, 2005, pp. 534–5), render Bathsheba a descendant from a well-known Judean family. Within the plot, that kind of information should have stopped David since any intercourse with a married woman would be called adultery with fatal consequences for both persons (cf. Ex. 20.14; Lev. 18.20; 20.10; similarly, Abasili, 2011, p. 8; Neely, 2020, p. 60). Moreover, adulterous behaviour with a woman of a leading family may impair the king's reputation and weaken the loyalty of his inner circle. Yet, David's reaction is told in a rapid pace that contrasts the lengthy introduction (with Abasili, 2011, p. 9), 'David sent messengers to fetch her; she came to him and he lay with her – she had just purified herself after her period – and she went back home' (2 Sam. 11.4).

King David has the power to command and get what he wants, not only concerning Bathsheba but also later Uriah, her husband. The verb *sh-l-kh*, 'to send', used nine times in 2 Samuel 11—12, signals that David is in command. None of his servants or messengers interferes; all follow his orders. Although David's emotions are not mentioned,[5] the narrator informs the readers that her beauty attracted his sexual desire, and he had sex with her. Without revealing any words or emotions of Bathsheba either, the narrator reports only her movements: she comes to David, and she returns to her house. Whether she deliberately came, or even knew for what purpose she was summoned to the palace, is not said.

Several interpreters have perceived gaps in the story and sought to fill them in imaginative ways. For example, already in the Greek translation of 2 Samuel 11.4 (cf. Abasili, 2011, p. 10, n. 39), one finds an interesting variant that attests to the role that imagination played for ancient readers. Instead of *wtbw' 'lyw*, 'she came to him', as attested in both the Masoretic Text and 4QSam^a, the Septuagint reads *kai eisēlthen pros autēn*, 'he went in to her' (codex B and A), thus alluding to the sexual intercourse as his deed and attributing to David even more blame while exonerating Bathsheba. Whether this is the original reading (Fincke, 2001, p. 192) or an interpretation that follows common expectations about a hegemonic male (Anderson, 1989, p. 151), its mere existence attests to some early examples of narrating rape.

The episode's context refers to a situation of war and aggression. While his army besieges Rabbah, the capital of neighbouring Ammon (2 Sam. 11.1), David stays in his palace in Jerusalem and assaults a married woman. When she gets pregnant, he tries to cover up his adultery by commanding her husband Uriah back so that he may have sex with his wife. When Uriah stays with the soldiers and does not visit his wife, David commands Uriah's heroic death and later marries Bathsheba.

With regard to Bathsheba, the narrator reveals only glimpses of her character in the following events. She mourns the death of her husband according to contemporary custom (2 Sam. 11.26–27). After their son has died, David is said to 'console' her by fathering another son whom she[6] calls 'Solomon'. This name in Hebrew means 'his replacement' and thus may refer to either her first son or her deceased husband (cf. McCarter, 1984, p. 303); only in the late tradition of 1 Chronicles 22.9 is it linked to Hebrew *shalom*, 'peace'. Solomon is said to be 'loved by the LORD' so that the prophet Nathan calls him *Jedidiah*, meaning 'Beloved one of YHWH' (2 Sam. 12.25).

Years later, when David's sons of different wives fight one another for the throne, Bathsheba enters the stage again as David's favourite consort, to whom the old and now impotent king (cf. 1 Kings 1.4) still listens. When Adonijah, the son of Haggith, plans to be crowned by gathering mighty men at a feast, Solomon's supporters led by the prophet Nathan[7] plot against him by urging Bathsheba to talk to David. In 1 Kings 1, Bathsheba has two memorable appearances: first, she enters the royal bedroom, bows before David, and in a long speech reminds him of his promise that Solomon will be his successor (1 Kings 1.15–21). This promise is not narrated earlier, Nathan utters it as a question, yet Bathsheba states it in David's presence as if it were a fact. Again, the reader may wonder whether Nathan and Bathsheba made it up assuming that David would be too senile to remember what he once said (cf. Cogan, 2000, p. 166). Then Nathan comes in and confirms that Adonijah has been declared king, a message to which David has Bathsheba called in again. In her presence, David swears that her son Solomon will succeed him as king (1 Kings 1.30). Bathsheba then prostrates herself before David, flattering him with the traditional wish 'May my lord King David live forever!' despite his old age and impotence. In what follows, David summons the party that favours Solomon and commands Solomon's coronation while Adonijah flees, but is later reprieved by Solomon. Thus, as a member of an influential party at David's court, Bathsheba plays an important role in securing the throne for her son Solomon.

After David's death, Adonijah's desire for power does not abate. He urges Bathsheba, now in the position of *gevirah*, 'queen mother', to ask Solomon that Abishag the Shunammite may be given to him in marriage. Solomon immediately rejects Bathsheba's request, arguing that marrying Abishag, David's last wife, would amount to inheriting David's position (1 Kings 2.22). Afterwards, Solomon eliminates the opposing party: Adonijah and the army general Joab are murdered by Benaiah, and the priest Abiathar is demoted to the Benjaminite town of Anathoth.

Bathsheba's rise to power is obvious in her speech to David, in which she negotiates Solomon as heir to the throne although he is not David's firstborn son. A closer look, however, reveals that she may also be a pawn in the power play of men (cf. Nelson, 1987, pp. 19–22). In 1 Kings 1, she is sent by Nathan who threatens her with the prospect that both her life and Solomon's life are endangered. He tells her what she shall say to David and she repeats his words before the king (1 Kings 1.13, 17). In 1 Kings 2, it is Adonijah who sends her to King Solomon on his own behalf, but this time her request is immediately declined. Therefore, the story demonstrates Bathsheba's limited authority within the royal court. Neither 2 Samuel 11 nor 1 Kings 1—2 reveal Bathsheba's intentions or emotions, so that her characterization remains ambiguous. In the context of the #MeToo movement, however, the interpretation of her rise to power gains some interesting new features.

Reading Bathsheba's story in the context of the #MeToo movement

The phrase 'Me Too' was initially used in 2006 on Myspace, by sexual assault survivor and activist Tarana Burke, a grassroots community organizer in New York City, to raise awareness of the pervasiveness of sexual abuse and assault in society (Harvard University, 2020). She aimed to empower young and vulnerable women of colour, through empathy, solidarity and strength in numbers, by visibly demonstrating how many have experienced sexual assault and harassment, especially in the workplace. In October 2017, #MeToo became a viral hashtag after the *New York Times* had revealed allegations of sexual harassment by film mogul Harvey Weinstein. Weinstein's history of sexual misconduct against many women was exposed by Jodi Kantor and Megan Twohey, investigative reporters of the *New York Times*, as well as by Ronan Farrow of *The New Yorker*. The *New York Times* article was published on 5 October 2017 after two women agreed to be named publicly as victims (Kantor and Twohey, 2017). After its release, 82 women came forward with their own allegations against Weinstein, leading also to workplace and legal reforms in other companies. Farrow's article was released online on 10 October and in print on 23 October 2017; he had talked to 13 women who were sexually harassed or assaulted by Weinstein between the 1990s and 2015.[8] In 2018, Kantor and Twohey as well as Farrow received the Pulitzer Prize for Public Service for a series of investigative articles on the sexual abuse of women.[9] In 2020, Weinstein was convicted of a criminal sexual act and of rape and sentenced to 23 years in prison. This conviction was overturned on April 25, 2024 by the New York Court of Appeals, who ordered a retrial. Since in February 2023 he was sentenced to 16 additional years in California on separate charges, he is unlikely to be released, although this verdict has also been appealed.[10]

In their non-fiction book *She Said*, published in 2019, Kantor and Twohey describe how after months of meticulous investigations they worked on their text and searched for women willing to testify against Weinstein.[11] Their book also documents the network of commercial interests, money, lawyers and assistants that protected an influential man despite all evidence of his predatory and illegitimate behaviour. In November 2022, the film *She Said* was released in the United States, based on the book, directed by Maria Schrader and with the screenplay composed by Rebecca Lenkievicz.

In what follows, I will compare Bathsheba's story of sexual abuse with the story told in *She Said*. In both cases, Connell's concept of hegemonic masculinity related to subordinated, complicit and marginalized masculinities is helpful to analyse the power relations around mighty men as well as between men and women.

Consensual sex or rape?

Whether Bathsheba consents to have sex with David or is raped has been fervently discussed, and many scholars point to her complicity in this adulterous act despite the power difference between her and the king (e.g. Klein, 2000, pp. 52–3). Compared with other rape stories – for example, Genesis 34 or 2 Samuel 13 – the Hebrew verbs *l-q-kh*, 'to take, fetch', and *sh-k-b* + *'im*, 'to lie with' used here do not explicitly convey force. Thus in 2 Samuel 11.1–5, the text is ambiguous and thus open to different interpretations. The narrator directs the reader's gaze on Bathsheba's assumedly naked body and produces many lacunas. Cheryl Exum calls this way of telling the story 'rape by the pen':

> The point is not what Bathsheba might have done or felt; the point is we are not allowed access to her point of view ... The denial of subjectivity is an important factor in rape, where the victim is objectified and, indeed, the aim is to destroy her subjectivity ... By denying her subjectivity, the narrator symbolically rapes Bathsheba, and by withholding her point of view, he presents an ambiguous portrayal that leaves her vulnerable to the charge of seduction. (Exum, 1993, pp. 173–4)

Read from the story's outcome, namely that Bathsheba became queen mother when her second son Solomon succeeded David on the throne, several interpreters, among them H. W. Hertzberg (1964, p. 309) and Steven McKenzie (2000, pp. 180–3), fill the gaps with the idea that Bathsheba may have planned to seduce David. While Alexander Abasili argues against this notion, he concludes from the phrase 'she came to him' (2 Sam. 11.4) that 'Bathsheba, though a victim of circumstances may not be declared entirely innocent; she does share minimally in the responsibility' (Abasili, 2011, p. 11). With regard to Connell's concept, Bathsheba would adopt the pattern of complicit behaviour and seek to benefit from it.

In Weinstein's case, several young women who consented to meet the producer reported that they hoped to get a role in a film or be promoted in their job within the company (Kantor and Twohey, 2019, pp. 33, 39, 72). From Weinstein's perspective, a woman's willingness to meet him would imply her consent to have sex with him. In contrast, several women felt trapped when realizing that Weinstein would meet them in his private hotel room, barely dressed, and some of them tried to escape.

Gazing at a female body

In 2 Samuel 11.2, the narrator focalizes Bathsheba through David's gaze: 'From the roof he saw a woman bathing. The woman was very beautiful.' That Bathsheba took a bath and thus exposed her naked body is just an interpretation of the common verb *r-kh-ts*, 'to wash', that is used twice more (cf. 2 Sam. 11.8; 12.20) in the story. What this female beauty entails rests solely in the eye of the beholder, who in this case is the reader imagining the scene. The manifold depiction of this scene in art, film and narrative signifies a strong male gaze on female nudity which is closely linked to male sexual desire (cf. Exum, 1996; Garroway, 2013).

Although the biblical narrator does not reveal Bathsheba's point of view, George Nicol (1997, p. 44) considers her bathing in the open as a provocative invitation to be seen by David. Randall Bailey (1990, p. 89) assumes that behind her bathing there is a strong political motivation to become queen. Given the time frame of the David story and the topography of Jerusalem, however, an informed reader could imagine the scene and come to a different conclusion: David stands on the roof of his palace located on top of Jerusalem's south-eastern hill with a view over the entire town. In early monarchic times, houses did not have indoor bathrooms with plumbing, and water was to be drawn and fetched from the Gihon spring. Thus, a woman may have washed herself in the inner courtyard of her house that was secluded from the street, but at least partly visible from the roof of a higher building in the neighbourhood. Contrary to Klein's suggestion (2000, p. 53), the text does not say that Bathsheba washed herself on the roof nor give any hint that she plotted anything (Tamber-Rosenau, 2017, p. 61). Therefore, in the plot of the story, the problem is not Bathsheba's bathing but David's voyeurism (so also Neely, 2020, p. 59).[12]

Concerning Bathsheba's intentions, interpreters argue about the function of the narrator's seemingly belated note in 2 Samuel 11.4, 'She had just purified herself after her period.' For Nicol (1997, p. 48) and Bailey (1990, p. 88), this note serves to exclude Uriah's paternity. Abasili (2011, p. 13) finds in it the reason for Bathsheba's bathing in the evening and an indication of her fertility, an interpretation that presupposes some knowledge about the referred action. While sexual intercourse with a woman who was menstruating is discouraged (Lev. 18.19; cf. Lev. 15.19–25), the texts in Leviticus focus on ritual purity – that is, being allowed to visit the sanctuary. Ritual purity can be re-established by washing oneself and one's clothes and waiting until the evening – that is, the beginning of the next day. Only in the case of a woman's unusual discharge should she wait another seven days after it stopped (Lev. 15.28–29). In the Mishnah tractate *Niddah*, this rule is applied to a woman's regular menstruation and her marital sexuality, but the beginning of the custom is not known. Neely (2020, p. 61) even argues that by presenting the sex and the purifying ritual, an 'engaging in ceremonial washing out of reverence for the presence of God', as simultaneous events, the narrator construes David's deed 'not only as an abuse of power, but as sacrilege, an impious violation not only of Bathsheba, Uriah, and her family, but as an affront to Yhwh himself'. While I consider this an over-interpretation, I concur with Neely that the narrator's strategy is to declare that David alone is guilty.

Concerning female nudity, as a result of hierarchical gender relations persisting until today, the issue of a woman's dressing or undressing is still a matter of debate – and a woman barely dressed is often blamed for demonstrating consent to sexual advances. Female actors in highly sexualized and/or minimal clothing present their bodies publicly at film festivals and parties. Such behaviour is, however, no invitation to any sexual act. Thus, the male gaze is still pertinent and gender hierarchy still ingrained in societal structures, especially in the contemporary film industry and its media.

Breaking the silence

In Weinstein's case, many women did not speak about what happened to them because of non-disclosure agreements that they had signed in exchange for money (Kantor and Twohey, 2019, pp. 57, 97–104). Weinstein used to threaten any woman that her career as an actress would be over; that she would lose her job in the film business. His lawyers negotiated agreements involving huge amounts of money to be paid by the company. As Kantor and Twohey reveal (2019, p. 91), one lawyer, David Boies, was introduced to the circle of film celebrities by Weinstein and also invested in a film production company: 'Time and again, he came to Weinstein's defense, and helped him to conceal, spin, and silence. He chose to believe Weinstein's claims that he was guilty only of philandering.' Being complicit with Weinstein's behaviour, a host of men and women around him managed to silence any victim and ward off any rumours of his misconduct. Any female victim of Weinstein would either leave the company or work with other producers, but would be silent in fear of ruining her career and perhaps her life.

Kantor and Twohey report in *She Said* that they struggled to encourage these women to speak out and start a series of trials in which judges in a court of law would place the verdict on the offender. While some of the victims admitted that they disregarded the rumours and met with Weinstein to talk about a film role, none of them said that they tried to seduce Weinstein in order to have a career. After Weinstein's case became public, many other women reported incidents of sexual misconduct by their bosses and peers so public opinion on such behaviour began to change (Kantor and Twohey, 2019, pp. 180–3).

Similarly, silence is an issue also in Bathsheba's story. She is not granted a point of view like the numerous women around Weinstein who were silenced by money and threats. She has no voice in what amounts to a series of traumatic events: sexual assault, possibly unwanted pregnancy, the death of her husband and her son. The only clue that Bathsheba is not only a victim of David's sexual harassment is her sending messengers to David announcing to him 'I am pregnant' (2 Sam. 11.5). While she does not speak after the sexual encounter – as does David's daughter Tamar after being raped by Amnon (2 Sam. 13.12–13, 16, 19) – Bathsheba informs David about the consequences of their intercourse and thus displays agency. Her announcement drives the plot forward, which leads to David's failed attempt to cover up his transgression and finally to Uriah's death. Imagining the situation then, what other option may Bathsheba have had? If her pregnancy became visible while her husband was away and serving in the army, she would likely have been accused of adultery. She might not have had the power to summon her husband home. Thus, her message to David can be seen as either a bold statement that he should take responsibility (Brueggemann, 1990, p. 274) or the last resort of a woman who does not know where else to go (Garland and Garland, 2011, p. 37). Again, the text neither reveals her emotions nor her intentions, and thus the readers fill the lacuna to their liking.

What is important for contemporary readers of the Bible is that Bathsheba's story is told at all, included in a collection of ancient narratives that reveal some aspects of women's lives in a patriarchal society based on strict gender hierarchy and hegemonic masculinity. Similarly, Mary Holland and Heather Hewitt, editors of a recent anthology entitled *#MeToo and Literary Studies*, argue:

> Much of the power of #MeToo lies in the power of storytelling: the voicing of individual traumatic experience, shared with others who

listen and support the victim; the creation of a community of individual victims who collectively bear witness to the larger problem of violence and in so doing dismantle silence, shame, and stigma; and the conviction that rape culture, while pervasive, is not acceptable, and that those who inflict harm and benefit from existing distributions of power must be held to account. (Holland and Hewitt, 2021, p. 3)

Thus, breaking the silence and revealing the system of patriarchal control and intimidation is key to any fight against sexual violence. Narrating rape and sharing experiences of sexual violence not only informs other women of potential threats but also helps survivors reclaim agency – at least to some degree.

The fall of a mighty male leader

Like King David in Israel's early monarchic period, Harvey Weinstein could be called a paragon of hegemonic masculinity: powerful and connected to a net of influential people in Hollywood's acclaimed film industry, persuasive, and a mentor of women who aspire to a career in the film business. Like David, Weinstein is an ambiguous figure and many people in his entourage must have noticed his flaws. For many years, there had been rumours about his sexual misconduct, but no woman dared to accuse him publicly. Like David's messengers who summon Bathsheba to the palace (2 Sam. 11.4), and his officer Joab who places Uriah on the front line of battle (2 Sam. 11.16), Weinstein was surrounded by many men, lawyers and assistants, who behaved complicitly and covered up his deeds. In both stories, the power relations around mighty men are detrimental to the women involved. In Weinstein's case, two female investigative reporters and one young journalist helped victims of sexual assault disrupt such toxic power structures.

In King David's case, the narrator announces God's verdict: 'The LORD was displeased with what David had done' (2 Sam. 11.27 (NRSV 12.1)) and has God send the prophet Nathan. Nathan tells a tale about a rich man who takes a poor man's only lamb to which the king responds with harsh words against such injustice. By identifying David with the rich man, Nathan finds the king guilty and David confesses his sin. Nevertheless, the son of the adulterous encounter dies and the series of transgressions darkens the portrait of David, the ideal king and hegemonic male. In 1 Kings 1—2, David is characterized as an old and impotent ruler who can no longer control his court. In retrospect, the murder of Uriah adumbrates David's reputation, but Bathsheba is no longer mentioned in 1 Kings 15.5: 'For David had done what was pleasing to the LORD and never turned throughout his life from all that He had commanded him, except in the matter of Uriah the Hittite.' In the later tradition of Chronicles, however, all of David's negative traits – including his assault on Bathsheba – are omitted (cf. Móricz, 2017).

Conclusion

To reveal the ambiguous character of mighty men both in the Hebrew Bible and today is, in my view, a starting point to criticize hegemonic masculinity that becomes toxic when privilege or force is used for personal interests. In Bathsheba's case, the narrator tells the story of her rise at David's court without revealing her viewpoint and allowing her to speak for herself. Yet, he portrays David as an ambiguous character and his deeds as an offence against God and has God through Nathan announce the verdict. Being caught, David surrenders to this mightier male character, who nevertheless has secured David's dynasty. The ancient story has many lacunas that are filled by scholars with various and even conflicting interpretations.

Kantor and Twohey narrate how they managed to break the silence of the women who were sexually harassed and raped by Harvey Weinstein and to prove that he tried to silence them by offering hush money and threatening to end their careers. In his case, the evidence the journalists gathered was so strong that even the most powerful lawyers could not repudiate it and Weinstein was convicted in court. At the same time, Kantor and Twohey revealed a system of toxic relationships of power, company structures, and complicit behaviour of numerous men and women. The result of the journalists' investigations pushed the #MeToo movement globally.

By criticizing the system of hierarchical gender relations and revealing the concept of hegemonic masculinity that allows men's dominance over women and other men to continue, Connell and others try to reveal the costs of this system for persons of all genders. Yet, they keep arguing that this system can change and needs to be changed. Revealing the unspoken assumptions and gender hierarchies in a story is the first step in changing the system. In the book's epilogue, Kantor and Twohey (2019, p. 260) come to the same conclusion:

> If the story was not shared, nothing would change. Problems that are not seen cannot be addressed. In our world of journalism, the story was

the end, the result the final product. But in the world at large, the emergence of new information was just the beginning – of conversations, action, change.

Analysing rape stories at a scholarly conference – and now in this present scholarly volume – are great subsequent steps towards bringing the voices and stories of biblical and contemporary women to public recognition. Narrating Bathsheba's story can break the silence around sexual harassment and help contemporary readers of the Bible talk about their experiences. Narrating how they managed to break the intimidating network around Harvey Weinstein, Kantor and Twohey summarize the consequences of breaking the silence:

> The key to change was a new sense of accountability: As women gained confidence that telling their stories would lead to action, more of them opened up. The volume and pain of those stories showed the scale of the problem and the way it had upended lives and undermined workplace progress. Businesses and other institutions investigated and fired their own leaders. Those consequences – the promise that telling the truth could lead to action – persuaded yet more women to speak up. (Kantor and Twohey, 2019, p. 182)

After breaking the silence and acting against cover-up and complicity, the next step would be to discuss how we all could cooperate in rendering women's spaces more secure in our communities and educating the next generation on how to disrupt and change the binary hierarchical social structures so that people of all genders can live safely together.

Bibliography

Abasili, Alexander I. A., 2011, 'Was it Rape? The David and Bathsheba Pericope Re-examined', *Vetus Testamentum* 61, pp. 1–15.
Anderson, Arnold A., 1989, *2 Samuel*, WBC 11, Dallas, TX: Word Books.
Bailey, Randall C., 1990, *David in Love and War*, JSOTSup 75, Sheffield: Sheffield Academic Press.
Brueggemann, Walter, 1990, *First and Second Samuel*, Interpretation, Louisville, KY: John Knox.
Clines, David J. A., 1995, 'David, the Man: The Construction of Masculinity in the Hebrew Bible' in *Interested Parties: The Ideology of Writers and Readers of the Hebrew Bible*, JSOTSup 205, Sheffield: Sheffield Academic Press, pp. 212–43.
Cogan, Mordechai, 2000, *1 Kings*, Anchor Bible, New York: Doubleday.
Connell, Raewyn, 2005, *Masculinities*, 2nd edn, Berkeley/Los Angeles, CA: University of California Press (original publication 1995).

Connell, Raewyn, and James W. Messerschmidt, 2005, 'Hegemonic Masculinity: Rethinking the Concept', *Gender & Society* 19, pp. 829–59.

Creangă, Ovidiu (ed.), 2010, *Men and Masculinity in the Hebrew Bible and Beyond*, Sheffield: Sheffield Phoenix Press.

Exum, J. Cheryl, 1993, 'Raped by the Pen' in *Fragmented Women: Feminist (Sub)versions of Biblical Narratives*, JSOTSup 163, Sheffield: JSOT Press, pp. 170–201.

Exum, J. Cheryl, 1996, 'Bathsheba Plotted, Shot, and Painted', *Semeia* 74, pp. 47–73.

Farrow, Ronan, 2017, 'From Aggressive Overtures to Sexual Assault: Harvey Weinstein's Accusers Tell Their Stories', *The New Yorker*, 23 October, available at https://www.newyorker.com/news/news-desk/from-aggressive-overtures-to-sexual-assault-harvey-weinsteins-accusers-tell-their-stories (accessed 27.12.2023).

Fincke, A., 2001, *The Samuel Scroll from Qumran: 4QSam^a restored and compared to the Septuagint and 4QSam^c*, Leiden: Brill.

Gardner, Anne E., 2005, 'The Identity of Bath-Sheba', *Revue Biblique* 112, pp. 521–35.

Garland, David E., and Diana R. Garland, 2011, 'Bathsheba's Story: Surviving Abuse and Loss', *Family and Community Ministries* 24, pp. 29–44.

Garroway, Kristine Henriksen, 2013, 'Was Bathsheba the Original Bridget Jones? A New Look at Bathsheba on Screen and in Biblical Scholarship', *Nashim: A Journal of Jewish Women's Studies and Gender Issues* 24, pp. 53–73.

Gilmour, Rachelle, 2022, 'Sex Scandal and the Politics of David's Throne', *Journal of Biblical Literature* 141/1, pp. 83–104.

Harvard University, 2020, 'Leading with Empathy: Tarana Burke and the Making of the MeToo Movement', Case #2197.0, 16 November, available at https://case.hks.harvard.edu/leading-with-empathy-tarana-burke-and-the-making-of-the-me-too-movement/ (accessed 20.07.2023).

Hertzberg, H. W., 1964, *I and II Samuel*, trans. J. S. Bowden, OTL, Philadelphia, PA: Westminster.

Holland, Mary K., and Heather Hewitt (eds), 2021, *#MeToo and Literary Studies: Reading, Writing, and Teaching about Sexual Violence and Rape Culture*, New York: Bloomsbury Academic.

Kantor, Jodi, and Megan Twohey, 2019, *She Said: Breaking the Sexual Harassment Story That Helped Ignite a Movement*, Penguin Random House.

Kantor, Jodi, and Megan Twohey, 2017, 'Harvey Weinstein Paid Off Sexual Harassment Accusers for Decades', *The New York Times*, 5 October, available at https://www.nytimes.com/2017/10/05/us/harvey-weinstein-harassment-allegations.html (accessed 20.07.2023).

Klein, Lilian R., 2000, 'Bathsheba Revealed' in Athalya Brenner (ed.), *Samuel and Kings: A Feminist Companion to the Bible (Second Series)*, Sheffield: Sheffield Academic Press, pp. 47–64.

McCarter, P. Kyle Jr, 1984, *II Samuel*, Anchor Bible, New York: Doubleday.

McKenzie, Steven L., 2000, *King David: A Biography*, New York: Oxford University Press.

Móricz, Nicolett, 2017, 'Beyond the Textual Gaps of Courtly Intrigues: The Story of Queen Bathsheba', *lectio difficilior* (1), pp. 1–23, http://www.lectio.unibe.ch (accessed 14.02.2023).

Neely, Winfred O., 2020, 'The Wife of Uriah the Hittite: Political Seductress,

Willing Participant, naïve Woman, or #BathshebaToo? The Preacher as Sensitive Theologian', *The Journal of the Evangelical Homiletics Society*, March, pp. 51–63.

Nelson, Richard D., 1987, *First and Second Kings*, Atlanta, GA: John Knox.

Nicol, George G., 1997, 'The Alleged Rape of Bathsheba: Some Observation on Ambiguity in Biblical Narrative', *Journal for the Study of the Old Testament* 73, pp. 43–54.

Schrader, Maria (director), 2022, *She Said*, Universal Pictures, 129 Minutes.

Tamber-Rosenau, Caryn, 2017, 'Biblical Bathing Beauties and the Manipulation of the Male Gaze: What Judith Can Tell Us about Bathsheba and Susanna', *Journal of Feminist Studies in Religion* 33/2, pp. 55–72.

Notes

1 See also Connell and Messerschmidt, 2005, where they discuss the appropriation of and criticism of the concept after 20 years and suggest some revisions. They explain 'practice' as 'things done not just a set of role expectations or an identity' (2005, p. 832).

2 In anthologies on masculinity in the Bible – for example, Creangă (2010) – about half of the articles use Connell's concept.

3 All translations of the Hebrew text are taken from the Jewish Publication Society's Tanakh 1985.

4 While most commentators consider Bathsheba a personal name, Gardner (2005, pp. 524–5) sees it as a patronym 'daughter of Sheba' changed to 'Bath-Shua' in 1 Chronicles 3.5 as a result of a scribal error. Sheba represents the Benjaminite region that was politically important for David (cf. Sheba's rebellion in 2 Sam. 20). Thus, Solomon would be of both Benjaminite and Judahite descent.

5 This is unusual as in the story of David's rise to power all his potential misdeeds are carefully explained to shed a favourable light on the David figure. See McCarter, 1984, p. 289.

6 Thus the *qere* reading in 2 Samuel 12.24; the *ketiv* refers to David as the subject of the naming.

7 Besides Nathan, there is Zadok the priest, Benaiah son of Jehoiada, the commander of the royal bodyguard, and David's men of his early career (1 Kings 1.8) who support Solomon's rise to the throne.

8 See https://www.newyorker.com/news/news-desk/from-aggressive-overtures-to-sexual-assault-harvey-weinsteins-accusers-tell-their-stories (accessed 27.12.2023).

9 See https://www.pulitzer.org/prize-winners-by-year/2018 (accessed 27.12.2023).

10 See https://edition.cnn.com/2024/04/25/us/harvey-weinstein-conviction-overturned-appeal/index.html (accessed 31.07.2024).

11 The book also reports the allegations to Supreme Court nominee Brett M. Kavanaugh (Kantor and Twohey, 2019, pp. 211–45) and a gathering of women in Los Angeles in 2019, some of them being harassed by Weinstein, others by Donald Trump (Kantor and Twohey, 2019, pp. 247–61).

12 Comparing the male gaze on Bathsheba and Susannah with Judith's bathing, which aims to titillate Holofernes and murder him in his chamber, Caryn Tamber-Rosenau (2017) plausibly shows how the figure of Judith manages to reverse the direction of the male gaze on female nudity.

4

Women Talking and Women Not Talking: Speaking *for* (?) in Fiction and Judges 21

ALEXIANA FRY

Introduction

For a period of about four years, until they were caught, nine men in a Mennonite colony in Bolivia raped around 130 people between the ages of 3 and 65. They were aided by a veterinarian from a neighbouring community who created an anesthetizing spray that the rapists used to sedate the rape victims and their families. At first, the victims, overwhelmingly women, were not believed, and were blamed for these stories as their own 'wild female imagination'. Two years later, the perpetrators, including the veterinarian, stood trial and were found guilty. Reporter Jean Friedman-Rudovsky (2013) adds there is evidence that the rapes have not stopped.[1] This story is still happening in real-time.

Seven years after the trial, former Mennonite Miriam Toews published a novel entitled *Women Talking* (2018), based on these events. Toews begins by offering her interpretation of the seemingly silent women, in that her work is 'both a reaction through fiction to these true-life events, and an act of female-imagination' (2018). In an interview published in *The Guardian*, Toews observes that the phrase 'wild female imagination' is 'used to discount and discredit what women do and say' (Onstad, 2018). This phrase that is meant to deter the women from talking is for Toews the starting point of her creative retelling.

The next page of Toews's novel displays in pictographs (since the women cannot read) the premise of the choices these women could have deliberated over: (1) do nothing, (2) stay and fight (an interesting addition involving a pacifist community), or (3) leave. The rest of the novel divulges the 'minutes' of the meetings that happened in order to choose just one of these options for a unified decision. The descriptions of the dialogues that could have happened among the women show the difficulty of moving forward with *any* of these choices. However, the minutes of these meetings are only recollected because of the narrator, August Epp, a man whose family was excommunicated from the colony when he was a boy but who returned to help teach this community and reconnect with his faith years later. The novel ends with the women choosing to leave the colony although danger clearly lies ahead no matter what decision is made.

Several years after its publication, Toews's novel was adapted into a film, directed by acclaimed feminist director Sarah Polley. The film adaptation begins with a shot of a long line of the women of the colony casting their votes between the three options. August Epp is no longer the narrator, nor the lens through which one 'sees' the story. In the film, August is shown to witness the women's discussion. After much deliberation, 104 minutes later, the women decide collectively to leave the colony, taking their children with them. Viewers are not aware of the fact that these women do not speak the language of everyone else outside of the colony; they are not given small, intimate details about August's own struggle of feeling implicated in the violence that happened to these women. Once again, leaving is where the story ends, however, with much more hope as the danger implicated in the book is erased.

The events of *Women Talking*, and the story behind it, can be productively compared with a similarly horrifying biblical story. Like *Women Talking*, Judges 21 narrates a mass rape event that also seems to be ignored and justified. Furthermore, any act of 'wild female imagination' that we might explore as a form of response is not present in the biblical text.

In Judges 20, inter-tribal war breaks out as a result of a gang rape and dismemberment of a Levite's concubine (Judg. 19) that was carried out by men of Gibeah from the tribe of Benjamin. All Israel (except for Benjamin and Jabesh-Gilead) is brought together at Mizpah to discuss what should be done (Judg. 20.1). Since they see this heinous act as narrated in Judges 19 to be an outrage and abomination (Judg. 20.8–10), they decide to punish the tribe of Benjamin. After much fighting, most Benjaminites are killed, except for 600 men. Although the men of Israel swore an oath not to give their daughters to any Benjaminite (Judg. 21.1),[2] they have compassion on the Benjaminites (Judg. 21.6). Realizing that the men of Jabesh-Gilead did not come to Mizpah and did not take part in the oath (Judg. 21.8), they enact *kherem*[3] on this town and capture its virgins to give them as an offering (exchange) of peace to Benjamin in an effort to repopulate this tribe (Judg. 21.12–15).

But these women were not enough. In recognizing that there is no other tribe to punish, all Israel prepares a workaround for the oath: they suggest to the Benjaminites that they should abduct the young women of

Shiloh when the girls go out dancing in an annual festival (Judg. 21.19–21). To the fathers and brothers of the women, they explain that this course of events would serve two ends: it would not breach the oath they had taken and help the Benjaminites to repopulate (Judg. 21.22). After the abduction of the women of Shiloh, everyone goes back home (Judg. 21.23–24). This is the end of the story and the end of the book of Judges. This story is told solely through a male lens, with seemingly only male interests. The women's point of view is not present.

Blurring the lines between these stories, the framework of the three choices from *Women Talking* referenced above may offer flexibility when rewriting and filling the lacuna pertaining to the missing perspectives of both the women of Jabesh-Gilead and the virgin daughters of Shiloh as told in Judges 20—21. Yet, in employing my own act of 'wild female imagination', I want to consider the realities of the Bolivian Manitoba colony as well as recognize that my desires may be different from the ones of these survivors. I will argue that the novel and the film insert their own hopes over and above these real women, ending in their fictional women making a unified decision after much debate to leave the colony and start over again, with a vision of 'liberal hope', not necessarily unhappy. Given that we have some accounts of what is actually occurring in the colony in the aftermath, there is literal, real space here for what Graybill (2021) calls 'after' terror. 'After' allows for still being affected by what happened and allows for multiple possibilities. Finally, once these stories are contrasted to highlight their differences for this constructed intertext, this chapter will re-read *Women Talking* alongside the current stories of the colony for 'an after' in Judges 21.

Taking care in rewriting

In employing my own act of female imagination, a common tool in feminist scholarship, one must reckon with Rhiannon Graybill's right critique in that these rewritings can be a tool that still uses women's bodies for one's own benefit. Graybill's work in *Texts After Terror* challenges what many have done to fill the gaps of women silenced in the biblical texts, from 'telling sad stories' to 'unhappy readings' (2021, pp. 146–51). The 'telling sad stories' practice often found in feminist scholarship follows Phyllis Trible, offering 'sympathetic readings' (Trible, 1984, p. 3) of women who are abused, mistreated, and otherwise silent in ancient texts. This is not necessarily something to discard entirely, however, and Graybill rightly adds that in taking up the helm to narrate a sympathetic reading, often we are participating in shaping these stories in how we 'have presumed is proper all along'. While Trible is correct in that our readings of these stories can alter the reader, sympathetic readings often prescind from the actual victims and/or survivors in the text. This is exactly what sympathy does: as Graybill puts it succinctly, 'interpreting *in sympathy with* or *on behalf of* can also mean speaking *in place of*' (Graybill, 2021, p. 147).

Some of this appraisal is founded in those sympathetic or, more accurately, salvific intentions of 'telling sad stories', implying that those who have moved through these awful and horrific situations are broken and need to be fixed. In interpreting these stories' silences, feminist interpreters usually create and curate 'in memoriam', *on behalf of* these victims and survivors, and they are found to be quite scripted. The salvific scripts often become what interpreters, including myself, want for those who have been harmed, which echoes throughout history how many liberal feminists have assumed and presumed a false universality (Graybill, 2021, p. 121). Agency, which we interpreters thought we were giving in the apparent lack of it, once again is taken away.

In our filling-of-the-gaps, there must be a resistance to resolution, beyond the binaries of curative, to allow people who have experienced tragedy to be fully human betwixt-and-between (Graybill, 2021, pp. 135–8).[4] This includes not only the recognition that people may not fit our scripts and have their own, but also the language we use. As it pertains to those who have had terrible things happen to them, calling someone a 'victim' as opposed to a 'survivor' in a zero-sum either/or is a problematic binary; a person either rises through their pain and 'gets over it' to become a survivor in triumph, while another is seen to be dwelling in their grief and pity, becoming a victim after truly being victimized. This is true whether or not we call things 'trauma' or, rather, an 'adversity'. In such constant language games that do not serve those who are harmed, we interpreters consistently serve the same systems that created these violent harms in the first place.[5] These binaries show more about *our* perspectives on particular connotations. Might we allow those who actually experienced what we feel so entitled to discuss the opportunity to decide for themselves? Instead of binaries, Graybill advocates for making space for our sadness – and maybe anger – to come through in our reading, recognizing them as feelings, enabling the creation of room for the 'surprise of otherness' (2021, p. 150). Graybill's 'unhappy readings' do not 'demand resolution, or inject fixed meaning into ambiguity, ambivalence, and discomfort' (2021, p. 151) and, in so doing, she teaches us how to be uncomfortable with *our* emotions about what other people choose to do with their stories.

On recognizing differences and allowing others to make decisions that are different from what *we* presume is best, there is a caution in being drawn to specific narratives of 'gratuitous terror'. Megan Goodwin's work in *Abusing Religion* notes that stories involving abuse inside religious settings often 'titillate audiences with gruesome depictions of sexual violation, reinforce anxieties about religious and sexual difference, and commodify violence against women and children while failing to meaningfully disrupt or prevent sex abuse' (Goodwin, 2020, p. 3). Goodwin's main point is to recognize which stories receive more attention in our context and why this is; it often points to our own feelings of discomfort about people's 'different' religious and lifestyle choices. Pinning abuse on religion is a scapegoat; however, 'religious belonging can make abusive situations and relationships harder to escape ... religion can make it harder to *recognize* abuse as such' (Goodwin, 2020, p. 147). Religious patriarchy statistically *does* make it more difficult to recognize abuse and leave it, thus making it easier to occur,[6] but we should not dictate women's choices of participation in religions regardless. Ensuring we are aware of our feelings while refusing to displace them on to the bodies of those we supposedly care about is vital in our re-readings and writings, and this also includes religious difference.

When assessing Toews's novel, it is important to recognize that, like any other religious group, Mennonites are not homogenous in how their beliefs are enacted and performed.[7] Some, like those I am specifically highlighting in this chapter, would prefer to carry out their faith in isolation, away from opportunities for assimilation that could threaten these tenets (Kraybill, 2008, pp. 888–90).[8] Migration, therefore, was a massive part of what it meant to preserve and keep their practices and lifestyles, in the name of religious freedom. A group of Russian Mennonites moved to Canada in the 1870s, but when Canada decided that they should send their children to public schools and have their men enlist in the military in the 1920s, they moved to Mexico, then to other South American nation-states to maintain their autonomy (Urry, 2006).[9] Further beliefs regarding women and sexuality within the particular community in Bolivia will be discussed below.[10]

With this foundation, I will first show how these cautions may have been ignored in both the novel and film *Women Talking*, then share in light of these interpretations the legitimate 'after'-math in the Mennonite colony in Bolivia. The divergences between these accounts will be of great help in attending to potential pitfalls in rewriting with 'wild female imagination' the women's perspective in the 'after' of Judges 21.

Women Talking by Miriam Toews (the novel)

Miriam Toews crafted a story of the women processing together, in ways she even experienced women talking when not 'policed' in Mennonite communities. In an extensive interview with Katrina Onstad (2018), she discusses *why* she wrote what she did in the novel: 'I felt an obligation, a need, to write about these women. I'm related to them. I could easily have been one of them.' Toews fled her community in Steinbach in Canada when she was 18. Her goal in *Women Talking* was to 'challenge the patriarchy, specifically of my Mennonite community, but I'm concerned with the suppression of girls and women especially, and any place in the world that falls under fundamentalist, authoritarian thinking' (Onstad, 2018). In the interview, Toews was also unsurprised by these events, calling the colony 'extremist, closed' and, because of that, 'ripe for violence'. Therefore, Toews's novel fills the obvious silence of these Mennonite women as their immediate conclusions were framed to be 'ghost rapes', even of demonic influence, as they could not recall what had happened to them.

And yet, as the interview reveals, Toews did not stop writing about Mennonites in both memoirs and even more fiction, remarking that she could not get the 'Mennonite thing' out of her system (Onstad, 2018). What is interesting – given these comments regarding the religiosity of *Women Talking* juxtaposed to the film – is Toews's commitment to some of the theological aspects of Christianity interwoven throughout. Alissa Wilkinson (2022) notes the blatant connections between the narrator of the novel, August Epp, to St Augustine. Toews's characters discuss that faith can mean many things, and sometimes faith does not make sense (Toews, 2018, pp. 214–15).

In order to flee, the women in the novel actually use the sedative, the 'belladonna spray', on some of the men who used it on them, to keep them unconscious and unable to prevent them from acting out their choice (Toews, 2018, p. 207). As August contemplates:

> Why does the mention of love, the memory of love, the memory of love lost, the promise of love, the end of love, the absence of love, the burning, burning need for love, need to love, result in so much violence? (Toews, 2018, p. 214)

Indeed, August's reflection leads one to consider further questions such as, 'What is evil?' and 'What is a necessary evil?' Is there such a thing as a necessary evil? Perhaps Toews herself may have been wrestling with that exact question in her gap-filling, or at least I would like to think she was alongside her characters. And yet, as the novel portrays the women unanimously choosing to flee the colony into what could potentially be even more dangerous, I also wonder if Toews acknowledges the harm that could be done in wanting something different for these women than what their choice was. Is this story one that simply becomes a soothing balm for Toews, using the survivors to save herself?

Women Talking by Sarah Polley (the film)

The film's perspective, as noted earlier, is *not* from the narration of August Epp as in the novel *Women Talking*. Instead, the narrator is Autje, a teenager who has been violated by her father and others unknown – and its focus is on the future. The film's viewer perspective, as noted by Christine Pasqua and Pamela Klassen (2023), is intentionally seated amid the women, allowing the viewers to become part of this conversation:

> In encountering these moments, the viewer is not a voyeur or a fly on the wall, but intentionally positioned in situ. We are meant to sit among the women, meet their gaze, and see them as they saw each other – without makeup, unplucked eyebrows and all. (Pasqua and Klassen, 2023)

Polley discusses in an interview the fact that her goal was decidedly *not* to make this a story only about the horrors of 'religious conservatism', giving a 'secular audience permission to say that this could never happen here' (Polley, 2023). None of the actors say the word 'Mennonite' in the film, and Polley intended to be authentic in the details while recognizing her outsider status to these communities; yet she claims 'it is about all of us'. Her point was not purposefully to point at religion as the problem, but universally at 'hierarchical power structures that allow terrible things to take place'.[11] Pasqua and Klassen note that 'the film also asks audiences to withhold judgment. Religion in the film is both a source of pain and of possibility' (2023). And yet, as noted earlier, August's character takes a backseat – faith is still present, but muffled – in washing one another's feet, in the hymns being sung, and biblical verses being quoted.

I applaud the fact that Polley refuses to give any screen time to the actual violent occurrences of rape, but solely on the women waking up from their induced/forced slumber, and coming to terms with what may have happened. They piece these things together as the women talk to one another, with clarity in conversation. However, some of the film's omissions that *were* present in the novel fail to encompass fully the dangers that surround many of their choices, although they were difficult already: being unable to read, write or speak the language of the country they reside in (Toews, 2018, p. 80); the concerns about those in colonies nearest to them (Toews, 2018, pp. 164, 191–2); or that there is a fire nearby that they may themselves be heading into (Toews, 2018, p. 196). Given what the film leaves out, and the more stick-it-to-the-literal-men emphasis at the end in hopes of female utopia elsewhere, the choice to leave seems much easier to make than the other options. Polley notes in her interview with Mead (2022) that, for the women, leaving would *not* be utopian, as they are breaking 'tenets of their faith' in leaving. Some Mennonites in the online discussions on the film agree that 'if the colony in the film is to be understood as a real place, then this story becomes one of western ideals being presented as superior' (Elliot, 2023). Different from the novel, there is a singular woman who stays behind: playing a nearly silent part – as one reviewer notes, 'precisely to show the diminishment that happens when we decide we simply must go on without talking at all … Not all women want to overturn the order of things' (Wilkinson, 2022). One could well ask, if this is a utopia, then for whom? This story is laudable and important, but may have erased the feelings of the people in Bolivia in favour of the red carpet (Braun, 2023), in favour of relieving the viewers' discomfort of the truth.

After the mass rapes: life in the Mennonite colony of Manitoba, Bolivia

The truth involving those who survived the rapes in the Mennonite colony in Bolivia, called Manitoba, is different from the novel and film adaptations. This colony adheres to more rigid articulations of what contemporary evangelical Christians would call 'complementarianism', where men and women are equal, but have different roles. Complementarianism certainly has degrees by which it can be practised, but here in Manitoba

> a woman's role in an Old Colony was to obey and submit to her husband's command. A local minister explained to me that girls are schooled a year less than boys because females have no need to learn math or bookkeeping, which is taught during the extra boys-only term. Women can neither be ministers nor vote to elect them.[12] They also can't legally represent themselves, as the rape case made painfully apparent. Even the plaintiffs in the trial were five men – a selected group

of victims' husbands or fathers – rather than the women themselves. (Friedman-Rudovsky, 2013)

In many Christian circles, adherence to purity involving sexuality also is of importance and has consequences. The lawyer for the colony, Oswaldo Rivera, mentioned that 'some women ... feared being ostracized ... some feared they would not be able to find a husband if it was known they had been raped, as women are expected to abstain from sex until marriage' (BBC, 2011).[13] Some of the women stopped going to church altogether because of shame (Friedman-Rudovsky, 2011). Stringent rules for women, as mentioned by 'different roles' for the genders, do not mean the same for the men. Anthropologist Paola Canova in her work on Mennonite colonies in Paraguay demonstrates how these men regularly seek out sex workers outside of their colony (Canova, 2020, pp. 116–17), and have married women who are not of their in-groups (Canova, 2020, pp. 28–9). Furthermore, Mennonite women's sexuality has been 'deployed to craft racial boundaries and sustain unequal relations toward outsiders' (Canova, 2020, p. 43).

In the real colony, instead of the consensus created in the novel and film, we see the three choices introduced in the novel happening at once: (1) do nothing, (2) stay and fight, or (3) leave. Regarding the first choice, some survivors found one another in their faith, in remaining, or 'do nothing'. Many of them 'doubled-down', 'in adherence to Mennonite rules and behaviours and expectations' (Epp, 2023). Friedman-Rudovsky (2013) adds that 'the safe space provided by such a segregated daily routine – offered comfort. Victims told me they leaned on their sisters or cousins, especially as they tried to adjust back to regular life in the wake of the trial.' Some said they had forgiven their rapists, granted that this was something they were confronted with in their faith, with the minister in the area adding 'if one woman didn't want to forgive, ... he would have simply explained to her that if she didn't forgive, then God wouldn't forgive her' (Friedman-Rudovsky, 2013). In light of the rapes continuing to occur, one of the survivors mentioned that they decided to stay, but moved to a new home, free from the memories of what happened there. Now that it is still occurring, she told the reporter (Friedman-Rudovsky, 2013): 'Maybe this is God's plan.' One of the grandmothers is noted to have windows on her house that now also don security bars, as 'a legacy of the rapes'. Psychological support was offered to the community, but the bishop refused it, stating they would not need it because they were not awake when these things happened. A woman notes (Pressly, 2019): 'A lot of people support the men in Palmasola [where the prison is located].

And if we – the victims – talk, those men in prison will hear, and families will be threatened.'

Interestingly, some have picked choice number two, stay and fight, but in their own way. The way some in this pacifist community stayed and fought was by building 'their own dissident church inside of Manitoba'. They believe what they were being taught is not actually in Scripture, and they want to become more 'biblically literate'. After the church broke ground and began to build, 'over 100 Manitoba men descended on the site and took it apart, piece-by-piece'. The Minister of the Old Colony wanted them to leave (Friedman-Rudovsky, 2013). All of the men convicted of these crimes are now denying their testimonies, and others still doubt that these rapes even happened. Some are now lobbying for the release of the rapists under that banner of forgiveness, and that what has happened may be punishment enough.[14] This movement has some members in the community who before used technology/smartphones to connect sparingly (if at all), but now are intentionally using WhatsApp to spread the word about what has happened in other communities within Bolivia and internationally. Some who were young girls when they were violated, and now are older, are now willing to testify (Pressly, 2019). One of the survivors' husbands warned them that if they were to return 'they will be lynched' (Friedman-Rudovsky, 2013). In fact, one of the members who was suspected to have taken part in the mass rapes was tied to a pole for nine hours, had to be hospitalized in the aftermath, and eventually died (*Canadian Mennonite*, 2009).

Some do choose the third option and leave, but there is much shame and loss associated with this decision. A woman named Erna Friessen and her spouse created 'Casa Mariposa', a shelter for abused Old Colony women and girls.[15] Friessen describes the implications of the women's decision to leave as follow:

> Aside from the challenges of making women aware of this space and convincing them that it's in their best interest to seek help, coming to Casa Mariposa often means leaving their families and the only world they've ever known. (Friedman-Rudovsky, 2013)

To summarize, if women left because of what happened, we obviously do not have their stories. The choice to leave the colony, however, is the least likely to have occurred. Given that this choice to leave is the one that both Toews and Polley have their characters unanimously choose, one asks how much of these specific Mennonite women's perspectives were left out.

Women Talking, in both the film and the novel version, are thus truly acts of fiction. Friedman-Rudovsky (2013) reminds us that 'in the years since the men were nabbed, there has never been a colony-wide discussion about the events. Rather, a code of silence descended following the guilty verdict.' And Pasqua and Klassen (2023) conclude their review of the film by stating, 'Knowing that the real women of the Manitoba Colony never held such a meeting and never left homes to start anew adds a sense of gravity to the story.'

I wonder what would have happened if the authors had been more honest about the Mennonite women's situation as it was playing out in real-time; how would those hidden conversations be imagined differently or, rather, more accurately? By introducing Judges 21, another story shrouded in silence about the women's perspective, I propose that the premise offered by the novel of the three *choices* may allow for 'wild female imagination' without full erasure, although readers will remain unsatisfied and uncomfortable, unhappy.

Narrating the mass rape in Judges 21

As noted above, the sexual violence narrated in Judges 21 is one consequence of the gang rape of a Levite's concubine[16] by men of the Benjamite town of Gibeah (Judg. 19). Understanding what is happening in the text of Judges 21 beyond an explanation of cyclical violence, as well as how there is any connection between *Women Talking* and the text, involves further explanation.

In order to make sense of the widespread and apparently justified rape in Judges 21, Katherine Southwood uses the anthropological category of marriage-by-capture.[17] This category, not an infrequent practice as one may assume, involves a process by which wives are procured by taking, stealing and kidnapping (Southwood, 2017, p. 67). However, marriage-by-capture happens on a spectrum, where there is more or less consent for the activity based on the involvement of the bride and her family (Southwood, 2017, p. 74). Southwood also notes that such an event may be more likely to occur in cultures where one finds 'an emphasis on virginity prior to marriage, the connection between virginity and male honour, the existence of a bride-price, male dominated regulation of marriages, and the significance of ethnicity and endogamy within such systems of marriage' (Southwood, 2017, p. 146). Southwood argues as follows regarding this practice, both in present manifestations and as referenced in Judges 21.22:

> Once the capture has taken place the family are [sic] forced into accepting the marriage, owing to the way marriage is culturally constructed in such cases. Particularly, once virginity is lost it is unlikely that a girl will find another partner let alone a bride-price. (Southwood, 2021, p. 167)

Because of the culture's emphasis on women's sexuality as something to safeguard, they inhabit a role that symbolizes the boundaries of large-group make-up. They are seen as the reproducers of their culture, both literally in providing offspring, but also in playing a specific role within a rigorous system of family honour. When these boundaries are crossed, then, even in marriage-by-capture practices that have some consent built in, 'an extra layer of complexity is added to the shame a bride would potentially face if she returned home after capture when the ethnic aspect of marriage by capture is considered' (Southwood, 2017, p. 206).[18] In many contexts where these boundaries are crossed, especially ethnically/tribally, the capturers would expect a fight of some sort from whichever group they took from (Southwood, 2017, pp. 83–6).

In Judges 21, not only the women are raped but, as Alice Bach notes, the fathers and brothers also incur an 'economic' rape by losing out on the bride wealth of these girls (Bach, 1998, p. 3). Here, in Judges 21, fight is not allowed, even considering the double loss incurred. Rather, any opposition of the Shiloh families is circumvented by assuming the complaint would be raised and a justification to pre-empt further issue provided by all Israel. For modern readers, this 'unity' of the Israelite tribes seems highly superficial, and the irony is that this story for ancient readers may have been understood as fictional. Furthermore, the text has many gaps and is narrated through a male lens.

Constructing the intertexts: differences and parallels

There are some obvious differences between Judges 21 and the Mennonite colony of Manitoba. War overwhelms the course of events narrated in Judges 21, with rape being a very regular occurrence and weapon in war (Bach, 1998, p. 10). In contrast, the colony entails a typically everyday peaceful setting. Marriage-by-capture was not what the rapists in Bolivia were attempting to do, as there was no seeming necessity to repopulate their community. However, the similarities of contexts do create a level of connection. As Southwood's work reveals, marriage-by-capture flourishes in communities that emphasize virginity, the connection between virginity and male honour, and endogamy; these rules and roles placed on *women*, negotiated by *men*, are important to acknowledge in both settings. These belief systems create a space in which sexuality and reproduction are understood as *owed* and *owned* by men.

As Bach (1998, p. 8) mentions that 'in biblical law, rape is a crime against the father or husband of the woman. A woman has no right to initiate a trial', we are similarly reminded of the *men* who were the plaintiffs in the rape cases of the *women* in the colony in Bolivia. The shame mentioned by Southwood that would happen if a girl returned home in Judges 21 reminds us of the shame in these Mennonite families, who refused to say that their daughters 'lost their virginity' via rape so they could still get married. Perhaps, shame was also a reason for those who decided not to leave the colony. Women, both in ancient Israelite and Mennonite culture, must be 'pure' in order to protect the group's identity. In both communities, the attacks and rapes are seemingly internal and still maintain endogamous structures. For different reasons, but nevertheless religious reasons, once such acts of sexual violence against women occur, people are not allowed to fight. It seems that although 'rules' remain for the women who have been violated in both communities, men are allowed to act in horrifying ways and be 'forgiven'. Once again, Goodwin reminds us that 'religion does not cause abuse, but religious communities frequently protect abusers while denying and enabling abuse, creating conditions for possibility for abuse, allowing abuse to flourish' (Goodwin, 2020, p. 147). Both of these settings have mainly advocated for 'keeping the peace' in the 'after'. In a trauma-informed language, dissociation can be an adaptation and option to such severe events, but so is revisionist history. Similar to Judges 21, some interpreters would prefer the gap, the lacuna.[19] Ultimately, in both the biblical text and *Women Talking*, we encounter a false unity; as we know from the actual colony, there is much tension.

Women Talking, in both the novel and the film, fills the silence, adding in fiction to placate readers' and viewers' feelings of horror at the situation, but eliding the truth and agency of women still in the colony. However, the novel begins with choices, even as it ends with the least likely choice for those women. The film adaptation then builds further upon the unified decision in favour of a universalized message. Feminism must acknowledge women's differences even in solidarity. In filling the gaps in Judges 21, I will take from Toews's initial framework the three choices as this fictional idea helps me to make sense of all possibilities, recognize the realities that were truly inhabited by the women in the Mennonite colony of Manitoba, and then to inform the similar, yet divergent, context of Judges 21, which may allow for an alternative understanding of agency.

Constructing an 'after': rewriting the mass rape of Judges 21

In reading the novel *Women Talking*, and watching the film, I resonate with Toews and Polley: I wanted these women to leave the colony. Although I know the dangers Goodwin portrays, I also wanted these women to leave their religion. But instead of using these survivors' bodies to only allow them to do what I would like, this 'after' will use the choices Toews gives to refuse full closure and maintain agency. Returning to Graybill's monograph, 'after' terror, for her, means many things: it 'names the immediate aftermath – what happens next in the narrative … and the larger space in and around the story', 'how we respond to rape stories', and 'acknowledging that not all rape stories have an after' (Graybill, 2021, p. 174). She also suggests (2021, p. 2) that we talk differently about rape stories. One of her strategies is explicitly to read through literature, to offer 'an alternative way of narrating sexual violence, rape, consent, harm, desire, and ambivalence' (2021, pp. 24–5). The literary works by Toews and Polley, however, demonstrate what Graybill critiques of biblical scholarship. Graybill mentions that some of the unhappiness is that what we do get in the 'after' is silence (Graybill, 2021, p. 174); and silence is how the narrative in Judges 21 ends. What about the women of Jabesh-Gilead and Shiloh? In taking from Toews the realities in Manitoba in Bolivia, I would like to offer some more wild female imagination in this 'after', which concurs with Saidiya Hartman's 'critical fabulation'.[20]

Do Nothing: These are the women in the story of Judges 21 who are always pictured as passive, yet moving in the supposed silence. They claim their faith as 'whole'; they decide their bodies will stay; they may even find purpose and meaning in their role as spouses of Benjaminites, although it was forced upon them and differently from how they may have imagined marriage and family to be. There might be wrestling, not only resignation to the situation, but a different kind of acceptance. Is this a 'holy' duty? Is there resentment? Do they like their new husbands? What does their relationship look like, as the men started it with an act of violation? Do the men feel guilty? How do they treat the women in their 'after'?

I want to imagine that these new brides find each other, leaning on one another for support, a sisterhood. When the men are not watching, and they are in their own spaces, they loosen a bit, not in disobedience, but sharing their own 'coded, rebellious exchange' (Onstad, 2018). They wash one another's feet too. Maybe they talk about what happened and gain clarity together in their conversations, but may also feel comfortable in the silence as well, in the knowledge that they do not have to explain or discuss. Some grow families inside their wombs, and some figure out what it means to live in this new space. Some still mourn their families, either alive or dead, the distance between them. Some are scared, fearful – and rightly so. Will this happen to their children too? Is this normal now? What happens when the time of year comes for their ritual performed in Shiloh? Do they still dance? Even for those who supposedly 'do nothing', they are not homogenous in response here. Is it spiritual bypassing, or is it an active hope? Can it be both, or neither? Allowing these women to fall on their faith in the remaking, maybe their faith will help them heal. At least, they persist.

Stay and Fight: These are the women in the story of Judges 21 who fight, raging against 'peace, peace' where there is no peace. They imagine creative ways of dissent, spinning the patriarchal narrative around in their fingers until they make their own web; they teach their children a new way of being even within this space. It seems what they were given is so black and white, so binary, but they stretch those ends out until the grey comes through and they expand in it. Maybe a Benjaminite spouse joins their captured bride in saying 'no more', in apologia, given that they too experienced loss and death (cf. Judg. 20.48). Maybe it turns out to be a constant domestic battle. Maybe even the families of Shiloh who were left to live decide they are not content with what happened, and they fight against the Elders who said otherwise. Maybe these families connect with other tribes, garnering more help for their cause, bringing their daughters back. Who knows, maybe they even claim that the rules and roles are not working, advocating for a new perspective. Maybe there is more violence, more stealing away.

And yet, as those in power pull away the bricks placed for a new way of belonging, a new way of understanding God, the next morning these women awake, and put the bricks back again in stubborn, determined hope for something different. Maybe it means they still worship YHWH. Maybe this means they must worship another god, a different one that would not endorse what happened to them, maybe they bake cakes for this god or goddess, burn incense, weave shrouds in hope of deliverance from their situation. They resist.

Leave: These are the women in the story of Judges 21 who leave their Benjaminite husbands, returning to the *beyt-'av*, 'the father's house'. Maybe they feel shame, or maybe they feel absolute relief. Maybe both, in waves. Some might return to their father's house to what could be a closed door, a refusal for their re-entry. What then? Some despair. Some dream up new worlds like the one in *Women Talking*, where they leave and create their own carved-out homes, a new tribe of women and their future children created by rape, and they will still love and love. Maybe they give birth to these children and do not want them either, and the grief of the mass amount of loss results in adding to the loss. Some children are adopted, maybe brought in by other tribes and kinship groups, maybe some are even enslaved. They might feel regret, they might linger on the what-ifs, or maybe they find hope. Maybe they find all of it. They insist.

And yet, amid these possibilities in the lacuna given by the initial framework of *Women Talking*, we settle in the unhappiness that overwhelms this situation. I offer the three choices, and I cannot help but hope for an amount of goodness in each to dissolve myself of my sadness, and my discomfort. While the religions portrayed did not cause this, 'abuse of power comes as no surprise'. Even if women choose a religion that does have gender hierarchy does not mean they made a poor decision; that would be to blame the victim if or when abuses occur. But when women talk, and even when women do not talk, we should listen.

Bibliography

Anonymous, 2009, 'Suspected Bolivian Rapist Killed by Colony Members', *Canadian Mennonite* 13/20, available at https://www.proquest.com/magazines/suspected-bolivian-rapist-killed-colony-members/docview/228224405/se-2?accountid=13607 (accessed 27.12.2023).

Bach, Alice, 1998, 'Rereading the Body Politic: Women and Violence in Judges 21', *Biblical Interpretation* 61, pp. 1–19.

BBC News Latin America, 2011, 'Bolivian Mennonites Jailed for Serial Rapes', 26 August, available at https://www.bbc.com/news/world-latin-america-14688458 (accessed 27.12.2023).

Bergen, Rachel, 2010, 'Grant us a Portion of their Pain: Manitoba Mennonites Come Together to Lament for their Suffering Bolivian Sisters', *Canadian Mennonite* 14/5, pp. 18, 10, March, available at chrome-extension://efaidnbmnnnibpcajpcglclefindmkaj/https://canadianmennonite.org/sites/default/files/past-issues/14-05small_618_2010-03-08.pdf (accessed 10.06.2024).

Braun, Will, 2023, 'Red Carpet Hayloft', *Canadian Mennonite* 27/4, 22 February, available at https://canadianmennonite.org/stories/red-carpet-hayloft (accessed 27.12.2023).

Canova, Paola, 2020, *Frontier Intimacies: Ayoreo Women and the Sexual Economy of the Paraguayan Chaco*, Austin, TX: University of Texas Press.

Elliot, Mandy, 2023, 'Film Review: Sorrow, Joy, Anger and Faith', *Canadian Mennonite* 27/4, 22 February, available at https://canadianmennonite.org/stories/film-review-sorrow-joy-anger-and-faith (accessed 27.12.2023).

Ellison, Christopher G., 2001, 'Religious Involvement and Domestic Violence Among U.S. Couples', *Journal for the Scientific Study of Religion* 40, pp. 269–86, available at https://doi.org/10.1111/0021-8294.00055 (accessed 27.12.2023).

Epp, Aaron, 2023, 'What About the Women of Manitoba Colony?', *Canadian*

Mennonite 27/4, 22 February, available at https://canadianmennonite.org/stories/what-about-women-manitoba-colony (accessed 27.12.2023).

Ewara, Eyo, 2022, 'Attempting Redress: Fungibility, Ethics, and Redressive Practice in the Work of Saidiya Hartman', *Theory & Event* 25/2 (April), pp. 364–91.

Friedman-Rudovsky, Jean, 2013, 'The Ghost Rapes of Bolivia', *VICE*, 22 December, available at https://www.vice.com/en/article/4w7gqj/the-ghost-rapes-of-bolivia-000300-v20n8 (accessed 27.12.2023).

Friedman-Rudovsky, Jean, 2011, 'A Verdict in Bolivia's Shocking Case of the Mennonite Rapes', *TIME*, 17 August, available at https://content.time.com/time/world/article/0,8599,2087711,00.html (accessed 27.12.2023).

Goodwin, Megan, 2020, *Abusing Religion: Literary Persecution, Sex Scandals, and American Minority Religions*, New Brunswick, ME: Rutgers University Press.

Graybill, Rhiannon, 2021, *Texts After Terror: Rape, Sexual Violence, and The Hebrew Bible*, New York: Oxford University Press.

Hamley, Isabelle, 2020, *Unspeakable Things Unspoken: An Irigarayan Reading of Otherness and Victimization in Judges 19–21*, Eugene, OR: Pickwick Publications.

Harding, Kate, 2020, 'I've Been Told I'm a Survivor, Not a Victim: What's Wrong with Being a Victim?' in *TIME*, 27 February, available at https://time.com/5789032/victim-survivor-sexual-assault/ (accessed 27.12.2023).

Hartman, Saidiya, 2007, *Lose Your Mother: A Journey Along the Atlantic Slave Route*, New York: Farrar, Straus & Giroux.

Hartman, Saidiya, 2008, 'Venus in Two Acts', *Small Axe* 26 (June), pp. 1–14.

Herman, Judith, 2023, *Truth and Repair: How Trauma Survivors Envision Justice*, New York: Basic Books.

Johnson, Breya M., 2023, 'Who Said We All Survived?', *Scalawag Magazine*, 25 May, available at https://scalawagmagazine.org/2023/05/victim-or-survivor-language/ (accessed 27.12.2023).

Klein, Lillian, 1988, *The Triumph of Irony in the Book of Judges*, Sheffield: Almond Press.

Kraybill, Donald B., 2008, 'Mennonites' in Richard T. Schaefer (ed.), *Encyclopedia of Race, Ethnicity, and Society*, volume 2, New York: Sage Publications, pp. 888–90.

Mead, Rebecca, 2022, 'Sarah Polley's Journey from Child Star to Feminist Auteur', *The New Yorker*, 14 November, available at https://www.newyorker.com/magazine/2022/11/21/sarah-polleys-journey-from-child-star-to-feminist-auteur?fbclid=IwAR2QZDjIwaCot_OC8dbpuljEkivSUoh_U2mOpKRMYznqSGxuaU25tpHlv-Y (accessed 27.12.2023).

Niditch, Susan, 2008, *Judges: A Commentary*, Louisville, KY: Westminster John Knox Press.

Onstad, Katrina, 2018, 'Interview: Miriam Toews', *The Guardian Europe*, 18 August, available at https://www.theguardian.com/books/2018/aug/18/miriam-toews-interview-women-talking-mennonite (accessed 27.12.2023).

Pasqua, Christina, and Pamela Klassen, 2023, 'Women Talking and Reimagining the World', *The Revealer*, 5 April, available at https://therevealer.org/women-talking-and-reimagining-the-world/ (accessed 27.12.2023).

Polley, Sarah, 2023, 'Interviewed by Tom Power, Making Women Talking: Sarah Polley Explains why Laughter was Key to Adapting Miriam Toews's Novel',

YouTube, 31 January, available at https://www.youtube.com/watch?v=DsvEcsk6bxU&t=984s (accessed 27.12.2023).

Polley, Sarah (director), 2022, *Women Talking*, United Artists Releasing, 104 Minutes.

Pressly, Linda, 2019, 'The Rapes Haunting a Community that Shuns the 21st Century', *BBC News Bolivia*, 16 May, available at https://www.bbc.com/news/stories-48265703.amp (accessed 27.12.2023).

Schwartz, Sarah, 2021, 'Law and Order in Judges 19–21', *Journal of the Ancient Near Eastern Society* 35, pp. 133–41, available at https://janes.scholasticahq.com/article/32972-law-and-order-in-judges-19-21 (accessed 27.12.2023).

Southwood, Katherine, 2017, *Marriage by Capture in the Book of Judges: An Anthropological Approach*, Cambridge: Cambridge University Press.

Toews, Miriam, 2018, *Women Talking*, New York: Bloomsbury.

Trible, Phyllis, 1984, *Texts of Terror*, Minneapolis, MN: Fortress Press.

Urry, James, 2006, *Mennonites, Politics, and Peoplehood: Europe-Russia-Canada 1525 to 1980*, Winnipeg: University of Manitoba Press.

Waroux, Yann le Polain de, et al., 2020, 'Pious Pioneers: The Expansion of Mennonite Colonies in Latin America', *Journal of Land Use Science* 16/1, pp. 1–17, available at https://doi.org/10.1080/1747423X.2020.1855266 (accessed 27.12.2023).

Wilcox, W. Bradford, 2004, *Soft Patriarchs, New Men: How Christianity Shapes Fathers and Husbands*, Chicago, IL: The University of Chicago Press.

Wilkinson, Alissa, 2022, 'What the film Women Talking loses (and preserves) from the 2018 Novel', *VOX*, 14 September, available at https://www.vox.com/culture/23345084/women-talking-review-tiff-augustine-oscars-best-adapted-screenplay (accessed 27.12.2023).

Yuval-Davis, Nira, 1997, *Gender & Nation*, London: Sage Publications.

Notes

1 While this is reported two years after the initial trial, Jean Friedman-Rudovsky (2011) was the reporter for *TIME* for the initial events as well; see also Pressly, 2019.

2 Interestingly, this information is *not* given in chapter 20. The oath replicates, to some extent, the Deuteronomic regulation against marrying foreigners such as Israel's archetypal enemy, the 'Canaanites' (Deut. 7.4; cf. Josh. 23.12; Judg. 3.5–6). The internal division of the tribes is much more fractured than assumed as the Benjaminites are seen in one instance as similar to 'foreigners'. The narration of events in Judges 19—21 is scattered, fragmented and redundant, which is not only a sign of redaction but also characteristic of a trauma narrative. Who is 'all Israel' when it seems, apparently, many of them were not there at Mizpah?

3 The word *kherem* means a 'devote to destruction', or a 'ban' which involves both property and people. The practice is most specifically outlined in Deuteronomy 13. In Judges 19, however, the ban is not acted out fully since the virgin girls are spared, and thus seems to be a pretence.

4 See Leah Lakshmi Piepzna-Samarasinha, 2018, *Care Work: Dreaming Disability Justice*, Vancouver: Arsenal Pulp Press.

5 Many have written on this topic, but two in particular have captured my attention: Johnson (2023) and Harding (2020).

6 See further Ellison, 2001, and also Wilcox, 2004, pp. 181–3.

7 There are 30 different Mennonite groups in just the United States (Kraybill, 2008, p. 888). Mennonites are Anabaptists; that is, they only baptize consenting adults, and they commit to pacificism. However, these 'different immigrant groups exude distinctive cultural, historical, and theological flavours'.

8 The term here would be that these groups are part of the 'Old Order'. Other groups are labelled as transitional and assimilated (Kraybill, 2008, p. 889).

9 It's important to note that because of their agrarian lifestyle, the receiving countries saw them as perfect settlers to take over indigenous land. Canada promised Anishinaabe and Métis land to them upon arrival. For research on this pattern of settling and uprooting in Latin America, see Waroux et al., 2020.

10 Finding sources for this work was made incredibly easy by the thorough journalism done by Pasqua and Klassen (2023).

11 Thoughtfully, she also 'hired an on-set therapist and ensured that each day of shooting ended at a reasonable hour so no one would have to miss time at home with their families' (Pasqua and Klassen, 2023). This should be the norm and not the exception to the rule.

12 If women are interested in voting, they *can* become 'nominal members, a status that comes with extra fees that stifle their interest in taking active participation'. However, some widows can vote 'in place of their deceased husbands' (Canova, 2020, p. 40).

13 The lawyer also said some families did not want to speak up if it happened to their daughter because of future marriage prospects (Pressly, 2019): 'So, many parents preferred to keep quiet and say, "Nothing happened in this house."'

14 This is not to understate that many survivors in general feel quite underserved by the systems of 'justice' as it pertains to sexual assault, even with a guilty verdict. Restorative justice movements are being sought instead; see Herman, 2023. Mennonite Will Braun (2023) also notes that there have been 'Circles of Support and Accountability, a case in which Mennonites have done courageous and creative work to rehabilitate sexual offenders and reduce sexual assault.' Braun mentions this in his work to 'beware the single story' (referencing Adichie's famous TED talk) about Mennonites.

15 Rachel Bergen (2010) writes that a lament service was done at Morrow Gospel Church in Manitoba in Canada to raise money for Casa Mariposa.

16 This term, *pilegesh*, is quite contested, and some would prefer the term 'secondary wife', because of the more racial tones that go with the term 'concubine'. However, the Levite in this text does not have a 'primary wife', which makes the 'secondary' term all the more difficult. Isabelle Hamley in *Unspeakable Things Unspoken* notes that, in the text, her position as *pilegesh* 'seems to be below even animals, as the Levite takes his donkeys first and the *pilegesh* second in Judg. 19.10–12' (Hamley, 2020, p. 137). For Lillian Klein, who views Judges as a tale of great irony, the Levite may have purchased the *pilegesh* 'for purposes of sexual gratification or housekeeping (or both), possibly because he could not afford the bride price of a wife' (Klein, 1988, p. 163). Both the notion of concubine and secondary wife do allow for an understanding that she would not be viewed in the status of 'wife', but closer to a slave instead.

17 For a critique of Southwood's important monograph, see T. M. Lemos's review in *Review of Biblical Literature* 03/2020.

18 Much of Southwood's understanding of this also coincides with my own readings of Nira Yuval-Davis's in *Gender & Nation*. Yuval-Davis argues (1997, p. 22) that maintaining an essentialist identity for groups, especially if groups feel threatened, has much to do with 'control of marriage, procreation, and sexuality' and, further, 'Women's positionings in and obligations to their ethnic and national collectivities, as well as in and to the states they reside in and/or are citizens of, also affect and can sometimes override their reproductive rights' (Yuval-Davis, 1997, p. 26).

19 Whereas Niditch notes that the end of Judges is *not* chaotic, but ends 'whole' because women were exchanged (Niditch, 2008, pp. 210–11), I argue that this end is a façade.

20 I must add that this work can also be seen as taking from Saidiya Hartman's 'critical fabulation'. She does this work in 'Venus in Two Acts', where she plays with and re-presents basic elements and events within the story, to imagine what cannot be verified (Hartman, 2008, pp. 11–12). Hartman does this by rewriting what she had initially written in her work *Lose Your Mother: A Journey Along the Atlantic Slave Route* (2007), where an unnamed Black girl is murdered on a ship and the trial mentions her as a fleeting moment and nothing more. In her attempts to redress this erasure, she writes in the gap, with a lot of purposeful self-reflection and reflexivity. Eyo Ewara (2022) helps to describe in detail what Hartman is doing.

5

Filling in the Gaps: Reading Hosea 1—3 with Francine Rivers's *Redeeming Love*

KIRSI COBB

Introduction

'That's what fiction is: it's an eye-level representation of universal truths' (Rivers and Hunt, 2020, loc. 2861). This quote penned by Francine Rivers comes from her 2020 companion study to her best-selling novel *Redeeming Love*. Originally published in 1991, *Redeeming Love* has become a worldwide phenomenon, selling over 3 million copies and having been translated into more than 30 languages (Law, 2020). Most recently, it has been adapted into a film of the same name, released in the United States in January 2022.

If, as Rivers claims, fiction represents universal truths, the question needs to be asked as to what these truths are and how they are represented in *Redeeming Love*. Based loosely on the story of Hosea and Gomer in Hosea 1—3, the book bears, in Rivers's words, 'a similarity to the path many of us take from brokenness to redemption and wholeness in Christ' (Rivers, 2020b, loc. 2861). Set as a fictional romantic Christian story of redemption, the aptly named *Redeeming Love* interprets the narrative of Hosea and Gomer as one where Hosea, or Rivers's fictional character Michael Hosea, represents Christ's love and self-sacrifice towards Gomer, in the book presented by Angel, a wilful and wounded prostitute in need of rescue. With Rivers's interpretation comes several preconceived notions of Hosea, Gomer and God, as well as those of marriage, agency and trauma. These presuppositions cause at times interesting twists and turns – at other times disturbing ones – in her narrative, inviting the reader to perceive the characters in particular ways. It is these 'truths' as presented by Rivers that this chapter seeks to address while pondering whether *Redeeming Love* in fact offers a love story of redemption or a tale of dysfunction.

Biblical retellings and Hosea 1—3

Since Rivers's book is only loosely based on the story of Hosea 1—3, one would be forgiven for asking what there is to gain by looking at fictional representations as opposed to the biblical narrative or associated academic works. While doing one does not exclude the other, we must remember that all interpretations (academic, fictional or otherwise) are ultimately exercises in gap-filling. Hebrew narratives are particularly curt, enticing the audience to make connections between the simplest elements to much more 'intricate networks' that are established and modified as the task of reading unfolds (Sternberg, 1987, p. 186). In her study of the reception history of Bathsheba, Sara Koenig (2018, p. 3) observes: 'No story can include every single detail, and a text that buttons up every answer and possibility is no longer really a story; it is something else, more akin to a dictionary entry than a narrative'. Narratives give space for speculation and imagination, creating a wealth of possibilities that in the realm of biblical interpretation give rise to various readings – academic, fictional or otherwise.

Different readings of biblical narratives can also open a window onto the concerns and cultural context of the interpreter as opposed to the ancient author. Meir Sternberg (1987, p. 188) famously called readings that were 'launched and sustained by the reader's subjective concerns ... rather than by the text's own norms and directives' as 'illegitimate gap-fillings'. While Sternberg is indeed correct that texts often invite us to fill in the gaps in ways congruent 'with the text's own norms' (Sternberg, 1987, p. 188; cf. Iser, 1974, pp. 274–94), subjectivity also remains part of the interpretative process (Clines, 1990, p. 12). After all, none of us interpret in a vacuum, and our cultural and communal contexts (Fish, 1980, pp. 338–55) will have a bearing on a text's interpretation as does its relevance and meaning for contemporary audiences (cf. Clines, 1990, pp. 11–12; Morse, 2020, pp. 2–3). As the Bible has offered inspiration for art, literature and music in the Western world, these retellings now often affect the way we understand the biblical text, as noted by Cheryl Exum (2007, p. vii). Of the more than 3 million readers of *Redeeming Love*, I wonder how many will understand the biblical story in view of Rivers's interpretation rather than vice versa? Based on her 3 million-plus readers, my guess is quite a few. Koenig (2020, p. 422) is quite right when she further notes: 'As much as biblical scholars might eschew "popular" interpretations of the biblical text, those retellings have the power to shape people's views about the content of the Bible.' Engaging with such retellings is therefore not a sideline venture or interesting trivia, but rather an important endeavour which engages readers of the Bible in new and imaginative ways.

The backstory: whose fault is it?

Rivers's *Redeeming Love* is set during the Californian Gold Rush in the 1850s. In the imaginary town of Pair-a-Dice, a local farmer named Michael Hosea comes to town on errands when God points out the person he is to marry: a young, attractive woman called Angel but, as Michael finds to his dismay, 'a soiled dove' (2013/1991, loc. 740). Not only is she beautiful but also the prized prostitute at the Palace, the biggest brothel in Pair-a-Dice. The illegitimate offspring of a Catholic mother and a married man, Angel was after her mother's demise sold at the age of eight to a man called Duke for his sexual pleasure (loc. 521–642, 3075). In time, Angel becomes a prostitute (loc. 3747), is forcibly sterilized (loc. 4138), and finally escapes from Duke to California, only to find herself back in prostitution to avoid starvation (loc. 675). In Pair-a-Dice, Michael tries to persuade Angel to marry him and eventually gets his wish while Angel is semi-conscious: Angel, depressed and suicidal, provokes her 'bodyguard' to beat her in the hopes of ending it all. While she is near to death, Michael pays the brothel for her and marries her on the spot. Angel is only vaguely aware of the commotion around her, and Rivers writes that she would even 'agree to wed Satan himself if it would get her out of the Palace'. To Michael's encouragement to accept his proposal, Angel simply replies, 'Why not?' (loc. 1419).

In this version of the Hosea-Gomer story, only the bare bones of the biblical narrative are visible – that is, God telling a man named Hosea to marry a promiscuous woman (Hos. 1.2). However, more inferences become obvious once we understand Rivers's reading of Hosea 1—3 as a narrative. In her companion study to *Redeeming Love*, she describes the Northern Kingdom as having fallen under the thrall of the god Baal and Gomer working as a prostitute at a temple (2020b, loc. 2012). Rivers hypothesizes that Gomer may have been taken to work at the temple as soon as she was sexually mature, perhaps at the age of 12 or 13. Her parents might have abandoned her as a result of financial hardship or their preference for raising sons but, whatever the reason, Rivers suggests that when Hosea offered Gomer a way out in the form of marriage, she willingly took it (loc. 2028).

The purpose of analysing biblical retellings is not, as Exum (2007, p. vii) reminds us, to study the biblical text and then evaluate whether the author of the retelling got the story 'right' or 'wrong'. There are in fact several ways in which Israel's so-called adultery against God can be understood,[1] of which religious transgression remains a contender (Macintosh, 1997, pp. 42, 48–50; Mays, 1969, pp. 25–6; Wolff, 1974, pp. 13–15, 34–5). What is problematic in Rivers's interpretation, however, is her equation of Angel with the sinful state of humanity from which redemption is needed in the evangelical Christian interpretation.

The book of Hosea begins with the prophet being told by God to marry an *'eshet zenunim*, 'a promiscuous woman' (1.2), later identified as Gomer (1.3). Following Phyllis Bird and others (Bird, 1989, pp. 75–94; Sherwood, 1996, pp. 19–20, n. 4), it seems that the Hebrew root *z-n-h* alludes to both pre- and extramarital sexual activity, and in the case of the abstract plural noun *zenunim* suggests habitual behaviour rather than a profession. In the biblical story, Gomer would have truly been a promiscuous woman as she would have knowingly rebelled against the prevalent gender norms. However, in Rivers's earlier portrayal of Gomer, it was her parents who took Gomer to the temple to work as a prostitute, similar to Angel's fate of being sold to Duke in *Redeeming Love*. In both of Rivers's readings, the women are the *objects* rather than the *subjects* of sexual sins. Admittedly, in her companion study Rivers (2020b, loc. 462) notes that Angel 'did nothing to deserve ending up in the clutches of people like Duke and the Duchess [the madam at the Palace]'. However, as per her evangelical roots (2020b, loc. 1512), Rivers claims that '[h]umans are sinful because we are born with a sinful nature' and this also applies to Angel who 'had no problem seeing herself as a sinner – after all, she was a prostitute' (loc. 1499). In *Redeeming Love*, Angel's state of sinfulness is further revealed in some of her choices (Rivers 2020a, loc. 800, 994). These include Angel describing herself as weak if in the face of hunger and homelessness she were to return to prostitution (Rivers 2013/1991, loc. 5511), and Angel confessing to Michael that 'the worst' she had ever done was to have sex with her father (loc. 4090). This happened when Angel was 16: Duke brought Angel's father to her as a client, knowing full well his identity (loc. 4090–122). When Michael asks Angel about her thoughts, she declares: 'I *knew* what I was doing, and I did it anyway! ... I did it with *relish*, just waiting for that moment when I'd tell him who I was' (loc. 4122, Rivers's italics). Later Angel's father commits suicide, seemingly at least in part because of this encounter (loc. 4122–38).

One of the more scathing reviews of *Redeeming Love* was a series of blogposts published between 2016 and 2018 by Samantha Field. Already in her initial posts, Field notes that Rivers seems to have little knowledge of trauma recovery (Field, 2016a) or the concept of survival sex (Field,

2016b), the latter of which is especially applicable to the examples used. By her own admission, Rivers did not research trauma or psychology before writing *Redeeming Love*. She notes (Rivers, 2020b, loc. 1966): 'I just opened my Bible, sat at my computer, and prayed, and God showed me Angel's life, inside and out.' Although what Rivers says might be true, further research may have been to her benefit.[2]

Survival sex is defined by Eugene Walls and Stephanie Bell (2011, p. 424) as 'the exchange of sex for food, money, shelter, drugs, and other needs and wants'. This exchange is needs-driven, even a 'subsistence strategy' (Walls and Bell, 2011, p. 424) in the face of economic hardship including homelessness (Clingan et al., 2020, pp. 2–3). In other words, it is sex exchanged for survival without interference from pimps or traffickers (Bigelsen and Vuotto, 2013, p. 6). In the first example, Angel's 'choice' of prostitution would have been the result of avoiding starvation and homelessness, and hence hardly a choice but a matter of survival. In the second, Angel was economically dependent on a man who considered her his sexual property. In this case, she could be classified as a victim of 'compelled sex trafficking' where the presence of a trafficker is coupled with the use of fraud, force and coercion (Bigelsen and Vuotto, 2013, p. 7). Regardless of how Angel may have felt about her situation, the facts of her circumstances remain unchanged. As Duke's property, her refusal to have sex with her father might not actually have made any difference, at least not to her trafficker. Rather, it might have induced punishment or eviction, so whether acknowledged or not her compliance to have sex with her father had an element of survival. In an analysis of Margaret Atwood's trauma novel *Alias Grace*, Laurie Vickroy (2015, loc. 1277) wonders whether 'victimization and personal agency ... can coexist in situations of powerlessness, of lack of choices under coercion, of the circumscription of women's lives and women's frequent subjection to violence or death'. In the case of Angel, her choices were not really choices because as a minor she had no real access to options or agency. Such situations make the evaluation of Angel's culpability highly problematic, perhaps even impossible (cf. Vickroy, 2015, loc. 1328).

One last example where Rivers's portrayal of Angel's culpability stretches credibility is in blaming Angel for her part in a sexual assault perpetrated by Paul, a man who was married to Michael's now deceased sister. In the book, Angel wishes to leave Michael and gets a lift from Paul back to Pair-a-Dice. Eventually, Paul reveals that he needs 'payment' for his troubles. In response to his constant goading, Angel taunts Paul – which seemingly fuels his ire, and eventually he pushes Angel to the ground and assaults her (Rivers, 2013/1991, loc. 2619–702). Afterwards,

Michael is grieved not only by Paul's duplicity but also by Angel's (loc. 2807–21). In fact, Paul even snaps at Angel, 'You're blaming me for what happened? Did I drag you off that wagon? Did I rape you? You'd like to think it was my fault, wouldn't you?' (loc. 5143). To this, Angel responds in her thoughts: 'She knew she had no defense' (loc. 5143). Later in the book Angel speaks with the somewhat transformed Paul who asks Angel if she knew she could have said no to him. Describing her inner dialogue, Rivers writes (loc. 6676): 'It was on her [Angel's] head. She had allowed it to happen. For whatever reason. What did it matter now? She couldn't cast blame on anyone but herself. The choice had been hers.'

Even though Angel blames herself, it is intriguing that the actual narration of the assault seemingly betrays this version of events. As per his words, Paul does not drag Angel down from the wagon; however, Paul's culpability is undeniable: 'Furious, he [Paul] grabbed her [Angel's] arm and propelled her a hundred feet off the road, into the shadows of a thicket. He was rough and quick, his sole desire to hurt and degrade her. She didn't make a sound. Not one' (loc. 2685). Rivers may have wanted to shift some blame on to Angel by adding subtle descriptions about her behaviour such as her taunting, climbing down from the wagon, resignation or perhaps even her 'cold, dead smile' (loc. 2680); yet the sexual act itself has Paul clearly in the position of the perpetrator while the only act Angel commits is her complete silence.

In a moment of sad irony, Rivers's reading of the rape as both Angel's fault and a deed committed by Paul could be suggested to have similarities to the book of Hosea. Although in Hosea 2.5 and 12 (Hebrew text: 2.7 and 14) it seems that Gomer chases willingly after her lovers, in Hosea 2.10 (Hebrew text: 2.12) Gomer also becomes the victim of a sexual assault.[3] In response to Gomer's/Israel's promiscuous conduct, Hosea/God declares: 'So now I will expose her lewdness before the eyes of her lovers; no-one will take her out of my hands' (NIV UK). The exposure of the woman's 'lewdness' (*navluth*) is a multifaceted term (Kelle, 2005, pp. 255–7); based on the Hebrew noun *nevalah* ('foolishness'), it could refer to the woman's adulterous conduct, but based on the Akkadian word *baltu/baštu*, the term could allude to the woman's genitals (cf. nakedness in Hos. 2.3 (Hebrew text: 2.5)). Since *navluth* only occurs here in the Hebrew Bible, study of the term *nevalah* could shed further light on the term. Intriguingly, several incidences of *nevalah* occur during (threatened) sexual violence perpetrated by men such as in Genesis 34.7 (the rape of Dinah), Judges 19.23 and 20.6 (the threatened violation of the Levite and the eventual gang rape of his concubine), and 2 Samuel 13.12 (the rape of Tamar) (Keefe, 1993, p. 82; Sherwood, 1996, p. 304). In a text that is declaring a seemingly justified punishment on Gomer/Israel for her misdeeds, the use of the term *navluth* is an interesting choice since, as noted by Yvonne Sherwood (1996, p. 304), the noun 'reverberates with memories of biblical rape scenes and reminds the reader of men's crimes just when the text requires he/she forget them'. In Hosea 2.10 (Hebrew text: 2.12), the woman Gomer/Israel is most severely punished for her sins, yet allusions to male-initiated rape create a moment of ambiguity where the audience is left wondering about the culpability of Gomer/Israel. In both Hosea and *Redeeming Love*, the respective authors' theological agenda needs a sinner for the message to hold (cf. Field, 2016c); yet the description of the rape in both cases casts suspicion on the woman's guilt. In *Redeeming Love*, the image we are left with is not that of an unrepentant sinner but a victim/survivor in need of safety and connection.

That both *Redeeming Love* and Hosea 2.10 (Hebrew text: 2.12) have the female victim assume at least some blame for the rape is worrying since, at least for contemporary readers, such readings can effectuate an understanding prevalent in rape myths (Stiebert, 2020, loc. 1509–1761) and purity culture (Cross, 2020; Shore, 2022); that a share of the responsibility for an assault should fall on to the (female) victim/survivor because, for example, of having behaved in ways that are 'provocative and, allegedly, rape-inciting' (Stiebert, 2020, loc. 1536; cf. Hos. 2.2, 5, 13 (Hebrew text: 2.4, 7 and 15)). According to this myth, had the female behaved 'appropriately', the rape need not have occurred. Victims/survivors are thus made to carry some or even 'a significant share' of the blame, be this in the form of, for example, what they said or did not say or what they did or did not do (Stiebert, 2020, loc. 1522, 1606–49). In *Redeeming Love*, one could argue that if Angel would have said 'no' or not taunted Paul, perhaps everything had been fine. Such an interpretation is, however, harmful as it leaves the victims/survivors to shoulder blame that belongs to the perpetrators alone. Moreover, it perpetuates what Johanna Stiebert (2020, loc. 1606, 1619) calls 'the myth of "real" rape', meaning: 'If there are no indications or evidence of concerted struggle (such as screaming, fending off, fighting, biting) and no signs of injury (such as scratches, bruises, or tearing) then whatever took place was not rape.' Making the victims/survivors responsible for the assault makes condemning perpetrators all the harder as the victims/survivors may not fit what society would describe as the image or the behaviour pattern of an 'ideal rape victim'. Both the book of Hosea and *Redeeming Love* seemingly support the notion that the woman is in some way responsible for the rape; yet one would be justified in asking what kind of an ideology of women, men or even God such a reading supports.

Who is in charge? Saving Angel from herself

In her review of the 2022 film of *Redeeming Love*, Anna Venarchik notes:

> For the film to function as a romance, the audience must accept that the only problem with the arrangement is Angel's inability to receive love due to her litany of past traumas: murder, forced sterilization, incest, sex trafficking – there's no trauma stone left unturned for the heroine. (Venarchik, 2022)

Comparing Venarchik's 'litany' with Judith Herman's reading of trauma, some significant overlap occurs. Herman defines traumatic events as those that

> overwhelm the ordinary systems of care that give people a sense of control, connection, and meaning ... Traumatic events are extraordinary ... because they overwhelm the ordinary human adaptations to life ... traumatic events generally involve threats to life or bodily integrity, or a close personal encounter with violence and death. (Herman, 2015/1992, p. 33)

Looking at Angel's life and events such as forced sterilization and sex trafficking on the one hand, and Herman's definition of traumatic events on the other, it seems well within the remit of the narrative to understand Angel as a traumatized character. Furthermore, as per Cathy Caruth's (2016, pp. 11–12) oft-quoted definition of trauma as 'an overwhelming experience of sudden or catastrophic events' to which the response frequently happens belatedly, it would not be impossible to envisage that Angel would remain haunted by her experiences later in life. In fact, in *Redeeming Love* we can note several traumatic responses, such as Angel's recurring nightmares (Rivers, 2013/1991, loc. 1883), the presence of triggers like her fear of the dark (loc. 1896–1928), feeling numb and hopeless (loc. 925, 970, 1309), hypervigilance (loc. 1433–1665; 1896–1912), and difficulty in forming trusting relationships (loc. 3445, 3516, 3865; Herman, 2015/1992, pp. 32–56) among others. In this way, Rivers succeeds in part by giving us a fleeting glimpse into the painful world of trauma, even if sometimes inadvertently (cf. Field, 2016d; 2017b).

Since trauma often disempowers victims and disconnects them from others, according to Herman (2015/1992, p. 133) recovery is likewise 'based upon the empowerment of the survivor and the creation of new connections'. However, Herman also notes that the victim/survivor 'must be the author and arbiter of her own recovery'. Since trauma robs its victim of power and control, these need to be restored to her (p. 159). While others can offer support, they should not try to 'cure' or pressure her. Rather, what is needed is care and support while the survivor finds her way. For this to happen, securing a place of safety is paramount as victims often feel unsafe in their own bodies as well as with others (pp. 159–63). Establishing a refuge so that the work of recovery can begin is therefore often the first task in the healing process (p. 159).

However, while Rivers may have at least in part succeeded in her description of trauma responses, sadly the way she envisages Angel's recovery leaves a lot to be desired. Rather than empowering Angel, she is constantly denied agency. As noted earlier, Michael marries Angel when she is only semi-aware of what is happening and is subsequently taken by Michael to his farm to recuperate. While Michael cares for Angel, he strips her of autonomy (cf. Field, 2016d; Shore, 2022): he takes her clothes since 'A farmer's wife doesn't wear satin and lace' (Rivers, 2013/1991, loc. 1558) and calls her Mara instead of Angel to allude to her assumed bitterness (loc. 878, 1433). In the end, Angel is utterly dependent on Michael for her needs, including provisions and shelter (loc. 1501). On a more intimate level, Michael even reveals that he wishes to consummate the marriage 'his way' rather than 'her way' – that is, when it means something more to Angel than payment (loc. 1589, 2223). Oddly reminiscent of the biblical text where upon marriage we do not know of Gomer's consent, or lack thereof, to sexual liaisons (Hos. 1.3), Michael does not wait for Angel to fall in love with him; rather, they have sex before any such event has occurred (Shore, 2022). During the act, Angel is seemingly trying to disassociate – that is, not be mentally present – while Michael is forcibly trying to make her so (Rivers, 2013/1991, loc. 2223–69). Overall, the picture is one where Angel needs a firm hand to guide her, and Michael's actions are justified as part of the divine plan to redeem Angel regardless of her thoughts, wants or feelings. Rather, as noted by Field (Field, 2016c, her italics; cf. Field, 2018a; Shore, 2022), '*ignoring consent* is an essential facet of both Micheal [sic] and God's character'.

From the perspective of trauma theory, Angel has not so much escaped her past than landed into another kind of servitude (cf. Rivers, 2013/1991, loc. 1501). However, since Angel is depicted as the sinner in need of a saviour and Michael as the emblem of the self-sacrificing love of Christ, domestic abuse and coercive acts are understood as signs of love and part of Angel's journey of redemption. Depicting Angel in this fashion finds similarities in the debate surrounding Hosea 1—3, where scholars have interpreted the character of God/Hosea as either an example of an entitled, abusive spouse or a paragon of forbearance – that is, a picture of a suffering male who will do anything and everything to save his wayward wife. Clearly, Rivers's interpretation supports the latter and arguably pushes it even further. Namely, if we read Hosea 2 with David Clines (1979) and Brad Kelle (2005, pp. 58–79, 239, 243, 247, 266) and argue that the various punishments that Hosea/God declares he will mete out on Gomer/Israel[4] are not a sequence of events, but threats or available options of which the only feasible one, and the one Hosea/God chooses, is reconciliation, then Rivers has made the story potentially[5] even worse by having Michael act out the threats. For example, as Hosea/God threatens to block Gomer's/Israel's path so she cannot find her lovers (Hos. 2.6–7 (Hebrew text: 2.8–9)), Michael disrupts Angel's escape attempt. As Hosea/God threatens to take away his provision (Hos. 2.9 (Hebrew text: 2.11)), all that Angel possesses is either destroyed or denied, making Michael her sole provider. As noted earlier, Paul takes advantage of Angel sexually which finds an echo in the sexual humiliation of Gomer/Israel in Hosea 2.10 (Hebrew text: 2.12). Since the Northern Kingdom was ultimately erased by Assyrian forces, it could be assumed that the threats in Hosea 2 were to some extent fulfilled; however, in *Redeeming Love* the threats are a reality from the beginning. They are not options but ways through which Michael can keep his defiant, bitter wife on her path to redemption.

In Hosea 1—3, Hosea's relationship with the faithless Gomer is in some way taken to be a metaphor of God's relationship with the fickle nation of Israel. Because of the brutality of some of the imagery in Hosea 2, some academics prefer to keep a distinction between God's treatment of Israel and human husbands' treatment of their wives. For example, Gale Yee (2012, p. 304) has stated that 'the human behaviors of Israelite husbands toward their wives are only the symbols of God's actions. God's actions are not a model for the behavior of Israelite husbands.' Although I appreciate Yee's sentiment and especially her attempt to raise awareness of abusive behaviour, I am not convinced that the distinction she makes is quite as clear cut. In Hosea 1—3, the imagery relies on patriarchal power distinctions both in marriage and human–divine relationships and, as noted by Sherwood (1996, p. 283), although a metaphor 'is a relation of similarities and dissimilarities, who decrees what is and is not transferable?' In fact, the entire metaphor relies on the fact that Hosea's/God's behaviour towards his wife is at the very least justifiable if not to be desired (cf. Blyth, 2021, p. 51; Day, 1999, pp. 175–6). Hence to reduce the violent imagery to merely a divine prerogative seems unwarranted.

In fact, Rivers's appropriation of abusive behaviour in *Redeeming Love* shows us that drawing the metaphorical line in the sand remains difficult if not impossible, and is a stark reminder of the kind of treatment the female characters in both Hosea and *Redeeming Love* are to endure seemingly for their own good.

In the end, Rivers and the author of the book of Hosea share a common goal: the submission of Angel and Gomer/Israel to the male authority in her life. In the book of Hosea, God will woo Israel back to himself, culminating in the renewal of the marriage (Hos. 2.14, 16, 19–20 (Hebrew text: 2.16, 18, 21–22)). In the novel, Angel gradually comes to recognize Michael's affection for her and, after a conversion experience and even beginning a ministry among prostitutes, she goes back to her relationship with Michael. However, in both texts there is a glimpse of an alternative path for the respective women. In the book of Hosea, it seems that Gomer/Israel wishes to retain her independence and sustain herself with the *'ethnah* (Hos. 2.12 (Hebrew text: 2.14)) – that is, a reward or payment of some kind from her lovers. Gomer/Israel is thus characterized 'as a prostitute by terming basic provisions her "hire"' (Sherwood, 1996, p. 301; cf. pp. 19–20, n. 4). Some intriguing insights into this interpretation could be garnered from Nancy Nam Hoon Tan's publication (2021), in which she reads several passages, among them Hosea 1—3, together with Hong Kong sex workers. Regarding the book of Hosea, several of the sex workers noted how they had entered their profession to 'put food on the table' to secure the financial well-being of their family. They imagined that perhaps Gomer had become a sex worker for similar reasons, but once the family had gained financial stability, 'Hosea had become ungrateful and jealous of her achievements' (Tan, 2021, loc. 2083). Some even commented that even though clients 'had offered to provide for them' if they stopped their profession, they had declined for various reasons, among them that 'it would be better to remain independent rather than to entrust their future to a man who would control everything' (Tan, 2021, loc. 2096). In fact, one of the sex workers read Hosea 1—3 'as a warning to working women. At the end of the day, the males would exert their control and claim that everything was theirs and blame every bad thing on their wives' (Tan, 2021, loc. 2096). Ultimately, the sex workers agreed that Gomer was successful in her own right and did not need Hosea, whom several of them described as a 'psychotic control freak' unable to 'comprehend what mutual love and respect in a relationship were' (Tan, 2021, loc. 1945, 2015).

In Rivers's *Redeeming Love*, Angel also dreams of freedom and independence. At the beginning of the book, her wish is to reclaim the money she is owed by the Palace:

[t]hen she would hire someone to build her a cabin ... far enough away from a town so she wouldn't hear the noise and smell the stench, but close enough that she could get what supplies she needed. She would buy a gun, a big gun, and plenty of bullets, and if any man came around knocking at her door, she would use it, unless she needed some money. (Rivers, 2013/1991, loc. 1589)

This dream of independence is, however, doomed by Rivers as a whisper from Satan (2013/1991, loc. 1589, 2038, 2237; Field, 2017a; cf. Shore, 2022). As noted by Alexiana Fry (2023), in *Redeeming Love* the kind of freedom Angel can have is 'dictated by others, including Michael Hosea, and Sarah [Angel] just needs to see it in his way'. In other words, Angel needs to find her 'freedom' in submission to Michael rather than as an independent agent. Likewise, in Hosea 1—3 Gomer's/Israel's only option is to return to her husband. Although both *Redeeming Love* and Hosea 2.14–23 (Hebrew text: 2.16–25) seem to imply that a loving reunion between the spouses ensues, it could also be argued that after the abuse the women in these stories have endured, this reconciliation is little more than the so-called honeymoon phase in abusive relationships. As noted by Julia O'Brien (2008, p. 73), 'In domestic violence situations, the cessation of violence does not mean that the dynamics of power within the relationship have changed; even in his apparent kindness, the man remains in control of the woman and of the relationship.' In patriarchal cultures such as those predicated in Hosea 1—3 and *Redeeming Love*, the female characters must relinquish their independence and submit to their spouses to find true happiness. While it is true that safe relationships can be a good starting place for healing for victims of trauma (Herman, 2015/1992, p. 133), it does not appear that in either text the relationship is particularly safe or empowering, at least not for the female characters. For contemporary readers, such interpretations can be particularly disturbing as they could encourage abused persons to stay or return to destructive relationships (Field, 2018b; Blyth, 2021, pp. 53–4). Since in both texts the abuse endured by the women is presented as being for their own good, an imbalance and abuse of power becomes justified at the expense of the women's agency. One would be quite justified in asking if the model of a patriarchal marriage even allows for 'love' that is mutual and respectful as indicated in Tan's work earlier (2021, loc. 2015) or if such a marriage will always exist at the expense of the other (cf. Cobb, 2020, pp. 118–19; Fry, 2023)?

Conclusion

How should Hosea 1—3 be read? Is it a love story of a long-suffering God and his fickle wife or a tale of horrific abuse? As an expression of cultural trauma as defined by Jeffrey Alexander (2012, pp. 9–30), Hosea 1—3 could be read as an explanation of the Northern Kingdom's downfall that found a way to sustain both the people and their identity as well as God and his sovereignty: since it was the people whose sin caused the punishment, the God of Israel remained in control (O'Connor, 2011, pp. 43–4; Stulman and Kim, 2010, pp. 14–15; Cobb, 2020, pp. 122–3; Smith-Christopher, 2004, p. 155). Read through this lens, Hosea 1—3 becomes an explanatory, even hopeful narrative since it implies that 'when one's own house is back in order, the defeat can be reversed' (Hos. 2.14-23 (Hebrew text: 2.16-25)) (Smith-Christopher, 2004, p. 155; cf. O'Connor, 2011, p. 44; Stulman and Kim, 2010, pp. 14–17; Cobb, 2020, pp. 122–3). However, creating meaning out of trauma is not a simple procedure. As noted by Kathleen O'Connor (2011, pp. 43–4), 'victims need interpretation. For their lives to rest on the most minimal order, they must have meaning, interpretation, explanation, even if the explanation is ephemeral, inadequate, partial, or outright wrong. Explanation puts order back in the world.' In the face of the collapse of one's system of meaning and belief, even a bad explanation is better than none.

One of the elements of this explanation that is ubiquitous in both Hosea 1—3 and *Redeeming Love* is the issue of self-blame. As a coping mechanism, self-blame can restore agency to the victim/survivor since the acknowledgement of one's guilt moves the trauma from something uncontrollable to the person's sphere of influence (Herman, 2015/1992, pp. 53–4; cf. Frechette, 2015, p. 25; 2017, pp. 245–6). As noted above, on a cultural level self-blame can also help in the creation of a masternarrative that explains the disaster without leaving the divinity or the people powerless. Ironically, such narratives could be read as creative attempts on behalf of 'defeated peoples to creatively reinterpret their defeat, and "disempower" their conquerors' (Smith-Christopher, 2004, p. 157). If Hosea 1—3 is understood in such a fashion, it raises the question of how one should interpret the theology of the book of Hosea or, to put it another way, how strongly should (or need) we hold on to the marital imagery in Hosea 1—3?

Redeeming Love rests on the premise that people are sinners needing redemption. As a traumatic text, Hosea 1—3 also understands the people of Israel as culpable. If read through the lens of cultural trauma, might these texts tell us more about the 'traumatic character of the human contexts out of which such texts emerged' as well as 'their limited psychological adaptive functionality in antiquity' (Frechette, 2017, p. 243).[6] Rather than give us universal truth or doctrine about God, these texts tell us about the trauma experienced by the community and the effort to rescue faith and identity amid its collapse. As a tale of communal suffering, we should therefore be careful not to treat the extremis of society as a template for our relationships with each other or even with the deity (cf. Smith-Christopher, 2004, p. 155). The presence of such a narrative in the Hebrew Bible may be uncomfortable; yet if understood as a creative reading of traumatic event(s), perhaps understandable. However, using Hosea 1—3 as a template of how we should relate to each other and God as per *Redeeming Love* swiftly becomes problematic. As noted by Ruth Poser (2021, p. 346; cf. Smith-Christopher, 2004, p. 155), texts that declare Israel's guilt and God as the righteous punisher 'come at a price': in addition to blaming the victim, one is left 'with an image of God that seems violent or even sadistic'. Even if such an image of God may have offered help or even hope to a recovering community, the question remains if such a text is useful to establish a story of redemption for contemporary readers. I would agree with Emily Shore (2022), who in her review of *Redeeming Love* notes that if Rivers's description of Michael and Angel is a reliable depiction of 'the relationship of God and his Church, then Angel is entitled to and *should* run far, far away and the further the better.'

Bibliography

Alexander, Jeffrey C., 2012, *Trauma: A Social Theory*, Cambridge and Malden: Polity Press.

Bigelsen, Jayne, and Stefanie Vuotto, 2013, 'Homelessness, Survival Sex and Human Trafficking: As Experienced by the Youth of Covenant House New York', pp. 1-28, available at https://humantraffickinghotline.org/sites/default/files/Homelessness%2C%20Survival%20Sex%2C%20and%20Human%20Trafficking%20-%20Covenant%20House%20NY.pdf (accessed 5.12.2022).

Bird, Phyllis A., 1989, '"To Play the Harlot": An Inquiry into an Old Testament Metaphor' in Peggy L. Day (ed.), *Gender and Difference in Ancient Israel*, Minneapolis, MN: Fortress Press, pp. 75-94.

Blyth, Caroline, 2021, *Rape Culture, Purity Culture, and Coercive Control in Teen Girl Bibles*, London: Routledge.

Caruth, Cathy, 2016, *Unclaimed Experience: Trauma, Narrative, and History*, 20th anniversary edn, Baltimore, MD: Johns Hopkins University Press.

Clines, D. J. A., 1979, 'Hosea 2: Structure and Interpretation' in Elizabeth A. Livingstone (ed.), *Studia Biblica 1978/ Sixth International Congress on Biblical Studies, Oxford 3–7 April 1978*, Sheffield: University of Sheffield Press, pp. 83–103.

Clines, D. J. A., 1990, *What Does Eve Do to Help? And Other Readerly Questions to the Old Testament*, Sheffield: JSOT Press.

Clingan, Sarah E. et al., 2020, 'Survival Sex Trading in Los Angeles County, California, USA', *The Journal of Sex Research* 57/7, pp. 943–52.

Cobb, Kirsi, 2020, 'Reading Gomer with Questions: A Trauma-Informed Feminist Study of How the Experience of Intimate Partner Violence and the Presence of Religious Belief Shape the Reading of Hosea 2:2–23' in Karen O'Donnell and Katie Cross (eds), *Feminist Trauma Theologies: Body, Scripture & Church in Critical Perspective*, London: SCM Press, pp. 112–33.

Cross, Katie, 2020, '"I Have the Power in My Body to Make People Sin": The Trauma of Purity Culture and the Concept of "Body Theodicy"' in Karen O'Donnell and Katie Cross (eds), *Feminist Trauma Theologies: Body, Scripture & Church in Critical Perspective*, London: SCM Press, pp. 21–39.

Day, Linda, 1999, 'Teaching the Prophetic Marriage Metaphor Texts', *Teaching Theology and Religion* 2/3, pp. 173–9.

Exum, J. Cheryl, 2007, 'Editorial Preface' in J. Cheryl Exum (ed.), *Retellings: The Bible in Literature, Music, Art and Film*, Leiden; Boston, MA: Brill, pp. vii–viii.

Field, Samantha, 2016a, 'Redeeming Love Review: Introduction', 11 July, available at http://samanthapfield.com/2016/07/11/redeeming-love-review-introduction/ (accessed 24.03.2023).

Field, Samantha, 2016b, 'Redeeming Love Review: Angel's Backstory', 8 August, available at http://samanthapfield.com/2016/08/08/redeeming-love-review-1-52/ (accessed 24.03.2023).

Field, Samantha, 2016c, 'Redeeming Love Review: Introducing Michael', 22 August, available at http://samanthapfield.com/2016/08/22/redeeming-love-review-introducing-michael/ (accessed 24.03.2023).

Field, Samantha, 2016d, 'Redeeming Love Review: Non-Consensual Marriage', 19 September, available at http://samanthapfield.com/2016/09/19/redeeming-love-review-non-consensual-marriage/ (accessed 24.03.2023).

Field, Samantha, 2017a, 'Redeeming Love Review: These Boots Are Made for Walking', 9 January, available at http://samanthapfield.com/2017/01/09/redeeming-love-review-boots-made-walking/ (accessed 24.03.2023).

Field, Samantha, 2017b, 'Redeeming Love Review: Family Love', 11 September, available at http://samanthapfield.com/2017/09/11/redeeming-love-family-love/ (accessed 24.03.2023).

Field, Samantha, 2018a, 'Redeeming Love Moral Relativity', 5 June, available at http://samanthapfield.com/2018/06/05/redeeming-love-moral-relativity/ (accessed 24.03.2023).

Field, Samantha, 2018b, 'Redeeming Love: The Abuser Wins', 21 June, available at http://samanthapfield.com/2018/06/21/redeeming-love-the-abuser-wins/ (accessed 24.03.2023).

Fish, Stanley E., 1980, *Is There a Text in This Class? The Authority of Interpretive Communities*, Cambridge, MA; London: Harvard University Press.

Frechette, Christopher G., 2015, 'The Old Testament as Controlled Substance: How Insights from Trauma Studies Reveal Healing Capacities in Potentially Harmful Texts', *Interpretation* 69/1, pp. 20–34.

Frechette, Christopher G., 2017, 'Two Biblical Motifs of Divine Violence as Resources for Meaning-Making in Engaging Self-Blame and Rage after Traumatization', *Pastoral Psychology* 66/2, pp. 239–49.

Fry, Alexiana, 2023, 'Redeeming Love 2 – with Dr. Alexiana Fry', hosted by D. L. and Krispin Mayfield, 6 July, *Prophetic Imagination Station* 8/7, available at https://www.propheticimaginationstation.com/episodes/texts-of-terror (accessed 17.11.2023).

Herman, Judith L., 2015/1992, *Trauma and Recovery: The Aftermath of Violence – From Domestic Abuse to Political Terror*, New York: Basic Books.

Iser, Wolfgang, 1974, *The Implied Reader: Patterns of Communication in Prose Fiction from Bunyan to Beckett*, Baltimore, MD: Johns Hopkins University Press.

Keefe, Alice A., 1993, 'Rapes of Women/Wars of Men', *Semeia* 61, pp. 79–97.

Keefe, Alice A., 2001, *Woman's Body and the Social Body in Hosea*, London; New York: Sheffield Academic Press.

Kelle, Brad E., 2005, *Hosea 2: Metaphor and Rhetoric in Historical Perspective*, Atlanta, GA: SBL Press.

Koenig, Sara M., 2018, *Bathsheba Survives*, Columbia, SC: University of South Carolina Press.

Koenig, Sara M., 2020, 'Bathsheba in Contemporary Romance Novels' in Susanne Scholz (ed.), *The Oxford Handbook of Feminist Approaches to the Hebrew Bible*, New York: Oxford University Press, pp. 407–23.

Law, Jeannie O., 2020, 'Bestselling Novel "Redeeming Love" to Be Turned to Movie Produced by Roma Downey', *The Christian Post*, 1 May, available at https://www.christianpost.com/news/bestselling-novel-redeeming-love-to-be-turned-to-movie-produced-by-roma-downey.html (accessed 14.03.2023).

Macintosh, A. A., 1997, *A Critical and Exegetical Commentary on Hosea*, Edinburgh: T&T Clark.

Mays, James L., 1969, *Hosea*, London: SCM Press.

Morse, Holly, 2020, *Encountering Eve's Afterlives: A New Reception Critical Approach to Genesis 2–4*, Oxford: Oxford University Press.

O'Brien, Julia M., 2008, *Challenging Prophetic Metaphor: Theology and Ideology in the Prophets*, Louisville, KY: Westminster John Knox.

O'Connor, Kathleen M., 2011, *Jeremiah: Pain and Promise*, Minneapolis, MN: Fortress Press.

Poser, Ruth, 2021, 'Embodied Memories: Gender-Specific Aspects of Prophecy as Trauma Literature' in L. Juliana Claassens and Irmtraud Fischer (eds), *Prophecy and Gender in the Hebrew Bible*, Atlanta, GA: SBL Press, pp. 333–57.

Rivers, Francine, 2013/1991, *Redeeming Love*, Oxford: Lion Hudson, Kindle Edition.

Rivers, Francine (with Karin Stock Buursma), 2020a, *A Path to Redeeming Love: A 40-Day Devotional*, Colorado Springs, CO: Multnomah, Kindle Edition.

Rivers, Francine (with Angela Hunt), 2020b, *Redeeming Love: The Companion Study*, Colorado Springs, CO: Multnomah, Kindle Edition.

Sakenfeld, Katharine Doob, 2003, *Just Wives? Stories of Power & Survival in the Old Testament & Today*, Louisville, KY: Westminster John Knox.

Sherwood, Yvonne, 1996, *The Prostitute and the Prophet: Reading Hosea in the Late Twentieth Century*, Sheffield: Sheffield Academic Press.
Shore, Emily, 2022, 'Is Redeeming Love Redemptive or Redundant Religiosity?', 24 January, available at https://emilybethshore.info/is-redeeming-love-redemptive-or-redundant-religiosity/ (accessed 24.03.2023).
Smith-Christopher, Daniel L., 2004, 'Ezekiel in Abu Ghraib: Rereading Ezekiel 16:37–39 in the Context of Imperial Conquest' in Stephen L. Cook and Corrine L. Patton (eds), *Ezekiel's Hierarchical World: Wrestling with a Tiered Reality*, Atlanta, GA: SBL Press, pp. 141–57.
Stark, Evan, 2007, *Coercive Control: How Men Entrap Women in Personal Life*, Oxford: Oxford University Press.
Sternberg, Meir, 1987, *The Poetics of Biblical Narrative: Ideological Literature and the Drama of Reading*, Bloomington, IN: Indiana University Press.
Stiebert, Johanna, 2020, *Rape Myths, The Bible, and #MeToo*, Abingdon; New York: Routledge, Kindle Edition.
Stulman, Louis, and Hyun Chul Paul Kim, 2010, *You Are My People: An Introduction to Prophetic Literature*, Nashville, TN: Abingdon.
Tan, Nancy Nam Hoon, 2021, *Resisting Rape Culture: The Hebrew Bible and Hong Kong Sex Workers*, London; New York: Routledge, Kindle Edition.
Venarchik, Anna, 2022, '"Redeeming Love": Evangelicalism's Toxic Patriarchal Tale Gets the Hollywood Treatment', *Daily Beast*, 19 January, available at https://www.thedailybeast.com/redeeming-love-evangelicalisms-toxic-slut-shaming-tale-gets-the-hollywood-treatment (accessed 24.03.2023).
Vickroy, Laurie, 2015, *Reading Trauma Narratives: The Contemporary Novel and the Psychology of Oppression*, Charlottesville, VA: University of Virginia Press, Kindle Edition.
Walls, N. Eugene, and Stephanie Bell, 2011, 'Correlates of Engaging in Survival Sex among Homeless Youth and Young Adults', *The Journal of Sex Research* 48/5, pp. 423–36.
Wolff, Hans Walter, 1974, *Hosea*, Philadelphia, PA: Fortress Press.
Yee, Gale A., 2012, 'Hosea' in Carol A. Newsom, Sharon H. Ringe and Jacqueline E. Lapsley (eds), *Women's Bible Commentary*, 20th anniversary edn, Louisville, KY: Westminster John Knox, pp. 299–308.

Notes

1 Alice Keefe (2001, pp. 191–5) has argued that in the Northern Kingdom there was an issue with 'two competing systems of land tenure'. One was latifundialization – that is, the monarchy and the urban elites' wish to create large estates and promote the production of 'cash crops'; this was not in accordance with the second, more traditional system of 'patrimonial land tenure' and its adjoining values. In a conversation with Sharon Moughtin-Mumby in January 2023, Keefe suggested that since the land in Hosea 1.2 is also committing 'prostitution' (*z-n-h*), it might be possible to understand this as the land being 'trafficked' by the elite. If so, then understanding Angel as a victim of human trafficking in *Redeeming Love*, and the land being 'trafficked' in Hosea, could strengthen the connection between the two texts.

2 Since *Redeeming Love* came out in 1991, it could be suggested that analysing the book by considering more recent trauma scholarship might be unfair to the text. In the 2022 film version of *Redeeming Love*, several traumatic elements have in fact been toned down if not eradicated. Even so, two issues remain: one is that the film's/book's premise still rests on a romance based on a patriarchal marriage and the unequal (ab)use of power, which makes both *Redeeming Love* and Hosea 1—3 highly problematic texts. Second, the book has not been updated and remains in circulation, which encourages conversation and criticism of the book's content in light of more recent research.

3 Daniel Smith-Christopher (2004, pp. 150–1) has alternatively suggested that the stripping could allude to the treatment of prisoners of war in ancient military practice. In this case, the stripping could be another way to humiliate prisoners in addition to rape, or apart from rape.

4 In Hosea 2.2–13 (Hebrew text: 2.4–15), it is not always clear as to whether the actions/threats are made by God or Hosea and consequently whether they are addressed to Israel or Gomer or both (Cobb, 2020, p. 114; Sakenfeld, 2003, p. 105).

5 Herman (2015/1992, p. 77); cf. Stark (2007, p. 251) notes how it is not necessary for the perpetrator to use violence 'to keep the victim in a constant state of fear … Threat against others are [sic] often as effective as direct threats against the victim.'

6 Frechette (2017, pp. 243, 246) refers here to biblical narratives that 'depict the biblical God as enacting violence against people', such as those narratives that include suffering of the people of God as divine punishment or imagine God as 'enacting violence against enemies'.

6

Will You Accept This Rose? The Magic Circle in the Book of Esther

STEED V. DAVIDSON

Introduction

Consent as a legal concept, let alone a philosophical notion, is a complex issue in the modern world. To bring consent into conversation with Hebrew Bible material where 'sex that is produced by patriarchy' (Srinivasan, 2020, p. 41) precludes any meaningful discussion of consent and may doom this chapter to failure, seems like a fool's errand. That this chapter exists in a volume on narrating rape in biblical texts can only mean several scholars share the same misguided ideas. This chapter goes a step further than the evident anachronism to join even more incongruous items: reality dating shows and the book of Esther. Esther has the quality of a fairy tale with a dreamy ending where the ordinary girl becomes queen. The debate about the precise nature of the book of Esther (Sun, 2021, p. 112, n. 74) tends to emphasize its humorous nature and, as a result, overlook deeply troubling aspects of the book, including the threat of violence and actual violence. One of the consequences of reading past disturbing aspects of the book, Randall Bailey posits, is to 'desexualize' Esther when the text goes out of its way to sexualize her (Bailey, 2009, p. 239). The narrative arc of Esther pairs well with the best romantic movies and the myth of reality dating shows, both of which can include bawdy elements. Both reality dating shows and the book of Esther raise implications around sexual consent. Reality dating shows create an artificial world that pretends it is real life where modern women who would otherwise be uncomfortable with a partner dating multiple women at the same time agree to be one among many women and to engage in different types of sexual activities they would refuse or at least be more judicious about engaging in their regular lives. Viewers can only guess at these sexual activities, since like the book of Esther they are never explicitly mentioned but are assumed for the plot to work. The fictive world of reality dating shows also invites viewers to participate in the altered reality, and through such participation to affirm the consent of the participants. After all, viewers hardly question whether anyone has given consent, and since no declaration appears at the start of each episode consent is assumed.

Interpretations of Esther that glamorize the book as a biblical fairy tale overlook the process of assembling young girls and grooming them for one man's sexual approval. Ericka Dunbar reads Esther as a tale of sexual exploitation from chapter 1 that intensifies in chapter 2 into sexual trafficking (Dunbar, 2022, p. 2). Applying the modern conception of sex trafficking raises the book to the level of 'biblical horror' as Dunbar categorizes it (Dunbar, 2022, p. 3). This association presents readers with stark choices about the book of Esther and possibly an uncomfortable position for viewers of *The Bachelor*. Such a position, though, too easily decides on matters of consent. After all, the unfettered power of the king to gather women from around the empire makes consent a moot point, and even more the question of the legality of his actions. Adding the veneer of marriage in these two contexts where certain forms of consent are assumed opens a different set of discussions to deal with disturbing aspects of sexual politics. The shared goal of marriage between several reality dating shows and Esther provides a specific social context within which to discuss consent. Marriage processes that make overt use of marriage markets (as these two contexts do) complicate consent since the goal is achieved through competitive means.

Marriage markets shape the way I read Esther and view reality dating shows. Simply put, marriage markets are the spaces of mate selection. Gayle Rubin's foundational work on the traffic in women proves a fruitful resource for thinking about these different, yet similar, marriage markets. The competitive nature of both markets means that some form of strategy determines the outcome more than romantic feelings. The Dutch historian Johan Huizinga's theory on play, where he explores the concept of the magic circle, the creation of a unique world where the normal rules of life no longer apply, forms a second resource for this work. The insights from these two sources lead me to make the point that Mordechai as Esther's guardian and owner of her sexuality trades her for proximity to the king. Securing her marriage to the king only serves as an initial step in a relationship where the idea of consent is blurred even as it could have operated in the narrative and cultural world of the book of Esther. Like viewers of a reality dating show, readers of Esther are invited to cheer on the marriage and ensure its success by conveniently ignoring several features of the narrative that Rhiannon Graybill would describe as 'fuzzy, messy, and icky' (Graybill, 2021, p. 11).

In the first section of this essay, I outline the similarities that I notice between Esther and reality dating shows. These similarities, though, lead me in the next section to pay attention to divergences rather than convergences. In that section, I show where consent exists, albeit in a murky way, in reality dating shows, and where refusal exists in Esther. Following these explorations, I introduce the two main theoretical foundations of this work: first, Gayle Rubin's traffic in women and, second, Johan Huizinga's notion of the magic circle. These works provide a useful intervention to describe the persistent ickiness of Esther and reality dating shows. Although fictive works, Esther and *The Bachelor* demonstrate the slipperiness of consent in a world structured around heterosexual male values. Such worlds accommodate women's sexual autonomy to the extent that it can be manipulated and controlled by men to affirm male power. As the modern 'text', *The Bachelor* masks consent with the seeming willingness of participants to engage in a process that shores up male conquest. Esther keeps readers fixed on the fantasy of a marriage that produces radical transformation for a people only to hide the murkiness of consent at various levels whether that be in the collection of young women, Esther's participation in the process, as well as the access Mordechai continues to have to her sexuality to influence the king.

Corresponding formulas

As reality television shows, sometimes called unscripted shows that are in effect so 'formulaic' as to make them almost scripted (Mukherjee and Pajé, 2022, p. 24), experienced a resurgence in the early 2000s, the reality dating genre garnered major audiences. In its first season in 2001, the now long-running *The Bachelor* captured a noteworthy 10.7 million viewers and in its second season achieved its highest audience of 13.93 million viewers. *The Bachelor* inspired several similar shows in addition to creating up to eight different spin-offs, the latest being *The Golden Bachelor* (2023). The simple premise of *The Bachelor* revolves around a single man selecting a mate from a collection of sometimes up to 20 women. By the end of the season, the man makes a formal proposal to one woman, leaving the show engaged with a future wedding to occur outside of the scrutiny of the show, but still within the view of the tabloid media. The basic premise of *The Bachelor* resembles the second chapter of the book of Esther: the king gathers women in a single place and over the course of time through one-on-one meetings discerns who he would marry as the replacement for the deposed Queen Vashti. Both *The Bachelor* and Esther do not announce themselves as competitions even though in essence they are. Jean-Daniel Macchi describes the process in Esther as a 'seduction contest' (Macchi, 2018, p. 118) and Michael V. Fox characterizes it as a 'beauty contest' (Fox, 1991, p. 27; Macchi, 2018, p. 43) and a 'sex contest' (Fox, 1991, p. 28). The competitive nature of *The Bachelor* is evident even from a cursory review of a single episode. There are several other similarities that emerge between *The Bachelor* and Esther 1—2 upon closer scrutiny.

The imperial palace in Susa, already known in chapter 1 for its extravagant parties, forms the setting for much of the book of Esther. The vast spread of the Persian Empire as told in 1.1, along with the displays of magnificence, affluence and grandeur (1.4), projects the king's power and the seductive appeal of the setting. *The Bachelor* similarly takes place in a luxurious location. From 2007, *The Bachelor* started filming in what has come to be known as the Bachelor Mansion. A 10,000-square-foot house with seven bedrooms and eight bathrooms, the mansion is in the exclusive scenic hillside community of Agoura Hills, California. The house is appropriately staged to give the impression of grandeur, wealth and splendour with modern touches. At the start of the season, the bachelor, dressed in a tuxedo, greets participants of the show as they arrive in a limousine at the mansion in elegant evening gowns. This staging suggests that the bachelor owns the property and will entertain the large number of participants as his guests over the course of the show. Each evening features receptions at the mansion topped off by 'rose ceremonies' where the bachelor announces his selections of those who will continue in the competition. This sense of luxury where all participants are well dressed resembles the lavish dinners that take place in Esther. In chapter 1, the king hosts two dinners. The first lasts for 180 days and includes powerful men from around the empire (1.3). The second banquet, though more inclusive and open to the people, lasts seven days but involves elaborate decorations and bottomless drinks (1.5). In addition, the queen, Vashti, hosts a separate event for women in the palace (1.9). Apart from the notice of its location, there are no comparable descriptions of the guest list, the décor, the menu, or other details to indicate where this event falls on the spectrum of luxury. Fox points out that women were not separated from men at Persian banquets (Fox, 1991, p. 20). This contrivance may be necessary for the plot to set the scene to summon Vashti into a room with intoxicated libidinous men.

The lure of power, wealth and luxury to achieve the seduction is common to both *The Bachelor* and Esther. The first chapter of Esther goes to great lengths to indicate that the assets of splendour and affluence belong to the king. These assets enable him to conquer not only vast territories but, as will be seen in chapter 2, the bodies of women. As Dunbar notes, the trapping of empire 'allows the sexual exploitation of female characters' (Dunbar, 2022, p. 18). Power is therefore gendered in Esther since it belongs exclusively to the king. And as seen in the comedic attempt of the male intelligentsia to ensure that Vashti's refusal does not lead to a contagion within the empire, shoring up male power throughout the empire requires the participation of the lowest male head of household to view themselves in the place of the king in order to affirm male royal power. Most certainly, the luxuries of the empire are not shared with the queen who merely has access to these assets as seen in the king's request for her to appear in the royal crown (1.11). At best, the queen functions as another sign of conquest for the king – in this case, the confirmation of his ability to wield his sexuality at will.

Ownership of wealth and luxury as distinct from access to these benefits also appears gendered in *The Bachelor*. One year after the start of *The Bachelor*, the spin-off *The Bachelorette* premiered and starred the runner-up of the male-focused season. *The Bachelorette* replicates most of the premise of *The Bachelor* with one notable exception being that the woman does not propose to the man she has selected. Maintaining this traditional sexual imbalance proves important to keep audiences who, as Anne Areias points out, are not accepting of a '"Princess" Charming' (Areias, 2013, p. 16). Bearing in mind that all the leads on *The Bachelorette* seasons have vied for the affection of a man in televised episodes of the partner show, the presentation of the lead women in their seasons focuses more upon their personality to sustain their likeability, gained from their previous appearance. As such, glamour and elegance serve as attractive features for these women who can project these traits through access to luxury and wealth rather than the unattractive prospect that they own the wealth and are therefore powerful. Both shows take participants on location to different parts of the world to engage in fun and exciting adventures. That the bachelor whisks women away to these locations, flying on private jets, staying in lavish hotels, all combine to increase his appeal as a powerful and wealthy individual. In the case of the bachelorette, her ability to entertain her suitors with these experiences speaks of her elegance, good taste and refinement. These traits, rather than the use or possession of raw power, reflect how Esther appears in the book and in several interpretive traditions. Esther remains demure except when she needs not to be and, in that case, only as encouraged by Mordechai.

Evidently smitten with Esther's beauty the king on two occasions (5.3, 6) readily offers half of the kingdom to Esther, who notably does not take him up on the offer.

Not surprisingly, Esther and *The Bachelor* both reflect heteronormative standards. Already in chapter 1, the queen's beauty serves as a source of pride for the king. Her appearance with the royal crown affirms her derivative status as queen as a benefit to the king. However, her physical appearance provides the king with a boast before the people and officials, in what Fox describes as 'a gathering of bibulous males' (Fox, 1991, p. 20). The text comments on her beauty in a way that provides the justification for the king's impulsive request (1.11). A specific standard of beauty appears to exist for the queen. The search for the replacement queen proceeds on criteria that recall the comments on Vashti's appearance: Vashti is 'attractive in appearance' *tovat mar'eh* (1.11) and the prospective queen must be 'attractive in appearance' *tovot mar'eh* (2.2, 3). Else Holt observes that this physical description of women occurs four times in Esther 1—2, emphasizing the persistence of this particular male gaze (Holt, 2021, p. 59). That the future queen should come with no prior sexual experience (*betulah*) also reflects heteronormative standards that privilege men as superior participants in sex and marriage. For most seasons of *The Bachelor*, contestants have been largely white women with body types that fall within a narrow range acceptable to dominant white male standards of beauty. As Rachel Dubrofsky (2011, p. 20) admits, 'the BI [Bachelor Industry] is a space that is raced'; by this, she means one that privileges whiteness. Even with more diverse casting, racial-ethnic women tend to be eliminated earlier and face more sexual stereotyping (Mukherjee and Pajé, 2022, p. 131). So far, the show caters only to opposite-gender couples, even though one male lead later came out as gay after the close of the season. Styled in some media as 'the first gay "Bachelor"' (Wagmeister, 2021), the former professional football player, despite struggles with his sexuality since his teens, checked most of the boxes of white masculinity that ensured his casting on the show. These selection values guarantee that the physical attractiveness of women plays a critical role in their casting. Unlike the careful mention of grooming processes in Esther (2.3) and their extensive duration (2.12), *The Bachelor* episodes reveal little of what it takes for women to maintain physical fitness as well as cosmetic treatments to ensure that they are camera-ready.

Marriage serves as an end goal for both the book of Esther and *The Bachelor*. Given the sexually permissive environments and capabilities of both contexts, that marriage becomes the container for these pairings places the matter of consent in the foreground. Sexual consent for an isolated encounter has its own problems. However, pursuing mate selection in the unusual circumstances in both contexts makes consent an even more troubling notion. In both cases, traditional marriages give the men relational power over the women to forestall women exercising choices that can publicly embarrass a man. The selection of a new queen comes precisely because the deposed queen exercised public power. The process for selecting a new queen sustains the already outsized imbalance of power to ensure that the king maintains the appearance of control. Not only do *The Bachelor* and Esther use marriage as a container, but they also make marriage a prize at the end of a contest. In both cases, mate selection occurs from the simultaneous interaction with several women rather than a serial process. The competitive nature of the process diminishes the power of the women over the course of the competition and, arguably, that of the winner who might emerge with the prize after having made several strategic and compromising moves to win.

Both *The Bachelor* and the search for a queen in Esther may seem like contrivances until they reflect several of the values and practices of male-organized societies. In my analysis of the similarities of these two situations, the ideas of game and play serve as the vehicle for the expression of masculinist practices of mate selection that compromise and complicate the consent of women as participants in marriage and other forms of romantic pairings. The issues of consent, while heightened in chapter 2 where Esther becomes queen through the outsized process set up by the empire, continue beyond this chapter. Arguably, Mordechai manipulates Esther long past his control of her sexuality to achieve her consent to use her sex in the furtherance of his agenda.

Consent and refusal

The notion of consent exists in the book of Esther. Consent, which implies the right of refusal as a practice by women, appears as an uncomfortable idea in the book. When women's consent rears its head in chapter 1 the imperial intellectual resources gather to consider how to eliminate it. Vashti's refusal demonstrates that the world of the book of Esther understands consent in some rudimentary form, albeit not with the nuanced legal understanding of modern jurisprudence. The crisp report of Vashti's 'no' contrasts with the elaborate transmission of the king's request via seven eunuchs (1.10–12). Readers can capture the force of Vashti's refusal and her assertion of bodily autonomy. This assertiveness provokes the king's fury. Vashti's refusal, though, is not the last time that consent appears in Esther. We see further evidence of refusal in Mordechai's rejection of the king's order to bow down to Haman (3.2). Mordechai's request to Esther to petition the king to stop Haman's destruction of the Jews acknowledges that she must consent to doing so or the consequences will be fatal (4.12–14). Even the king exercises the choice to say yes to Esther when she breaks protocol to meet with him (5.2). Within the story world of Esther, that the king certainly has the discretion not given to other mortals to choose (4.11) provides further indication of an understanding of consent. Yet this form of consent only expects positive responses since negative responses receive severe consequences. Graybill describes this as a form of 'consenting to avoid rape' (Graybill, 2021, p. 13) since not consenting also results in injury.

The perception of consent as a bulwark against sexual violence and exploitation is not only a modern one but commonplace. The expectation of clear verbal assent to sex disappears when consent takes the form of a frame of mind especially accompanied by unexpected oral and bodily acts (Mukherjee and Pajé, 2022, p, 126). This is not merely a case of 'she changed her mind'. Rather, what Graybill sees as the limitation of consent discourses (Graybill, 2021, pp. 34–9) reflects the murky areas around sex in reality shows as well as the narratives of the Hebrew Bible. What either appears as, or is assumed to be, consent hardly goes through the scrutiny of determining how that consent is acquired. Reality shows require legal consent from participants that also spell out enforcement agreements that may involve participation in 'awkward, uncomfortable activities and encounters' (Mukherjee and Pajé, 2022, p. 126). The gender imbalance that is at the heart of *The Bachelor* and Esther means that women as the social inferiors do not provide consent on equal terms. Graybill (2021, p. 37) makes the point, 'Consent does not share power so much as it reiterates relations of domination.' The gap between Esther with the mockery of Persian-era sexual practices and *The Bachelor* is both broad and narrow. Broad in the sense that the assumption that women who appear on *The Bachelor* own their sexuality can be taken for granted. Not so with Esther who is controlled by a series of men, with her surviving guardian Mordechai continuing to influence her sexuality long after she is married. The gap is also narrow, in that Esther and the women of *The Bachelor* are susceptible to overt and subtle forms of coercion that Graybill (2021, p. 36) highlights as 'discomfort'. Mordechai's constant presence, whether pacing nervously outside the women's house (2.10) or cajoling Esther to get together with the king, constitutes the type of discomfort that makes it almost impossible for her to say 'no' to him and the high stakes of saving her race. *The Bachelor* contestants experience discomfort from different areas: the man, the producers, the event, and the viewers. Reality shows are voyeuristic endeavours. To lose on a show like *The Bachelor*, even with its stylized rose ceremonies, amounts to what Areias (2013, p. 18) calls 'a public dumping ceremony'.

The book of Esther presents consent when exercised by women – or, better put, refusal – as a problem. Men certainly make choices within the book. The book seduces readers with the idea that consent is neither desirable nor possible in the way that it generates the crisis around Vashti and resolves it with Esther. The contrasts in the presentation of the two women can easily ignore the fact that what draws them together is the notion of women's consent to their sexual autonomy. Vashti's vilification for not playing along with the king's party games places her as the villain who is ousted from the kingdom. Esther's willingness and availability to men for their purposes accompanies her presentation as a gorgeous woman. With her desirability heightened by her willingness, the book shows how Esther calculates the consequence of refusal which is placed as a central plot device in the book. Not to cooperate means losing the prize. In this case, the book makes saving the race the ultimate prize.

In the book of Esther, the consequence of refusal for women is extraordinarily high. Since the book thrives upon exaggerations, the hyperbolic response to Vashti should not seem unusual. Yet the response is not so much to Vashti as it is to women in general given that the king proceeds to acquire many women in his home. For Vashti, refusal leads to her expulsion from the palace, and this sets off the chain reaction centred on tightening the control of women (1.19). The consequences are not nearly as dire for men who refuse to comply. Vashti remains the spectre that hovers over the book precisely because she is removed from the plot of the book through what Timothy Beal refers to as 'exscription', a form of 'writing out' from the text. Beal states that 'exscription serves to mark territory by naming that which belongs outside it; yet precisely in this process of marking off for oblivion, Vashti and her refusal are also indelibly *written* into the story in a way that will be difficult to forget' (Beal, 1997, p. 25, emphasis in the original). Vashti, therefore, stands as an object lesson for Esther, functioning as implicit coercion to go along to advance the plot.

The presumption that consent exists in reality dating shows like *The Bachelor* allows viewers to exercise another form of coercion over the women on the show. Viewers of reality shows – in fact, superfans – do not passively consume the episodes. They become active on social media as commentators on several aspects of the show but, most significantly, about contestants on the show. The threat of slut-shaming or other forms of name-calling by viewers through social media places external pressure upon participants to generate suitable content for the show. Suitable content can range from the party girl persona to more sexually permissive behaviour with the understanding that such stand-out behaviour induces financial and other rewards. Invariably, this means that participants must play to heteronormative, coercive codes since failure to conform to these expectations of the show can lead to the critique from other participants of not being on the show for 'the right reasons'. This critique, especially if it comes to the bachelor's attention, has the potential of expulsion from the show.

Legal considerations dictate that participants on *The Bachelor* provide informed consent for their participation. The legal waivers notwithstanding, the unwritten expectations of being a contestant on *The Bachelor* determine consent and coercion. These expectations, though, are clear, since they emerge from the social contexts of mate selection except that there is little attempt to prevent these expectations from tipping the range of power against the man. Participants in any reality show must do so fully and enthusiastically. Their capacity to meet these expectations would have been critical to their casting for the show. This enthusiasm means granting access to deeply personal areas of their life as the means to generate content for the show. The first episode of *The Bachelor* sets the bar for the show along with the expectations to succeed. Not only does this episode have the largest number of contestants, but it also includes 'the impression rose'. Participants therefore vie to make the best impression on the man to secure their place in the next episode and hopefully advance as far as possible. The 'impression rose' goes to the woman whom the bachelor selects as his top pick for a potential mate. The rose guarantees her place on the show, for at least one episode, which precludes her from competing for the bachelor's attention. In much the same way, the women in Esther need to make a good first impression in order to gain a second night with the king (2.14). Making the best first impression on *The Bachelor* can range from goofy performances to being willing to kiss the stranger that she has only spent five minutes talking to. The more good content a participant generates, the longer they can last in the competition and the more money they can gain. Participants sustain their time in the show at great expense since much of the glamour on the screen does not always translate off-screen. For instance, women are expected to share rooms with other participants who are also rivals. No hair and make-up stylists are on call to assist their preparations. There are long days of filming. And bodily privacy and boundaries can be compromised by film crews who might continue to shoot consensual sexual activity not intended for the show (Mukherjee and Pajé, 2022, p. 124).

The heteronormative sexual scripts operative in shows like *The Bachelor* place expectations on participants to engage in activities that they would not normally do in their real life. The obvious consequence for not living up to expectations is being sent home from the show. Participants must vie for the attention, affection and, most of all, the time of the man to ensure that they are seen as viable prospects for a marriage proposal. Unenthusiastic participants who are reluctant to be physically affectionate can face derogatory religious and racial comments. After several seasons of the show, ready physical intimate contact in forms that can be shown on television have become commonplace among all participants. Participants on the show invest in the search to find their 'person', at times without serious consideration of their compatibility with the man. As a participant on the show, women come with the seal of being marriageable and failure carries with it the tragic verdict of singleness. The high stakes of the show, never mind its abysmal success rate for marriages, subject the women both to advocate a sincere interest in the man, the process, and what it takes to succeed – even if that success is not really guaranteed. The contours of the show fall within permissible yet coercive practices of heteronormative culture. Consent therefore at best can be seen as 'enforced voluntary participation' (Mukherjee and Pajé, 2022, p. 126).

The vagueness of consent does not mean that coercion that results in sexual violence cannot be adjudged. Consent exists in forms that are evident or, as Pamela Haag offers, 'consent is always an interpreted idea' (Haag, 1999, p. xv). Exactly what sexual autonomy Esther possesses in a culture that does not see her as a subject leads Cheryl Kirk-Duggan to describe Esther's actions in the book as 'the politics of seduction' (Kirk-Duggan, 1999, p. 205). Holt includes the king and Haman in the orbit of Esther's seduction (Holt, 2021, p. 33), a circle necessitated by the circumstances that Mordechai laid on her. Controlled by other men, Esther has little choice but to play within the parameters established for her, moving through the processes of time in the woman's house, to marriage, to being queen. Bailey (2009, p. 241) indicts 'cover up translation' of not providing readers with a view into her seductions and the use of her sexuality over the course of the book. The challenge of consent as an 'interpreted idea' for both Esther and *The Bachelor* consists in the hiding of the sexual content. Readers and viewers, therefore, engage the material without calling attention to the troubling aspects of sexual consent.

The traffic in women

The competitions that exist in Esther and *The Bachelor* end with marriage as the prize. To situate marriage within discourses of consent requires avoiding romantic sentiment around marriage. Instead, I examine marriage from the perspective of its origins as a benefit designed for men. A seminal work such as Gayle Rubin's 'The Traffic in Women' proves useful in reading Esther with its ancient mate selection practices alongside *The Bachelor*, which contrives to create traditional mating practices while trying to appear as an equal opportunity show. Rubin premises the concept of traffic in women on the creation of the category 'woman'. As a result of this category, which is biologically and otherwise differentiated from men, marriage provides men with the opportunity to stabilize kinship and other relationships. For Rubin, kinship, though having some basis in biology, is really an artificial creation, even 'an imposition of cultural organization' (Rubin, 2004, p. 777). As an organization, kinship therefore functions as a form of power that allows men to exchange gifts among themselves, namely women. As gifts, women 'are in no position to realize the benefits of their own circulation' (Rubin, 2004, p. 779). Those benefits, instead, accrue to men who negotiate these exchanges and facilitate social organization. Rubin concludes from this analysis that the oppression of women arises from social organizations rather than from biology, with marriage being one of the primary sites where the oppression occurs (Rubin, 2004, p. 2004). Rubin's less-than-sanguine analysis of the origins of marriage leaves little room for consent in the ways that make marriage a meaningful institution within modern life. To understand consent as an interpreted idea, according to Haag, means that even in modern marriages women can acquiesce as subordinates in social systems to achieve some measure of benefit.

I find Rubin's ideas appealing for their invocation of travel, a practice common to both *The Bachelor* and Esther. As stories that have aspects of 'finding Prince Charming', traversing geographical lands in search of a mate seduces readers/viewers to view these women as invested in a process. That effort, whether they travel on their own volition or not, provides a veneer of consent. Rubin's idea of 'traffic' has little to do with geography and more with movements across social terrain and systems that create women as the prize. Those imperceptible movements make it quite easy to miss some of the more insidious aspects of marriage that Rubin describes. For one thing, the exchange of women involves trading access to sex but not simply as sexual intercourse. Rubin sees how sexual access allows men 'genealogical statuses, lineage names and ancestors, rights and people – men, women, and children – in concrete systems of social relationships' (Rubin, 2004, p. 780). From this perspective, the Persian king embarks on a reckless path to choose a mate who would add little to his power, emphasizing the fiction of the book. And the process of *The Bachelor*, as focused as it is on sex and sexual intercourse, consistently falls flat in the creation of viable marriages, given that the participants cannot sustain even these rudimentary elements of marriage in the complexities of the modern world. Of the 26 men who appeared on *The Bachelor*, only one remains married to the woman he proposed to at the end of the show. Even though another four men remain in relationships with their final picks, the success rate for the franchise is less than 4 per cent. The rates are somewhat better for *The Bachelorette* at 22 per cent, consisting of four women who remain married to the men they picked at the end of the show. Despite the risk of making a mockery of marriage, I think that Esther and *The Bachelor* use it as a prize because marriage raises the stakes around consent and offers the opportunity to demonstrate rituals of male control over women.

Like several aspects of the book of Esther, the process of mate selection is exaggerated or caricatured, depending upon one's perspective. The imperial-sized process of mate selection suggests not so much an inclusive process, nor even tokenism, implied in the sampling of different varieties of women. Rather, the scope of the king's reach for women throughout the expanse of the Persian Empire demonstrates the various forms of power available to the king, including sexual power. This traffic in women across the empire, as advised, should confirm the king's power not simply over the kingdom but over women in general and the one whom he selects as queen. We can read Mordechai's active interest in this process as the means to exploit the benefits of sexual access. Instead of handing over Esther's sexuality, Mordechai retains controlling interests in ways that allow him entry into the social systems of the Persian Empire. Unlike other male guardians whose consent to hand over their girls is taken for granted, Mordechai exercises a form of refusal to go along with the stated imperial process. The unchallenged power of the king to acquire women without the consent of their male guardians may seem extraordinary within the scope of biblical literature. The closest parallel to the mass acquisition of women occurs in Judges 21 where the men of Shiloh are forced to relinquish the women under a gentleman's agreement that allows the men of Shiloh not to incur guilt (Judg. 21.22). Presumably, men throughout the Persian Empire consent to this mass collection of young women in agreement with the logic of Esther 1.20 which requires women to honour their husbands. From this perspective,

Esther shows how men continue to benefit through marriage even when consent works against them.

Social systems traditionally benefit men. Whether in the case of Shiloh (Judg. 21) or in Esther, men create the social system within which women are moved around as prizes. To contain the potential spread of women refusing their husbands, the king needs to enlist men in this campaign. As a result, they are expected to willingly surrender their daughters or female charges for this serious empire-wide campaign. Male consent to the potential marriage of daughters is assumed, given what is at stake for men in the maintenance of sexual social systems. Mordechai participates in this social system, albeit with different objectives and even ones that are opposed to the king. As the book shows, marriage without his consent proves to be an advantageous investment for Mordechai as he emerges as the mastermind who saves the people.

Reality dating shows prefer marriage as the outcome of the show. Not only is marriage a tangible goal for the pairing process, but it allows sex to surface as part of the drama of the show only to be hidden under the murkiness of consent. *The Bachelor* and its viewing audience understand, as Rubin points out, 'marriages are a most basic form of gift exchange, in which it is women who are the most precious of gifts' (Rubin, 2004, p. 778). *The Bachelor* attracts a larger audience than *The Bachelorette* largely because, as Areias argues, a 'woman in power is not necessarily seen as attractive in the eyes of society' (Areias, 2014, p. 18). The dynamics of 25 women vying for a man means an expansion of the prize for the man in a way that a single woman selecting a mate does not. Centring women in the mate-selection allows for the type of tension around women's chastity, and the use of their sexuality, to emerge that are not the same as men's sexual activity. The potential for this type of drama opens the matter of consent, given that these women are assumed as sexually autonomous. In this case, the questions revolve around what happens off-screen that enables various participants to advance in the process. The advance of participants assumes a compromise with coercion and control. Audiences at best guess at what these compromises are but even in their ignorance are willing to consent to them for the sake of the show's outcome – a marriage. Mukherjee and Pajé suggest that reality dating shows like *The Bachelor* present love as 'sexual conquest characterized by coercion and control' (Mukherjee and Pajé, 2022, p. 124).

The magic circle

Competition lies at the heart of both Esther and *The Bachelor*. Participants employ strategies designed to win the prize of marriage. Reading these contexts from the perspective of game-play makes sense. Johan Huizinga theorizes the idea of the magic circle as part of the world of play. Huizinga sees play serving important cultural functions, such as the way 'society expresses its interpretation of life and the world' (Huizinga, 1964, p. 46). The magic circle represents an environment where the normal rules of the real world do not apply, and special ones take over. As a fictive or unreal space, the magic circle can seem real to players who are not aware that they have stepped out of the real world into this unique space. Huizinga defines the magic circle as 'temporary worlds within the ordinary world, dedicated to the performance of an act apart' (Huizinga, 1964, p. 10).

At the heart of the fantasy of *The Bachelor* lies the Bachelor Mansion. As the magic circle, the Bachelor Mansion functions as the gathering place but also the site to achieve the prize, namely a marriage proposal. As a fictive site that holds a tenuous resemblance to the real world, since participants engage in several activities outside of the mansion that align with the fiction of luxury, participants on *The Bachelor* do what it takes to 'win'. Since the rules of the real world are suspended in the magic circle, participants' pursuit of the goal does not always resemble their real lives or their normal standards around mate selection. In the magic circle, consent is at best ambiguous consent that can lead to practices such as sleeping with a stranger, kissing or other intimate forms of touch that would otherwise be unwelcomed or, as Mukherjee and Pajé (2022, p. 128) believe, 'outside the RDS [reality dating shows] environment ... would be considered violent'. Relaxation of these standards within the magic circle allows participants to advance in the game in a way that Huizinga (1964, p. 10) regards as 'a limited perfection'. Reinforcing systems that make participants fear failure that would confirm them as failures in love create distortions of consent. The participation of what has been called 'Bachelor Nation', the community of dedicated viewers who engage through social media and other forums in support of the show, serves as another layer that derives ambiguous consent from participants. Heightened social media activity occurs after episodes are taped and aired. Although the season is technically over, online discussions that pertain to that season have a chilling effect on future shows and participants. Since most participants have a social media presence, they receive feedback and comments from superfans over the course of the season that can be either complimentary or negative. In either case, the fan base signals expectations to potential participants of what success can look like either to receive the proposal from the man or become the lead in the next season of *The Bachelorette*. The stakes are high for women to leave the show either with a proposal, a positive social media profile or, if they are savvy enough, some other tangible win that can be converted into their benefit. Johan Huizinga understands winning as not just supremacy but that someone 'won esteem, obtained honour' (Huizinga, 1964, p. 50). The most successful participants are those who enthusiastically immerse themselves into the fiction of the show and produce appropriate content.

In the real world, according to heteronormative sexual scripts, women are the objects to be conquered but not without their consent. Reality shows like *The Bachelor* create the scenario for sexual conquest to occur but require women to give ambiguous consent and for the men to accommodate that ambiguous consent, or at least to proceed on the assumption of consent as the means to burnish their sexual credentials. Each episode of *The Bachelor* ends with the rose ceremony, a ritualization of consent that signals approval for what has already happened and prepares the way for the ultimate marriage proposal. By accepting the rose when asked, ostensibly a woman agrees to continue in the process. The conferral of the rose functions as a preliminary award of the ultimate prize that blurs the issue of consent. The choice of a rose as the token of consent with its associations of affection, romance and intimacy further distorts consent since it is never clear whether her 'yes' is an approval of all that has happened and the willingness to do what it takes to go the distance or acceptance of the man's affections and attentions.

The king's palace and specifically the women's house (2.3) serve as the magic circle in Esther. The process of selection of a replacement queen also shares in the unreality of the process of becoming queen, the true prize in Esther. Unlike *The Bachelor*, Esther has the complication of Mordechai's involvement in the process. The text remains unclear how Esther enters the process, apart from the passive 'taken' (2.8), a word that has generated in the minds of some interpreters Esther as being an unwilling participant and victim of rape. This is the case among rabbinic interpreters uncomfortable with the idea of a Jewish woman in a consensual relationship with a Gentile. Interpreters like Ibn Ezra absolve Mordechai of any guilt for not rescuing Esther since he understands she was forcefully removed (Carruthers, 2008, p. 110). In any event, Mordechai takes an active interest in her success and, when she becomes queen, exploits his access to her to gain favour with the king. Because the book only focuses on Esther, we see the additional male help she receives that ensures her success. To discuss consent in Esther requires including the input of Mordechai to a great extent, and to a lesser extent that of Hegai whose advice Esther follows to ensure her success and favour (2.15). As Holt observes, 'the power play in Esther, then, is staged in the shape of male–female gender play, as well as in the male–male rivalry between Mordecai and Haman' (Holt, 2021, p. 33). While Holt's idea of male–male rivalry makes sense, Randall Bailey calls attention to possible homoerotic features of the relationship between these men (Bailey, 2009, pp. 242–4). In any event, Esther sits within a matrix of men who manipulate her advancement in the process since they too want to share in the prize. If the prize is marriage in Esther, that prize comes with the title of queen with presumably limited access to the king. But as Mordechai's constant urgings prove, Esther could expand that access to the king and with that gain access to the power of the empire.

The fiction within the world of Esther that constitutes the magic circle revolves around the king's access to the most beautiful, pure, available women in the empire. The extravagant desire to have his pick of the beauty elite confers upon participants the high stakes of the process as well as its unreality. As Esther advanced in the process through the favour of Hegai (2.9), she lives in the artificially created world where her ethnicity neither exists nor matters, as it would in the real world of the Persian Empire. Of course, she inhabits the magic circle as guided by Mordechai (2.10). This positive feedback from Hegai and his attention manufactures Esther's consent to do what it takes to win since not winning means sharing Vashti's fate. If winning for Esther means becoming queen, for Mordechai it means living into the power of the position of queen. As such, Mordechai manipulates the ambiguity of consent to have Esther perform further acts for his purpose. When she reports the attempted threat upon the king's life from Bigthan and Teresh (2.21), Esther has already been living in the fantasy world where her husband hosts banquets and declares holidays in her honour (2.18). To live in the fantasy world of the magic circle created by the book, Esther needs to act outside the norms of the palace that require that even she as queen could only be in the king's presence when asked (4.10). Despite the agonized decision-making (4.16), Esther succumbs to Mordechai's pressure to go to the king. Ultimately, subsequent requests outside of the norms are easier for her to accept.

Esther follows the heteronormative script where attractive women serve as props for powerful men. Regardless of the homoerotic overtones, the men in the book recognize the value of Esther's physical attractiveness and use it for their purposes. The book masks a great deal of the sexual content, so much so that sexual power never appears on the surface of the text. Hegai advances Esther ahead of the other participants in the competition and directs her appearance and her performance arguably in a way to ensure that she wins. His familiarity with the king's sexual preferences leads Bailey to enquire about the source of his knowledge. That she becomes queen testifies to everyone that the king is satisfied with her in every way deemed desirable or, as Bailey puts it, 'the one who sexes him the best becomes queen' (Bailey, 2009, p. 237). As the king falls over himself in Esther's presence, readers see the evidence of heteronormative sexual scripts in the form of the king flattered by his sexual conquest as an assurance of his political power. Of course, the book pokes fun at the thinness of the king's boast, but readers are not expected to subvert the sexual scripts, only to see the buffoonery of the Persian king sexually manipulated by other men (Bailey, 2009, p. 246).

Conclusion: persistent ickiness

The analysis of these two contexts shows that marriage functions as the way to emphasize male power. Sexual conquest gives the Persian king the semblance of control that is otherwise absent from his vast territorial conquest. The pursuit of that conquest shows him as both shallow and vulnerable. The marriage to Esther will no more advance his geopolitical interests nor prove his sexual prowess. Whatever sexual satisfaction he derives speaks to Esther's ability both to please him sexually and discreetly burnish his ego. Marriage as a plot device for a reality show has proven a durable concept what with the tenure of *The Bachelor* and the proliferation of similar shows in the United States and other parts of the world. Even with limited success in the creation of marriages, the shows persist. Reality dating shows are not really interested in marriage as much as the idea of marriage, particularly in its patriarchal forms with the in-built gender tensions that arise in the modern world. As Areias observes, marriage permits the show to exist in a space where 'to create real-life couples become secondary to creating good drama' (Areias, 2014, p. 22). Both Esther and *The Bachelor* sustain the heteronormative sexual scripts for the audience which mean keeping consent as an ambiguous concept that thrives in the world of play. Mordecai finds Esther's willing consent to his continued negotiation of her sexuality useful to accomplish the larger goal of freedom. His role as owner of her sexuality continues long after he involuntarily gives it up, which allows him to eke out consent from the king at every turn. Esther is guided by male help to advance in the competition for the king's prize of queenship. Her beauty, charm and wisdom combine to have her follow careful male advice on how to thrive upon the heteronormative sexual script. All this is to say that, once set up in the palace, Esther achieves major accomplishments that render her a more complex character than her use of sex as a strategy would suggest. Angeline Song makes the point that Esther should be seen as more than 'a bimbo in a colonizer's world – gorgeous, unintelligent, and oh so willing to be invaded and tamed in both body and mind, in this case by the Persian king' (Song, 2018, p. 134).

Reality dating shows nibble around the edges of gender and sexual politics of the modern world. These forays require representation of sexual conquest as a male skill that becomes even more thrilling when it skirts the edges of consent. These depictions engage the contours of patriarchal marriage and sex for a largely female viewing audience who readily identify with the disappointments, hurts, frustrations and brief moments of sweetness. Sustaining the social sexual systems that thrive upon the impression of consent while negotiating consent away is an important production value for these shows. Mordechai's continued involvement in Esther's sexuality is critical to freedom, not simply the people's but also Esther's. Far from being the woman moved around several men in a sex contest, by the end of the book Esther gains the type of stature that demonstrates her own emancipation. Of course, as a character in an ancient text, she does not escape the limitations placed upon her sexual autonomy, but her forays into the public role speak to another arena where the position of queen gives her more independence.

Bibliography

Areias, Anne, 2013, 'The Bachelor Embraces the American Fairytale', *New Errands* 1, pp. 15–24.

Bailey, Randall C., 2009, '"That's Why They Didn't Call the Book Hadassah!": The Interse(ct)/(x)ionality of Race/Ethnicity, Gender, and Sexuality in the Book of Esther' in Randall C. Bailey, Tat-siong Benny Liew and Fernando Segovia (eds), *They Were All Together in One Place? Toward Minority Biblical Criticism*, Atlanta, GA: SBL Press, pp. 227–50.

Beal, Timothy K., 1997, *The Book of Hiding: Gender, Ethnicity, Annihilation, and Esther*, London: Routledge.

Carruthers, Jo, 2008, *Esther Through the Centuries*, Hoboken, NJ: Wiley Blackwell.

Dubrofsky, Rachel E., 2011, *The Surveillance of Women on Reality Television: Watching The Bachelor and The Bachelorette*, Lanham, MD: Lexington Books, 2011.

Dunbar, Ericka Shawndricka, 2022, *Trafficking Hadassah: Collective Trauma, Cultural Memory, and Identity in the Book of Esther and in the African Diaspora*, London: Routledge.

Fox, Michael V., 1991, *Character and Ideology in the Book of Esther*, Columbia, SC: University of South Carolina Press.

Graybill, Rhiannon, 2021, *Texts After Terror: Rape, Sexual Violence, and the Hebrew Bible*, New York: Oxford University Press.

Haag, Pamela, 1999, *Consent: Sexual Rights and the Transformation of American Liberalism*, Ithaca, NY: Cornell University Press.

Holt, Else K., 2021, *Narrative and Other Readings in the Book of Esther*, London: T&T Clark.

Huizinga, Johan, 1964, *Homo Ludens: A Study of the Play-Element in Culture*, Boston, MA: Beacon Press.

Kirk-Duggan, Cheryl A., 1999, 'Black Mother Women and Daughters: Signifying Female-Divine Relationships in the Hebrew Bible and African-American Mother-Daughter Short Stories' in Athalya Brenner (ed.), *Ruth and Esther: A Feminist Companion to the Bible (Second Series)*, Sheffield: Sheffield Academic Press, pp. 192–210.

Macchi, Jean-Daniel, 2018, *Esther*, International Exegetical Commentary on the Old Testament, Stuttgart: Kohlhammer.

Mukherjee, Sreyashi, and Dacia Pajé, 2022, '"You Can't Force Someone to Want You": Investigating Consent, Tokenism, and Play in Reality Dating Shows' in Stephanie Patrick and Mythili Rajiva (eds), *The Forgotten Victims of Sexual Violence in Film, Television and New Media Turning to the Margins*, Cham, Switzerland: Palgrave Macmillan, pp. 123–42.

Rubin, Gayle, 2004, 'The Traffic in Women' in Julie Rivkin and Michael Ryan (eds), *Literary Theory: An Anthology*, Malden, MA: Blackwell, pp. 770–94.

Song, Angeline M. G., 2018, 'Not Just a Bimbo: A Reading of Esther by a Singaporean Immigrant in Aotearoa New Zealand' in Jione Havea (ed.), *Sea of Readings: The Bible in the South Pacific*, Atlanta, GA: SBL Press, pp. 131–45.

Srinivasan, Amia, 2020, *The Right to Sex*, London: Bloomsbury.

Sun, Chloe T., 2021, *Conspicuous in His Absence: Studies in the Song of Songs and Esther*, Downers Grove, IL: InterVarsity Press.

Wagmeister, Elizabeth, 2021, 'Colton Underwood, the First Gay "Bachelor" Confronts His Controversial Coming Out', *VARIETY*, 12 May, available at https://variety.com/2021/tv/features/colton-underwood-the-bachelor-netflix-1234970331/ (accessed 15.12.2023).

7

Rape Jokes, Sexual Violence and Empire in Revelation and *This Is the End*

MEREDITH J. C. WARREN

Introduction[1]

The book of Revelation is one of the most borrowed-from texts of the New Testament when it comes to popular culture. Although there are dozens of other ancient apocalyptic writings, it is John's apocalyptic visions that directly inform contemporary ideas of apocalypse.[2] The apocalyptic comedy *This Is the End* (directors Seth Rogen and Evan Goldberg, 2013) not only invokes imagery from Revelation (filtered through 2,000 years of culture) but also adapts portions of the text in its portrayal of the end times. However, it also reproduces and expands the use of sexualized violence as a means of punishment found in Revelation.[3] To head off objections that analysing issues of consent or sexual assault in antiquity is anachronistic, I would propose that the tools for analysis of antiquity, historical-critical or otherwise, are all technically anachronistic (Schüssler Fiorenza, 2001, pp. 22–3); and, further, that if 'consent' as we approach it today does not exist in antiquity, that is in part because of the active silencing of women and enslaved men whose perspectives on their own bodily autonomy (or lack thereof) are not well represented in ancient texts (see Graybill, 2021). As Rhiannon Graybill points out, rape stories in the Bible are part of the 'cultural scaffolding' that supports a system in which rape and sexualized violence are normalized: 'The Bible helps us understand contemporary rape culture; contemporary rape culture helps us read and understand rape in the Bible' (Graybill, 2021, pp. 12, 20). Cinema represents one place where examples of rape culture, and their relationship to the Bible, can be found. Using methods outlined by other scholars of Bible and film, drawing attention to the film's quotation of the Bible as text and its use for elements of the plot (see Reinhartz, 2003), this chapter will examine the mechanisms of sexualized violence in Revelation as they are interpreted in *This Is the End*. I will argue that in the same way that Revelation imagines itself as challenging the status quo that is the Roman Empire (see Portier-Young, 2014), and yet reinforces violence against women as normative, the rape jokes in *This Is the End* (even ones that purport to invert narratives) prop up a system commonly called 'rape culture',[4] in which sexualized violence is understood as deserved punishment.

The premise of the film *This Is the End* is that several celebrities, playing themselves, become trapped together as the apocalypse begins, after attending a party at James Franco's Hollywood mansion. The characters are exaggerated caricatures of the actors or their typical roles, or sometimes inversions of themselves. Jonah Hill plays a 'sensitive new-age guy' who is in touch with his emotions, as if his character in *Superbad* has matured a few years; Danny McBride plays a selfish, hyper-masculine 'bro' reminiscent of his roles on *Eastbound & Down* and *Vice Principals*; Michael Cera, on the other hand, plays a rage-filled, coked-up arsehole who sexually assaults Rihanna at the party and shortly after meets his death by falling into the giant crevasse that opens up on the front lawn of the mansion. Those who survive the party – James Franco, Jonah Hill, Seth Rogen, Jay Baruchel, Danny McBride and Craig Robinson – attempt to survive and to figure out what is going on.

Writers Rogen and Goldberg are Jewish, as are many of the main cast. However, I want to be clear that the sexualized violence in the film is not the result of Jews reading an otherwise benevolent Christian text. The New Testament texts are not benevolent: the New Testament includes many examples of Jesus calling for violence, including – but not limited to – Revelation (Mroczek, 2021). The film's interpretation of Revelation instead emerges from a culture that has been steeped in Christian dominance for generations, and is especially coloured, consciously or otherwise, by American Dispensationalist readings of Revelation (Boxall, 2020, pp. 376–93; Rossing, 2004). This particular cinematic iteration of the intersection of the Bible and rape culture emerges from specifically Christian notions of gender and apocalyptic violence, despite the writers' identity.

The film consciously evokes imagery from Revelation, and the characters at one point quote the biblical text to support their suspicion that they are experiencing the biblical end times. That the text itself is highlighted in the film indicates the special location that the book of Revelation has as a cultural icon of apocalypse, interpreted or imagined by its readers in light of the various cultural readings of the last two millennia. Baruchel gestures with a Bible and proceeds to try to convince his friends that the disasters they are experiencing are located in the book of Revelation.[5] He proceeds to 'read' aloud from the Bible in order to prove his point:

> Jay Baruchel: I think I know what it is.
> Craig Robinson: Let's hear it.
> JB: I think it's the Apocalypse.
> All: What?
> JB: I'm serious, boys. It's all in here, in the Book of Revelations.
> James Franco: You took my Bible?
> JB: Well, just hear me out, and you tell me that what I'm describing isn't what's going on right now. 'And the skies shall open up, and the light of the Lord shall shine down, and those of good heart shall be brought into my kingdom of heaven.' That's the Rapture, those are the gigantic beams of blue light. 'And there will be a great mountain burning in fire.' I mean, the Hollywood Hills are literally engulfed in flames as we sit here right now.
> CR: The Hollywood Hills ain't no mountain. It's a hill. Takes about 10 minutes to get across that motherfucker with no traffic. [A discussion about LA traffic ensues, interrupting Baruchel's reading.]
> JB: Boys, can I just fucking finish? [...] 'And out of the pit rose a great red dragon having seven heads; that old serpent called the devil and Satan, which deceiveth the whole world, was released onto the earth.'

The careful reader may have noticed some creative additions to the text as read by Baruchel, since to establish a biblical precedent for the Rapture, for example, requires some flexibility. Regardless, the film clearly and intentionally locates its apocalyptic mythology in the book of Revelation. It establishes a direct connection for the viewer between the apocalyptic events on the screen and in the Bible, so that viewers assume a continuity between the text and the film.

There are several rape jokes in *This Is the End*. I've counted at least four, but I will focus my analysis on two examples. The film came out in a time when rape had not yet become as widespread a topic within public discussion as it has now become, in particular since the #MeToo movement.[6] However, there were several discussions going on at the time of, and just prior to, the film's release on the function of rape jokes in society. Notably, in the summer previous to *This Is the End*, comedian Daniel Tosh had been under fire for responding to a woman heckler at a live comedy show by suggesting that it would be funny if that woman were raped by five men right then and there.[7] This incident brought the issue of rape jokes to the fore; Roxane Gay responded to the Tosh event in an essay for *Salon*, saying, 'Rape humor is not "just jokes" or "stand-up." Humor about sexualized violence suggests permissiveness – not for people who would never commit such acts, but for the people who have whatever weakness that allows them to do terrible things unto others' (Gay, 2012). Scholars of humour have likewise pointed out how jokes function to communicate social and political meaning; Elise Kramer (2011, p. 163) writes, 'In order to fully understand the social meaning of rape jokes ... one must understand the culturally specific ideological framework within which "types" of jokes are associated with "types" of people.' The implication is twofold: first Gay suggests that social acceptance of rape jokes signals to rapists that their actions are socially accepted as well; second, Kramer observes that negative reactions to rape jokes emerge from the perception that those who tell rape jokes or find rape jokes funny lack critical understanding of rape culture.[8]

Rape's function as a tool of power and control points to the dynamics that make rape jokes potent communicators of social values (Brownmiller, 1975); such jokes perform tacit reminders to women that they are rapeable. This claim can also be made of Roman antiquity. Sexually aggressive jokes made at the expense of victims were commonplace in ancient Roman society, as I will illustrate briefly below. Amy Richlin has pointed out that such comments are not 'locker-room talk', ignored by women or addressed only to other elite men; rather, she approaches these texts as having 'descriptive validity' that represents a current within a culture that is only sometimes explicitly voiced (Richlin, 1992, p. xxv).

Revelation's apocalypse depicts a dualistic battle between God and the forces of evil (see Frey, 2014, pp. 271–94). Likewise, the characters in *This Is the End* must fight back against material demons as well as their own personal shortcomings in order to survive. As a weapon of power and control, rape in the context of war has a long, sordid and ongoing history as both reality and as metaphor (see Brownmiller, 1975, pp. 31–113; Gaca, 2011). The Trojan War, after all, centres on the euphemized rape of Helen, and a sizeable portion of *The Iliad* revolves around Achilles' pouting because the woman he has captured to rape is going to be raped by someone else.[9] Greeks and Romans also used the threat of rape as a metaphor for conquest, as in the examples I offer here of a Greek vase and a Roman coin depicting the subjugation of Judea. The so-called Eurymedon Vase (Figure 1), from around 460 BC, depicts a nude man in Thracian cape and not much else holding his erect penis while gesturing at another man on the other side of the jug.[10]

The other man, marked as a foreigner by his clothing and his hat, is bent over in surrender. The inscription on the vase reads 'I am Eurymedon /

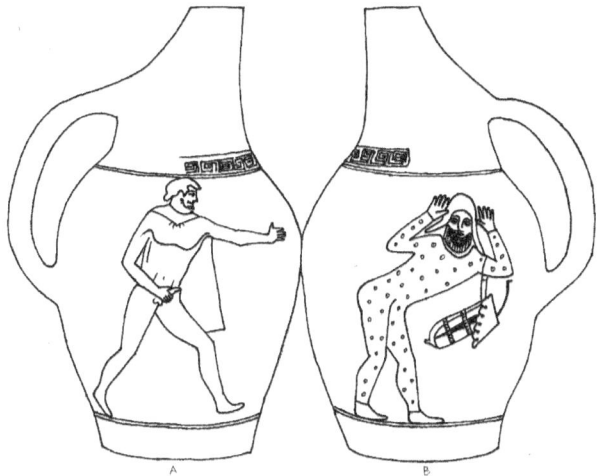

Figure 1: By M. Warren after The Eurymedon Vase (Museum für Kunst und Gewerbe, Hamburg).

I stand bent forward.' The overall impression is that the conquered is made to submit to the sexual assault of the victor. While initial interpretations of the vase hypothesized that the entire caption was attributed to the clothed man (Schauenburg, 1975, pp. 97–121), subsequent readings have challenged that understanding. Rather, as Amy C. Smith has demonstrated, the position of the text in relation to the figures likely indicates that the first part of the text, 'I am Eurymedon', is spoken by the nude man, while the second portion, 'I stand bent forward', should be attributed to the other figure (Smith, 1999, p. 135). The meaning of the name Eurymedon has been controversial, with Schauenburg initially assuming that the clothed figure represented the site of the Battle of Eurymedon and that the nude figure represented the army; however, especially in combination with the attribution of the speech, it is also unlikely that the clothed figure represents the river after which the battle was named (Smith, 1999, p. 135). Rather, he likely represents the personification of the battle itself, while the other figure stands in for the conquered locale. Acknowledging the multiple layers of meaning that are possible in artistic representation, including sex, satire and comedy, Smith observes that the dress of the nude figure marks his identity as a hunter and that 'a hunter is a pursuer, whether in the context of game, sex, or war' (Smith, 1999, p. 136). Thus, the conquest of the foreign location by the 'hunter' is imagined in the context of sexual pursuit. The posture of the clothed man indicates that the vase's political commentary relies on rape to make its point. While James Davidson suggests that the bent-over position is suggestive of promiscuity, and thus that the bent-over figure is indicating his extreme sexual desire (Davidson, 1998, pp. 180–1), most other scholars disagree with this view. His clothing, marking him as foreign, and his weaponry, indicating that he is an archer who kills from afar rather than up close, already mark him as feminized in the context of the vase. He holds his arms up in alarm, in a posture commonly used to depict women about to be raped in other artistic representations (Zeitlin, 1986, p. 128; Smith, 1999, p. 138). As Karim Arafat (2002, p. 190) concludes, 'I do not find it possible to interpret the vase in any other way than as using rape as a metaphor for victory. As such, it is highly appropriate, since if the pursuit is the battle, the rape is the victory.' Rape's use to represent military conquest has a long lineage,[11] then, one that extends well beyond Revelation's era.

The Judea Capta coin (Figure 2) likewise presents a virile conqueror towering over a small, hunched-over woman. Davina Lopez points out that the coin uses gendered bodies to illustrate the masculine power of Rome over and against the feminized weakness of Judea, the conquered land.[12] As Lopez observes, 'the positioning of his dagger in his groin area appears to be no accident' (Lopez, 2007, pp. 121–3; see also Rodgers, 2004, pp. 69–93). The sword the soldier carries at his hip suggests both the threat of further violence, including, especially because of its phallic

Figure 2: By M Warren after LIMC 'Iudaea' no. 14 (+ BMCRE 117).

placement, the very real possibility of rape. This tactic is prevalent in Roman discourse and iconography; gendered modes of depicting inferiority were (and continue to be) a mechanism by which elite men prop up, or attempt to impose, their own claims to authority and power (Wilson, 2015, pp. 28, 42).

It is also the case that Revelation uses the threat of sexual violence as a tool against those whom the author views as the enemies of God. Threats of sexualized violence are used against two female characters in Revelation, Jezebel and Babylon, as part of how the Seer imagines God's war against the evils of the Roman Empire (see Marshall, 2010, pp. 17–32; Young, 2022, pp. 239–59). Revelation is a text of resistance against the violence of Rome. It attempts to muster rhetorical weapons against that empire as a means of challenging its dominance. It is in this context that we should read the threats of sexualized violence that the text contains.

The first example, as several scholars now recognize (Pippin, 1995, pp. 191–8; Huber, 2013, p. 43; Emanuel, 2020, p. 110; Young, 2022, pp. 241–6), is in the letter to the assembly at Thyatira, which is dictated to John by Jesus himself. Part of this letter, Revelation 2.22–23, condemns a woman called Jezebel for what the text claims is fornication and false prophecy: 'Beware, I am throwing her on a bed, and those who commit adultery with her I am throwing into great distress, unless they repent of her doings; and I will strike her children dead.'[13] Her fornication, her *porneia*, is unspecified; the Greek covers a range of inappropriate sexual activities, including – but not limited to – sex work. In this context, the significance of the threat to throw her on a bed should not be overlooked; while the exact act threatened is glossed over, it makes her lovers very upset. Her children, presumably the (real or metaphorical) products of her *porneia*, Jesus threatens to kill. Whether Jezebel stands in for a faction within John's community which holds different attitudes in its relationship with Rome, or whether she represents a historical leader of such a group, her gender – and thus vulnerability to forcible penetration – is implicated in the threat of punishment. Just as in the example of the Judea Capta coin, women's vulnerable bodies are a locus for arguments about colonial power and resistance (Marshall, 2010, pp. 22–5). But likewise, as in the Eurymedon vase, the text attempts to make humorous the sexualized violence it describes; Jezebel is the butt of the joke, whose punchline relies on her sexual humiliation as well as other ancient intertexts, as Emanuel points out (Emanuel, 2020, p. 115). In threatening sexual assault against Jezebel as a means of upholding John's interpretation of how best to resist Rome, the text mimics imperial modes of expressing power, including by using humour.

The Seer's violent response to Jezebel in chapter 2 is magnified later in the vision when he turns his attention to Babylon. These two female enemies of God are connected in how they are described: as sexually immoral, as connected with inappropriate food, and as encouragers of behaviour that John despises (Duff, 2001, pp. xiii, 89–92, 189; Marshall, 2010, p. 27). Direct sexualized violence takes place in Revelation 17.16–17, where the angel explains to John that 'they will make her desolate and naked; they will devour her flesh and burn her up with fire'. Make no mistake: stripping someone naked is a sexualized punishment (Tombs, 2023, pp. 8–26; Huber, 2013, p. 64). Here, the A CITY IS A WOMAN metaphor is employed, using Babylon, a city historically the enemy of Jerusalem, to map conceptually the characteristics of Babylon on to the city/woman in the text, but also the negative associations attached to sex work in antiquity (Huber, 2013, p. 62). In refiguring the conquering Rome as a conquered and humiliated woman instead of the virile soldier of official coinage, John explicitly inverts political imagery used by the Empire in his critique (Marshall, 2010, pp. 27–8), but in doing so replicates the threats of sexual assault used by Rome in establishing and maintaining its imperial power. Again, Babylon, as a sexualized Rome, is the object of ridicule as well as sexualized violence (Emanuel, 2020, pp. 149–63). Importantly, the casual reader is implicated in this violence, and in the text's sexualized derision of her, since its portrayal as the downfall of the enemy, Rome, makes it tempting to join in with Revelation in celebrating Babylon's ruin at the hands of the powerful God (Pippin, 1992, p. 75).

To sum up what I have established so far, Revelation as apocalyptic text uses women and sexualized violence in similar ways to the Empire it seeks to resist. As Lynn Huber suggests, the boundaries between human women and metaphorical women in antiquity isn't always easy to discern (Huber, 2013, p. 59), making this imagery all the more volatile in the biblical context, as well as in its afterlives. Sarah Emanuel's work points out the role that humour plays in the sexualized derision of both Jezebel and Babylon in their respective sexual assaults. The 2013 comedy film *This Is the End* invokes Revelation as the blueprint for its apocalyptic landscape. The next section of this chapter will discuss the ways in which Revelation's sexualized violence is replicated for comedic effect in *This Is the End*, and how its rape jokes function, like the threats in Revelation, to reinforce rather than critique rape culture. I will look at two representative scenes from the film in order to showcase how the film uses rape jokes.

Example 1 *Women exaggerate and blame good guys*

In the first scene I will examine, Emma Watson has just broken into the house to find the protagonists alive and more or less well. She needs food and water, which the men have, and her appearance suggests that she has been on the run for a while, trying to find safety. She is relieved when they offer her a place to stay. When she is in her bedroom with the door closed, the men have a conversation about how they should *not* rape her, which Watson overhears, or mishears:

> Jay Baruchel: Guys, listen, listen. I think we need to address the elephant in the room.
> Seth Rogen: Whoa. Jay, don't talk about Craig like that. That's fucked up.
> Craig Robinson: I'm right here, man.
> SR: Yeah.
> JB: I'm not calling Craig an elephant.
> James Franco: Wow, that's fucking weird. What does that even mean?
> JB: Yeah, no.
> JF: That's racist.
> JB: I wasn't referring to him. I was referring to the issue that's on all of our minds.
> JF: What?
> JB: This is one girl in a house with six males.
> JF: Yeah. Really safe.
> SR: Ideal scenario.
> CR: She's like a little sister.
> JB: I think that she needs ... It's important that she feels safe.
> JF: Yeah.
> JB: And comfortable. And we should be mindful.
> CR: Who's making her not feel safe?
> JB: Well, I'm just saying, we should ... We don't want to give off a bad vibe.
> SR: Vibe?
> JF: Vibes? I ain't giving no vibes.
> SR: Yeah, wait, what kind of vibes are you talking about, man?
> Danny McBride: He's talking about us giving off a rapey vibe.[14]
> Everyone: Hey! Shh! Whoa! What? Jesus.
> JF: Jay, what the fuck, man?
> SR: Chill out, dude.
> JF: Why you putting that shit in the mix? Yeah.

JB: He fucking said it.
DM: You're the one saying it. No one here is thinking about raping anyone.
JB: Shh!
JF [waving a gun]: Well, you talking about vibes is the only thing that's rapey going on right now.
SR: Dude, nothing was rapey till you brought up the rapey vibes.
JF: Fucking one who smelt it dealt it, dawg.
SR: True that, dude.
JF: One who denies it supplies it.
JB: I know, it's farts, I get it.
Jonah Hill: Guys, guys, guys. Jay's not rapey. Jay couldn't rape a fly. He probably could.
CR: Maybe we should just stop this entire conversation right now.
JF: If anyone's gonna rape anyone here, it's probably gonna be Danny.
DM: What the fuck, Franco?
JF: What?
DM: Why do you think I'm gonna rape somebody?
JF: I'm just trying to lay it out there.
DM: I'm not gonna rape anyone, all right? If anyone's gonna rape somebody, it's Jay.
[Cut to Emma Watson, overhearing]
[Off-screen:
JB: What?
DM: He came up with the rape idea.] [return screen to men in hallway]
And his face looks like the police sketch of a fucking rapist.
JF: True.
JB: What the fuck does that mean?
DM: If anybody's raping Emma Watson, it's fucking Sir Rapes-a-Lot over here.
JB: Chill out!
[Emma Watson kicks open the door to confront them]
EW: Hey!
Men: Whoa!
JF: Easy. Easy.
EW: Back the fuck up!
JF: Emma. What's wrong?
SR: Wait, what's wrong?
EW: What's wrong? I just heard you guys talking about which one of you is gonna get to rape me.
Men: No, no, no, no!

SR: Guys, I got it. I got it. No. It's funny. It's funny. We were specifically talking about not raping you.
[EW hits SR in the nose with the butt of her axe]
Men: Jesus! Holy shit!
EW: Back up!
JH: It's me, Jonah! It's me, Jonah Hill. America's sweetheart. J-bug, J-bone. Your friend. I would never hurt you.
EW: Get back!

As the audience, we are party to both the 'true' conversation that the men have, and the 'false' conversation that Watson thinks she hears. As the audience, we are supposed to empathize with the men and laugh at the misunderstanding. Really, it was Jay Baruchel's concern about a woman's safety that is at fault for the whole misunderstanding; Baruchel's attempt to encourage his fellow men to be 'mindful' about how Watson might perceive her safety is what creates the problem. Seth Rogen even explains the 'joke' to Watson, telling her that it actually is funny if only she would try to understand. But the punch-line – that women misunderstand men's intentions and overreact to the imagined threat of rape – is at Watson's expense. It is a punchline that makes use of anti-feminist narratives about women not being funny (Hitchens, 2007), or not being able to take a joke, exaggerating about sexual harassment, and lying about sexual assault. In an interview, the directors discuss their decision to include this scene, and their decision to 'embrace that rapiness' (McGrath, 2013). The conversation comes about as the result of the interviewer querying why they chose not to include any women in the core cast. For Rogen and Goldberg, the answer is simple: including women changes the tone of the film from neutral to sexual. In other words, in their view, the very presence of a woman automatically sexualizes a scene and brings the possibility of rape to the fore: 'We kept saying like, "If we have a girl, it will start to feel rape-y"' (McGrath, 2013). The directors' justification for the scene provides important additional context: the film's engagement with rape culture emerges from the widespread view that women are inherently sexual and inherently rapeable.

Example 2 Men's rape is funny

The next example is the depiction of the rape of Jonah Hill by a demon. In this example, the wording is less important than the cinematography, and so I will forgo the transcription in favour of spending some time describing the way the scene was shot. The assault opens with a camera shot from the point of view of the demon, so that we, the audience, experience the demon's approach to Hill firsthand. We can hear the demon's growl as it/we loom over the bed. The camera then shifts and we see the silhouette of a human-shaped demon with an erect penis before the point of view collapses demon and viewer once more. It is a scene that consciously evokes a similar scene of demonic rape from Roman Polanski's *Rosemary's Baby* in its lighting, camera position and direction. Even if the scene is a conscious allusion to Polanski's infamous scene and not something created *ex nihilo* by the writers, Rogen and Goldberg made a decision not only to include a scene of rape as a comedic moment, but also, in some sense, to pay homage to a film directed by Polanski, an alleged rapist (see Sherlock, 2021, for other film references). As in *Rosemary's Baby*, the viewer experiences the assault in part from the point of view of the demonic being. Hill is sleeping in his bed when the assault occurs, and at first, like Rosemary, he is unsure if what is happening is a dream or real. The audience, as in the scene with Watson, are in the know; we understand that the rape is real. This knowledge is supposed to make the scene humorous as we watch Hill's unconscious reactions to the demon's touches. Hill, still asleep, thinks that the person touching him and scratching him is his friend Craig Robinson, the film's only Black leading actor.[15] The punch-line for this rape joke resides in the idea that men's rape is somehow funny, and likewise plays on Hill's character's effeminate behaviours before and after the rape: he is affectionate, peace-making, negotiating tensions among the group using words and, in his post-assault 'confession' to the video-camera, talks about his experience as if he is discussing it with a therapist. Hill's rape also directly echoes Revelation's use of sexualized violence as end-time punishment. Demonic divine beings are precisely those beings who, in the biblical text, mete out the punishment for Babylon in Revelation 17.16–17:

> And the ten horns that you saw, they and the beast will hate the whore; they will make her desolate and naked; they will devour her flesh and burn her up with fire. For God has put it into their hearts to carry out his purpose by agreeing to give their kingdom to the beast, until the words of God will be fulfilled.

Whereas in Revelation 2 the rape threat is uttered by Christ himself, in this excerpt God uses the Beast to punish Babylon. Especially in the context of a film whose resolution occurs when the main characters attempt genuine remorse for past bad actions and, when successful, are taken up in beams of light, the use of rape by demons presents a world in which wrongdoers are punished with sexual assault at the will of God.

Conclusion

Not all rape jokes are created equal. There is debate among feminists about the difference between a rape joke that makes *rapists* the butt of the joke and a rape joke that makes *rape victims* the butt of the joke. The question is whether the joke reinforces rape culture and victim blaming or whether it makes wry observations in a critical way about a culture that seems not to care about how prevalent sexual harassment and violence is.[16] In the examples that I have covered here from *This Is the End*, there is no critique of the existing rape myths; instead, Hill's rape and Watson's reaction to the threat of rape both make the victims the object of the humour. The audience, who view Hill's rape through the eyes of the demon, are made complicit in his assault, similar to how readers of Revelation 17 might become caught up in the sexual assault of Babylon. In the case of Watson, because viewers are party to the whole conversation, we are intended to empathize with the men in the scene, who are 'falsely' accused of plotting Watson's assault. This is also the case for the other rape jokes in the film, although there is insufficient space to cover them all here: in one scene, James Franco admitting to having sex with Lindsay Lohan when she was so intoxicated that she thought he was someone else,[17] and another where Channing Tatum is shown naked and bound in chains, as the sex slave of Danny McBride. As such, the film's punch lines reinforce rape culture rather than critique it.

Writing about rape jokes in an entirely different context – ancient Rome – Richlin (1992, p. xxviii) writes, 'Cultures where rape is a joke are cultures that foster rape. We need to know our history and our present.' She points out how punitive rape, such as that encountered by Jonah Hill or by the Whore, is a common threat in joking representations of sexualized violence (Richlin, 1992). Like the Eurymedon vase (Arafat, 2002, p. 189), the jokes in *This Is the End* are at the expense of the victim; we as viewers are invited to join in making fun of the victims and to identify with the attacker or potential attackers. Likewise, Revelation invites us as readers or hearers of its depictions of sexualized violence to ally ourselves with the attackers, who are either divine or agents of God. The mockery of the victim emerges from the ironic inversion of circumstances experienced by Jezebel and by the Whore (Yarbro Collins, 1980, pp. 185–204; Barr, 2009, pp. 20–30); where once they are described as figures whose adultery was intentional, the Seer imagines the removal of their agency in acts of sexualized violence.

The film's use of rape in this particular way is similar to how sexualized violence is used in the biblical text from which it explicitly draws its vision of the end times. Comparing these two texts helps to clarify the significance of the sexualized violence in the biblical text. Revelation is certainly an anti-empire text, but it uses the same modes of enforcing power that Rome does. Just as the imperial coin commemorating the subjugation of Judea uses the threat of the phallus as a symbol of Roman might, Revelation likewise envisions its enemies as the victims of sexual assault. Like the dominated 'outsider' community around the text of Revelation, the actors James Franco, Seth Rogen, Jonah Hill and the other stars of the film are known for their style of 'outsider comedy', sometimes called 'comedy of the bullied' (Waxman, 2007), that resists mainstream humour. The actors and their directors have made an industry of portraying 'hapless losers as heroes' (Waxman, 2007). Their oeuvre presents itself as rejecting mainstream modes of joke-making which are often at the expense of 'losers', and the actors emerged in their earliest projects as underdogs; *Freaks and Geeks*, *Superbad*, *Knocked Up*, and other films and television shows that starred Franco, Rogen, Hill, and the rest of the *This Is the End* cast, focused on uplifting the nerds and outcasts. But the film's purported challenge to the status quo is limited, if it is present at all; the system of social power that makes these actors and their characters feel like bullied underdogs is not broken down but simply inverted.[18] The film employs those hierarchical structures in order to construct its humour; the rape jokes are part of how that humour and its social capital function. Revelation likewise uses sexual assault to bring down a status quo, only to imagine its author and his allies as the new violent power in control. As Sarah Emanuel writes, 'As God and Christ become the new overlords of the New Jerusalem, we are haunted by images of the Roman past. Just as Rome was secured via war, rape, and conquest, so too is Christ's New Kingdom' (Emanuel, 2020, p. 51). In challenging the Roman Empire, the text reinforces violence against women as normative, just as the rape jokes in *This Is the End* prop up a system wherein sexual assault is punishment. In both cases, biblical and cinematic, the apocalyptic imagination tolerates and emboldens those who purport to be underdogs to empower themselves through the use of sexualized violence.

Bibliography

Arafat, K. W., 2002, 'State of the Art – Art of the State' in S. Deacy and K. F. Pierce (eds), *Rape in Antiquity: Sexual Violence in the Greek and Roman Worlds*, London: Duckworth, pp. 180–223 (original publication 1997).

Arieti, J. A., 2002, 'Rape and Livy's View of Roman History' in S. Deacy and K. F. Pierce (eds), *Rape in Antiquity: Sexual Violence in the Greek and Roman Worlds*, London: Bloomsbury, pp. 374–407.

Barr, D. L., 2009, 'John's Ironic Empire', *Interpretation* 63/1, pp. 20–30.

Boxall, I., 2020, 'Reception History and the Interpretation of Revelation' in C. R. Koester (ed.), *The Oxford Handbook of the Book of Revelation*, Oxford: Oxford University Press, pp. 376–93.

Brinkley, E., 2013, 'Is Robin Thicke's "Blurred Lines" a "rapey" song?', *Wall Street Journal*, 8 August, available at https://www.wsj.com/articles/BL-SEB-76254 (accessed 2.12.2023).

Brownmiller, S., 1975, *Against Our Will: Men, Women, and Rape*, New York: Bantam.

Darby, J. N., 1839, *Notes on the Book of Revelations: To Assist Inquirers in Searching into that Book*, London: Central Tract Depot.

Davidson, J., 1998, *Courtesans and Fishcakes*, London: HarperCollins.

Davidson, J., 2001, 'Dover, Foucault and Greek Homosexuality: Penetration and the Truth of Sex', *Past & Present* 170, pp. 3–51.

Duff, P. B., 2001, *Who Rides the Beast? Prophetic Rivalry and the Rhetoric of Crisis in the Churches of the Apocalypse*, Oxford: Oxford University Press.

Emanuel, S., 2020, *Humor, Resistance, and Jewish Cultural Persistence in the Book of Revelation: Roasting Rome*, Cambridge: Cambridge University Press.

Frey, J., 2014, 'Apocalyptic Dualism' in J. J. Collins (ed.), *The Oxford Handbook of Apocalyptic Literature*, Oxford: Oxford University Press, pp. 271–94.

Gaca, K. L., 2011, 'Telling the Girls from the Boys and Children: Interpreting Παῖδες in the Sexual Violence of Populace-Ravaging Ancient Warfare', *Illinois Classical Studies* 35–36, pp. 85–109.

Gay, R., 2012, 'Daniel Tosh and Rape Jokes: Still Not Funny', *Salon*, 12 July, available at https://www.salon.com/2012/07/12/daniel_tosh_and_rape_jokes_still_not_funny/ (accessed 2.12.2023).

Graybill, R., 2021, *Texts After Terror: Rape, Sexual Violence, and the Hebrew Bible*, New York: Oxford University Press.

Hitchens, C., 2007, 'Why Women Aren't Funny', *Vanity Fair*, January, available at https://www.vanityfair.com/culture/2007/01/hitchens200701 (accessed 2.12.2023).

Huber, L. R., 2013, *Thinking and Seeing with Women in Revelation*, London: Bloomsbury.

Huber, L. R., 2007, *Like a Bride Adorned: Reading Metaphor in John's Apocalypse*, London: Bloomsbury.

Kotrosits, M., 2018, 'Penetration and Its Discontents: Greco-Roman Sexuality, the Acts of Paul and Thecla, and Theorizing Eros without the Wound', *Journal of the History of Sexuality* 27/3, pp. 343–66.

Kramer, E., 2011, 'The Playful is Political: The Metapragmatics of Internet Rape-Joke Arguments', *Language in Society* 40/2, pp. 137–68.

Lampen, C., 2022, 'All the Allegations Against James Franco', *The Cut*, 13 July, available at https://www.thecut.com/2022/07/all-the-sexual-misconduct-allegations-against-james-franco.html (accessed 2.12.2023).

Lopez, D. C., 2007, 'Before Your Very Eyes: Roman Imperial Ideology, Gender Constructs, and Paul's Inter-Nationalism' in T. Penner and C. Vander Stichele (eds), *Mapping Gender in Ancient Religious Discourses*, Leiden: Brill, pp. 115–62.

Marshall, J. W., 2010, 'Gender and Empire: Sexualized Violence in John's Anti-Imperial Apocalypse' in A.-J. Levine and M. M. Robbins (eds), *A Feminist Companion to the Apocalypse of John*, London: Bloomsbury, pp. 17–32.

Masterson, M., 2014, 'Studies of Ancient Masculinity' in T. K. Hubbard (ed.), *A Companion to Greek and Roman Sexualities*, London: Blackwell, pp. 17–30.

McGrath, M., 2013, 'Seth Rogen, Evan Goldberg and Craig Robinson Discuss "This is the End"', *Daily Californian*, 13 June, available at https://www.dailycal.org/2013/06/13/seth-rogen-evan-goldberg-and-craig-robinson-discuss-this-is-the-end (accessed 2.12.2023).

Mroczek, E., 2021, 'Mean, Angry Old Testament God vs. Nice, Loving New Testament God?', Class handout, available at https://docs.google.com/document/d/1BG5PvCO5pTTATcgBF-Da5j9p0myFgg9wj1ECkrRhFbI (accessed 2.12.2023).

NosIsBack, 2013, 'Wanda Sykes – Detachable Pussy', *YouTube*, 5:06, 12 April, available at https://youtu.be/Jv5pjSRSLGQ (accessed 2.12.2023).

Owens Patton, T., and J. Snyder-Yuly, 2007, 'Any Four Black Men Will Do: Rape, Race, and the Ultimate Scapegoat', *Journal of Black Studies* 37/6, pp. 859–95.

Pippin, T., 1992, 'The Heroine and the Whore: Fantasy and the Female in the Apocalypse of John', *Semeia* 60, pp. 67–82.

Pippin, T., 1995, '"And I Will Strike Her Children Dead": Death and the Deconstruction of Social Location' in F. Segovia and M. A. Tolbert (eds), *Reading from This Place, Volume I: Social Location and Biblical Interpretation in the United States*, Minneapolis, MN: Fortress Press, pp. 191–8.

Portier-Young, A., 2014, 'Jewish Apocalyptic Literature as Resistance Literature' in J. J. Collins (ed.), *The Oxford Handbook of Apocalyptic Literature*, Oxford: Oxford University Press, pp. 145–62.

Reinhartz, A., 2003, *Scripture on the Silver Screen*, London: Westminster John Knox.

Richlin, A., 1992, *The Garden of Priapus: Sexuality and Aggression in Roman Humor*, Oxford: Oxford University Press.

Ricker, A., 2010, 'The Devil's Reading: Revenge and Revelation in American Comics' in A. D. Lewis and C. H. Kraemer (eds), *Graven Images: Religion in Comic Books and Graphic Novels*, New York: Continuum, pp. 15–23.

Rodgers, R., 2004, 'Female Representation in Roman Art: Feminizing the Provincial Other' in S. Scott and J. Webster (eds), *Roman Imperialism and Provincial Art*, Cambridge: Cambridge University Press, pp. 69–93.

Rossing, B. R., 2004, *The Rapture Exposed: The Message of Hope in the Book of Revelation*, Boulder, CO: Westview Press.

Schauenburg, K., 1975, 'εὐρομέδον εἰμί', *Mitteilungen des deutschen Archäologischen Instituts, Athenische Abteilung* 90, pp. 97–121.

Schüssler Fiorenza, E., 2001, *Jesus and the Politics of Interpretation*, New York: Continuum.

Smith, A. C., 1999, 'Eurymedon and the Evolution of Political Personifications in the Early Classical Period', *The Journal of Hellenic Studies* 119, pp. 128–41.

Tombs, D., 2023, *The Crucifixion of Jesus: Torture, Sexual Abuse, and the Scandal of the Cross*, London: Routledge.

Warren, M. J. C., 2023, 'Rape Jokes, Sexual Violence, and Empire in Revelation and *This Is the End*', *Journal of Religion & Film* 27/1, Article 59, pp. 1–32.
Waxman, S., 2007, 'Giving the Last Laugh to Losers', *New York Times*, 6 May, available at https://www.nytimes.com/2007/05/06/movies/moviesspecial/06waxm.html (accessed 1.12.2023).
Wilson, B. E., 2015, *Unmanly Men: Refigurations of Masculinity in Luke-Acts*, Oxford: Oxford University Press.
Yarbro Collins, A., 1980, 'Revelation 18: Taunt-Song or Dirge?' in J. G. Lambrecht and R. Beasley-Murray (eds), *L'Apocalypse Johannique et l'apocalyptique dans Le Nouveau Testament*, Gembloux, Belgium: J. Duculot; Louvain: Leuven University Press, pp. 185–204.
Young, S., 2022, 'Revelation Naturalizes Sexual Violence and Readers Erase It: Unveiling the Son of God's Rape of Jezebel' in C. Cobb and E. Vanden Eykel (eds), *Sex, Violence, and Early Christian Texts*, London: Lexington Books, pp. 239–59.
Zeitlin, F., 1986, 'Configurations of Rape in Greek Myth' in S. Tomaselli and R. Porter (eds), *Rape*, Oxford: Blackwell, pp. 122–51.
Zinoman, J., 2012, 'Toe-to-Toe at the Edge of the Comedy Club Stage', *New York Times*, 17 July, available at https://www.nytimes.com/2012/07/18/arts/television/when-the-comic-and-the-heckler-both-take-offense.html (accessed 2.12.2023).

Notes

1 A version of this chapter first appeared as Warren, 2023, pp. 1–32.

2 While the original meaning of the Greek term *apokalypsis* means the revealing of something, the prevalence in ancient apocalyptic literature, developed especially in Christian apocalypses, is that what is revealed is God's coming judgement of the world. In popular culture, the word 'apocalypse' has come to refer to the end of the world rather than something revealed per se, but such popular apocalypses do in the end reveal much about our own society and its social ills.

3 Sexualized violence is an umbrella term which includes sexual assault, sexual abuse and sexual harassment, including both physical and emotional violence.

4 Graybill (2021, p. 28) gives the following definition: '"Rape culture" is a term drawn from feminist scholarship and activism around sexual violence. It describes the social, cultural and ideological structures that sustain and nourish sexual violence. The concept of "rape culture" insists that rape is not an act of incomprehensible violence that suddenly ruptures the social fabric, but rather an extreme expression of what is culturally acceptable, salient, even ordinary: it stands on a continuum with other acts of "everyday rape culture".'

5 Baruchel says Revelations with an 's', a common misspelling which coincidentally also occurs in Dispensationalist theologian John Nelson Darby's *Notes on the Book of Revelations: To Assist Inquirers in Searching into that Book* (1839).

6 #MeToo was coined by activist Tarana Burke in 2006 and came into widespread use in 2017 when it began trending on social media. The 2017 use of the hashtag was in response to the allegations about Harvey Weinstein, notably used by actress Alyssa Milano. As a movement, #MeToo raises awareness about experiences of sexual abuse and harassment and was a way to empower survivors of sexual violence to share their stories; in doing so, the movement demonstrates the

prevalence of sexual abuse and harassment in society. Regarding this movement, see also Chapter 3 by Christl M. Maier in this volume. Several scholars, many of whom are cited in this chapter, had already published works on sexual violence in the Bible (e.g. Johanna Stiebert, Renita Weems and Phyllis Trible) and in Revelation specifically (e.g. Tina Pippin, Lynn R. Huber and John Marshall) before the #MeToo movement; and the Shiloh Project, a research theme dedicated to exposing the relationship between rape culture and the Bible, housed within the Sheffield Centre for Interdisciplinary Biblical Studies, was founded in 2016.

7 The woman shouted, 'Rape jokes are never funny!' Tosh responded: 'Wouldn't it be funny if that girl got raped by, like five guys right now?' (Zinoman, 2012).

8 The fact that James Franco, one of the film's main stars, has been accused of sexual exploitation and inappropriate sexual behaviour by at least five women suggests that he lacks critical understanding of rape culture (Lampen, 2022).

9 When Agamemnon demands Briseis, she is already in Achilles' tent, suggesting that Achilles has already raped her (*Iliad* 1.311); Agamemnon denies raping Briseis in 19.163, 239–40; Achilles is explicitly depicted as sleeping in the same bed with Briseis in 24.660.

10 The fact that this vase exists as a rape joke/threat is separate from the issue of penetrator/penetrated in ancient Greek and Roman sexuality (See Kotrosits, 2018, pp. 343–66; Masterson, 2014, pp. 17–30; Davidson, 2001, pp. 3–51).

11 Including, of course, Livy's invocation of the Rape of the Sabine women to establish the city of Rome; here the mass rape is a means of conquering the indigenous population while at the same time colonizing the land with new offspring (Arieti, 2002, p. 379).

12 For discussion of the metaphor A City is a Woman in antiquity, particularly in Revelation, see Huber, 2007, pp. 89–112.

13 Translations of biblical texts are from the New Revised Standard Version Updated Edition (NRSVUE).

14 The word 'rapey' reached its second-highest search ranking on Google in June 2013, corresponding with the film's release (cf. https://trends.google.com/trends/explore?date=all&q=rapey&hl=en-GB (accessed 6.06.2024)). Only three months earlier, Robin Thicke's song 'Blurred Lines' was released, leading to widespread discussion about what seemed to many to be its casual support for rape culture (Brinkley, 2013).

15 The darkness of the demon's form, both in shadow and in complexion, combined with enduring racist stereotypes about Black men as rapists of White victims, adds to the already problematic scene. See Owens Patton and Snyder-Yuly, 2007, pp. 859–95.

16 An example of a rape joke that critiques rape culture is Wanda Sykes' 'detachable pussy' joke: https://youtu.be/Jv5pjSRSLGQ (accessed 6.06.2024).

17 This is sexual assault! It is particularly heinous coming from the character of James Franco since, as I mentioned above, actor James Franco has, as of 2023, been accused by at least five women of sexually exploitative behaviour.

18 On Revelation and its reception in American popular culture as a 'revenge fantasy' of underdogs merely reversing existing modes of violent oppression against the oppressor, see Ricker, 2010, pp. 15–23.

PART 2

Rape and Sexual Violence in Ancient and Contemporary Contexts

8

Resistance, Rage and Re-enactment: Trauma Responses in the Sumerian Rape Narratives

RENATE MARIAN VAN DIJK-COOMBES

Introduction

The earliest known narratives about rape are from Mesopotamia, which is broadly speaking modern-day Iraq. These narratives were written in the Sumerian language and date to the Old Babylonian Period (c. 1894–1595 BC). There are three such narratives: *Enki and Ninḫursaĝa*,[1] in which the goddess Uttu[2] is raped by the god Enki; *Inana and Šukaletuda*,[3] in which the goddess Inana is raped by the mortal human gardener Šukaletuda; and *Enlil and Ninlil*,[4] in which the goddess Ninlil is raped by the god Enlil.[5]

Today there are various definitions of rape. For example, the Metropolitan Police of Greater London define 'rape' as 'when a person intentionally penetrates another's vagina, anus or mouth with a penis, without the other's consent'.[6] This definition is quite narrow in that only penile penetration is considered, and therefore only men can be perpetrators of rape. The United States Department of Justice has a more inclusive definition in which 'rape' is 'the penetration, no matter how slight, of the vagina or anus with any body part or object, or oral penetration by a sex organ of another person, without the consent of the victim'.[7] This definition is more inclusive in that not only penetration by a penis is considered, and therefore all sexes and genders may be the perpetrators of a rape. What is consistent in these definitions is the lack of consent of the victim.[8] In this chapter, rape will therefore be broadly defined as 'sexual penetration without consent',[9] following the modern understanding of the term. It must, however, be noted that in all three instances under discussion, penile penetration of the vagina occurs.

In Sumerian, the language in which the three narratives were written, the term for 'rape' is ĜIŠ AZIG, which literally means 'violence of the penis'.[10] This term, however, is not used in any of the three narratives under discussion to describe the sexual encounters that are recounted. Because none of the sexual activity in these narratives is explicitly said to be rape, there has been debate over whether these sexual encounters should be considered to be rape or not.[11] For example, Leick (1994, p. 51) has claimed that it is 'inappropriate' to call them rapes because the narratives in which they are portrayed concern the activities of deities, and human social conventions and understandings of terms should therefore not be applied.[12] Scurlock (2003) similarly concluded that the sexual intercourse in the narratives should not be considered to be rapes, but approached the question of rape differently. She asked of Ninlil's sexual experience in *Enlil and Ninlil*, 'But was it rape?', by analysing laws both ancient and modern. According to Scurlock, the concept of rape (as a legal matter and in the modern sense of the term) did not exist in Mesopotamia at the time when the laws were written. Instead, these narratives portray the 'ruination of an unmarried girl' in which an unmarried woman has sex and thereby becomes undesirable and 'ruined' for marriage (Scurlock, 2003, pp. 90, 103). In response to Scurlock, Gadotti (2009) answered 'Why it was rape' by arguing that there was indeed a concept of rape in Mesopotamia. She did this by analysing the same narrative (i.e. *Enlil and Ninlil*) in relation to the other Sumerian-language literary sources (i.e. *Enki and Ninḫursaĝa*, and *Inana and Šukaletuda*).[13] There has also been disagreement over the sexual intercourse in the individual narratives (see below).

For the purposes of this chapter, it is somewhat of a moot point whether the people of ancient Mesopotamia would have understood the sexual encounters in these three narratives to have constituted rape or not. By our modern understanding, they can be understood as rapes, because consent either is not or cannot be given (see below for each case). Therefore, instead of asking whether the acts of sexual intercourse were considered rapes at the time when the narratives were written, this chapter assumes that they are rapes in the modern sense of the word – sexual penetration without consent. Rather than questioning whether the sexual intercourse constituted rape, this chapter instead seeks to explore how the three victims are portrayed and how they behave after their sexual encounters. As such, it seeks to provide a psychological portrait of the three victims by analysing how they respond to and deal with the trauma of their rapes. This will allow for comparisons between the ways in which these three victims respond to their rapes and a modern understanding of trauma responses.

Rape can be defined as a traumatic event. Contemporary trauma theory seeks to understand the impact that trauma has on an individual (Goodman, 2017, p. 188). Morrow (2011, p. 281) defines trauma 'as (violent) stress that is sudden, unexpected, or nonnormative, exceeds the individual's perceived ability to meet its demands, and disrupts various psychological needs'. 'Trauma', however, does not only refer to the traumatic event, but also the emotional and psychological response to that event. As Van der Kolk (2014, p. 24) states, 'Trauma is not just an event that took place sometime in the past; it is also the imprint left by that experience on mind, brain, and body. This imprint has ongoing consequences for how the human organism manages to survive in the present.'[14] Trauma can have devastating and long-lasting effects on an individual's psyche which may include dissociation,[15] issues with attachment,[16] re-enactment(s),[17] and an impairment in emotional capacities (Goodman, 2017, pp. 187–8). In psychology, the development of these and other such symptoms after experiencing a traumatic event is recognized as 'post-traumatic stress disorder' (PTSD).[18]

This chapter will use contemporary trauma theory as a framework within which to analyse the three Sumerian rape narratives. I wish to stress that I am not trying to ascertain whether the people of ancient Mesopotamia would have viewed the women in these narratives as exhibiting symptoms of trauma;[19] instead, my intention is to show that such symptoms are nonetheless evident in the narratives. The three Sumerian rape narratives will each be discussed in turn: first *Enki and Ninḫursaĝa*, then *Inana and Šukaletuda*, and finally *Enlil and Ninlil*. First, a brief summary of the narrative will be given,[20] and thereafter the sexual violence and the victim's response to that violence will be discussed.

Enki and Ninḫursaĝa

Enki and Ninḫursaĝa takes place in the semi-mythical land of Dilmun. It chronicles a series of incestuous sexual relations between Enki and his successive daughters. Enki first has sex with the mother goddess Ninḫursaĝa, who gives birth to Ninnisig. Enki then has sex with Ninnisig, and she gives birth to Ninkura. He then has sex with Ninkura, who gives birth to Ninimma. He then has sex with Ninimma who gives birth to Uttu. Once Uttu comes of age, Ninḫursaĝa advises her against having sex with Enki. The text is unfortunately broken at this point, but when it resumes Enki disguises himself as a gardener and has sex with Uttu. She cries out in pain. Ninḫursaĝa then removes Enki's semen from Uttu's thigh or lower body[21] and discards it on the ground. Plants grow from the semen. Enki eats these plants and is cursed by Ninḫursaĝa. He then becomes ill and is in a lot of pain. Ninḫursaĝa then helps Enki to give birth to eight deities, each one from a part of his body that is in pain. The narrative ends with praise for Enki.

While the sexual encounters between Enki and Ninnisig, Ninkura, Ninimma and Uttu respectively are all clearly incestuous, there have been many differing opinions over whether one or all of these unions constitute rape.[22] These range from none of the sexual encounters in the narrative being rapes[23] to all of them being rapes,[24] and from all of the daughters except Uttu being raped[25] to Uttu being the only daughter raped by Enki.[26] I would argue that Uttu is raped, but that Enki's other daughters are not. The encounter with Uttu is told in some detail. Ninḫursaĝa advises Uttu not to have sex with Enki, and presumably this refusal is recounted in the lacuna.[27] In comparison, the descriptions of the sexual encounters between Enki and his other daughters are short and very formulaic, with each successive union being recounted almost verbatim. Enki sees his daughter, becomes aroused by the sight of her, embraces her, kisses her and has sex with her. She immediately falls pregnant and gives birth after nine days. Although consent is not explicitly stated in these encounters, they stand in contrast to Enki's union with Uttu.[28] Uttu has been advised to reject Enki, and there is therefore a lack of consent in their union. The detail with which Enki's sexual encounter with Uttu is told suggests that both the sexual intercourse and the rejection can be seen as extraordinary. Therefore, in comparison, the sexual unions between Enki and his other daughters constitute the norm. Because it is the norm and therefore expected, it is not necessary to recount the consent in these cases.[29]

The matter of Uttu's consent or lack thereof hinges upon line 186 of the narrative.[30] In this line, either while Enki and Uttu are having sex, or immediately after, she cries out, 'Ah! My thighs! (she cried out,) Ah! My body! Ah, my heart/belly!'[31] The Sumerian for 'ah!' or 'oh!' is the phonogram A, although A_2 has been used in this line. The Sumerian A is an interjection or expression of pain, and it can refer to both physical and moral pain (Attinger, 2019d, p. 1).[32] Attinger (1984, p. 43) has noted the play on words between A and A_2, which can mean power or force,[33] which further underlies the violence inherent in this sexual encounter. There may be further play on words, because A is also the sign for semen or sperm.[34] If this is the case, then Uttu's crying out 'ah!' encapsulates well the pain, the violence and the sexual nature of her encounter with Enki.

When Uttu cries out, she calls out the parts of her body that are in pain. These are her ḪAŠ₂, her BAR, and her ŠAG₄. ḪAŠ₂ is usually translated as 'thigh' (ePSD: HAŠ; Attinger, 2019d, p. 92), but it may also be translated as 'lower body' or 'abdomen' (ePSD: HAŠ). BAR refers to the body (ePSD: BAR; Attinger, 2019d, p. 20). ŠAG$_4$ is usually translated as 'heart', but may additionally refer to the belly (ePSD: ŠAG; Attinger, 2019d, p. 176). In Uttu's cry, ŠAG$_4$ has been translated by Dickson (2007, p. 18) as 'belly/womb' and by Attinger (1984, p. 23) as 'ventre', belly. The pain of the sexual intercourse is therefore centred around the area of Uttu's lower body, precisely the area that would be in pain during and after a rape.

Uttu's crying out in pain is her immediate reaction to her rape. After Ninḫursaĝa removes the semen from Uttu's thigh, Uttu is not mentioned again. Instead, the focus is on Enki. The plants that Enki eats are the direct result of his own semen which Ninḫursaĝa has wiped away from Uttu's thighs or lower body. His own pain is therefore indirectly caused by his rape of Uttu. While Uttu is not mentioned again, her crying out in pain is an apt representation of the pain that a rape victim may feel during and immediately after their rape.

Inana and Šukaletuda

In *Inana and Šukaletuda*, Šukaletuda is a somewhat inept human gardener: he is supposed to water his plants, but he pulls them up by the roots instead. After a long journey around the earth, Inana lays down in Šukaletuda's garden to rest, and she falls asleep in the shade of a Euphrates poplar tree. Šukaletuda sees her and recognizes her, and while she is sleeping he undresses her and has sex with her. When she wakes up, she realizes what has happened to her, and she determines to get justice. She sends three types of catastrophes as punishment and to try and flush out the perpetrator so that she may have that justice: first she fills the wells of the land with blood rather than water, thereafter she sends a massive storm to devastate the earth, and finally she blocks the roads, causing chaos. Each time Šukaletuda evades her with the help of his father by hiding in the city. Frustrated at not being able to find the perpetrator, Inana goes to her father Enki and pleads her case.[35] He agrees and allows Inana to find Šukaletuda, who is hiding in the mountains. Šukaletuda admits to Inana what he has done, and Inana determines his destiny. She puts him to death, but allows his name to live on in songs.[36]

If rape can be defined as sexual penetration without consent, then the sexual encounter between Inana and Šukaletuda must be a rape: she was asleep when it occurred and therefore could not consent.[37] Her reaction when she wakes up also points to this act being a violation.[38] After she wakes up, she inspects herself, and is outraged by what has happened. Immediately before Inana fills the well of the land with blood, lines 129–30 recount, 'this is what the woman destroyed because of her vagina; this is what pure Inana did because of her vagina',[39] making it clear that her actions are a direct reaction to her rape. These two lines are repeated before the next two catastrophes that she sends to devastate the land: the massive storm and blocking the roads.[40] These punishments are therefore a direct response to her rape, and a physical manifestation of her rage. Anger is one of the most common emotional reactions of rape victims, but the relationship between the two is also sorely under-studied (Harris, 2019, pp. 256–7). 'Heightened and even uncontrollable anger' (Lemos, 2015, p. 103) is also one of the most common emotional reactions to all types of trauma, and is a symptom of PTSD. It is further linked to other negative emotions like blame and disgust (Lemos, 2015, pp. 103–4, 120). This blame and disgust are evident in Inana's further actions: when none of the three plagues flush Šukaletuda out of hiding, Inana calls out, 'Oh! Who will compensate me? Oh! Who will repay me?'[41] These lines also express her desire for justice and revenge. As Goldner, Lev-Wiesel and Simon (2019, p. 2) state, 'The desire for revenge; namely, to cause the perpetrator to suffer, does not cease until it is recognized and released in one way or another. The greater the harm and transgression caused to the victim, the more the victim perceives the perpetrator's responsibility for the harm, the greater the desire for revenge.' The desire for revenge may also foster in the victim an 'obsession with the perpetrator and the hurt' (Simon, 2018, p. 3), which is evident in Inana's search for Šukaletuda, and the repeated references to what she did 'because of her vagina'. Inana's anger and desire for justice and revenge are also well portrayed in her sending of the three catastrophes, as well as her demand for restitution. She goes to her father Enki in his shrine in the Abzu,[42] and she implores him, 'Father Enki, something should be given, someone should pay! When this man has been delivered into my hands from the Abzu, I will return appeased to my shrine Eanna.'[43] When Inana cannot exact revenge herself, she desperately goes to Enki to seek justice. He allows her to find Šukaletuda and she is able to find peace through punishing him with death.

Inana (and her Akkadian counterpart Ištar) is the goddess of sexuality and warfare, and sex and violence are fundamental to both her character and this narrative. She is raped, and she is enraged at what happens, sending devastation to the earth. Her rage at her violation is well portrayed in the narrative. While her angry retaliation could be seen as an extension of her sphere of war and violence, this should not diminish the importance of her rage in this narrative. Inana's actions after her rape reflect the shock, anger and desperate yearning for justice or retribution that many rape victims feel: they are a response to the trauma of her rape.

Enlil and Ninlil

The final narrative is *Enlil and Ninlil* which begins in the city of Nippur, where Ninlil is a young woman. Her mother, Nisaba, advises her not to go to the river, because Enlil will see her and want to have sex with her. Ninlil disobeys her mother and goes to the river, where Enlil sees her and propositions her. She rejects him, stating that she is too young and still a virgin. Enlil ignores this and has sex with her. She becomes pregnant with the god Sîn. Enlil is arrested and banished from Nippur as punishment. As he leaves, he tells the gatekeeper not to tell Ninlil where he is. However, Ninlil follows Enlil, and Enlil, disguised as the gatekeeper, has sex with her. As a result, Ninlil becomes pregnant with the god Nergal-Meslamtaea. Enlil leaves again and goes to the Netherworld, where he tells the 'man of the river of the Netherworld' not to tell Ninlil where he is. Yet, Ninlil follows him once more, and again they have sex, this time with Enlil disguised as the 'man of the river of the Netherworld'. Ninlil becomes pregnant with the god Ninazu. Enlil leaves again, and tells the ferryman of the Netherworld not to tell Ninlil where he is. Again, Ninlil follows Enlil, and again they have sex, this time with Enlil disguised as the ferryman of the Netherworld. Ninlil falls pregnant for a fourth time, this time with the god Enbilulu. The narrative ends with praise for Enlil and Ninlil.[44]

In this narrative, the first sexual encounter between Ninlil and Enlil can be described as rape, because Ninlil has clearly and explicitly rejected Enlil – there is not only a *lack* of consent,[45] but Ninlil actively *does not consent* to having sex with Enlil. The matter of consent in the subsequent three sexual encounters is less clear. In each of these three encounters, it is Ninlil who propositions Enlil. However, Enlil is in disguise each time – first as the gatekeeper, then as the 'man of the river of the Netherworld', and finally as the ferryman of the Netherworld. There is no indication in the narrative whether Ninlil is aware that her sexual partner is Enlil or the man who he is impersonating in each instance. Therefore, while force is used in the first encounter, trickery and deception are used in the final three: although Ninlil ostensibly consents to these encounters, and indeed does instigate them, it is not clear to whom she is consenting.[46]

Cooper (1980, p. 180) describes *Enlil and Ninlil* as 'The psychological portrait of Ninlil, who followed the man who raped her, yet had to be tricked into repeated acts of intercourse with him, [and which] is an early attestation of the well-known ambivalence of the victim towards the oppressor, especially in sexual contexts.' Indeed, Ninlil's behaviour after her first sexual encounter with Enlil has many of the hallmarks of PTSD.

I propose that Ninlil's behaviour can be read as an example of 'hypersexuality' as a trauma response to her rape. Hypersexuality is 'a compulsive attitude towards sexual activities derived from a major psychological suffering' (Fontanesi et al., 2021, pp. 631–2) and is marked by the 'compulsive-like pursuit of sex to manage emotional dysregulation' (Wright, 2021, p. 236). The defining features of hypersexuality are 'the excess of sexual activities, the obsession of sex and the related consequences' (Fontanesi et al., 2021, p. 631). The way in which Ninlil follows Enlil and repeatedly has sex with him illustrates this well.

Furthermore, Ninlil's sexual encounters with Enlil after her initial rape may also be understood as 'repetition compulsion' or 're-enactments'. In these re-enactments, an individual who has been the victim of a traumatic event may recreate that past trauma, or elements of that past trauma, in the present (Levy, 1998, pp. 227, 228). While the traumatic event itself may be re-enacted, the repetitive behaviour may also include thoughts, images, emotions, feelings, dreams, flashbacks, and other types of behaviours (Bowins, 2010, p. 283; Levy, 2000, p. 46). These re-enactments are not necessarily conscious or a 'choice'; Chu (1992, p. 267) has theorized that they occur as a result of both a psychological and a biological need or compulsion. Regarding re-enactments of sexual trauma, Bowins (2010, p. 291) contends that a victim, particularly a victim who experienced the sexual trauma at a young age, 'sexualizes her relationships with men, having multiple casual encounters and no emotional investment from her partners'. This describes Ninlil and her subsequent sexual encounters with Enlil well. First, Ninlil cites her youth and sexual inexperience as her reasons for rejecting Enlil's advances:

> My vagina is too small, it does not know how to widen,
> My lips are too young, they do not know to kiss
> My mother would find out and she would hit my hand
> My father would find out and he will beat me
> Speaking to my girlfriend straight away, I'll stop existing to her.[47]

Ninlil's youth is further highlighted by her repeatedly being described in the narrative as a KI-SIKIL,[48] a young woman or virgin (ePSD: KISIKIL; Attinger, 2019d, p. 110). Ninlil therefore would be classified as a 'young victim' of sexual trauma, and may therefore have been more susceptible to developing this type of trauma response.

Second, when Enlil has been banished from Nippur and Ninlil follows him, she has sex three times, each time with Enlil who is in disguise. These can be described as 'casual encounters' with 'no emotional investment' on the part of her male companion – whether she sees through Enlil's disguises or not. That Enlil is not emotionally invested is evident from the way in which he keeps abandoning her and instructing first the gate keeper, then the 'man of the river of the Netherworld', and finally the ferryman of the Netherworld to lie to Ninlil about his whereabouts.[49] This ties in with hypersexuality where 'seeking sexual experiences can represent an attempt to forge a connection with someone (or one's self), where trauma has severed one's former familiarity with one's place in the world in relation to others' (Wright, 2021, p. 236). This is portrayed through Ninlil leaving behind what is familiar (i.e. her home in Nippur) to follow Enlil, trying to 'forge a connection' with him.

Fontanesi et al. (2021) find a relationship between trauma, hypersexuality, depression, shame and guilt. Similarly, Levy (1998, p. 206) notes that 'reenactments often lead to revictimization and related feelings of shame, helplessness, and hopelessness'. Nisaba, Ninlil's mother, specifically told her not to go to the river because Enlil would want to have sex with her, and Ninlil disobeyed her mother and went to the river, and was subsequently raped. Because Ninlil had been warned about what would happen, she may have feelings of self-blame, and would likely therefore have feelings of guilt and shame. Furthermore, she follows a man who keeps abandoning her, potentially reinforcing these feelings.[50] On the other hand, Bowins (2010, p. 292) notes that 'identification with the aggressor greatly distorts the experience such that some positive emotional reactions are linked to the trauma, as opposed to emotions like fear, shame, guilt and sadness that actually arose from the trauma'. If Ninlil identifies with Enlil and feels positive emotions towards him, it would explain well the psychological desire to follow him. However, his shunning of her may further traumatize her, and her repeatedly pursuing him may be indicative of complex trauma.

Ninlil's actions may also be reflective of an insecure attachment style, another hallmark of PTSD. Furthermore, Ciocca et al. (2021, p. 399) have found that insecure attachment styles played a fundamental role in the development of hypersexuality. They found that insecure attachment has a causal relation to hypersexuality, which means that people who have insecure attachment are more likely to become hypersexual. Ninlil's repeated following after Enlil who repeatedly shuns her does represent insecure attachment, albeit after the fact. Issues with attachment are a fundamental part of trauma. As Goodman (2017, p. 187) notes, complex trauma 'impacts a person's ability to develop healthy interpersonal relationships and to establish trust, leading to impairment in the abilities to form secured attachment with others'. Ninlil certainly displays these symptoms in her continued pursual of a man who repeatedly lies to her, has sex with her, and abandons her.

Ninlil's behaviour after her first sexual encounter with Enlil therefore exhibits a complex interweaving of hypersexuality, repetition compulsion (i.e. re-enactments) and an insecure attachment style. These combine to form a profound portrayal of a trauma response to sexual assault.

Conclusion

The three Sumerian rape narratives are the oldest known rape narratives. Although nearly 4,000 years old, they portray modern understandings of trauma and trauma responses, although each is different. Uttu's crying out in *Enki and Ninḫursaĝa* perfectly encapsulates the pain and anguish that a victim feels during rape and in its immediate aftermath, while simultaneously indicating the physical locus of that pain. Inana's reactions in *Inana and Šukaletuda* portray the consuming rage and yearning for justice and revenge that a victim of rape may feel. Ninlil's characterization in *Enlil and Ninlil* is the most complex of the three narratives. Hers is a profound depiction of hypersexuality, re-enactment(s) and impairment to attachment as trauma responses. They would not have been understood as such at the time, but these narratives represent accurate portrayals of what is now understood as complex psychological reactions to trauma. Despite being some of the oldest narratives in the world, they portray remarkably 'modern' understandings of trauma and trauma responses.

Bibliography

Abdul-Hamid, W. K., and J. Hacker Hughes, 2014, 'Nothing New Under the Sun: Post-Traumatic Stress Disorders in the Ancient World', *Early Science and Medicine* 19, pp. 1–9.

Alster, B., 1978, 'Enki and Ninhursag: The Creation of the First Woman', *Ugarit-Forschungen* 10, pp. 15–27.

Alster, B., 2005, *Wisdom of Ancient Sumer*, Bethesda, MD: CDL Press.

American Psychiatric Association, 2013, *Diagnostic and Statistical Manual of Mental Disorders*, 5th edn, Washington DC: American Psychiatric Publishing.

Asher-Greve, J. M., and J. G. Westenholz, 2013, *Goddesses in Context: On Divine Powers, Roles, Relationships and Gender in Mesopotamian Textual and Visual Sources*, Orbis Biblicus et Orientalis 259, Fribourg: Academic Press and Göttingen: Vandenhoeck & Ruprecht.

Attinger, P., 1984, 'Enki et Ninḫursaĝa', *Zeitschrift für Assyriologie und Vorderasiatische Archäologie* 74/1, pp. 1–52.

Attinger, P., 2019a. *Enki et Ninḫursaĝa (1.1.1)*. Zenodo, available at https://doi.org/10.5281/zenodo.2667747 (accessed 7.09.2023).

Attinger, P., 2019b, *Innana et Šukaleduda (1.3.3)*. Zenodo, available at https://doi.org/10.5281/zenodo.2599591 (accessed 7.09.2023).

Attinger, P., 2019c, *Enlil et Ninlil (1.2.1)*. Zenodo, available at https://doi.org/10.5281/zenodo.2667749 (accessed 7.09.2023).

Attinger, P., 2019d, *Lexique sumérien-français*. Zenodo, available at https://doi.org/10.5281/zenodo.2585683 (accessed 7.09.2023).

Behrens, H., 1978, *Enlil und Ninlil: Ein sumerischer Mythos aus Nippur*, Studia Pohl: Series Maior 8, Rome: Biblical Institute Press.

Besnier, M.-F., 2002, 'Temptation's Garden: The Gardener, a Mediator Who Plays an Ambiguous Part' in S. Parpola and R. M. Whiting (eds), *Sex and Gender in the Ancient Near East: Proceedings of the 47th Rencontre Assyriologique*, Helsinki: Neo-Assyrian Text Corpus Project, pp. 59–70.

Bowins, B., 2010, 'Repetitive Maladaptive Behavior: Beyond Repetition Compulsion', *The American Journal of Psychoanalysis* 70, pp. 282–98.

Chu, J. A., 1992, 'The Revictimization of Adult Women with Histories of Childhood Abuse', *The Journal of Psychotherapy Practice and Research* 1/3, pp. 259–69.

Ciocca, G. et al., 2021, 'Hypersexual Behavior and Attachment Styles in a Non-Clinical Sample: The Mediation Role of Depression and Post-Traumatic Stress Symptoms', *Journal of Affective Disorders* 293, pp. 399–405.

Cooper, J. S., 1980, 'Review of "Enlil und Ninlil: Ein sumerischer Mythos aus Nippur" by Behrens, H.', *Journal of Cuneiform Studies* 32/3, pp. 175–88.

Cooper, J. S., 1989, 'Enki's Member: Eros and Irrigation in Sumerian Literature' in H. Behrens, D. Loding and M. T. Roth (eds), *DUMU-E$_2$-DUB-BA-A: Studies in Honor of Åke W. Sjöberg*, Occasional Publications of the Samuel Noah Kramer Fund 11, Philadelphia: The University Museum, pp. 87–9.

Couto-Ferreira, M. E., 2021, 'Disturbing Disorders: Reconsidering the Problem of "Mental Diseases" in Ancient Mesopotamia' in U. Steinert (ed.), *Systems of Classification in Premodern Medical Cultures: Sickness, Health, and Local Epistemologies*, London; New York: Routledge, pp. 261–78.

Dickson, K., 2007, 'Enki and Ninhursag: The Trickster in Paradise', *Journal of Near Eastern Studies* 66/1, pp. 1–32.

Edzard, D. O., 2003, *Sumerian Grammar*, Handbook of Oriental Studies 71, Leiden; Boston: Brill.

Fontanesi, L. et al., 2021, 'Hypersexuality and Trauma: A Mediation and Moderation Model from Psychopathology to Problematic Sexual Behavior', *Journal of Affective Disorders* 281, pp. 631–7.

Frymer-Kensky, T., 1992, *In the Wake of the Goddesses: Women, Culture and the Biblical Transformation of Pagan Myth*, New York: Fawcett Columbine.

Gadotti, A., 2009, 'Why It was Rape: The Conceptualization of Rape in Sumerian Literature', *Journal of the American Oriental Society* 129/1, pp. 73–82.

Goldner, L., R. Lev-Wiesel and G. Simon, 2019, 'Revenge Fantasies After Experiencing Traumatic Events: Sex Differences', *Frontiers in Psychology* 10/886, pp. 1–9.
Goodman, R., 2017, 'Contempoary Trauma Theory and Trauma-informed Care in Substance Use Disorders: A Conceptual Model for Integrating Coping and Resilience', *Advances in Social Work* 18/1, pp. 186–201.
Harris, C., 2019, '"For Rage": Rape Survival, Women's Anger, and Sisterhood in Chaucer's Legend of Philomela', *The Chaucer Review* 54/3, pp. 253–69.
Jacobsen, T., 1976, *The Treasures of Darkness: A History of Mesopotamian Religion*, New Haven and London: Yale University Press.
Jacobsen, T., 1987, *The Harps that Once… Sumerian Poetry in Translation*, New Haven, CT; London: Yale University Press.
Kurtz, J. R., 2018, 'Introduction' in J. R. Kurtz (ed.), *Trauma and Literature*, Cambridge: Cambridge University Press, pp. 1–17.
Leick, G., 1994, *Sex and Eroticism in Mesopotamian Literature*, London; New York: Routledge.
Lemos, T. M., 2015, 'The Apotheosis of Rage: Divine Anger and the Psychology of Israelite Trauma', *Biblical Interpretation* 23, pp. 101–21.
Levy, M. S., 1998, 'A Helpful Way to Conceptualize and Understand Reenactments', *The Journal of Psychotherapy Practice and Research* 7/3, pp. 227–35.
Levy, M. S., 2000, 'A Conceptualization of the Repetition Compulsion', *Psychiatry* 63/1, pp. 45–53.
Mitchell, J., 2014, 'Dissociation' in D. A. Leeming (ed.), *Encyclopedia of Psychology and Religion*, 3rd edn, New York: Springer Reference, pp. 509–11.
Morrow, W., 2011, 'Deuteronomy 7 in Postcolonial Perspective: Cultural Fragmentation and Renewal' in B. E. Kelle, F. R. Ames and J. L. Wright (eds), *Interpreting Exile: Displacement and Deportation in Biblical and Modern Contexts*, Atlanta, GA: SBL Press, pp. 275–93.
Scurlock, J., 2003, 'But Was She Raped? A Verdict Through Comparison', *NIN: Journal for Gender Studies in Antiquity* 4, pp. 61–103.
Simon, G., 2018, 'Revenge Fantasies Following a Human-Made Hurtful Event: Women vs. Men', MA thesis, Haifa: University of Haifa.
Stol, M., 2016, *Women in the Ancient Near East*, Boston; Berlin: De Gruyter.
Van der Kolk, B., 2014, *The Body Keeps the Score: Mind, Brain and Body in the Transformation of Trauma*, London: Penguin Books.
Volk, K., 1995, *Inanna und Šukaletuda: Zur historisch-politischen Deutung eines sumerischen Literaturwerkes*, SANTAG 3, Wiesbaden: Harrassowitz Verlag.
Wright, J., 2021, 'The "Grey Area" of Consent: Understanding the Psychological Impacts of Trauma on Sexual Consent', PhD dissertation, University of Toronto, Canada.

Abbreviations

ePSD   Electronic Pennsylvania Sumerian Dictionary, available at http://psd.museum.upenn.edu/

ETCSL   Electronic Text Corpus of Sumerian Literature, available at https://etcsl.orinst.ox.ac.uk/

Notes

1 ETCSL 1.1.1. See Attinger, 1984, for the critical edition, and Attinger, 2019a, for the most recent translation.

2 Uttu, a goddess of weaving, is not to be confused with Utu, the sun god.

3 ETCSL 1.3.3. See Volk, 1995, for the critical edition, and Attinger, 2019b, for the most recent translation.

4 ETCSL 1.2.1. See Behrens, 1978, although somewhat outdated, for the critical edition of this narrative, and see Attinger, 2019c, for the most recent translation.

5 Brief summaries of these narratives will be given below.

6 Metropolitan Police, available at https://www.met.police.uk/advice/advice-and-information/rsa/rape-and-sexual-assault/what-is-rape-and-sexual-assault/ (accessed 1.12.2023).

7 The United States Department of Justice Archives, available at https://www.justice.gov/archives/opa/blog/updated-definition-rape (accessed 1.12.2023). A similar definition is followed by the Criminal Law (Sexual Offences and Related Matters) Amendment Act of the Republic of South Africa, No. 32, 2007, 'Any person ("A") who unlawfully and intentionally commits an act of sexual penetration with a complainant ("B"), without the consent of B, is guilty of rape.'

8 See, however, Wright, 2021 (especially pp. 165–97), for the complexities and 'messiness' of consent, particularly as related to traumatized individuals. Concerning 'consent', see also Steed Davidson's Chapter 6 in this volume.

9 This differs from the definition of rape provided by Gadotti (2009, pp. 73–4) when discussing the same narratives that I am, 'the act of forcing a woman or a man to submit to sexual intercourse against her or his will', in that force is not a prerequisite. Indeed, Gadotti's definition does not apply to all three narratives that she discusses, as she concedes regarding *Inana and Šukaletuda*, 'In this case, the rapist uses stealth rather than force' (Gadotti, 2009, p. 78).

10 See, for example, the *Instructions of Šuruppak*, ETCSL 5.6.1 line 62, DUMU LU₂-RA ĜIŠ₃ A₂-ZIG₃ NA-AN-E-EN KISAL-E BI₂-ZU-ZU which Alster (2005, p. 69) translates as 'Don't rape a man's daughter; the courtyard will find out about you', and which Stol (2016, p. 354) translates more literally as 'Do not commit violence of the penis on a man's daughter. The inner courtyard will get to know of it.'

11 There is also debate in the case of *Enki and Ninḫursaĝa* over which sexual encounters in the narrative should be considered to be rape (see below).

12 In this regard, Leick (1994, p. 51) is referring specifically to *Enki and Ninḫursaĝa* and *Enlil and Ninlil*.

13 According to Gadotti (2009, p. 73), 'a better way to interpret the rape of Ninlil is by comparing it with similar episodes in analogous compositions' – that is, literary texts rather than laws.

14 See, similarly, Kurtz, 2018, p. 2, who defines 'trauma' as 'a pathological mental and emotional condition, an injury to the psyche caused by catastrophic events, or by the threat of such events, which overwhelm an individual's normal response mechanisms'.

15 'Dissociation' is the 'splitting off of clusters of mental contents from conscious awareness' (American Psychiatric Association, 2013, p. 820) in which 'Streams of thought or consciousness are kept apart and communication between them is restricted, resulting in a discernible alteration in thoughts, feelings, or

actions' (Mitchell, 2014, p. 509). See Van der Kolk, 2014, pp. 77–9, for more on dissociation.

16 'Attachment' refers to an individual's ability to form an emotional bond in relationships.

17 For more on re-enactment(s), see below.

18 See American Psychiatric Association, 2013, pp. 271–80, for a full discussion on PTSD.

19 Indeed, see Couto-Ferreira, 2021, for an overview on the problems with the application of psychology to ancient Mesopotamian cuneiform sources. However, see, for example, Abdul-Hamid and Hacker Hughes, 2014, who argue that cases of PTSD were recorded in Mesopotamian sources. It must be noted that these cases of PTSD are all related to trauma in battle, and not to trauma of sexual assault.

20 These are not intended to be comprehensive retellings of the narratives, but instead summaries of the events that are relevant to the rapes.

21 Her ḪAŠ$_2$; see below for more on this term.

22 The same author may even have differing opinions. For example, Jacobsen first reads the narrative as Enki seducing Uttu with promises of marriage, after which he 'used her and left her' (Jacobsen, 1976, p. 113), and later states that Enki takes Uttu 'by force' (Jacobsen, 1987, p. 184) – in other words, he rapes her.

23 For example, as mentioned above, Leick (1994, p. 51) considers the term 'rape' to be 'inappropriate', arguing that the behaviour of deities should not be framed in human terms or morals, and Scurlock (2003) argues that the concept of rape did not exist at the time the narrative was composed. Frymer-Kensky (1992, pp. 22–3) similarly does not understand any of these sexual encounters as rape, but rather sees the narrative as an aetiology of marriage.

24 For example, Cooper (1989, pp. 88–9) and Dickson (2007, pp. 13–14), although Dickson (2007, p. 13, n. 16) couches this by stating that he uses 'the term "rape" advisedly, as a kind of shorthand for intercourse initiated by one partner without any *apparent* willingness on the part of the other' (Dickson's emphasis).

25 For example, Gadotti argues that Ninnisig, Ninkura and Ninimma were raped, but that Enki's encounter with Uttu was 'not an attempted rape, but rather a failed sexual encounter' (Gadotti, 2009, p. 76).

26 For example, Alster (1978) understands the narrative to recount a series of irregular sexual behaviours, which culminates in the rape of Uttu.

27 See also Gadotti, 2009, p. 75: 'It is clear that Uttu is advised about a specific course of action, which she duly follows.' If Uttu has been advised against having sex with Enki, her rejection of him would presumably have been recounted in the lacuna.

28 Besnier (2002, p. 62, n. 13) similarly suggests that 'consent is tacit at least' and that 'even if the text does not specify their reaction, we can assume they are not reluctant'.

29 Consent is also actively not given, and recounted as such, in *Enlil and Ninlil*; see below. It must be noted, however, that the willingness or lack thereof of Enki's other daughters is not recorded, and it is possible that these were also not consensual acts. Be that as it may, the sexual intercourse between Enki and Uttu can – and should – be understood as rape (at least in the modern sense of the word), as will become evident below.

30 See here especially Attinger, 2019a, p. 10, n. 57, 'L'hypothèse qu'Enki prend Uttu de force... est la seule à render compte de la l. 186, traduite de manière inexacte ou laisse en général non commentée ... par ceux qui pensent qu'Uttu était consentante.'

31 ETCSL 1.1.1 line 186, A₂? ḪAŠ₂-ĜU₁₀ IM-ME A₂? BAR-ĜU₁₀ A₂? ŠA₃?-BA-ĜU₁₀ IM-[ME].

32 In this regard, see, for example, Attinger, 1984, p. 23, who translates the phonogram as 'hélas', and Edzard (2003, p. 167) who renders it as 'woe' or 'ouch'.

33 ePSD: A 'arm; labor; wing; horn; side; strength; wage; power'; Attinger (2019d, p. 4), 'bras, force, vigueur; tranchant'. Attinger (1984, p. 43) records it as 'bras; force'.

34 ePSD: A 'water; semen; progeny'; Attinger (2019d, p. 1), 'eau, boisson; semence, sperme'.

35 Enki is not consistently Inana's father in the Mesopotamian thought-world; more commonly her father is Nanna or An.

36 Šukaletuda's name living on is not necessarily a blessing: it probably means 'covered in warts' (Volk, 1995, p. 171), and he is therefore to be remembered by an insult.

37 Contrast with Leick, 1994, p. 53, who argues that Inana was not angry because she was raped, but because she is the goddess of sexual love, 'the hubris is his [i.e. Šukaletuda's] failure to give her pleasure' and that 'intercourse during a deep sleep is not what she [i.e. Inana] would call an erotic experience worth having'. In other words, Leick believes that the problem is not that Inana was raped, but that she did not enjoy the sex.

38 See, similarly, Gadotti, 2009, p. 77, 'That this was not consensual sex is proven by Inana's reaction when she wakes up.'

39 ETCSL 1.3.3 lines 129–130 UD-BA MUNUS-E NAM GAL₄-LA-NA-ŠE₃ A-NA IM-GU-LU-U₈-A-BI / KUG ᴰINANA-KE₄ NAM GAL₄-LA-NA-ŠE₃ A-NA IM-AK-A-BI. The Sumerian GALA (GAL₄-LA) refers to female genitals (ePSD: GALA) and can be translated as either 'vulva' or 'vagina' (Attinger, 2019d, p. 60). I have chosen to use 'vagina' instead of 'vulva' because the vagina is the focus of rape, not the vulva.

40 ETCSL 1.3.3 lines 185–6 and 214–15 respectively. The lines are also repeated by Šukaletuda to his father in lines 168–9, 197–8 and 224–5, although with minor variation.

41 ETCSL 1.3.3 lines 242–4 E ĜA₂-A A-BA-A MA-AB-SIG₁₀-GE / E ĜA₂-A A-BA-A MA-AB-AĜ₂-E

42 The Abzu is the subterranean waters, and the home of Enki.

43 ETCSL lines 247–8 A-A ᴰEN-KI ḪE₂-EN-GA-MU-E-/SIG₁₀\ {/ḪE₂-EN\-GA-MU-E-AĜ₂} / LU₂-BI ABZU-TA ŠA-ĜA₂ U₄-MU-E-RE-ZE₂-EĜ₃/ EŠ₃ E₂-AN-NA-ĜU₁₀-ŠE₃ ZE₂-BA-BI DA-AN-KUR₉.

44 Although there are 11 lines of praise for Enlil, and only one for Ninlil. See also Asher-Greve and Westenholz, 2013, p. 147, 'The final passage contains a four-fold praise for Enlil but nothing equivalent for Ninlil.'

45 As, for example, in *Inana and Šukaletuda* where there is no consent because Inana is asleep and therefore cannot consent.

46 Note also Scurlock, 2003, p. 66, n. 27, 'It is, of course, perfectly conceivable that Ninlil recognized her lover and played along in the spirit of fun and/or to help him deceive the queen of the netherworld.' While 'conceivable', this is conjecture

as there is no indication in the narrative that this was the case, nor that either was necessarily having 'fun'.

47 ETCSL 1.2.1 lines 30–4 GAL$_4$-LA-ĜU$_{10}$ TUR-RA-AM$_3$ PEŠ$_{11}$ NU-MU-UN-ZU / ŠU-UM-DU-UM-ĜU$_{10}$ TUR-RA-AM$_3$ ŠE SU-UB NU-UN-ZU / AMA-ĜU$_{10}$ BA-ZU-ZU ŠU-ĜU$_{10}$ MU-UN-SAG$_3$-GE / AD-DA-ĜU$_{10}$ BA-ZU-ZU ŠU SA$_2$-BI MU-UN-E / A-DA-LAM MA-LA-RA DUG$_4$-GA-ĜU$_{10}$-UŠ NU-ME-E BA-NA-SILIG-GE-EN. I follow Attinger's (2019c, p. 27, n. 77) translation of the final line.

48 ETCSL 1.2.1 lines 11, 13, 38, 64, 92 and 118.

49 See also Asher-Greve and Westenholz, 2013, p. 147, 'Ninlil is described as a girl dismissing her mother's advice, becoming pregnant and *pursuing a lover who shuns her*' (my emphasis).

50 See, for example, Van der Kolk, 2014, p. 37, 'Repetition leads only to further pain and self-hatred. In fact, even reliving the trauma in therapy may reinforce preoccupation and fixation.'

9

Things Too Indecent to be Recorded: The Soldiers Mocking the Death of Herod Agrippa

DAVID TOMBS

Introduction

Herod Agrippa – known as Agrippa I (c. 11 BC–AD 44) – lived a tumultuous life.[1] Josephus acknowledges this when he says, 'It may also be edifying to tell the story of Agrippa, which is in the highest degree remarkable' (*Ant.* 18.129).[2] Well-known events from Agrippa's life in Rome are included in the popular BBC television series *I Claudius* (1976), which is based on the two fictionalized historical novels by Robert Graves: *I, Claudius* (1934), and *Claudius the God* (1935). The focus of this chapter is on an event that is less well-known. It looks at the public mockery that Josephus says accompanied Agrippa's death and explores how this incident is instructive in terms of how indecent acts were narrated in the ancient world, and how this can supply contextual detail for understanding the opportunities for sexualized violence during the mockery of Jesus by a cohort of soldiers in the *praetorium* (Mark 15.15–20; Matt. 27.26–31).

When Agrippa was a teenager, he moved with his mother to Rome in about AD 5 and grew up in the Augustan court. In AD 37, in his late forties, he was made king and ruled over some of the territories that had previously been ruled by his grandfather Herod the Great (37 BC–4 BC). Additional territories in Palestine were granted to him in AD 39 (Galilee and Perea) and AD 41 (Judea, Samaria and Idumea). By the time of his death in AD 44 he ruled over a significant territory as a client king for the Romans. Josephus praises him as a wise ruler who benefited both the Jewish and non-Jewish populations of his kingdom.[3] He seems to have enjoyed the confidence of the emperor Claudius and, according to Josephus, he managed to remain on good terms with Rome and do well for his subjects. He died in Caesarea in AD 44 as a result of a violent illness, or possible poisoning, that lasted five days. His death is described in Acts 12.20–23, and *Ant.* 19.343–52. After news of Agrippa's painful death broke, both he and his daughters were subjected to a dramatic display of public hostility. Josephus records in his *Jewish Antiquities* (written in c. AD 93) that the townspeople and soldiers of Caesarea and Sebaste celebrated his death with hostile open mockery. To express their hatred for Agrippa, soldiers set up statues of Agrippa's young daughters on the roofs of brothels, and offered them 'every possible kind of insult, doing things too indecent to be reported' (*Ant.* 19.358). This chapter examines two notable lacunae in relation to the Josephus passage and suggests how awareness of these two lacunae might, in turn, help recognition of another possible lacuna in the mockery of Jesus.

The first lacuna is signalled by Josephus himself. It is explicitly indicated in his statement that some of the soldiers' actions were 'too indecent to be reported' (*Ant.* 19.358). Although the reticence of Josephus means that specific details in the mockery remain unclear, he leaves little doubt that the soldiers' insults against the statues took a sexual form. The first lacuna stems from the offensive nature of these abuses and is indicative of how sexualized violence was often only referenced obliquely when narrated in antiquity.

The second lacuna to be addressed is the relative neglect and/or misrepresentation of the passage in New Testament studies. Biblical scholars have shown surprisingly little interest in the Josephus passage and some of what has been written is perplexing. This second lacuna shows the lack of attention that the first lacuna has received.

With these two lacunae in mind, I turn in the second part of this chapter to consider how both the mockery itself and the fact that it has been largely overlooked might help towards a better understanding of the mocking of Jesus during his crucifixion. How might the outrageous acts in the Josephus passage illuminate the biblical texts? Might the lacuna that is explicit in Josephus' account of Agrippa's mockery point to a possible lacuna – the third lacuna considered in this chapter – that covers insults 'too indecent to be reported' in the mocking of Jesus?

This third lacuna is of particular interest to me because in other work I have argued that modern torture reports and recent testimonies of prisoner abuse can offer a helpful lens to consider the mistreatment of Jesus in the *praetorium* and during crucifixion. I suggest torture reports help to understand Roman crucifixion as a form of torture, an instrument of sexual violence, and an open opportunity for sexual harm (Tombs, 1999; Tombs, 2023a). Modern torture reports have much to offer on how soldiers frequently abuse, mock and mistreat their victims during detention and/or torture, and sexual violence often plays a prominent role in this mockery and humiliation (Tombs, 2023b). However, modern reports must always be used with caution when used to interrogate past events. They cannot reveal anything directly about Jesus' own experience, but they can encourage generative questions about neglected aspects in the narratives. These neglected aspects can then be investigated further. Josephus' description of the mockery of Agrippa is significant because it narrates the disturbing behaviour of soldiers who were very close in time and place and background to the soldiers involved in the mockery of Jesus. Josephus' account of Agrippa's mockery therefore offers an especially valuable contextual resource for a consideration of the soldiers' mockery of Jesus. As an historical account Josephus must be used with caution since he wrote with biases and interests. Nonetheless, his account in *Jewish Antiquities* deserves more attention than it has so far received, and is valuable both for what it explicitly says and for what it intentionally omits and leaves to the imagination of the reader.

The mockery following Agrippa's death

In *Jewish Antiquities*, Josephus describes the public celebrations in Caesarea and Sebaste that met the news of Agrippa's death. He writes (*Ant.* 19.353–59):

> But when it became known that Agrippa had departed this life, the people of Caesarea and of Sebaste, forgetting his benefactions, behaved in the most hostile fashion. They hurled insults, too foul to be mentioned, at the deceased; and all who were then on military service – and they were a considerable number – went off to their homes, and seizing the images of the king's daughters carried them with one accord to the brothels, where they set them up on the roofs and offered them every possible sort of insult, doing things too indecent to be reported. Moreover, they reclined in the public places and celebrated feasts for all the people, wearing garlands and using scented unguents; they poured libations to Charon, and exchanged toasts in celebration of the king's death.

The general picture offered in this passage is clear enough but many of the specific details are left unexplained. For example, the townspeople are described as behaving 'in the most hostile fashion' and hurling insults 'too foul to be mentioned'. Josephus makes their antagonism to Agrippa clear, while leaving the exact words and actions quite vague. However, for the purpose of this chapter, it is the insults of the soldiers – rather than the townspeople – that are particularly relevant. For the soldiers, Josephus also provides some important details but still leaves some things unsaid – indeed, things apparently unspeakable. He explains that the soldiers seized the images – most likely statues – of Agrippa's daughters and set them up on the roofs of the brothels. The soldiers then offered 'every possible sort of insult'. What this involved is left largely to the imagination of the reader, but the mention of brothels strongly suggests a sexual dimension to the insults, even though exactly what was involved is not spelt out. To add to the complexity, Josephus makes clear that his sense of propriety has caused him to deliberately omit some of the most offensive details. He refers to these as 'things too indecent to be reported'. The word *porneia*, translated as 'indecent', reinforces the impression that the mockery took a sexual form. However, Josephus is intentionally reticent on what exactly was involved. Thus, while there can be little doubt that Josephus understood the mockery as both publicly performed and offensively sexualized, the reader is left to imagine the specifics of how this might have been enacted.

Public insults against Agrippa's daughters would have been a powerful way to mock the deceased king as well as the daughters. Josephus provides the ages of Agrippa's children in the sentences just before this passage. The young age of the three daughters further reinforces the offensiveness of the scene (*Ant.* 19.354):

> He [Agrippa I] left one son Agrippa [II], in his seventeenth year, and three daughters. Of these, one, Berenice, who was sixteen years old, was married to Herod [Chalcis] her father's brother, and two were unmarried, namely Mariamme and Drusilla, aged respectively ten and six years.[4]

Whatever Josephus is alluding to as 'unspeakable' therefore seems to have involved sexualized insults directed against – or upon – the statues (or images) of a teenager and two even younger girls. While the immediate targets are the statues and the three daughters they represent, Josephus presents the primary target of the mockery as Agrippa himself. Both the statues and the daughters are a way for the soldiers to express their hatred and bitterness against Agrippa.

In *The Herods: Murder, Politics, and the Art of Succession*, Bruce Chilton (2021, p. 207) suggests that the soldiers 'raped and sodomized' the effigy of Berenice. It is not clear why Chilton only mentions Berenice (also spelt as Bereniké) at this point. The clear implication in the Josephus passage is that the statues of all three daughters were insulted in the same way, because the Josephus text reads 'daughters' (plural). However, Chilton makes no mention of Mariamme or Drusilla. A comment Chilton offers on Berenice a few pages earlier risks suggesting that Berenice was in some way to blame for the insults to which she was subjected. Chilton notes that the soldiers set up the statues of the daughters for public humiliation, but he then singles out Berenice. He writes:

> The defamation of Bereniké was grotesque. Having been married off twice in order to further Agrippa's connections, the sixteen-year-old was a ready target for the crowds' outlandish attacks. She was dismissed as a whore and her father as a pimp in obscene pantomimes with the statues posed in various sexual positions in displays of violation. (Chilton, 2021, p. 207)[5]

The young ages of Mariamme and Drusilla might make it harder to impute such victim-blaming against them. This could explain why Chilton's account identifies Berenice but omits the outrages against the younger daughters, even though there is no justification for this distinction in the Josephus passage.[6]

The uncertainty as to how exactly the soldiers insulted the statues can be considered further in light of a story associated with the statue of Aphrodite of Knidos. This statue was sculpted by Praxiteles in c. 360 BC and is recognized as the first nude female Greek statue (Havelock, 1995; Beard, 2018). It was created at a time when heroic male figures might be depicted nude in Greek sculptures but there were no nude female figures. According to Pliny, the statue was originally offered to Kos but the people of Kos felt a nude female statue was too scandalous and opted instead for a clothed alternative (Spivey, 1999, p. 205). The naked Aphrodite statue was therefore offered to Knidos (a Greek town on the western coast of Turkey and also known as Cnidus) instead. It was housed in a temple shrine and became a major attraction and was copied and imitated in other statues. Sadly, the original statue has not survived but the many copied images give a good sense of the original.[7] Aphrodite is fully nude and seems to be captured as if emerging from her bath. In her left hand, she holds a towel or sheet in front of her. At the same time, her right hand partially covers her breasts. The statue therefore reveals at the same time as it conceals (Beard, 2018, p. 88).

Many visitors travelled to Knidos to behold the beauty of Aphrodite. A strange tale of three friends, Lycinus, Charicles and Callicratidas, who visited the statue is included in Lucian's *Amores*.[8] This second-century book is also known as *Erotes* or, in English, as 'Affairs of the Heart', or 'Loves', or 'Two Kinds of Love'. It is a contest dialogue traditionally attributed to the satirist Lucian of Samosata (c. 120 to after c. AD 190), but usually seen as likely to be Pseudo Lucian. *Amores* (11–19) recounts that the three travellers wishing to see the statue arrived at Knidos and made their way to the Temple of Aphrodite (*Amores*, 11). After admiring the statue from the front, they wished to see her also from behind (*Amores*, 13). A female temple attendant opened a door to allow them to do this. The three men then admired the statue from behind and remarked on its beauty (*Amores*, 14). At this point, they noticed a blemish on one of Aphrodite's thighs just under her buttock. At first, they supposed that this must have been an imperfection in the marble that Praxiteles had skilfully sculpted around. However, the woman attendant who had admitted them corrects them by telling 'a strange, incredible story' (*Amores*, 15). She recounts that a young man from a distinguished family had often visited the precinct and fallen in love with the statue. He became so inflamed that one night when the Temple was closing he concealed himself inside the Temple when its door was locked. He then consummated his passion with the statue. The next morning 'the marks of his amorous embraces' were discovered on the statue (*Amores*, 16).

The dialogue frames the story in terms of the young man's love inflaming his uncontrollable sexual desire. However, the man's subsequent sense of shame, and some of the language of the attendant, suggest at least some awareness on the author's part that this is not a harmless story of unrequited love and innocent ardour. The attendant speaks of 'the reckless deed of that unmentionable night' and 'the goddess had that blemish to prove what she'd suffered'. The young man's name has not been preserved and it is said that 'his deed has caused him to be left nameless'. As Mary Beard (2018, p. 90) points out, the story is not a harmless romantic tale. It should be read as a tale of sexual violence and rape: 'It shows how a female statue can drive a man mad but also how art can act as an alibi for what was – let's face it – rape. Don't forget, Aphrodite never consented.'

Although the image was a stone sculpture the young man's forceful action was understood by the attendant and those who discovered the marks (and by the young man himself) as a violation of the goddess.[9] A statue was not seen as dead stone or marble, but a meaningful representation of the figure it depicted. The young man is so ashamed that he forced himself on a goddess in this way that he takes his own life by jumping from a high cliff into the sea. He is said to utterly vanish in the waves (*Amores*, 16).

Despite some clear differences between the behaviour of the young man and the behaviour of the soldiers, the story in *Amores* is suggestive in a number of ways. First, it gives an example of how sexualized acts with statues might be performed. Second, it shows how in antiquity these acts were likely to be viewed as violations of the person (or goddess) the statue represented. Third, it illustrates how sexual violence can be narrated in ways that require an attentive reading if the elements of violence are to be properly acknowledged.

The mockery of Agrippa in modern and ancient scholarship

In view of Agrippa's status as a Jewish king, and the severity of the mockery directed against him through the mockery of his daughters, it might be supposed that biblical scholars would give this passage quite detailed treatment in discussions of the mockery of Jesus. It could be read as a salutary warning of just how far soldiers in Palestine might go in their offensive mockery. However, the passage has received relatively little attention.[10]

Chilton is unusual in giving the mockery in AD 44 explicit attention but, as noted above, some questions might be raised as to why he limits his comments to Berenice. His treatment borders on blaming Berenice for being a target and does little to interrogate the actions of the soldiers.

The distinguished scholar Raymond Brown falls short in his treatment of the passage in a different way. He lists the mockery of Agrippa as described by Josephus as relevant to the mockery of Jesus, but his summary of the event is very limited. He writes: 'The people of Caesarea on the Palestinian coast and of Samaria quickly forgot his benefactions and indulged in public mockery of him, wearing garlands and using perfumes' (Brown, 1994, pp. 874–5). To focus on the problem of the mockery as the 'wearing of garlands and using perfumes', and not make any mention of the insults against the statues, serves to erase the sexualized violence that Josephus reports.

In his commentary on Matthew, Ulrich Luz starts his discussion in a promising way by describing the Josephus passage as 'historically the closest parallel' for understanding the mockery of Jesus in Matthew 27.26–31 (Luz, 2005, p. 513). Furthermore, Luz notes that both the mockery of Jesus and the mockery of Agrippa involve mocking 'the King of the Jews'. In addition, Luz recognizes a crucial connection in that both scenes involve 'the same non-Jewish auxiliary troops' (Luz, 2005, p. 513). However, despite making these three important points, Luz omits any specific mention of the statues or the sexualized insults. The result is that the disturbing issue of sexual violence in the Agrippa mockery is erased, and the opportunity to draw sexual violence as a potentially relevant context for a consideration of the mockery of Jesus is lost.[11] This erasure may be unintentional, but it reflects an important dynamic that serves to marginalize sexual violence as an issue.

The poor representation and relative silence on the Josephus passage in recent biblical scholarship can be contrasted with at least one example of it being given candid attention in earlier times. Photios, the ninth-century patriarch of Constantinople, stands out in this regard. Photios was a leading scholar of his day and undertook to compile a *Bibliotheca* or collection of ancient writings, which mainly featured significant extracts or abridgements of ancient works. Most of the 280 volumes he gathered have been lost. However, in what remains there is the passage from Josephus on the mockery of Agrippa (*Cod.* 238). In this version of the text, Photios appears to have added his belief that it was not the statues, but the daughters themselves who were abused by the soldiers. There is no reason to believe that Photios had any evidence for this interpretation beyond the passage in Josephus. The alteration he presents makes the passage even more disturbing, but it is hard to believe that Claudius would have been so lenient to the soldiers if the outrage had taken the form Photios suggests (see more on the reaction of Claudius below). None the less, the version offered by Photios is important as a historical record of what a significant church leader saw as believable when reading an ancient source, and might be how he understood the lacuna that Josephus says is in the passage.

Reading the mockery of Agrippa alongside the mockery of Jesus

The relevance of the mockery of Agrippa for the mockery of Jesus has been recognized in previous work but has not been discussed in depth (Tombs, 2023a, pp. 38–9; Tombs, 2023b). In this section, I suggest that addressing this lacuna in the scholarly literature can make a helpful contribution to a new area of discussion on sexualized elements in the mistreatment of Jesus.

Recent work has argued for acknowledgement of Jesus as a victim of sexualized violence (Reaves, Tombs and Figueroa, 2021). The stripping and forced naked exposure of Jesus on the cross is recorded in all four Gospels. This provides clear grounds for identifying Jesus as a victim of sexual violence or sexual abuse. This understanding is further supported, and its importance reinforced, by the additional strippings recorded by Mark (15.15–20) and Matthew (27.26–31) that Jesus experienced in the *praetorium* (Tombs, 2020).

Beyond this clearly attested evidence, there is a further question on whether or not there may have been additional sexual violence beyond the stripping and exposure. The likelihood of this additional violence is much harder to assess because it is not directly attested in the text. However, the historical possibility that there might have been further violence in the *praetorium*, or at the cross, that is omitted in the biblical narration can hardly be dismissed as irresponsible speculation (Tombs, 2021, 2022, 2023a).[12] A naked man in the hands of a cohort of soldiers would have been an open invitation to additional violence. Many examples can be given from recent times that support the concern that a prisoner who is stripped and subjected to forced nudity may also be subjected to other forms of sexual violence (Human Rights Watch, 2013, p. 39). Although this additional violence is not explicitly attested to in the stripping of Jesus, this lack of direct attestation is not unusual. Even when sexual violence is known to have taken place it is often absent in modern reports (Tombs, 2006). It is quite common for sexual violence to be omitted from written records or to be referenced with reticence or indirectly through euphemisms (Human Rights Watch, 2013, p. 22).

During Jesus' time as a detainee, he was in a position of extreme vulnerability. The possibility of further violence – beyond the stripping and forced nudity – therefore requires critical investigation. As in modern times, it would not be strange for explicit mention of disturbing acts to be omitted or understated in ancient sources. References to sexual violence were 'obscene' in the literal sense that they should be left 'off-scene' or mentioned only very discreetly. Ancient authors observed a widely shared convention and etiquette around this. As Hultin says:

> From such diverse individuals as Democritus, Isocrates, the author of the *Rhetorica ad Alexandrum Charondas*, and Aeiius Aristides, we find the warning that what was shameful to do was shameful also to mention. According to Herodotus, the Persians had forbidden even naming those things they ought not do. (Hultin, 2008, p. 186)

Since shameful acts would typically go unmentioned or understated it was left to the reader to be attentive and pick up on discreet clues. In the biblical accounts of the mocking of Jesus, it is possible that oblique clues are offered in the same wording used for the mocking as for the abuse of the Levite's wife in Judges 19 in the Septuagint (Tombs, 2021, pp. 155–7). This terminology may also echo the death of Saul and his fear of sexualized violence at the hands of the Philistines (Thiede, 2022, pp. 79–80).

If used carefully, modern torture reports can help develop this critical awareness. For example, attention to what is often left unsaid in reports of modern torture can frame questions to guide a more critical investigation of silences and omissions in ancient sources. In particular, three modern features of prisoner mistreatment offer lessons that might be useful when enquiring about Jesus' experience. First, sexualized violence is so common in recent torture that it cannot be considered odd or exceptional. Rather, it should be viewed as routine and normalized. It can be described as a 'standard operating procedure' in recent times. The purpose of this violence is less likely to involve sexual gratification and much more likely to be intended to humiliate, degrade and psychologically damage. As the Iranian filmmaker and activist Shirin Neshat (cited by Jansen, 2023) explains: 'Once you're captured and in the hands of the government, they want to break you – and the way to break you is to psychologically destroy you by sexually violating you.' Sexual violence in detention should not be viewed as surprising. Second, although sexualized violence is well known as a prevalent element in contemporary torture it commonly remains unspeakable. Victims are often unwilling to speak of their torture in anything but general terms, and they frequently self-censor the acts of sexualized violence or refer to these experiences without naming them directly as sexual (Human Rights Watch, 2013, p. 22). A victim's sense of private humiliation is commonly reinforced by a sense of public shame and the victim may feel a burden of stigma if their experience is named. Third, those who hear and record accounts of torture may designate sexualized violence under the more generic heading of torture. This more generic categorization may be well intended to protect those who report it but it usually reduces the visibility of sexualized violence. These three concerns drawn from modern reports – that sexualized violence during detention should not be seen as surprising, that reticence and silence often impact reporting, and that there are further opportunities for sexual violence to be erased by the way it is recorded – can be used to re-read the crucifixion accounts. Each of these concerns can be identified in the mocking of Agrippa as discussed earlier. Josephus disapproves of the soldiers, but he does not feel the need to explain their behaviour; he narrates the passage in a way that leaves the most disturbing details unclear, and modern scholars will often further erase the most troubling aspects of his account.

The soldiers of Caesarea and Sebaste

To further appreciate the relevance of Agrippa's mockery for an understanding of the mockery of Jesus it is helpful to examine the connection between the soldiers involved in the two incidents, and their standing in the military and political landscape of first-century Palestine. In Matthew 27.27 the soldiers are described as 'the soldiers of the governor'. However, there is more to this than first appears. The 'soldiers of the governor' in Matthew 27.27 were comprised of auxiliaries recruited locally in Palestine and drawn especially from the non-Jewish populations in Caesarea and Sebaste.

Christopher Zeichmann (2018, pp. 1–21; 2019, p. xi) explains that the soldiers who served the Roman Empire in the area belonged to three different groups. First, there were the Roman legionaries; they were Roman citizens and recruited primarily from Italy. In the Eastern Empire, the legions that oversaw Palestine were based in Syria and Egypt. The legionaries were involved in the conquest of Palestine by Pompey in 63 BC and assisted Herod the Great and his forces in the campaign against Antigonus in 37 BC. They also returned when there was major trouble following the death of Herod in 4 BC. Apart from that, legionaries had little further involvement in Palestine until the outbreak of the Jewish War starting in AD 66.

A second category of soldiers was the locally recruited Roman auxiliaries. Auxiliaries were often garrisoned with the legions as support on threatened frontiers. During major campaigns, auxiliary cohorts would typically accompany and fight alongside the legions. Auxiliaries could also be tasked with the oversight of law and order in more peaceful territories. This allowed the legions to concentrate their presence on areas of greatest need. From AD 6 to AD 41, Judea and Samaria were under direct imperial rule by a Roman prefect.[13] During this time, and through to the outbreak of the revolt in AD 66, there was little need for interventions into Palestine by the legions based in Syria. It is probable that there were barely any legionaries in Palestine during this period of direct administration. The Roman prefects who oversaw Judea, Samaria and Idumea commanded five cohorts, usually based in Caesarea. When the prefect travelled to Jerusalem, he took a cohort with him. These soldiers were locally recruited auxiliaries rather than Italian legionaries. Most of the recruitment came from non-Jewish populations in Caesarea and Sebaste. The pay and conditions for auxiliaries was not as favourable as for legionaries, but one of the attractions for serving as an auxiliary was the promise of Roman citizenship after 25 years of service.

The third type of soldier, the royal troops, was found in territories ruled by client kings. Under Herod the Great, Herodian royal troops maintained the peace and could assist in Roman campaigns if needed, but they were under Herodian authority, not under direct Roman authority. The pay, conditions and career prospects of these royal troops might vary depending on which client king they served, but generally they would not have been as favourable as the pay and conditions of Roman auxiliaries, even though the service they gave might be very similar. Of particular importance was that, unlike the auxiliaries, royal troops did not automatically qualify for Roman citizenship after their service.

When Pilate (c. AD 26 to c. AD 36) travelled to Jerusalem for Passover in the year that Jesus was crucified (c. AD 30 to AD 33) the soldiers who accompanied him were almost certainly Roman auxiliaries and largely drawn from the non-Jewish populations of Caesarea and Sebaste. When Pilate handed Jesus over to 'the soldiers of the governor' (Matt. 27.27), he was handing Jesus over to about 500 auxiliary soldiers (a 'whole cohort') who probably had special hostility towards a Jewish king.

While there are still questions on how auxiliary soldiers were deployed in territories like Judea and Samaria, the evidence from Josephus suggests a strong connection between the soldiers involved in the mocking of Agrippa and the mocking of Jesus. When Claudius granted oversight of Judea, Samaria and Idumea to Agrippa in AD 41 the local auxiliaries would probably have been redesignated as Agrippa's royal troops. The close association in both incidents between the soldiers involved and the cities of Caesarea and Sebaste explains Luz's comment that both the mocking of Jesus and the mocking of Agrippa involved 'the same non-Jewish auxiliary troops' (Luz, 2005, p. 513). The troops were essentially the same but in c. AD 30 they were serving Pilate as auxiliaries whereas in AD 44 they were serving Agrippa as royal troops.

Josephus gives no explanation for why the townspeople and soldiers of Caesarea and Sebaste were so hostile towards Agrippa. The antagonism of non-Jewish soldiers to a Jewish king would explain some hostility. In addition, if the soldiers who served the Roman prefect had enjoyed the status of auxiliaries since AD 6, and some veterans had benefited from the achievement of citizenship for the completion of their 25 years, the transfer of serving troops to Agrippa in AD 41 had likely been a devastating blow. Those who were near the end of their 25-year term would have been especially bitter that the prize that was so close had been taken from them and the future would have been less certain for all the soldiers. The non-Jewish populations in Caesarea and Sebaste would probably have shared this disappointment and frustration.

Josephus says that the people of Caesarea and Sebaste simply forgot Agrippa's good treatment of them. Given the depth of their hostility, it seems that something more visceral than forgetfulness motivated their anger. The demotion of the auxiliary soldiers to royal troops and a loss of the promised citizenship in return for military service would be a more plausible explanation for the strength of their antagonism.[14]

The probability that the auxiliary cohorts were simply transferred by Claudius to Agrippa in AD 41 and redesignated as royal troops is further supported by what happened when Claudius heard of the mockery in AD 44. According to Josephus, when Claudius learned of the soldiers' behaviour, he was furious. His initial inclination was to order that the soldiers be sent to serve away from their homeland as a punishment. However, the soldiers sent an appeal to Claudius, and Claudius relented. Instead of sending them elsewhere he decided to make them Roman auxiliaries and allowed them to continue their service in Palestine (*Ant.* 19.366). Claudius' designation of the cohorts as auxiliaries in AD 44 shows how cohorts could be transferred collectively from one status to another. In this case, he was redesignating them back to a status that they had enjoyed only a few years before.

To sum up, Luz's statement that the soldiers involved in the two incidents are largely the same is essentially correct, even though their status was different in the two incidents. They would have been serving as auxiliaries under Pilate and then royal troops under Agrippa. The collective identity of the two groups is a close cultural match and some soldiers may even have been present at both events. This connection provides further reinforcement for viewing the mockery of Agrippa as a highly relevant first-century local context for the earlier mockery of Jesus.

Conclusion

Sexual violence against male victims in biblical texts is often erased or passed over unnoticed (Greenough, 2021). The insults of the soldiers against Agrippa and his daughters, and the statement by Josephus on 'things too indecent to be reported', strengthen the concern that the Gospel writers might be exercising some discretion in their accounts of what took place in the *praetorium*. Since sexualized violence against Jesus beyond the stripping is not directly attested to in the Gospels any verdict about additional violence must remain cautious and tentative; however, there are reasons to take the possibility seriously. It should not be dismissed as groundless speculation or irresponsible supposition.

Attention to the mocking of Agrippa and consideration of its relevance to the mockery of Jesus is an example of why disturbing events should not be overlooked or passed over in silence. The outrageous acts of the soldiers from Caesarea and Sebaste, and the ways these are described, strengthen the argument for further investigation on whether, or not, the Gospel writers have exercised discretion on what they have included, and what they may have decided to leave as a discreet lacuna, in the mockery of Jesus by auxiliaries recruited from Caesarea and Sebaste.

Bibliography

Barclay, John M. G., 1996, *Jews in the Mediterranean Diaspora: From Alexander to Trajan (323 BCE–117 CE)*, Edinburgh: T&T Clark.

Beard, Mary, 2018, *How Do We Look? The Body, The Divine, and the Question of Civilisation*, New York: Liveright.

Brown, Raymond E., 1994, *Death of the Messiah*, vol. 1, Anchor Bible Reference Library, New York: Doubleday.

Chilton, Bruce, 2021, *The Herods: Murder, Politics, and the Art of Succession*, Minneapolis, MN: Fortress Press.

Feldman, Louis H. (trans.), 1965, Josephus, *Jewish Antiquities, Volume VIII: Books 18–19*, Loeb Classical Library 433, Cambridge, MA: Harvard University Press.

Graves, Robert, 1934, *I, Claudius*, New York: Modern Library.

Graves, Robert, 1935, *Claudius the God*, New York: Harrison Smith and Robert Haas.

Greenough, Christopher, 2021, *The Bible and Sexual Violence Against Men*, London: Routledge.

Havelock, Christine Mitchell, 1995, *The Aphrodite of Knidos and Her Successors: A Historical Review of the Female Nude in Greek Art*, Ann Arbor, MI: University of Michigan Press.

Hultin, Jeremy F., 2008, *The Ethics of Obscene Speech in Early Christianity and Its Environment*, Leiden and Boston, MA: Brill.

Human Rights Watch, 2013, *"We Will Teach You a Lesson": Sexual Violence against Tamils by Sri Lankan Security Forces*, New York: Human Rights Watch, available at https://www.hrw.org/report/2013/02/26/we-will-teach-you-lesson/sexual-violence-against-tamils-sri-lankan-security-forces (accessed 18.12.2023).

Jansen, Charlotte, 2023, '"I Want to Unleash Rage": Iranian Exile Shirin Neshat on her Film about Veils, Prison and Rape', *The Guardian*, 2 October, available at https://www.theguardian.com/artanddesign/2023/oct/02/iranian-exile-shirin-neshat-fury-film-veils-prison-rape (accessed 3.12.2023).

Kenan, T. Erim, 1982, 'A New Relief Showing Claudius and Britannia from Aphrodisias', *Britannia* 13, pp. 277–81.

Luz, Ulrich, 2005, *Matthew 21–28: A Commentary*, trans. James E. Crouch, Minneapolis, MN: Fortress Press.

Pseudo Lucian, 1967, *Amores (Affairs of the Heart)* in *Soloecista. Lucius or The Ass. Amores. Halcyon. Demosthenes. Podagra. Ocypus. Cyniscus. Philopatris.*

Charidemus. Nero. vol. VII, trans. M. D. Macleod, Loeb Classical Library 432, Cambridge, MA: Harvard University Press.

Reaves, Jayme, David Tombs and Rocío Figueroa (eds), 2021, *When Did We See You Naked? Jesus as a Victim of Sexual Abuse*, London: SCM Press.

Spivey, Nigel, 1999, 'Christ and the Art of Agony', *History Today* 49 (August 1999), pp. 16–23.

Thiede, Barbara, 2022, *Rape Culture in the House of David: A Company of Men*, London; New York: Routledge.

Tombs, David, 1999, 'Crucifixion, State Terror, and Sexual Abuse', *Union Seminary Quarterly Review* 53 (Autumn), pp. 89–109.

Tombs, David, 2006, 'Unspeakable Violence: The Truth Commissions in El Salvador and Guatemala' in Iain Maclean (ed.), *Reconciliation: Nations and Churches in Latin America*, Aldershot: Ashgate, pp. 55–84, available at https://doi.org/10.4324/9781315603957-4 (accessed 6.06.2023).

Tombs, David, 2020, 'Hidden in Plain Sight: Seeing the Stripping of Jesus as Sexual Violence', *Journal of Interdisciplinary Biblical Studies* 2/1 (Autumn), pp. 224–47, available at https://dx.doi.org/10.17613/ek9a-mx94 (accessed 6.06.2023).

Tombs, David, 2021, 'Reading Crucifixion Narratives as Texts of Terror' in Monica Melanchthon and Robyn Whitaker (eds), *Terror in the Bible: Rhetoric, Gender, and Violence*, Atlanta, GA: SBL Press, pp. 139–60.

Tombs, David, 2022, 'Asking the Right Questions: Noticing and Naming Sexual Abuse' in Jione Havea, Emily Colgan and Nasili Vaka'uta (eds), *Theology as Threshold: Invitations from Aotearoa/New Zealand*, Lanham, MD: Lexington Books/Fortress Academic, pp. 85–105.

Tombs, David, 2023a, *The Crucifixion of Jesus: Torture, Sexual Abuse, and the Scandal of the Cross*, London: Routledge, available at https://doi.org/10.4324/9780429289750 (accessed 6.06.2023).

Tombs, David, 2023b, 'Alone and Naked: Reading the Torture of Jesus alongside the Torture of Miriam Leitão', *International Journal of Public Theology* 17 (4), pp. 537–57, available at https://doi.org/10.1163/15697320-20230102 (accessed 6.06.2023).

Zeichmann, Christopher B., 2018, *The Roman Army and the New Testament*, Lanham, MD: Lexington Books/Fortress Academic.

Zeichmann, Christopher B. (ed.), 2019, *Essential Essays for the Study of Military in First-Century Palestine: Soldiers and the New Testament Context*, Eugene, OR: Pickwick.

Notes

1 His full name was Marcus Julius Agrippa. In this chapter, for simplicity and brevity, I use the name Agrippa rather than Herod Agrippa or Agrippa I, and I use the name Agrippa II for his son.

2 All references to Josephus in this chapter are taken from the Loeb translation by Louis Feldman (1965).

3 On Agrippa's death, the Romans returned Judea, Samaria and Idumea to direct rule under a procurator, and Agrippa II inherited other parts of his father's territory. Agrippa II was the last of the Herodian line to rule.

4 Berenice's first husband had died earlier in the year, and she had married Herod Chalcis as a second marriage, which lasted until his death in AD 48. Josephus adds that Agrippa had promised Mariamme (sometimes spelt as Mariamne) in marriage to Julius Archelaus, son of Helcias, and Drusilla to Epiphanes, the son of Antiochus king of Commagene (*Ant.* 19.354).

5 Chilton's comments on Berenice may be influenced by salacious rumours that were associated with Berenice later in her life. Agrippa II and Berenice lived together for some years after the death of Herod Chalcis (AD 48) and there were rumours that their close relationship was incestuous (Juvenal, *Satires*, VI). According to Josephus, Berenice requested a third marriage to put an end to these rumours. Her third marriage was to Polemon II of Pontus, king of Cilicia, but this marriage was short-lived and she subsequently deserted him.

6 Another troubling passage by Chilton on Berenice (given in the context of Agrippa promising her as a ten-year-old for marriage to Marcus Julius Alexander) reads (Chilton, 2021, p. 179), 'At this point, Bereniké, owing to her age, was not quite a sexual pawn, but she showed the promise of becoming one; with time she would yield power with talents that included – but were by no means limited to – the deft use of sexuality.'

7 A good illustration is offered in Beard, 2018, p. 86.

8 All references are to the Loeb translation by M. D. Macleod, in the volume Pseudo Lucian, *Soloecista. Lucius or The Ass. Amores. Halcyon. Demosthenes. Podagra. Ocypus. Cyniscus. Philopatris. Charidemus. Nero. Volume VII.*

9 A different illustration of an association between statues and sexual violence is provided by a statue to Claudius marking the conquest of Britannia (AD 43); see Kenan, 1982, and Tombs, 2023a, p. 67.

10 The relative silence in scholarship on the mockery in AD 44 is more notable when compared with the attention that scholars often give to the mockery of Agrippa by the people of Alexandria when Agrippa visited the city in AD 38, as told by Philo (*Flaccus*, 36–39). See, for example, Barclay, 1996, pp. 52–3.

11 This omission is made worse because in the English translation of Luz's work, the 'daughters' (plural) in German are rendered as 'daughter' (singular). In addition, mistaken mention is made of a man representing Agrippa, which is most likely taken from the earlier mockery of Agrippa when he visited Alexandria in AD 38 (Luz, 2005, p. 513). This mistake is not present in the German original. I am grateful to Christl M. Maier for information on the German original.

12 Since this chapter is in a volume on narrating rape, it should be noted that the understanding of indecent acts to which Jesus might have been subjected is much broader than just rape. Sexualized violence against male detainees takes a wide variety of forms. Rape (including rape with instruments or weapons) is a possibility that should always be considered; however, reports suggest other forms of sexual violence are usually more common against male detainees.

13 During this time, the Roman governor was appointed from the equestrian class, and had the status of a prefect. After Agrippa, the governor was a procurator, a more senior rank appointed from the senatorial class.

14 Christopher B. Zeichmann, '"Forgetting the Kindnesses Bestowed upon Them": The Death of Agrippa I and Patronage in Herodian and Roman Armies'. The contents of this unpublished paper were generously shared by the author.

10

'Slaves of Christ': Rape Culture in the New Testament

JEREMY PUNT

Introduction

Associating the Pauline call to become slaves of God or Christ (Rom. 6; 1 Cor. 7) with rape culture may come across as disturbing – but engaging with rape culture does exactly that: trouble and upset. After all, the New Testament had its origins in what can be called ancient rape culture: a world where power was gendered, and sexual violence a mechanism for exercising social control, normalized to the extent that divine rape formed the inspiration for many works of art. It was a slaveholding world, with slaves in some places estimated to have been as many as half the local population. The history of sexuality is a vast research area. In particular, the conditioning and formative influence of slavery on sexuality in world systems requires more investigation, given how ancient sexuality notions reigned until the early modern period, and how human trafficking or slavery persists today[1] (Richlin, 2013, p. 307). The focus here, though, is slavery's entanglement with rape culture.

Defining rape culture as '[a]n environment in which sexual assault and gendered violence remain consistently prevalent due to systemic patriarchy' (Parks, Sheinfeld and Warren, 2022, p. 331) makes slavery's influence difficult to deny.[2] Slavery was ubiquitous in the ancient world and impacted every aspect of people's lives. Biblical texts have no outright condemnation of slavery but, instead, at times its endorsement (Marbury, 2023). Even if not its only dimension, slavery has been a vital component of the rape culture of the first century and an enduring connection over many centuries. Situating first-century rape culture is complex and requires attention as to how slaves – but also women and marginalized men – were implicated in an era of domesticity[3] that saw many free persons become complicit in 'the system'. Another challenge is to identify rape in a world with different understandings of consent, where enslaved people were none the less bodily subjected to their owners, to be used as surrogate bodies, corporeally open to insult, violence and various kinds of abuse, including sexual abuse (Glancy, 2002, p.93).

Not aspiring to a comprehensive account of ancient sexuality or a historiography of slaves' sexual lives, my contribution is grounded in a first-century socio-historical context as an imperial, kyriarchal and slaveholding world. Cognisant of the challenges brought about by the tenuous relationship between texts and reality, my contribution explores the rhetorical impact of the New Testament call for Jesus followers to be(come) slaves of Christ and its relevance for rape culture. I intend to show how the construction of a discourse built upon slavery may for all its rhetorical force provide a normalizing framework in which sexual abuse is obfuscated for the sake of other interests such as obedience.

Slavery in the first century AD: various lives, different experiences

Slavery was one of the most determining aspects of ancient Greek and Roman society (Briggs, 2000, p.110). While on one level it is important to record significant differences between the slavery of the first century and of later colonial times,[4] as an institution slavery was, regardless of the period under discussion, the 'permanent, violent domination of natally alienated and generally dishonored persons': the constant threat and actions of violence, natal alienation and loss of honour as the characteristic elements of slavery meant it was 'social death' (Patterson, 1982, p. 13; see Martin, 2005, p. 228). Slaves belonged to the households of their owners, often included with the members of the family without being considered part of the family (Osiek, 2005, pp. 208–11). Amid the many ways power and control were exerted over first-century people, institutionalized slavery was the ultimate 'displacement' (see Punt, 2009).

As an ancient institution but also in its more recent and contemporary worldwide practices devoid of freedom, human dignity or rights it is difficult to think about slavery in any but negative terms. Ancient slavery's impact cannot be smoothed over by references to self-imposed slavery, palatable treatment in some instances or manumission possibilities; ancient (here, first-century) slavery was a mixed bag in the sense of a wide range of experiences, also for slaves' sexual lives.[5] Owners typically exercised control over slaves' lives including their sexual availability, while legal and practical realities impacted on slaves' experiences and owners' erotic advances.[6] In Athens, financial situation, gender, living arrangements and ownership affected slaves' sexual experience: state-owned slaves could sexually exploit free persons, male slaves could frequent brothels or be forced to work in them, female slaves could work as prostitutes in addition to domestic duties, while slaves living outside the household could have their own dwellings cohabiting in ongoing monogamous relationships. Rome offered an equally varied context, with some slaves in monogamous relationships with others, wealthy and powerful slaves acquiring their own slaves, and others living at some distance from their owners (see Cohen, 2014, pp. 184–5; Daniel-Hughes, 2019). However, while differences existed in rank and influence among slaves, it did not necessarily exempt those of higher status from the (threat of) abuse and maltreatment typically meted out to slaves (Byron, 2008, p. 143).[7]

Roman-era authors reveal the sexually vulnerable position of slaves (see Marchal, 2011, p. 749), notwithstanding the prevalence of a consistent elite male voice.[8] The Greek poet Herodas (*Mimes* 5.6) has a slave say, 'Bitinna, I am a slave: use me as you wish.' In Chariton's novel *Chaereas and Callirhoe* (2.6.2), the owner's role towards the slave is put in stark terms: 'You are her master, with full power over her, so she must do your will whether she likes it or not.'[9] Petronius' fictive work leaves no doubt when a slave says, 'For fourteen years I pleasured him; it is no disgrace to do what a master commands. I also gave my mistress satisfaction' (*Satyricon* 75.11), and Horace's simple statement has slaves in mind: 'I like sex that is easy and obtainable' (*Satires* 1.2.119). Seneca summarizes the contemporary spectrum of perspectives when it comes to sex: 'Unchastity is a crime in the freeborn, a necessity for a slave, a duty for the freedman' (*Controversies* 4, *Praef.* 10).[10]

However, the traditional binary model of all power resorting in the elite to the exclusion of the marginalized who included slaves may be too one-sided. Similar to the long androcentric tradition imposed by generally male-authored texts as well as such textual rhetoric taken to reflect the real-life circumstances of women in antiquity, the study of slaves faces an analogous if more pronounced challenge.[11] Katherine Shaner (2018, p. xv) argues that the rhetoric of some texts and archaeological materials jeopardizes the consensus that slaves (like women) were 'clearly identifiable and clearly subordinate'.[12] Resisting both kyriarchy and kyriarchal interpretation that accepts, stabilizes and even promotes the construal of social structures' unequal power dynamics in favour of a certain group,[13] Shaner pushes back both by exploring slaves' influence notwithstanding their ostensibly subordinated status, to consider how such influence challenged social hierarchies that advantaged wealthy slave owners.[14]

However, slaves' sexual vulnerability seems beyond dispute even if the overwhelmingly elite portrayal of and expectations for slavery is acknowledged. Amid reigning perceptions of slaves being inherently untrustworthy and open to physical assault,[15] their ubiquitous sexual availability was unexceptional (Marchal, 2011).[16] Sexual availability was not restricted to female slaves, who were at a particular disadvantage in an androcentric society. In the ancient Greek and Roman world, a woman's most important characteristic was considered sexual restraint. However, this was not expected from female slaves, except in the context of household sexual relationships, as permitted or required by the owner. While it is unclear what motivated the household codes found in various texts (e.g. Col. 3.22—4.1; Eph. 6.5–9; 1 Tim. 6.1–2; Did. 4.9–10; Ign. Pol. 4.3), they reinforce the idea that slaves should obey their owners, and there is no good reason for thinking that enslaved Christians were exempt from the duty to submit to their owners' sexual advances (Glancy, 2019, p. 640).

Ambiguities of violence and sex in the ancient world and in the New Testament

Violence was not incidental to slavery, maintained as it was by threat and practice, including punishment, torture and even execution (Osiek, 2005, p. 206). In the history of interpretation, attention to the physical aspects of slavery, including the sexual exploitation of the enslaved body and its susceptibility to physical mistreatment, has been sparse (Glancy, 2002, p. 154).[17] Given interpretive tradition's allergic reaction to dealing with embodiment, gender, and especially sexuality, least of all sexual violence, inattention to slaves' sexual use surpasses scholarly disaffection for slavery. The ancient context shows keen awareness of many sexual dangers to which slaves were exposed, perhaps more for commercial than compassionate reasons. Roman laws allowed for redress and compensation to owners, not slaves, where a third party sexually assaulted a slave, or a purchaser's sexual actions towards a slave lowered the slave's value, while sexual attacks upon a slave leading to disorder among the household's other slaves evoked sanction (Bradley, 1994, p. 49).

The ancient world provides ample evidence in literary texts and other material artefacts of the intersections between violence and sex.[18] Sexual violence was aided and abetted by the agonistic context, replete with strong masculine warrior images, with bravery related to the battlefield, and dominance extended over the women, children and marginalized men – often portrayed on material artefacts from the time. A volume on rape in the ancient world (Deacy and Pierce, 2002) portrays the various ways in which ancient authors narrated rape, how sexual acts seen as rape by people today would have been understood in antiquity, and how already in Herodotus, sexual overpowering was seen as rape only if the perpetrator was of lower class (Harrison, 2002). A telling example is Livy's account of Roman history, etched in various accounts of what we would call rape, with those of the Sabine women led by Rome's mythological founder, Romulus, probably best known.[19] Vital for the story of Rome, rape became ambiguous and contested, as both destructive (of women physically and psychologically) and constructive (in the sense of new life, especially in divine rape narratives) (Arieti, 2002, pp. 209–29).[20]

Investigation of the entanglements of rape culture, gender violence and the Bible (Blyth, Colgan and Edwards, 2018) tends to consider the Hebrew Bible/Old Testament as problematic when it comes to sexual violence; the New Testament is resolved by simplistically equating Jesus and God with peace, concealing problematic issues (on this point see, for example, Warren, 2017).[21] Notwithstanding its calls for peace, the New Testament is not devoid of violence or its promotion, and 1 Peter 2.18–21 confirmed slaves' corporal punishment (see Punt, 2009). Sexualized and sexual violence is not entirely absent and at times is implied and even explicitly promoted.[22] The intersection of sex and violence extends to the overt imperial context even if sexual violence is more subtly present. Scholars, for example, suggested that Jesus' birth may have been the result of Mary being raped by a Roman soldier (Van Aarde, 2001); that Jesus' explicit disrobing at crucifixion, twice, suggests sexual assault as part of the sustained humiliation of the victim (Reaves, Tombs and Figueroa, 2021); that Paul's negotiations with Philemon about Onesimus may have been about the sexual use (*euchrēstos*) of a slave (Frilingos, 2014, p. 48); and the story about the woman caught in adultery (John 8) raises many questions, especially about the absent (male) partner. In Revelation, sex and violence intersect explicitly but at times they are disguised by interpretive practices, such as when 'one like a son of man' (Rev. 1.13) threatens rape against Jezebel: 'look, I will throw her on a bed' (Rev. 2.22).[23] In Revelation 17—18, the Great Whore or Prostitute's account is enveloped in *porneia* (sexual immorality, Rev. 17.2, 4; 18.3), and her end marked by sexualized violence.[24]

Notwithstanding different classical and biblical understandings of *porneia*, its New Testament and early Christian use shows the entanglement of gender, sex and violence, and its relevance for slavery. The original use of *porneia* as prostitution without a broader range of immoral activities may conceal its innovative nature among Jewish and early Christian communities. The concept was immersed in cultures where acceptability of heterosexual relationships was less determined by marital status than by a particular woman's social standing (Harper, 2012, p. 383). Historical records show that Hellenistic Jewish writers did not employ the term *porneia* to describe a male slave owner's abuse of their slaves. These writers support sexual intimacy between married couples while accepting non-marital sexual relations between slave owners and their female slaves. In early Christian texts, *porneia* becomes more expansive, including forms of extramarital sexual behaviour otherwise accepted in Greek and Roman cultures. However, earlier texts such as the Pauline writings provide no evidence of challenging the sexual availability of slaves or the power dynamics of slavery (Glancy, 2015, p. 215).

Paul and slavery

Paul's slavery metaphors are embedded in the socio-cultural world of the first century and also intertextually in his writings.[25] The metaphorical use of slavery is especially prominent in the Pauline letters and early Christian thought (Kartzow, 2018b, p. 1). Paul introduced himself and his co-workers as slaves (Phil. 1.1 and Rom. 1.1), slavery metaphors were supported by servile (e.g. 1 Cor. 4.1) or imprisonment (Philemon 1) terminology, and narratives of Paul's suffering underscore his service to God (2 Cor. 11.23–33). Paul's slavery metaphor was a subtle invocation of the cross since slaves were more likely to be the victims of crucifixion.[26] In what O'Collins (1992, p. 1208) described as a 'sadistically cruel' and 'utterly shameful death', crucifixion was the Empire's way to uphold authority, preserve law and order and instil fear among rebels, criminals and slaves. With few exceptions, Roman rulers crucified foreigners, those from lower classes and, first and foremost, slaves. Known as the 'slaves' punishment' (*supplicum servile*)[27] in Jewish reference, crucifixion was a reminder to the Jewish people of enslavement to Rome as a foreign power.

Scholars tend to conclude positively about Paul's use of slavery metaphors, that his appropriation of the slave title may have allowed for submission to God and acting as God's representative (e.g. Kartzow and Martinsen, 2019; see Bartchy, 1973; Martin, 1990). Such conclusions, however, may obscure the larger socio-cultural and literary context of Paul's work. While Paul also used slavery terminology with negative implications – for example, in relation to sin (Rom. 6.6)[28] – his slavery metaphors are mostly affirmative. In Romans 6.22 the believers' freedom from sin is paralleled by *doulōthentes de tō theō* (becoming enslaved to

God) which allowed them to 'have their fruit of sanctification' and its 'end or goal of eternal life'. The centrality of the slavery metaphor is remarkable, but surprising given his insistence in the passage on freedom through Christ.[29] The audience for the Romans letter may have included slaves, which would have entailed tensions between metaphorical and real slavery as pronounced elsewhere: 'For he who was called in the Lord as a slave is a freedman of the Lord; likewise, he who called as free man, is a slave of Christ' (1 Cor. 7.22, my paraphrase). Slavery metaphors introduced a paradox: while all Jesus followers were depicted as the Lord's slaves, some had to live as real-life slaves (Kartzow, 2018b),[30] for whom Paul's emphasis on avoiding sexual sin may have created further problems.[31]

Even if slaves engaged in such authoritative roles like religious specialists, priests and leaders in cultic groups, including early Jesus-follower groups, Roman-era slavery was no benign institution, nor is there evidence that all early Christians were kinder and more egalitarian to slaves (Shaner, 2018).[32] Some scholars implicate Paul more radically in the link between slavery and sex. Frilingos (2014) refers to the use of *euchrēstos* by Lucian of Samosata (second century AD) to express sexual servitude in a context of slavery (*Amores* 25, 27).[33] Frilingos suggests that Paul and Philemon may have quarrelled over claims to the sexual use of Onesimus, given Paul's frequent use of familial rhetoric such as *tou emou teknon* (Philemon 10; cf. Gal. 4.19; 1 Thess. 2.7, 11–12).[34] Aware that ancient slavery entailed more than physical labour, including the sexual exploitation of slaves, Pauline agency cannot be ruled out; even if it is, Paul's position remains ambivalent and, if nothing else, situated within slavery discourse.

New Testament slavery terminology and rape culture

The scholarly trend to find more positives than negatives in ancient slavery, 'a benign form of mass employment for the under classes as well as an effective means of integrating foreigners' (Byron, 2004, p. 116), are changing.[35] With scepticism about positive sentiments already mounting for a few decades,[36] scholars note that ancient slavery was a mixture of protection, provision, abuse and exploitation (see Barclay, 1991, p. 167). Previous acclaim for the Septuagint's notion of slave of God as rendering service to God was seen to mean more than fulfilling divine directives in favour of 'total dependence and submission toward God deriving from his relationship with men [sic] (e.g., cf. Judg. 10.13,16; Ps. 2.11;

99.2; 101.23)' (Malina, 1978, p. 72). Taking up 'slave' as title may have Jewish origins (Kartzow and Martinsen, 2019), and without dismissing the LXX's influence, the New Testament's use of *doulos* metaphors derives from Jewish as much as Greek and Roman worlds (Goodrich, 2013). Upwardly mobile slaves were exceptions to the continuously maltreated, dehumanized and worked-to-death slaves, and slavery amounted to exploitation of the powerless and 'relationship of violent domination' (Byron, 2008, p. 140).[37]

The ubiquity of slavery, like the item in plain sight most difficult to spot, played into slaves' sexual abuse remaining unremarked upon. Throughout the cityscape, the unfree were relatively unseen in their pervasive presence (Shaner, 2018, p. 27), which is significant for the early Jesus-follower communities of Paul's urban ministry in particular. When it comes to slavery, more important than the obscurity of the obvious is the naturalization of the abominable through discourse. '[T]he use of social relations to make a theological point is successful to the degree that the metaphor reinscribes the social relation, rather than calling it into question' (Castelli, 1994, p. 294). The metaphorical reach of slavery is only understood if the somatic dimensions of its New Testament deployment are adequately referenced.[38] Conceptual metaphor theory explains how a metaphor is more than a comparison, as it also creates meaning (Lakoff and Johnson, 2003). Metaphors put one reality next to another, to contribute to understanding and experiencing the world anew across different dimensions.[39] Expressions like 'slave of God' or 'slave of Christ' fit into a complex socio-linguistic network,[40] which with a material display of sexual violence against women and slaves meant their symbolization served to reinforce behaviour that the authors presented as appropriate (Parks, Sheinfeld and Warren, 2022, p. 232).[41]

Masculinity and by extension patriarchy were built on gender patterns that allocated men pride of place, informed constellations of power, and impacted social systems like slavery and perceptions about violence, sex and gender. With what some have described as the reign of the phallus (Keuls, 1993), men – and in particular those from elite classes – were socialized with a disposition of unchallenged dominance, in a society where men were unalterably different and superior to slaves, women and barbarians (Brown, 1988, p. 9). The link between masculinity and sexual violence was not only established through socialization processes but 'the study of such texts in school facilitates the internalization by boys of the links between violence and masculinity' (Gale and Scourfield, 2018, p. 20).[42] In the Jesus-follower contexts, too, ascribing a dominant male, patriarchal role to God sanctioned such gender patterns.

Besides the ubiquity of slavery and the naturalization of slavery discourse, obscuring practices in ensuing traditions served to entrench a favourable picture of slavery, avoiding negative portrayals. This is underscored by widespread practices of translating slaves-slavery as servant-servanthood in today's translations of the Bible. Marbury (2023) argues for good intentions, wishing to avoid associations between African people, slavery and Blackness as evil. Believers (re)claim slavery texts on spiritual or devotional grounds without acknowledgement of slavery's devastating effects, and without identifying slavery texts as 'texts of terror'.[43] However, the spiritualization of slave-of-God language is dangerous in that 'prioritization and "authoritization" of vertical enslavement served to remove the focus from the oppression of horizontal slavery, and thus serves in favor of the persistence of horizontal slavery' (De Wet, 2018, p. 20). When early Christians eventually denunciated slaves' sexual exploitation, it did not amount to shunning the surrounding luxurious, violent Roman society. Early Christians' concern about their community's pollution carried more weight than concern about slaves' welfare, sexually or otherwise. In the early texts of the Christian era, not only were free Christian women regarded as superior to their enslaved counterparts but bishops cautioned male householders against sexual relations with female slaves to prevent them from becoming insolent – not to prevent their exploitation (Clark, 2019, p. 43).

Conclusion

My argument is not that Paul was an overt advocate for rape culture, a heartless slave keeper, or sexual pervert (see Punt, 2022).[44] Rather, I argue that affirmative slavery terminology in the absence of slavery's condemnation in the Pauline letters, and the New Testament generally, have aided and abetted ancient rape culture, even if unintentionally, and has the potential to continue doing so, especially in its intersection with male prerogatives. Even if sexual assault was identifiable as a legal and social offence during the Greek and Roman eras, the standards used to establish what constituted sexual assault in ancient Rome, who had the authority to give consent, or could be considered as the injured party, and penalties or compensations imposed were considerably different from contemporary notions (Reeder, 2017, p. 366). While the sexual exploitation of slaves became a moral conundrum for early Christians (De Wet, 2018, p. 3), the New Testament appears to reflect an early stage where the exploitation of slaves went unaccounted, or even assumed (e.g.

1 Pet. 2.18–25; Eph. 6.5–8; Col. 3.22). An important difference between sexual violence and violence in general is that unlike the latter which tends to attract people's attention, sexual violence elicits avoidance, denial and disavowal (Heister, 2022, pp. 187–8). Rape culture work in the Bible also adds a critical element, in joining concerns about trauma theory's tendency towards individualist and extraordinary event-based disposition that betrays a Eurocentric bias (Andermahr, 2016, pp. 1–6; see Craps, 2013, on postcolonial trauma); rape culture work is concerned about the everyday, ongoing trauma of groups, of oppressed, enslaved and colonized peoples.[45] Rape culture endures in our modern context where rape is addressed through strategies of containment and disregard for victims' felt experiences, stalling broader claims for justice (Larson, 2021). Discourses in the ancient world, notwithstanding differences in contents and circumstances, such as the New Testament's onboarding of slavery discourse, show analogous containment (and appropriation?) strategies that have been influential for centuries.[46] The persuasive nature of discourse rooted in slavery can create an environment where sexual abuse is normalized. Unpacking the New Testament's favourable slavery discourse requires first and foremost recognition for the potential of slavery discourse to downplay or even condone sexual abuse, alongside the manipulative nature of such discourse and its potential to obscure the severity of sexual abuse within a system of oppression. Even if sexual abuse was not the primary aim of all ancient slavery, slavery discourse can create a context in which it is more likely to occur or be tolerated. This distinction is crucial, as it acknowledges the complex factors that contribute to sexual abuse and avoids simplistic or deterministic explanations.

Bibliography

Andermahr, Sonya, 2016, 'Decolonizing Trauma Studies: Trauma and Postcolonialism – Introduction' in Sonya Andermahr (ed.), *Decolonizing Trauma Studies: Trauma and Postcolonialism*, Basel: MDPI AG, pp. 1–6.

Arieti, James A., 2002, 'Rape and Livy's View of Roman History' in Susan Deacy and Karen F. Pierce (eds), *Rape in Antiquity: Sexual Violence in the Greek and Roman Worlds*, paperback edn, London: Duckworth, pp. 209–29.

Barclay, John M. G., 1991, 'Paul, Philemon, and the Dilemma of Christian Slave Ownership', *New Testament Studies* 37, pp. 161–86.

Bartchy, S. Scott, 1973, *ΜΑΛΛΟΝ ΧΡΗΣΑΙ. First-Century Slavery and the Interpretation of 1 Cor 7:21*, Missoula, MT: Scholars' Press.

Beard, Mary, and John Henderson, 1998, 'With This Body I Thee Worship: Sacred

Prostitution in Antiquity' in Maria Wyke (ed.), *Gender and Body in the Ancient Mediterranean*, Oxford: Blackwell, pp. 56–79.

Belser, Julia Watts, 2014, 'Sex in the Shadow of Rome: Sexual Violence and Theological Lament in Talmudic Disaster Tales', *Journal of Feminist Studies in Religion* 30/1, pp. 5–24.

Blyth, Caroline, Emily Colgan and Katie B. Edwards (eds), 2018, *Rape Culture, Gender Violence, and Religion: Biblical Perspectives*, Religion and Radicalism, Cham: Palgrave Macmillan.

Bradley, Keith R., 1987, *Slaves and Masters in the Roman Empire: A Study in Social Control*, New York: Oxford University Press.

Bradley, Keith R., 1994, *Slavery and Society at Rome*, Key Themes in Ancient History, Cambridge; New York: Cambridge University Press.

Bradley, Keith R., 2003, 'Slavery and Gender' in Jane Schaberg, Alice Bach and Esther Fuchs (eds), *On the Cutting Edge: The Study of Women in Biblical Worlds: Essays in Honor of Elisabeth Schüssler Fiorenza*, New York/London: Continuum, pp. 171–92.

Bradley, Keith R., and P. Cartledge, 2010, *The Cambridge World History of Slavery, Volume 1: The Ancient Mediterranean World*, Cambridge: Cambridge University Press.

Briggs, Sheila, 2000, 'Paul on Bondage and Freedom in Imperial Roman Society' in Richard A. Horsley (ed.), *Paul and Politics: Ekklesia, Israel, Imperium, Interpretation: Essays in Honor of Krister Stendahl*, Harrisville, PA: Trinity Press International, pp. 110–23.

Briggs, Sheila, 2003, 'Slavery and Gender' in *On the Cutting Edge: The Study of Women in Biblical Worlds. Essays in Honor of Elisabeth Schüssler Fiorenza*, ed. Jane Schaberg, Alice Bach and Esther Fuchs, New York/London: Continuum.

Brooten, Bernadette Joan, and Jacqueline L. Hazelton (eds), 2010, *Beyond Slavery: Overcoming Its Religious and Sexual Legacies*, Black Religion/Womanist Thought/Social Justice, New York: Palgrave Macmillan.

Brown, Peter R. L., 1988, *The Body and Society: Men, Women and Sexual Renunciation in Early Christianity*, New York: Columbia University Press.

Byron, John, 2004, 'Paul and the Background of Slavery: The *Status Quaestionis* in New Testament Scholarship', *Currents in Biblical Research* 3/9, pp. 116–39.

Byron, John, 2008, *Recent Research on Paul and Slavery*, Recent Research in Biblical Studies 3, Sheffield: Sheffield Phoenix Press.

Castelli, Elizabeth, 1994, 'Romans' in Elisabeth Schüssler Fiorenza (ed.), *Searching the Scriptures, Volume 2, A Feminist Commentary*, New York: Crossroad, pp. 273–300.

Charles, Ronald, 2020, *The Silencing of Slaves in Early Jewish and Christian Texts*, Routledge Studies in the Early Christian World, London; New York: Routledge, Taylor & Francis.

Clark, Anna, 2019, *Desire: A History of European Sexuality*, 2nd edn, London; New York: Routledge, Taylor & Francis.

Cohen, Edward C., 2014, 'Sexual Abuse and Sexual Rights: Slaves' Erotic Experience at Athens and Rome' in Thomas K. Hubbard (ed.), *A Companion to Greek and Roman Sexualities*, Blackwell Companions to the Ancient World, Chichester: Wiley Blackwell, pp. 184–98.

Concannon, Cavan W., 2021, *Profaning Paul*, Class 200: New Studies in Religion, Chicago, IL; London: University of Chicago Press.

Cook, John Granger, 2014, *Crucifixion in the Mediterranean World*, Tübingen: Mohr Siebeck.

Craps, Stef., 2013, *Postcolonial Witnessing: Trauma Out of Bounds*, London: Palgrave Macmillan.

Daniel-Hughes, Carly, 2019, 'Prostitution' in Benjamin H. Dunning (ed.), *The Oxford Handbook of New Testament, Gender, and Sexuality*, Oxford: Oxford University Press, pp. 644–60.

Davis, Stacy, 2023, 'Jezebel from an African-American Perspective', *Bible Odyssey* (blog), February, available at https://www.bibleodyssey.org/passages/related-articles/jezebel-from-an-african-american-perspective/ (accessed 7.12.2023).

De Wet, Chris L., 2018, *The Unbound God: Slavery and the Formation of Early Christian Thought*, Routledge Studies in the Early Christian World, London; New York: Routledge, Taylor & Francis.

Deacy, Susan, and Karen F. Pierce (eds), 2002, *Rape in Antiquity: Sexual Violence in the Greek and Roman Worlds*, paperback edn, London: Duckworth.

Du Toit, Louise, 2012, *A Philosophical Investigation of Rape: The Making and Unmaking of the Feminine Self*, New York; London: Routledge.

Dube, Musa W., 2000, *Postcolonial Feminist Interpretation of the Bible*, St Louis, MO: Chalice Press.

Forsdyke, Sara, 2021, *Slaves and Slavery in Ancient Greece*, Key Themes in Ancient History, Cambridge; New York: Cambridge University Press.

Frilingos, Christopher A., 2014, 'Children, New Testament' in Julia M. O'Brien (ed.), *The Oxford Encyclopedia of the Bible and Gender Studies, Volume 1*, Oxford: Oxford University Press, pp. 44–9.

Gale, Monica R., and J. H. D. Scourfield (eds), 2018, *Texts and Violence in the Roman World*, Cambridge; New York: Cambridge University Press.

Garnsey, Peter, and Richard Saller, 1987, *The Roman Empire: Economy, Society and Culture*, London: Duckworth.

Glancy, Jennifer A., 2002, *Slavery in Early Christianity*, New York: Oxford University Press.

Glancy, Jennifer A., 2015, 'The Sexual Use of Slaves: A Response to Kyle Harper on Jewish and Christian Porneia', *Journal of Biblical Literature* 134/1, pp. 215–29.

Glancy, Jennifer A., 2019, 'Slavery and Sexual Availability' in Benjamin H. Dunning (ed.), *The Oxford Handbook of New Testament, Gender, and Sexuality*, Oxford: Oxford University Press, pp. 626–44.

Goodrich, John K., 2013, 'From Slaves of Sin to Slaves of God: Reconsidering the Origin of Paul's Slavery Metaphor in Romans 6', *Bulletin for Biblical Research* 23/4, pp. 509–30.

Graybill, Rhiannon, 2021, *Texts after Terror: Rape, Sexual Violence, and the Hebrew Bible*, New York: Oxford University Press.

Graybill, Rhiannon, Meredith Minister and Beatrice Lawrence (eds), 2019, *Rape Culture and Religious Studies: Critical and Pedagogical Engagements*, Feminist Studies and Sacred Texts Series, Lanham, MD: Lexington Books.

Greenough, Chris, 2021, *The Bible and Sexual Violence against Men*, Rape Culture, Religion and the Bible, Abingdon; New York: Routledge.

Harper, Kyle, 2012, 'Porneia: The Making of a Christian Sexual Norm', *Journal of Biblical Literature* 131/2, pp. 363–83.
Harrill, J. Albert, 2006, *Slaves in the New Testament: Literary, Social, and Moral Dimensions*, Minneapolis, MN: Fortress Press.
Harrison, Thomas, 2002, 'Herodotus and the Ancient Greek Idea of Rape' in Susan Deacy and Karen F. Pierce (eds), *Rape in Antiquity: Sexual Violence in the Greek and Roman Worlds*, paperback edn, London: Duckworth, pp. 185–208.
Healicon, Alison, 2016, *The Politics of Sexual Violence: Rape, Identity and Feminism*, Houndmills, Basingstoke, Hampshire; New York: Palgrave Pivot.
Heister, Chantel R., 2022, 'Jezebel's Punishment in Revelation 2: Research and Trends', *Currents in Biblical Research* 20 (2), pp. 186–99.
Hengel, Martin, 1977, *Crucifixion: In the Ancient World and the Folly of the Message of the Cross*, London: SCM Press.
Hezser, Catherine, 2005, *Jewish Slavery in Antiquity*, London; New York: Oxford University Press.
Hezser, Catherine, 2016, 'Greek and Roman Slaving in Comparative Ancient Perspective: The Level of Integration' in Stephen Hodkinson, Marc Kleijwegt and Kostas Vlassopoulos (eds), *The Oxford Handbook of Greek and Roman Slaveries*, Oxford; New York: Oxford University Press.
Huber, Lynn R., 2013, *Thinking and Seeing with Women in Revelation*, Library of New Testament Studies 475, London: Bloomsbury T&T Clark.
Hurlbert, Brandon, 2023, 'The Slave Bible: For Slavery or Salvation?', *The Torah. Com* (blog), January, available at https://www.thetorah.com/article/the-slave-bible-for-slavery-or-salvation (accessed 7.12.2023).
Kartzow, Marianne Bjelland, 2018a, 'Slave Children in the First-Century Jesus Movement' in Reidar Aasgaard, Cornelia B. Horn and Oana Maria Cojocaru (eds), *Childhood in History: Perceptions of Children in the Ancient and Medieval Worlds*, Abingdon: Routledge, pp. 111–26.
Kartzow, Marianne Bjelland, 2018b, *The Slave Metaphor and Gendered Enslavement in Early Christian Discourse: Double Trouble Embodied*, Routledge Studies in the Early Christian World, New York: Routledge.
Kartzow, Marianne Bjelland and Anders Martinsen, 2019, 'Man, Men. III. New Testament' in *Encyclopedia of the Bible and Its Reception*, vol. 17, Berlin: De Gruyter, pp. 650–6.
Keuls, Eva C., 1993, *The Reign of the Phallus: Sexual Politics in Ancient Athens*, Berkeley, CA: University of California Press.
Lakoff, George, and Mark Johnson, 2003, *Metaphors We Live By*, Chicago, IL: University of Chicago Press.
Lalumiere, Martin L., et al., 2005, *The Causes of Rape: Understanding Individual Differences in Male Propensity for Sexual Aggression*, Washington: American Psychological Association.
Larson, Stephanie R., 2021, *What It Feels Like: Visceral Rhetoric and the Politics of Rape Culture*, Rhetoric and Democratic Deliberation 27, University Park, PA: Pennsylvania State University Press.
Loughlin, Gerard, 2005, 'Biblical Bodies', *Theology & Sexuality* 12 (1), pp. 9–27.
Malina, Bruce J., 1978, 'Freedom: A Theological Inquiry into the Dimensions of a Symbol', *Biblical Theology Bulletin* 8, pp. 62–76.

Marbury, Herbert R., 2023, 'The Legacy of the Bible in Justifying Slavery', *Bible Odyssey*, available at https://www.bibleodyssey.org/people/related-articles/the-legacy-of-the-bible-in-justifying-slavery/ (accessed 7.12.2023).

Marchal, Joseph A., 2011, 'The Usefulness of an Onesimus: The Sexual Use of Slaves and Paul's Letter to Philemon', *Journal of Biblical Literature* 130/4, pp. 749–70.

Marchal, Joseph A., 2020, *Appalling Bodies: Queer Figures before and after Paul's Letters*, New York: Oxford University Press.

Martin, Clarence J., 2005, 'The Eyes Have It: Slaves in the Communities of Christ-Believers', in Richard A. Horsley (ed.), *Christian Origins*, vol. 1: A People's History of Christianity, Minneapolis, MN: Fortress Press, pp. 221–40.

Martin, Dale B., 1990, *Slavery as Salvation: The Metaphor of Slavery in Pauline Christianity*, New Haven, CT: Yale University Press.

Meyers, Carol L., 2014, 'Was Ancient Israel a Patriarchal Society?', *Journal of Biblical Literature* 133/1, pp. 8–27.

Milnor, Kristina, 2005, *Gender, Domesticity, and the Age of Augustus: Inventing Private Life*, Oxford: Oxford University Press.

Müller van Velden, Nina, 2022, 'How Far Does God's Violence Go? John's Jezebel in Conversation with Rape Culture' in Manitza Kotzé, Nadia Marais and Nina Müller van Velden (eds), *Sexual Reformation? Theological and Ethical Reflections on Human Sexuality*, Eugene, OR: Wipf & Stock, pp. 143–56.

Neutel, Karin B., 2012, 'Slaves Included? Sexual Regulations and Slave Participation in Two Ancient Religious Groups' in Stephen Hodkinson and Dick Geary (eds), *Slaves, Cults and Religions*, Cambridge: Cambridge Scholars, pp. 133–48.

O'Collins, Gerald, 1992, 'Crucifixion' in David Noel Freedman (ed.), *Anchor Bible Dictionary*, New York: Doubleday, pp. 1207–10.

Osiek, Carolyn, 2005, 'Family Matters' in Richard A. Horsley (ed.), *Christian Origins*, vol. 1: A People's History of Christianity, Minneapolis, MN: Fortress Press, pp. 201–20.

Owens, William M., 2019, *The Representation of Slavery in the Greek Novel: Resistance and Appropriation*, Routledge Monographs in Classical Studies, New York: Routledge.

Parks, Sara, Shayna Sheinfeld and Meredith J. C. Warren, 2022, *Jewish and Christian Women in the Ancient Mediterranean*, Abingdon; New York: Routledge.

Patterson, Orlando, 1982, *Slavery and Social Death: A Comparative Study*, Cambridge: Harvard University Press.

Punt, Jeremy, 2009, 'Cross-Purposes? Violence of the Cross, Galatians, and Human Dignity', *Scriptura*, no. 102, pp. 446–62.

Punt, Jeremy, 2021, 'Revelation, Economics and Sex: The Bible and Sex Work in South Africa', *Journal of Early Christian History* 11/2, pp. 76–95.

Punt, Jeremy, 2022, 'Paul's pro-Sex, Anti-Desire Stance', *Akroterion* 67, pp. 43–64.

Reaves, Jayme, David Tombs and Rocío Figueroa (eds), 2021, *When Did We See You Naked? Jesus as a Victim of Sexual Abuse*, London: SCM Press.

Reeder, Caryn A., 2017, 'Wartime Rape, the Romans, and the First Jewish Revolt', *Journal for the Study of Judaism* 48/3, pp. 363–85.

Richlin, Amy, 2013, 'Sexuality and History' in Nancy F. Partner and Sarah Foot (eds), *The SAGE Handbook of Historical Theory*, Los Angeles: SAGE, pp. 294–310.

Scaer, Peter J., 2005, *The Lukan Passion Narrative and the Praiseworthy Death*, Sheffield: Sheffield Phoenix Press.
Scholz, Susanne, 2010, *Sacred Witness: Rape in the Hebrew Bible*, Minneapolis, MN: Fortress Press.
Schüssler Fiorenza, Elisabeth, 1994, 'The Rhetoricity of Historical Knowledge: Pauline Discourse and Its Contextualizations' in Lukas Bormann et al., *Religious Propaganda and Missionary Competition in the New Testament World: Essays Honouring Dieter Georgi*, Supplements to Novum Testamentum 74, Leiden: Brill, pp. 443–69.
Schüssler Fiorenza, Elisabeth, 1999, *Rhetoric and Ethic: The Politics of Biblical Studies*, Minneapolis, MN: Fortress Press.
Shaner, Katherine Ann, 2018, *Enslaved Leadership in Early Christianity*, New York: Oxford University Press.
Smith, Merril D. (ed.), 2004, *Encyclopedia of Rape*, Westport, CT: Greenwood Press.
Sommar, Mary E., 2020, *The Slaves of the Churches: A History*, New York: Oxford University Press.
Strasser, Ulrike, and Heidi Tinsman, 2005, 'Engendering World History', *Radical History Review* 91, pp. 151–64.
Thornhill, Randy, and Craig T. Palmer, 2000, *A Natural History of Rape: Biological Bases of Sexual Coercion*, Cambridge, MA: MIT Press.
Trouillot, Michel-Rolph, 2015, *Silencing the Past: Power and the Production of History*, Boston, MA: Beacon Press.
Tsang, Sam, 2005, *From Slaves to Sons: A New Rhetoric Analysis on Paul's Slave Metaphors in His Letter to the Galatians*, New York: Peter Lang.
Van Aarde, Andries G., 2001, *Fatherless in Galilee: Jesus as Child of God*, Harrisburg, PA: Trinity Press.
Vikman, Elisabeth, 2005, 'Ancient Origins: Sexual Violence in Warfare, Part I', *Anthropology & Medicine* 12/1, pp. 21–31.
Vitanza, Victor J., 2011, *Sexual Violence in Western Thought and Writing: Chaste Rape*, New York: Palgrave Macmillan.
Warren, Meredith, 2017, 'Sexual Violence and Rape Culture in the New Testament', *The Shiloh Project* (blog), 31 May, available at https://www.shilohproject.blog/sexual-violence-and-rape-culture-in-the-new-testament/ (accessed 7.12.2023).
Williams, Craig A., 2010, *Roman Homosexuality*, 2nd edn, New York and Oxford: Oxford University Press.
Zachariah, George, 2022, 'Legitimising Sexual Violence: Contesting Toxic Theologies that Valorise Suffering as Redemptive', *The Shiloh Project* (blog), 9 April, available at https://www.shilohproject.blog/legitimising-sexual-violence-contesting-toxic-theologies-that-valorise-suffering-as-redemptive/ (accessed 7.12.2023).

Notes

1 In colonial slavery 'European' patriarchal ideas conflicted with African agricultural customs and gender roles, with women playing a predominant role in farming, influenced slave-based agriculture in the Americas, and impacted the 'dynamics between masters, mistresses, and slave servants, underscoring the (often sexual) violence of domestic work' (Strasser and Tinsman, 2005, p. 160).

2 Various larger studies have been done on rape from historical (Thornhill and Palmer, 2000) and philosophical (Du Toit, 2012) perspectives; and also on sexual violence against men (Greenough, 2021). The literature on rape is vast, and includes studies on the causes of rape (Lalumiere et al., 2005), the politics of rape and sexual violence (Healicon, 2016), the literary presentation of rape (Vitanza, 2011), rape culture (Graybill, Minister and Lawrence, 2019) and even an encyclopaedia of rape (Smith, 2004).

3 The New Testament finds itself in the midst of a Roman era of domesticity, signalled perhaps most clearly in the Augustan laws regarding family, children, adultery (even if for the benefit of the elite), and evident in social arrangements (e.g. Milnor, 2005).

4 First-century AD slavery generally allowed the possibility of manumission, and in exceptional cases even possibilities beyond just freedom, but always with some attachment to former owners (Garnsey and Saller, 1987, p. 200).

5 'Slavery ... was a principal social institution in the ancient Mediterranean ... Ancient slaves were also open to various forms of physical, including sexual, manipulation and abuse' (De Wet, 2018, p. 1).

6 'Owners' control over the sexual availability and experience of slaves and masters' erotic use of slaves are tempered by legal and practical realities and coexist with servile sexual experience sometimes similar to that of the free population' (Cohen, 2014, pp. 184–5).

7 Roman authors' acknowledgement of slaves' humanness did not lessen their hardship, since food could be used as an incentive for labour and obedience amid hunger, or sexual intercourse and possible concubinage when slaves desired companionship and intimacy (De Wet, 2018, p. 3); see Cohen, 2014, on slaves' sexual abuse and rights.

8 Part of the difficulty in dealing with ancient (and modern) slavery has to do with the power differentials in historiography and, more pointedly, the silence of the past (Trouillot, 2015).

9 Bradley (1994, p. 49) comments, 'The significant point here is that the owner's sexual access to slaves was regarded as conventional, a norm made explicit.'

10 See also *Ad Lucilium Epistulae Morales* 47.7 about a slave having to divide 'his time between his master's drunkenness and his lust; in the chamber he must be a man, at the feast a boy'. With slaves' bodies at their masters' disposal, it was assumed that among the services they might expect was the satisfaction of their sexual desires (Williams, 2010, p. 31).

11 In Shaner's words, 'materials about enslaved persons do not provide windows into reality; rather, they advance arguments that reinforce certain social hierarchies' (Shaner, 2018, p. iv; Forsdyke, 2021). However, on the silencing of slaves see also Charles, 2020.

12 Early Greek novelists may challenge and undermine, and later novelists affirm elite stereotypes, because the authors and their readers included literate ex-slaves. Their interests and needs shaped the emerging genre, making the protagonists' slavery a key motif, and slavery a theme that helped define the genre (Owens, 2019).

13 The rhetorical nature (rhetoricity) of the Pauline texts is argumentative literature, building arguments intended to persuade rather than offering 'objective' descriptions (Schüssler Fiorenza, 1999, pp. 105–28; 1994, pp. 443–69). For criticism of privileging gender oppression over imperialism, see Dube, 2000, pp. 26–30; 34–9.

14 '[I]n slave societies sexual status and civil status are impossible to separate, but slave texts are rare, never mind slave texts about sex' (Richlin, 2013, p. 302). See also Meyers, 2014, on the postulation of an all-pervasive patriarchy in the ancient Near East.

15 Crucifixion was the basic *supplicum servile* (slave punishment), used in the early principate against slaves, *liberti* (freed persons) and *peregrini* (non-citizens), and occasionally against citizens (Cook, 2014, pp. 358–9).

16 The Torah's tolerance of slaves' sexual use (Ex. 21.7–11; Lev. 19.20–22; Deut. 21.10–14), and preservation of male privilege, provide the tradition for the Pauline writings; Hebrew Bible/Old Testament slave and slavery metaphors are part of a long tradition (Hezser, 2005, pp. 140–5).

17 Slaves were not able to refuse the sexual attention of their slaveholders and were reliant on food and rest in order to cope with their workload and to avoid punishment (Glancy, 2002, pp. 154–5).

18 Texts include Herodotus, Hist. 8.32–33; Polybius 21.38; Diodorus Siculus 13.58.1–2, 17.35.7; Livy 21.13, 21.57, 26.13, 29.17; *Tacitus, Agr.* 15, 31, and *Hist.* 4.14; Plutarch, *Mulier. virt.* 259–60; Appian, *Bell. civ.* 1.13, *Hist. rom.* 7.7.9; and visual depictions of rape: for example, the Gemma Augustea, the Claudius and Brittania relief from Aphrodisias, the Column of Marcus Aurelius, and the Clementia sarcophagus.

19 Major political developments in the early books of Livy's *Ab Urbe Condita* are preceded by rape (Arieti, 2002, p. 209). See Belser, 2014, on the 'pervasive Roman symbolism of imperial dominance as a form of "sexual conquest"'.

20 The debate continues as to whether rape was an accompaniment and consequence of war rather than strategy; on the latter, see Vikman, 2005.

21 For longer studies on rape in the Hebrew Bible/Old Testament, see, for example, Graybill, 2021, and Scholz, 2010. Valuable work on rape culture and Bible is done by the Shiloh Project, available at https://www.shilohproject.blog (accessed 7.06.2024).

22 In sexualized violence the focus is on the violence aspect, where the latter has a sexual connotation; not so much sexual acts in themselves as the sexual symbolic of violent acts such as penetration by foreign objects (sword or knife), or stripping off clothes (Parks, Sheinfeld and Warren, 2022, pp. 232–7). In sexual violence, the focus is on the sexual and coercive sexual acts committed against an unwilling victim. The meaningfulness of distinctions for victims is another question.

23 All translations of New Testament texts are my own unless indicated otherwise. The interpretive history rendering *klinē* as 'sick bed' (e.g. RSV; ESV; NASB) testifies to the embarrassment of sexual violence and its divine connections (see also Rev. 19.1–2). Parks, Sheinfeld and Warren (2022, p. 237) and Müller van Velden (2022) warn against the assumption that texts, especially in polemical mode, render accurate renditions of situations. 'The Jezebel stereotype remains a reminder of the ways a dominant culture can use a biblical image as a justification for racism and sexism' (Davis, 2023).

24 The sexualization of the prostitute is equalled only by the violence of her portrayal (Rev. 17.6; see 18.24), but the violence meted out, far worse (see Punt, 2021).

25 Slavery in the ancient world, and also the time of the New Testament, is a wide area of scholarship; more generally; see, for example, Byron, 2004; 2008;

Bradley, 1987; 1994; Glancy, 2002. For more sustained treatments of slavery as *topos* in Paul, cf. e.g. D. B. Martin (1990) and Tsang, 2005. Broader debate ranged between slavery-positive positions such as Bartchy (1973) and Martin (1990) to the more recent slavery-condemning positions of Glancy (2002) and Harrill (e.g. 2006).

26 Roman literature is replete with references to the connection between slavery and crucifixion, after revolts or violent confrontations (Livy 22.33.2; 33.36.3); see Glancy, 2002, p. 152. Even frivolous infringements made slaves prone to crucifixion: falling out of favour with owners (Juvenal, *Sat* 6.223), tasting the soup (Horace, *Sat* 1.3.80–83), or consulting astrologers (Petronius, *Sat* 53.3).

27 Cf. Cicero (*Verr* 2.5.169); Tacitus referred to crucifixion as *servile modum* (a slave-type) punishment (*Hist* 2.72.1–2). See also Hengel, 1977, pp. 51–63, and Scaer, 2005, p. 1. Some scholars point to the sexual abuse that accompanied crucifixion (e.g. Reaves, Tombs and Figueroa, 2021).

28 Cf. Kartzow and Martinsen (2019, p. 654): 'The metaphor [of enslavement] elsewhere describes the changing of masters, from being enslaved to sin to being the slave of God (Rom 16:12–23).'

29 Paul's emphasis on freedom and its connections with Christ is an equally prominent notion in the Pauline writings; see, for example, Rom. 8.2; Gal. 5.1, 13; 2 Cor. 3.17 etc.

30 To this day, the translation of the last two words of 1 Cor. 7.21 is contested: *mallon chrēsai*.

31 The emphasis on abstaining from sexual sin seems to override including slaves in the Pauline communities when conditions for participation were the same for all (Neutel, 2012, p. 146).

32 Mary Sommar's study shows how the Church sought to establish norms for slave ownership and regulate behaviour towards slaves. Church leaders' impulse to protect the Church's heritage for the benefit of future generations compelled them to retain firm control over their enslaved workforce so that their opportunities for freedom were more curtailed inside the Church than outside it (Sommar, 2020).

33 Adult–child sexual activity was common at the time, with pederasty (not to be simply rolled into modern-day understandings of paedophilia) deriving from Greek practices but frowned upon by Romans (Frilingos, 2014). On slave children in the Jesus movement, see, for example, Kartzow, 2018a.

34 Other scholars have argued convincingly about the sexual availability of slaves in antiquity (e.g. Glancy, 2002; 2015; 2019; Marchal, 2011).

35 See also Byron for an overview of different scholarly positions in New Testament studies: Byron, 2004, pp. 116–39; and, more extensively, 2008; also, more broadly, Bradley, 1987; 1994; Bradley and Cartledge, 2010. For slavery in the Jewish context, see also Hezser, 2005; 2016.

36 Reasons for the change of heart include greater apprehension about the extent to which written sources (legal, novel, satire and others) reflect the social context or merely conjure up a narrative world by and for the consumption of the elite.

37 And with attention to the social world, the economic value of slaves exposed the ambivalence of a situation where slaves' exploitative position and their economic value for their owners would have created tension.

38 While the metaphorical use of the cross/crucifixion was limited to the Roman world with the Greek world apparently finding it offensive (Hengel, 1977, p. 68),

the use of slavery as metaphor was found more regularly in literature (see Briggs, 2003, p. 185).

39 In Israelite and Roman cultic and political discourse, female symbolism was applied to victory and peace as well as to domination and defeat, but also functioned as an index of moral and social health (Huber, 2013, pp. 45, 48). Scholars challenge the notion of sacred or cultic prostitution and criticize the use of the bodies of women in such myth-making (Beard and Henderson, 1998, pp. 56–79).

40 Distinguishing between horizontal or normal slavery and vertical or metaphorical enslavement to God rendered 'a complex system or network of doulological classifications' (De Wet, 2018, p. 19).

41 '[T]he editors of the Slave Bible did not remove liberative portions or emphasize servitude … A contingent benefit to the conversion of slaves … was that the Christian faith was understood to emphasize certain virtues favorable to slavery' (Hurlbert, 2023, p. 3).

42 According to Loughlin (2005, p. 13), '[B]iology is cultural, and our ideas of sex are gendered, and God's gender affects his sex, and this becomes all too evident when divinity is used to underwrite certain human orderings.' On toxic theologies see Zachariah, 2022.

43 Scholars have investigated ways to trouble and undermine slavery's religious and sexual legacies (e.g. Brooten and Hazelton, 2010).

44 And indeed, 'Paul rarely singles out women or female characters as temptresses or evil harlots; the apostles' admonitions against sexual immorality were addressed to men and women alike' (Clark, 2019, p. 45). Others are more critical of Paul and his legacy: 'It would be foolish to expect Paul, who was born, raised, and socialized in the patriarchy, misogyny, hierarchies, slaving, and violence of the first-century Mediterranean, to share the values of modern liberal Westerners. Slavery seemed natural to him' (Concannon, 2021, p. 3; cf. Marchal, 2020, for his deliberate anachronistic juxtapositions).

45 Craps faults trauma theory's founding texts on four grounds: marginalizing traumatic experiences of minority cultures, postulating universal validity for Western modernity's experience of trauma, privileging a modernist aesthetic of fragmentation and aporia for experiencing trauma, and ignoring connections between metropolitan and 'non-Western traumas' (Craps, 2013, p. 2).

46 Larson emphasizes rhetoric, how language privileges male perspectives and, more deeply, how it is shaped by systems of power – patriarchy, white supremacy, ableism and heteronormativity. In contrast, 'African Americans responded to a world shaped by white supremacy by honing a sophisticated and self-reflective hermeneutics that refused to accept arguments for biblical affirmations of slavery' (Marbury, 2023, p. 3).

11

'Madoda Sabelani' and Matthew 2.18: Lamenting Hegemonic Masculinity

DEWALD JACOBS

Introduction

Matthew 2.18 recounts the order of King Herod the Great to 'kill all the boys in Bethlehem and its vicinity who were two years old and under'. Herod issues this violent order in the interest of safeguarding his own claims to kingship upon learning of the birth of the Messiah, who was perceived as the legitimate king of the Jews. This passage has become synonymous with resistance movements, sermons and conferences against gender-based violence (GBV). In 2019, the late Professor Mary-Anne Plaatjies van Huffel, Professor of Ecclesiology and Church Law, reflected on this text during a silent protest-action at the Faculty of Theology, Stellenbosch University. She spoke out against an upsurge in rape and murder cases in South Africa and directly addressed President Ramaphosa, stating:

> Mr President, throughout South Africa a sounding voice of lament, of weeping, of mourning is heard ... in the townships ... on farms ... on universities ... on schools, factories, over the hill tops ... up into the corridors of the parliament. Women are weeping for her children, and the children of others, the boy and girl child ... the LGBTQIA community. We are weeping for mutilated and decomposing human bodies and uncared dead female bodies in the land and will not be comforted, because they are no more (Matt. 2.18).[1]

This chapter argues that the musical cry of singer/songwriter Lloyiso in his song 'Madoda Sabelani' (Men, heed the call) echoes the lament found in Matthew 2.18 (NIV): 'A voice is heard in Ramah, weeping and great mourning'.[2] Claus Westermann contends that a characteristic of lament is that it typically has three dimensions, namely: an accusation or complaint against God, a complaint against an enemy, and/or towards the lamenter himself (Westermann, 1974, p. 27). Given the crisis of gender-based violence in the context of South Africa, this chapter will proceed to direct the complaint against men and hegemonic masculinity by focusing on the figure of King Herod the Great. I will proceed to draw from the lament of 'Madoda Sabelani', for men to heed the call, to lament the hegemonic masculinity found in the actions of Herod. This will be done according to the structure of Psalms of Lament: (1) an address to God, (2) complaint, (3) request, (4) motivation (why God should act), and (5) confidence in God (Lewis Hall, 2016; Brueggemann, 1986; Westermann, 1974).

Importantly, the Matthean text of the New Testament is an ancient text written centuries ago and the concept of hegemonic masculinity is a contemporary concept of the late twentieth and twenty-first centuries. While recognizing the historical distance between the two, this chapter contends that the two can meaningfully be considered together in lamenting masculinity of the past and present. Furthermore, lament generally has a transition or transformation in mind – from lament to praise. According to Jones, Walter Brueggemann would suggest, it could be seen as a shift from Orientation to Disorientation to New Orientation (Jones, 2007, p. 49). This chapter will showcase how the movement through the structure of lament is important to address hegemonic masculinity.

Men, heed the call

The voice of singer/songwriter Lloyiso Gijana echoed through South Africa in June 2020 when he released the song 'Madoda Sabelani' (Men, heed the call) in memory of his friend Uyinene Mrwetyana, who was gruesomely murdered in 2019. Uyinene was raped and murdered in the local Claremont Post Office in Cape Town by Luyanda Botha, an official of the Post Office. The circumstances surrounding Uyinene's murder sparked resistance movements against gender-based violence across the country as women were raising their voices in solidarity through movements such as #AmINext and #EnoughisEnough.

The song was released in the wake of the news of another gruesome murder of a young woman, Tshegofatso Pule, in 2020. Notably, at the start of the music video of 'Madoda Sabelani', the lamenting voice of Lloyiso is coupled with the picture of Pule.[3] The country had been particularly shocked by the death of Pule, whose body was found hanging from a tree in Roodepoort, west of Johannesburg. Pule was eight months pregnant at the time she was murdered by Muzikayise Malephane, who confessed to have been contracted to murder her by Ntuthuko Shoba, Pule's estranged boyfriend and father of her unborn child. When Shoba was sentenced to life in prison in July 2022, acting judge Stuart Wilson stated that despite 'his productive career, strong family background and his previous good character', the presented evidence overwhelmingly pointed to Shoba as the prime driver of the murder of Pule (The State and Ntuthoko Ntkozo Shoba, 2022, Case No: SS36/2021). Shoba grew up in a loving and supportive environment and eventually became a financial analyst on the Johannesburg Stock Exchange. Evidently, Pule's vulnerability as a young pregnant woman seeking emotional and financial care from Shoba proved to be an inconvenience to him. Moreover, he exploited her vulnerability and dependence on him to orchestrate her abduction and murder and was eventually the one to hand her over to her killer.

This all happened during the time of the National Lockdown, when a spike in GBV cases in South Africa occurred. According to Police Minister Bheki Cele, in the first week of the National Lockdown telling amounts of 2,230 cases and 87,000 complaints relating to GBV were recorded (Mlambo, 2020; Tshangela, 2020). Pule was not alone, but was one of thousands of the most vulnerable: women, children, the LGBTQIA+ community, elderly people, and people living with disabilities who were trapped in violent and abusive environments. In this regard, the words of President Cyril Ramaphosa regarding GBV in 2019 remain true. President Ramaphosa called upon men to respond to GBV and acknowledge it as a men's problem, as men are the ones who rape and kill women.

In the song 'Madoda Sabelani', we find an example of how Lloyiso responds to the passing of his friend and the crisis of GBV in South Africa. Reflecting on the song in an interview, Lloyiso mentions that the song is a call for action to men to start talking about the role men can play in our societies to protect women (Bambalele, 2020). In this regard, 'Madoda Sabelani' isn't only a song, as Aphiwe Mhlangulana and Leballo Tjemolane (2022) rightly observe: '"Madoda Sabelani" is a common phrase used to encourage men to respond to the prevalence and growing numbers of cases of gender-based violence (GBV) in the country.' Furthermore, 'Madoda Sabelani' serves as a lament which expresses the frustration, grief and anger of many in the country, but it also calls upon men in the country to put a stop to the violence and acknowledge that, as men, 'we are the danger'.

Lamenting hegemonic masculinity in Matthew 2

Elizabeth Lewis Hall argues that lament can serve as a 'verbalization of suffering' to help those who are suffering to express and articulate their suffering in words (Lewis Hall, 2016, p. 224). This verbalization of the suffering allows a personal and interpersonal process of meaning-making amid suffering. In this sense, lament does not only reflect the experience of suffering, but it also helps shape this experience and evidently imagines and calls upon a new and alternative reality. Throughout the structure of the psalms of lament space is created for those who are suffering to clearly express their voices, minds, hearts and emotions towards God, enemies, neighbours and/or themselves. Logan Jones notes that in the tradition of lament, a tradition of honest dialogue with God is found which dares to dwell in the depths of pain and relentlessly expresses the unspeakable and unnameable hurt of life (Jones, 2007, p. 49). In South Africa, GBV has become the too familiar and normalized hurt of life and requires a relentless and honest response and dialogue, such as seen in 'Madoda Sabelani'. This section follows the structure of the psalms of lament in an attempt to provide an honest and raw engagement with hegemonic masculinity found in Matthew 2 and in our contemporary context. But first it is important to give a short overview of what is understood under this term.

Defining hegemonic masculinity

The term and concept of hegemonic masculinity originated in the 1970s and 1980s and is largely attributed to the work of Raewyn Connell and James Messerschmidt in the field of gender theory. In the article 'Hegemonic Masculinity: Rethinking the Concept' (2005), Connell and Messerschmidt do well to flesh out the origin, formulation and application of hegemonic masculinity. Hegemonic masculinity is essentialized as the 'most honoured way of being a man', distinguishing itself from subordinate and complicit masculinities (Connell and Messerschmidt, 2005, p. 832). Evidently, hegemonic masculinity exerts pressure on men to align themselves according to a structure of power, a specific set of societal norms and practices, and ultimately an identity stereotypically associated with what it means to be a man. Ideologically, it understands and legitimates itself in relation to the subordinate being, identity and place of women and all other groups in society. This position of hegemonic masculinity is further strengthened by the patriarchy that is prevalent in most societies globally but is also subject to varying circumstances in various contexts. This leads South African scholars such as Madipoane Masenya, Sarojini Nadar, Karen Graaff and Lindy Heinecken to assert, in the words of Masenya, that 'what and how a man is, becomes and should be, is constructed by his own society' (Masenya, 2019, p. 399; Nadar, 2009, p. 552; Graaff and Heinecken, 2017, p. 623). Graaff and Heinecken highlight the following aspects of hegemonic masculinities that are common across contemporary societies: the need to be the providers of the family, a supposedly insatiable sex drive, and displaying physical strength and toughness, often with the ability to inflict violence (Graaff and Heinecken, 2017, p. 623). They emphasize how these aspects pave the way for men to resort to violence and aggression to solve problems, confrontations and conflict. Moreover, they stress how these aspects are intensified in the context of South Africa with a history of apartheid and the normalization of violence, income inequality, militarization and gender inequality (Graaff and Heinecken, 2017, pp. 624–7).

Most often, the struggle to attain this most desired and often unattainable hegemonic masculinity of power in patriarchal contexts paves the way for sexism, homophobia, ableism and violence against women and children. Turning to the Matthean text, the citation of Jeremiah 31.15 in Matthew 2.18 becomes significant in the context of hegemonic masculinity, as it breaks what Tinyiko Maluleke and Sarojini Nadar have coined as 'the covenant of silence' (Maluleke and Nadar, 2002, p. 7). The citation of Jeremiah reads as follows in Matthew:

> A voice is heard in Ramah,
> weeping and great mourning,
> Rachel weeping for her children
> and refusing to be comforted,
> because they are no more.
> (Matt. 2.18, NIV)

The address

Lament typically begins with a distress call to God: 'My God, My God, why have you forsaken me' or 'How long, Lord? Will you forget me forever?' (Lewis Hall, 2016, p. 225; Westermann, 1974, p. 28). This address and cry to God is indicative of the interpersonal and covenant relationship between the people and God as those who are suffering are allowed to bring the entirety of their situation before God. In 'Madoda Sabelani' this call is directed towards men who are identified as the danger. This chapter unequivocally identifies and addresses King Herod the Great in

Matthew 2 as being the danger. He serves as an example of one who was committed to the endless pursuit of hegemonic masculinity and who was willing to go to the extreme of killing innocent infants in his struggle to remain dominant in power.

M. J. Mans highlights the various references that are made to Herod by the early church fathers and identifies the characterization of the fifth-century author Chrysologus as the most damning. Chrysologus describes Herod as 'a murderer of helpless infants, a robber breaking up families, a commander in chief of evil, a military bully' (Mans, 1997, p. 95). Even Herod's immediate family was not spared from his cruelty as it was generally known that Herod's pig was more cared for than his wife and sons (Carter, 2013, p. 64). Evans recalls that even though the literary character of King Herod in Matthew 2 could refer to his son Archelaus who governed from 4 BC to AD 6, it was only Herod the Great, who ruled from 37 BC to 4 BC, who was officially known as the King of the Jews (Evans, 2012, p. 50). Herod was declared 'King of the Jews' in 40 BC by the Roman Senate, upon the recommendation of the Roman general Mark Anthony (Marcus Antonius). In 37 BC, Herod would gain control of Judea and be appointed by the Romans as a client king in the province of Judea and reign till his death in 4 BC (Basser, 2015, p. 49; Evans, 2012, p. 11). Mans mentions that questions still exist regarding the historicity of the infanticide of Bethlehem and King Herod's role in it. It is however clear that the Matthean author's designation of King Herod as literary character calls on the historical figure of King Herod, the client king of Rome, who was known to the Matthean audience. Importantly, he held a place of power and influence in the patriarchal and hierarchal structure of power of the emperor and the imperial cult. To a great extent, he always had to perform to remain in power as he was tasked to foster loyalty to Roman power and govern over a system that benefited a small elite at the expense of the majority non-elite (Carter, 2013, p. 5). Additionally, this was in a time when the emperor was regarded as the *Pater Patriae* ('Father of the Fatherland') and the 'figurehead' of a male-centred and male-dominated structure of power (Carter, 2006, p. 4).

In her studies on hegemonic masculinity in the Hebrew Bible, Susan Haddox recognizes that masculinities are bound to context and should also be cognisant of the intersection of race, religion and class. She proceeds to identify the following traits commonly observed in patriarchal cultures (Haddox, 2016, pp. 179–82): military might, bodily integrity, honour, virility, provisioning and spatiality. Focusing on the hegemonic masculinity of Herod, the categories of military might and honour are considered especially important and will be examined in this chapter.

First, it is suggested that military might is indicative of hegemonic masculinity. This relates to the connection between masculinities, violence and power that has marked human experience throughout the ages, ranging from domestic violence to world wars. The possibility of his position of power as a Roman client king being threatened leads Herod to orchestrate a plan to remain in power. In the process, he calls on the resources that are available to him and he abuses his power and alliances with the imperial cult, the Jerusalem elite, the chief priests and scribes to locate the birthplace of Jesus and instruct the murders of the children of Bethlehem. His position as a client king of Rome enabled Herod to have access to the resources of the Roman army to inflict violence on innocent children and further threaten colonial subjects with the mere possibility of inflicting violence. Madipoane Masenya notes that power enables those in power to 'both build and destroy' (2019, p. 414). From a Roman client king to a financial analyst of the Johannesburg Stock Exchange and an official in a local post office, hegemonic masculinity and power lead to violence and death.

Second, Masenya (2019, p. 411) mentions that honour is considered to be a value that should be embodied by adult males and is intricately tied with male ideologies. Honour in this sense refers to the male's ability to exert control over women and exercise authority over his family. Furthermore, honour in the ancient context existed within a binary sex and gender system that rendered men at the apex of the power hierarchy, serving as active agents rather than passive followers who submitted to the power of other people. Other men, in contrast, were deemed 'less than male figures', with women perceived as 'incomplete versions of the ideal male' and slaves as 'unmen, compared to the free male citizen' (Conway, 2016, p. 16). Notably, the significance of children's lives was only recognized when they could contribute to the economy, implying that the lives of non-elite infants from Bethlehem would likely not have concerned Herod. Upon hearing that his own sons were plotting against him to overthrow him, Herod did not hesitate to have them killed. Even before his death, Herod had his eldest son Antipater imprisoned and had him executed four days before his own death (France, 2007, p. 138).

In the context of hegemonic masculinity, the possibility of Herod being deceived by his own sons and wives, and by the magi with regard to the birth of Jesus, leads to violence and, ultimately, death. In light of his position in the Roman Empire, he was inclined to show loyalty to the imperial cult and ensure that there was peace in Judea. The birth of a rightful heir to the throne of the king of the Jews would possibly lead to Herod's authority being questioned and resisted. At that point, the Jews already disapproved of Herod as king, perceiving his ascent to power as illegitimate and viewing him as a mere puppet king under Rome's influence (France, 2007, p. 142). Herod and Shoba are worlds apart, yet both resorted to violence when their societal positions faced potential threats. The imperative here for the contemporary reader lies in acknowledging and lamenting the destructive impact of hegemonic masculinity, which in its extreme form can lead to violence and harm innocent lives. Through the citation of Jeremiah 31, the Matthean author does well to invite the intended ancient audience of the Matthean text to communally lament the loss of innocent lives.

The complaint

The cry of 'Madoda Sabelani' prophetically acknowledges that 'we [men] are the danger'. The second component of lament addresses the cause of the suffering that is brought before God and expresses the disorientation experienced in the face of suffering (Lewis Hall, 2016, p. 226). This aspect of lament does not shy away from the suffering that is experienced but instead embraces the grief in an attempt to make sense of the situation. Lewis Hall underscores that engaging with suffering confronts us with the discomfort of attending to the pain of others and ourselves. This stance contradicts the cultural and religious status quo of our societies, challenging the prevalent tendency to distract those in pain or direct their attention to the potential 'good' that might arise from their current circumstances (Lewis Hall, 2016, p. 227).

The citation of Jeremiah 31.15 in Matthew 2.18 serves as an editorial comment on a traditional story, strategically employed to amplify the significance of the Messiah's birth. Through this citation, the Matthean author creatively interprets the received narrative, referring to the matriarch Rachel, who weeps for her children who were killed or exiled. This quote prompts the reader to discern the significant underlying patterns of fulfilment unfolding in the narrative. Evans suggests that the character of King Herod too is employed by the Matthean author to draw a typological comparison between the birth narratives of Jesus and Moses. In doing so, the author recalls the initial commands of the Pharaoh of Egypt to the Hebrew midwives Shiphrah and Puah, and subsequently to all his people, to kill every Hebrew boy that is born in Egypt (Ex. 1.15—2.10). This typological connection is strengthened when the parents of Jesus flee with him to Egypt, to escape Herod's wrath, and in doing so fulfil the prophecy of Hosea 11.1: 'Out of Egypt I have called my son.' Moreover, just as Moses delivered the Israelites from Egypt, Jesus too departs from Egypt to initiate his ministry of deliverance (Evans, 2012, p. 57).

The complaint aspect of lament challenges us as contemporary biblical readers to pause and contemplate the gruesome killings of innocent children. Evidently, this unsettling episode in Matthew's Gospel plays a significant role in drawing a comparison between Jesus and Moses and fulfilling the words spoken by the prophet Hosea. However, it also disrupts the seamless transition to the birth and life of the promised Messiah. Through this inclusion of Rachel's mourning voice, the Matthean author breaks the covenant of silence. According to Maluleke and Nadar, when societies remain silent about violence, especially violence against women and children, they commit themselves to a deadly covenant of silence. This covenant cultivates and reinforces attitudes, teachings, practices and rituals which tear human societies apart (Maluleke and Nadar, 2002, p. 7). Such silence plays out in families, neighbourhoods, churches and workplaces. Moreover, this societal covenant of violence is often illegitimately endorsed through 'the unholy trinity of religion, culture, and the subsequent power of gender socialization' (Maluleke and Nadar, 2002, p. 14). In this regard, sacred texts and religious traditions may be called upon in societies to justify violence experienced at the hands of men.

However, in this sacred text, the Matthean author breaks away from the covenant of silence by not turning a blind eye to the actions of political leaders like Herod, who seem to establish a normative pattern of male behaviour in the given society. The infanticide of Bethlehem and the weeping of mothers like Rachel confront the reader to acknowledge the harm that has been done. It serves as an act of lament that protests against the normativity of violence. Westermann (1974, p. 30) notes that laments serve as protests that refuse to endure and to accept absurdity. Moreover, acknowledging this inhuman violence calls the readers to stand with those who have suffered.

Matthew 2 acknowledges the weeping of the mothers at Bethlehem and the tragedy of the Israelite exiles who were forcefully gathered in Ramah to march to Babylon in 586 BC (France, 2007, p. 140). Likewise, the music video of 'Madoda Sabelani' acknowledges the passing of Tshegofatso Pule, Uyinene Mrwetyana, and many other women and children. In this context, lament functions as a communal acknowledgement of suffering that reverberates through the entire community and calls this community to formulate an appropriate response to such suffering.

The request

Laments in the Hebrew Bible typically do not remain stuck in the experience of the suffering but move beyond to appeal to the one who can remove the suffering (Brueggemann, 1986, p. 58; Westermann, 1974, p. 22; Lewis Hall, 2016, p. 228). Typically, hope is central to making sense of the suffering and inaugurates a movement from complaint to request. This hope is founded on the imagined possibility that God will intervene, deliver, and save those who are suffering (Jones, 2007, p. 48). The song 'Madoda Sabelani' also moves from addressing men to heed the call, to praying to God and asking God to intervene and answer our prayers (*Ndiyathandazi nkosi, Uphendule imithandazo yethu*).

This chapter, however, seeks to continue addressing men, especially cis-gendered, heterosexual, able-bodied men. In the current climate of violence against women, children and people who identify as LGBTQIA+, elderly and differently abled people, these men are the ones who can combat the suffering inflicted by hegemonic masculinity. Laments are generally built on the premise that God must and will respond because humans share in the covenant relationship with God. In this relationship with God, all human experiences can be brought before God, who will embrace all of what humans experience (Jones, 2007, p. 50). Through the act of lamentation, we speak to the heart of God, as the cry of lament speaks the terrible truth of disorientation and disrupts what we consider to be normal. Significantly, in the Gospel of Matthew, the celebrated nativity story of Jesus is disrupted and intertwined with the terrible truth of the infanticides at Bethlehem and a great weeping heard in Ramah.

According to Richard France, the citation of Jeremiah 31.15 serves as a message of hope beyond this tragedy as it recalls the time of the exile and the return from exile (France, 2007, p. 141). Furthermore, the Matthean author also refers to Jeremiah 31.31 ('my blood of the covenant') in Matthew 26.28 as Jesus has his last meal with the disciples and establishes a new covenant community (France, 2007, p. 862). Jeremiah 31 thus plays a crucial role in the fulfilment theme of Matthew, underscoring how the suffering of the infants of Bethlehem is woven into the birth of the Messiah and the establishment of a new covenantal relationship. The early church fathers regarded these infants as the first martyrs who 'were worthy of dying for the sake of Christ' (Mans, 1997, pp. 96–7). However, this interpretation neither excuses Herod's violent acts nor justifies a patriarchal hierarchical system that would allow such deeds. Instead, it urges us as contemporary biblical readers to recognize that the birth of the Messiah and the new covenant relationship will forever be entwined with the tragic loss of innocent lives in Bethlehem.

In the context of hegemonic masculinity and the violent covenant of silence, all human suffering at the hands of men must be brought before men, and men must respond to the suffering and brokenheartedness that is caused by hegemonic masculinity in our societies. The danger is that people become too familiar with the cries, weeping and protests of women, and are no longer moved by it. Lamenting hegemonic masculinity confronts us to heed the call and acknowledge that we are entangled in structures and systems of violence.

Furthermore, 'Madoda Sabelani' also serves as Lloyiso's response to the murder of his friend, and as much as his art form is an expression of his grief and suffering, it also becomes an expression of hope against injustice and suffering in South Africa (Mlamla, Dlamini and Shumba, 2021, p. 109). While at first the song was a private and personal response of Lloyiso, it became a public response that caught the attention of the country and demanded a response.[4] Currently, 'Madoda Sabelani' has over two million views on YouTube. It is now known globally and has inspired responses by many others. The Matthean author responded in writing to the violence inflicted by Herod; Loyiso responds through his voice, body and art. Both responses testify to the relentless nature of lament to demand a response from their addressees (Jones, 2007, p. 47). Moreover, by means of lament, the question of justice is kept alive, visible and legitimate, resisting the normalization of unjust actions and circumstances (Brueggemann, 1986, p. 63). Through lamenting hegemonic masculinity, the question of justice is kept alive, visible and legitimate, resisting the normalization of violence against women, children, the LGBTQIA+ community, elderly people and people living with disabilities.

The motivation

The motivation element of lament refers to the reasons why God should answer the petition, as the one suffering proceeds to remind God of why God should act and intervene. Lewis Hall (2016, p. 228) emphasizes that the motivation element serves as a reminder of who God is, by referring to God's reputation, past actions, the guilt or innocence of the speaker, and the promise of praise and trust in the Lord. The question now arises: Why should we, men especially, act against hegemonic masculinity?

In the Matthean text, the birth of the Messiah, Jesus, the son of God, will always be connected to the deaths of the infants of Bethlehem, and the weeping of their mothers interrupts the biblical reader to simply move towards the birth of the Messiah. The act of crying out to God shapes us relationally, reminding us of who God is, and who we are in the covenant relationship with God. Brueggemann emphasizes that the loss and absence of lament in the covenant relationship with God would harm its integrity and authenticity (Brueggemann, 1986, p. 60). The covenant relationship without the presence of lament would become a pretentious covenant that denies and covers up the terrible truth of the hurt and suffering of life. By means of lament, believers are not only able to initiate honest dialogue with God and demand the response of God, but they themselves become responsible and mature covenant partners who engage with both the joy and hurt of life (Brueggemann, 1986, p. 61).

In contemporary contexts, questions regarding hegemonic masculinity and labels such as #menaretrash will always be connected with gender-based violence in our societies, and will always implicate that 'men are the danger'. Andrea Waling mentions that occurrences of gender-based violence have led to the conceptualization and differentiation of healthy and toxic masculinities. In this regard, toxic masculinity is associated with aggressive and predatory heterosexual behaviour leading to acts of sexual and domestic violence perpetrated by men. She problematizes how the concept of toxic masculinity positions masculinity as a disease that infects the male population in any given society and seems to be incurable (Waling, 2019, p. 368): 'Men are thus victims of such a disease, unable to break away from the contamination masculinity brings, unavoidable due to the circumstance of their assigned sex and gender.' On the other hand, no consensus is reached on what precisely healthy masculinity is and how it relates to the intersections of class, sexuality, gender, culture, race and disability. Most often, it is only understood in light of toxic masculinity, meaning that men who do not rape and kill can claim that they do not have toxic masculinity – pointing fingers to the Herods of the world under the guise of 'not all men'.

'Madoda Sabelani' and lamenting hegemonic masculinity demand a response from all men, to become mature, responsible, and accountable in breaking the violent covenant of silence that covers up and denies the hurt of gender-based violence in our societies. Waling highlights that hegemonic and toxic masculinities can have a dire and devastating impact on communities if they are not recognized and attended to (Waling, 2019, p. 368). Given the violent history and lasting legacy of colonialism and apartheid in South Africa and its influence on masculinities, attending to hegemonic masculinity in our communities could foster a culture of communal healing from generational trauma. Importantly, bell hooks emphasizes in her essay 'Understanding Patriarchy' (2004) that patriarchal and hegemonic masculinity promotes insanity and leads to 'male pain' as it undermines and denies the emotional and mental well-being of men. She highlights that men are already indoctrinated and nurtured into the rules of patriarchy and hegemonic masculinity from a young age through practices that force them to endure pain and deny their feelings. Furthermore, she cautions that if the problem of patriarchal hegemonic masculinity remains unaddressed, men will continue to suffer 'male pain', unable to be emotionally inclined beings and continue to feel an overwhelming dissatisfaction with the lives they live (hooks, 2004, p. 4).

Herod and Shoba exemplify the severe consequences of a life lived in pursuit of this most desired and often unattainable hegemonic masculinity of power. Herod's preoccupation with power, control and greed led to a lonely life of fear, paranoia and insanity to the point of having his own wife and sons killed. In the proceedings before Shoba's sentencing, prosecutor Faghre Mohammed noted that Shoba did not show any sign of remorse for the contracted murder of Pule (Koka, 2022). As a result of the hegemonic masculinity of power, he was, however, calculated and strategic in using his power and influence to have someone contracted to murder his infant and its mother. If we do not resist these violent systems and acknowledge the problem of hegemonic masculinity, we will continue to have a problem of violence in our communities. Lamenting hegemonic masculinity thus also becomes a necessity for men and the society at large to flourish and live healthy and meaningful lives.

The expression of confidence

The final element of lament is often marked by the word 'but', as it signifies a contrast and a movement into a new way of experiencing reality (Lewis Hall, 2016, p. 230). This 'but' indicates that the lamenting person will not remain in brokenness and grief, but in an act of boldness will move from plea to praise, pointing towards the possibility of transformation (Jones, 2007, p. 48). This movement from disorientation to a new orientation – grounded in the covenant relationship with God – remains a mystery, but attests to the fact that life has been transformed and health has been restored (Jones, 2007, p. 53). Typically, this element signifies utter confidence that God will deliver and save the one who is suffering, leading to a new place and orientation where praise is generated from the heart because the old orientation is overcome.

Lewis Hall attests to the mystery of this transformation of life in referring to the psalms of lament that are often silent about how the movement to praise takes place. She does, however, highlight the importance of such movement (Lewis Hall, 2016, p. 239): 'As we pray through the psalms, our desires, affections, and perspectives are reshaped.' At this point, we may not know how the situation of hegemonic masculinity and the violent covenant of silence in our communities may be transformed. The lament of the Matthean author recording the cruel acts of Herod and Lloyiso singing 'Madoda Sabelani' do however confront us with the terrible truth of our current situation of hegemonic masculinity. Moreover, they challenge us to heed the call for our desires, affections and perspectives to be reshaped in lamenting. Being confronted with hegemonic masculinity, the following questions may lead to further necessary conversations.

Do we have confidence that men have the will to change? Do we have confidence that we can break the violent covenant of silence? Do we have confidence that life will be transformed and the old orientation of hegemonic masculinity will be no more?

Only if we are willing to break the violent covenant of silence we maintain in our families and communities. Only if we are willing to learn that we can love, care, be vulnerable, and be compassionate, and not only strong, courageous and protective. Only if we are willing to be moved by the weeping of women and children, who are at a point where they refuse to be comforted. Only if we are willing to accept that we are the danger and we are complicit to hegemonic masculinity in the private and public spheres of life. Only if we are willing to heed the call.

Conclusion

Lewis Hall argues that the act of lament assists in the process of understanding suffering and in bridging the gap between the understanding of the cause of the suffering and the worldview that is held in relation to the suffering. This gap can either be bridged by changing the view of the cause or by changing one's worldview of the suffering (Lewis Hall, 2016, p. 231). In lamenting hegemonic masculinity in Matthew 2 and with a thorough engagement of the song 'Madoda Sabelani', this chapter has foregrounded hegemonic masculinity as the cause of gender-based violence in our societies and has invited men to heed the song's call by acknowledging that 'we are the danger'. The movement through the structure of lament serves as a transformative process that has allowed us to be confronted with the honest reality of hegemonic masculinity and has challenged us to reconsider our desires, affections, perspectives and worldviews.

Bibliography

Bambalele, P., 2020, 'Song against Femicide a Big Hit', *Sowetan Live*, 19 June, available at https://www.sowetanlive.co.za/entertainment/2020-06-19-song-against-femicide-a-big-hit/ (accessed 9.12.2023).

Basser, H., and M. B. Cohen, 2015, *The Gospel of Matthew and Judaic Traditions: A Relevance-based Commentary*, Leiden: Brill.

Brueggemann, W., 1986, 'The Costly Loss of Lament', *Journal for the Study of the Old Testament* 11, pp. 57–71.

Carter, W., 2006, *The Roman Empire and the New Testament: An Essential Guide*, Nashville, TN: Abingdon.

Carter, W., 2013, 'Between Text and Sermon, Matthew 2:1–12', *Interpretation: A Journal of Bible and Theology* 67/1, pp. 64–7.

Connell, R. W., and J. W. Messerschmidt, 2005, 'Hegemonic Masculinity: Rethinking the Concept', *Gender & Society* 19/6, pp. 829–59.

Conway, C. M., 2016, 'Was Jesus a Manly Man? On Reading Masculinity in the New Testament', *Word & World* 36/1, pp. 15–23.

Evans, C. A., 2012, *Matthew*, Cambridge: Cambridge University Press.

France, R. T., 2007, *The Gospel of Matthew*, Grand Rapids, MI: Eerdmans.

Graaff, K., and L. Heinecken, 2017, 'Masculinities and gender-based violence in South Africa: A study of a masculinities-focused intervention programme', *Development Southern Africa* 34/5, pp. 622–34, DOI: 10.1080/0376835X.2017.1334537

Haddox, S. E., 2016, 'Masculinity Studies of the Hebrew Bible: The First Two Decades', *Currents in Biblical Research* 14/2, pp. 176–206.

hooks, bell, 2004, 'Understanding Patriarchy', *The Anarchist Library*, December, available at https://theanarchistlibrary.org/library/bell-hooks-understanding-patriarchy.pdf (accessed 19.12.2023).

Jones, L. C., 2007, 'The Psalms of Lament and the Transformation of Sorrow', *Journal of Pastoral Care & Counseling* 61/1–2, pp. 47–58.

Koka, M., 2022, 'Prosecutor Calls for Harsh Sentence for Tshegofatso Pule's Killer Shoba', *Sowetan Live*, 22 July, available at https://www.sowetanlive.co.za/news/south-africa/2022-07-28-prosecutor-calls-for-harsh-sentence-for-tshegofatso-pules-killer-shoba/ (accessed 19.12.2023).

Lewis Hall, M. E., 2016, 'Suffering in God's presence: The Role of Lament in Transformation', *Journal of Spiritual Formation and Soul Care* 9/2, pp. 219–32.

Maluleke, T., and S. Nadar, 2002, 'Breaking the Covenant of Violence Against Women', *Journal of Theology for Southern Africa* 114, pp. 5–17.

Mans, M. J., 1997, 'The Early Latin Church Fathers on Herod and the Infanticide', *HTS Teologiese Studies/Theological Studies* 53/1–2, pp. 92–102.

Masenya, M., 2019, 'Reading Hegemonic Masculinities in 2 Samuel 11 in the South African Contexts', *Stellenbosch Theological Journal* 5/3, pp. 399–420.

Mhlangulana, A., and L. Tjemolane, 2022, '"Madoda Sabelani": A Cry for Men to

Heed the Call against Gender-based Violence', *News24*, 28 November, available at https://www.news24.com/news24/opinions/columnists/guestcolumn/opinion-madoda-sabelani-a-cry-for-men-to-heed-the-call-against-gender-based-violence-20221128 (accessed 9.12.2023).

Mlambo, S., 2020, 'SAPS Received 87 000 Gender-based Violence Calls during First Week of Lockdown – Cele', *IOL*, 2 April, available at https://www.iol.co.za/news/south-africa/saps-received-87-000-gender-based-violence-calls-during-first-week-of-lockdown-cele-46024648 (accessed 9.12.2023).

Mlamla, N. E., Z. Dlamini and K. Shumba, 2021, '"Madoda Sabelani"! Engaging Indigenous Music in the Fight Against Toxic Masculinities and Gender-Based Violence in South Africa: A Critical Discourse Analysis', *Acta Criminologica: African Journal of Criminology & Victimology* 34/3, pp. 101–17.

Nadar, S., 2009, 'Palatable Patriarchy and Violence Against Wo/men in South Africa – Angus Buchan's Mighty Men's Conference as a Case Study of Masculinism', *Scriptura: Journal for Contextual Hermeneutics in Southern Africa* 102/1, pp. 551–61.

Ramaphosa, C., 2019, 'President Cyril Ramaphosa: Address to the Nation on Public and Gender-based Violence', *South African Government*, 5 September, available at https://www.gov.za/speeches/president-cyril-ramaphosa-address-nation-public-and-gender-based-violence-5-sep-2019-0000 (accessed 9.12.2023).

The State and Ntuthoko Ntkozo Shoba, 2022, Case No: SS36/2021, available at https://lawlibrary.org.za/akn/za-gp/judgment/zagpjhc/2022/877/eng@2022-07-29 (accessed 9.12.2023).

Tshangela, L., 2020, 'More than 87 000 GBV Complaints Received during Lockdown', *SABC News*, 3 April, available at https://www.sabcnews.com/sabcnews/more-than-87-000-gbv-complaints-received-during-lockdown/ (accessed 9.12.2023).

Waling, A., 2019, 'Problematising "Toxic" and "Healthy" Masculinity for Addressing Gender Inequalities', *Australian Feminist Studies* 34/101, pp. 362–75.

Westermann, C., 1974, 'The Role of the Lament in the Theology of the Old Testament', *Interpretation* 28/1, pp. 20–38.

Notes

1 Since the passing of Professor Mary-Anne Plaatjies van Huffel in 2021, I have come to cherish this passage and the memory of attending the silent protest in 2019 as a student.

2 Lloyisa Gijana, 2020a, 'Madoda Sabelani (Lyrics)', available at https://www.musixmatch.com/lyrics/Loyiso/Madoda-Sabelani/translation/english (accessed 9.12.2023).

3 Lloyisa Gijana, 2020b, 'Madoda Sabelani (Music Video)', *YouTube*, available at https://www.youtube.com/watch?v=jAN6Dv3KSWw (accessed 9.12.2023).

4 The music video of Madoda Sabelani was viewed when this essay was delivered at the conference 'Narrating Rape: Lacunae and Shifting Perspectives in (Biblical) Literature and Popular Culture' at the Faculty of Theology, Stellenbosch University. Listening to the lament in the academic setting transgressed the normal way of doing things at a conference in an academic setting.

12

The Poetics of Redacted Absence as Presence: Kin Eyes Hearing Tamar (2 Samuel 13)

GERALD O. WEST

Introduction

In 1996 what is now the Ujamaa Centre for Community Development and Research was summoned by organized groups of women to facilitate a workshop on 'Women and the Bible in South and Southern Africa'. On the third day, under the sub-theme 'Women and Violence', we used the story of Tamar in 2 Samuel 13.1–22 for the first time (West and Zondi-Mabizela, 2004; West, 2021c, pp. 186–7). Among the factors that suggested that this text might be an appropriate text for a Contextual Bible Study dialogue between text and context was Phyllis Trible's pioneering analysis of this text in her seminal work *Texts of Terror*.

In her chapter 'Tamar, the Royal Rape of Wisdom' (Trible, 1984, pp. 37–63), Trible not only drew this text from the margins to the centre of biblical studies, she also offered a literary-narrative reading of this text, acknowledging those who had undertaken literary-narrative analysis of this text before her (Trible, 1984, p. 57). At the time socio-historical method dominated biblical studies, even feminist biblical studies (see, for example, Schüssler Fiorenza, 1983; Meyers, 1988). Trible's method demonstrated the potential for ordinary readers of the Bible, including the women in our workshop, for whom the Bible is a significant and sacred resource, to engage with the literary dimensions of the text. They did not need socio-historical information in order to collaborate with this biblical text for social transformation.

The tendency within liberation theologies and their biblical hermeneutics from the 1970s to the 1980s was to begin with the socio-historical dimensions of the biblical text (see the overview provided by Míguez, 2006). While offering significant ideologically useful information on the socio-historical sites of production of biblical text, the use of historical-critical and sociological methods meant that ordinary readers of the Bible required scholarly mediators in their engagement with the Bible. Trible offered us other avenues of access when we turned to this text in the mid-1990s.

Trible is of course aware of the socio-historical dimensions of 2 Samuel 13.1–22, but she relegates this information to footnotes. Literary-narrative analysis holds sway over her analysis. Socio-historical resources, cited in her first endnote (Trible, 1984, p. 57), are used to separate this text from its surrounding literary environment. From this point onwards her focus is on the 'well-ordered design' of the literary unit, its 'plot', its 'episodes', and her task, which is 'to explore the artistry and meaning of this literary unit as we attend to its single female character' (Trible, 1984, p. 37).

The cadence of Trible's prose is itself unusually poetic for biblical scholarship. This feature of Trible's work was part of what drew me to her analysis when I first read it at the University of Sheffield in 1985. Her writing style enhanced the literary and poetic dimensions of the texts she analysed. I came to biblical studies from an English language and linguistics background and so was fortunate to do postgraduate studies within a Biblical Studies department that embraced an emerging literary-narrative method within the discipline. The poetic resonance between Trible's analysis and Tamar's text remained with me and led me to suggest to Ujamaa Centre colleagues that we might attempt a Contextual Bible Study (CBS) using this text for the third day of the workshop.

Our 'Tamar' CBS (see below), as it has come to be called, has since been used thousands of times around the world (see, for example, FECCLAHA, 2017). The reception by participants has been the same: this story resonates with and enables the articulation and sharing of similar contemporary stories (see also Kalmanofsky, 2017). What enables this resonance is the remarkable voice of Tamar. Our CBS foregrounds Tamar's voice, and it is her poetic voice that summons women (and many men) to hear and speak out.

My colleagues in the Ujamaa Centre and I have reflected on this work often (for recent collating examples, see West, 2019; 2021a; 2021b; 2021c). In this chapter I return to the text again, but this time with a more overtly socio-historical orientation (see also West, 2013). My analysis has a significant focus on the literary-narrative – specifically the poetic – aspects of the story, but I put them to a different methodological purpose, discerning more than one socio-historical redacted story of rape.

The poetics of absence (lacunae)

The chapters in this volume invite us to reflect on the poetics of absence, with the narration of rape as the focal reality. Over 30 years ago, Itumeleng Mosala, working within South African Black Theology's understanding of 'racial capitalism' (Sebidi, 1986, p. 31), offered a similar invitation, asking Black Theology to consider the poetics of absence with respect to a marginalized class and/as race presence in the Bible. Mosala argued that the re-use of 'text' (whether oral or written) through successive redactions tended to co-opt marginalized economic sectors in the interests of dominant economic sectors. In attempting to recover voices that have been co-opted, Mosala invokes the notion of 'absence'. His two case studies are Micah, from the Hebrew Bible, and Luke, from the New Testament, though his analysis pertains to every biblical text. Mosala laments 'the absences in the text of material concerning the experiences of the oppressed in ancient society' (Mosala, 1989, p. 152), but recognizes that 'while the oppressed and exploited peasants, artisans, day laborers, and underclasses of Micah's Judah are entirely absent in the signifying practice that the wider text of Micah represents, something of their project and voice has almost accidentally survived' in the redacted texts that have co-opted their struggles and projects (Mosala, 1989, p. 152).

For Mosala, the absence of the voices of the most marginalized in the biblical text is a reality that contemporary readers of the Bible must accept. For it is only 'through struggle with the dominant forces inscribed in the text itself' that 'the oppressed and exploited people today can seek to discover kin struggles in biblical communities' (Mosala, 1989, p. 188). These redacted biblical struggles offer two sets of resources for contemporary communities of struggle, both of which relate to Mosala's concept of absence. First, biblical struggles 'serve as a source of inspiration for contemporary struggles' (Mosala, 1989, p. 188), for absence is never total, as 'Ideology is not a lie. It is rather a harmonization of contradictions in such a way that the class interests of one group are universalized and made applicable to other classes.' There are, therefore, Mosala continues, always 'aspects of the texts that provide hermeneutical links with the struggles and projects of the oppressed peoples of biblical communities' (Mosala, 1989, p. 152). Second, recognition of co-optation by dominant ideologies serves also 'as a warning' to contemporary struggles 'against their co-optation' by the dominant forces in their contemporary context (Mosala, 1989, p. 188). In sum, Mosala concludes, 'The category of the "black struggle" as a hermeneutical factor draws its poetry from a future that in ... [the] struggle with the [biblical] text ... is experienced as an "absence".' The visions and ideals of the black struggle are eloquent in the [biblical] text by the text's silences about the struggles and aspirations of the oppressed and exploited people of the ancient world (Mosala, 1989, p. 188).

Mosala's hermeneutic of contemporary reception interprets ancient textual absence as a potential contemporary future actual presence. The experience of the Ujamaa Centre with the Tamar CBS is that this is precisely what takes place as contemporary women read the absences and silences within the text, finding and forging their own futures of resilience, resistance and transformation.

But what if the residual remnant is 'accidentally' present in contradictions of a patriarchally co-opted text? Trible finds such prophetic fragments within Tamar's story and their summons: 'compassion for Tamar requires a new [contemporary] vision', for not only is 'Israel found wanting' by this story, notwithstanding its co-optation for male matters, but '*so are we* [contemporary readers]' (Trible, 1984, p. 57). The text invokes compassion in the reader. But how does the text do this?

In the next section of this chapter, I interrogate the residual presence that remains of Tamar's voice, interrogating both its presence and absence. My argument is that it is the poetry that retains both her present elite voice and her sisters' absent subaltern voices.

The poetics of presence

Trible has appropriately identified the poetic qualities of the text, noting its overall chiastic structure (Trible, 1984, p. 61, n. 50), within which an internal chiasm foregrounds the rape (1984, pp. 43–4), which she eloquently refers to as 'a flawed chiasmus that embodies irreparable damage for the characters' (1984, p. 43). Framing the rape there is a pre-rape 'Conversation between Amnon and Tamar (13:11b–14a)' and a post-rape 'Conversation between Amnon and Tamar: Amnon's command to Tamar and her response (13:15c–16)' (Trible, 1984, p. 44). Trible analyses these with her usual close and careful reading. She notes, for example, that, 'Precisely now [13.12], when Tamar speaks for the first time, the narrator hints at her powerlessness by avoiding her name.' This is in contrast to the male speeches, for as Trible goes on to state: 'Repeatedly, the introductions to direct speech of male characters use their proper names ... By contrast, the name of Tamar never prefaces her speeches, here or later (13:16a); only the pronoun *she* obtains.' 'This subtle difference',

Trible continues (1984, p. 46), 'suggests the plight of the female. Without her name, she lacks power. Nonetheless, she speaks reason and wisdom.'

This acknowledgement by Trible of a pervasive patriarchal narrative point of view leads me to my focus for this chapter. Is the rape of Tamar a narrative construct of a male narrator whose primary purpose is to provide a reason for the enmity between Amnon and Absalom? Clearly, within the larger literary-narrative context, the narration of the rape serves a patriarchal political agenda. But does it 'accidentally' (Mosala) include an already existing narrative of female resistance to rape? Has a poetic re-membering of female resistance to rape moved from the realm of a hidden transcript among subaltern women into the public realm of men by being connected, first, to a royal woman, and then, second, to male political matters? Is there more than one narration of rape?

My use of notions of a hidden and public transcript invokes the incisive analysis of James Scott, who insists that the dominated are never absent from the discourses of the dominant, being always present in the infrapolitics of the public realm, through their arts of resistance (Scott, 1990; for the use of Scott's work within biblical studies, see, for example, Horsley, 2004). Of relevance to my argument are particular aspects of the hidden transcript. First, the hidden transcript 'is specific to a given social site and to a particular set of actors' (Scott, 1990, p. 14). Second, the language Scott uses here to describe his first characteristic of the hidden transcript connotes a poetry of presence, for Scott acknowledges that though the hidden transcript includes 'a whole range of practices', its primary form is 'speech acts' (Scott, 1990, p. 14). Third, Scott emphasizes that the hidden transcript is 'rehearsed again and again' and 'rehearsed in various forms' among the sequestered safety of 'a restricted "public" that excludes – that is hidden from – certain specified others' (Scott, 1990, pp. 8, 14). However, when dignity demands a response in the public realm, a particular hidden transcript irrupts into the public realm (Scott, 1990, pp. xi, 113–14).

The poetic dimensions of Tamar's verbal response in particular, as well as the poetic dimensions of the internal chiasm and the chiastic shape of the story as a whole identified by Trible, may indicate a discourse of resistance to rape forged and rehearsed 'offstage' by women. As Scott argues, subordinate groups 'create and defend a social space in which offstage dissent to the official transcript of power relations may be voiced' (Scott, 1990, p. xi). My argument in this chapter is that the poetic shape Tamar's voice takes provides form-critical indications of a site in which women have organized to articulate a hidden transcript of resistance to rape.

The anonymity of Tamar's speech, noted by Trible, may be an indication, in Scott's terms, of a hidden transcript making its way into the public realm. When Tamar's poetic resistance identifies a public site in which it can speak with relative safety it enters the zone of infrapolitics; it takes on 'a politics of disguise and anonymity that takes place in public view but is designed to have a double meaning or to shield the identity of the actors' (Scott, 1990, p. 19). The politics of infrapolitics is a politics for disguise. While the primary oppressive system that both Scott and Mosala address is the economic, their analysis holds for the 'interlocking' (Collective, 1977) systems of patriarchy and dominant economies – econo-patriarchy. Scott's following formulation may reflect a reality that resides behind Tamar's textual presence:

> A subordinate conceals the hidden transcript from powerholders largely because he [and she] fears retaliation. If, however, it is possible to declare the hidden transcript while disguising the identity of the persons declaring it, much of the fear is dissipated. Recognising this, subordinate groups have developed a large arsenal of techniques that serve to shield their identity while facilitating open criticism, threats, and attacks. (Scott, 1990, p. 140)

Scott then goes on to list '[p]rominent techniques that accomplish this purpose', including 'spirit possession, gossip, aggression through magic, rumor, anonymous threats and violence, the anonymous letter, and anonymous mass defiance' (Scott, 1990, p. 140). To these, I would add anonymous resisting poetry. In enumerating actual subordinate examples of each of these 'arts of resistance', Scott notes that his examples 'have hardly begun to exhaust the many forms of anonymity deployed by subordinate groups' (Scott, 1990, p. 148). A common feature, Scott notes, of all types of resisting anonymity is that they hide the identity of the real actors and thereby make possible a far more direct expression of verbal resistance (Scott, 1990, p. 148). Where better for ordinary subaltern women to talk back about rape than through the voice of a royal princess, David's daughter Tamar.

As indicated, the analysis that follows begins with the anonymous poetry attributed to Tamar. I will then reflect on plausible textual indications of a series of socio-historical co-optations of this anonymous poetry.

The poetry of resistance

In a recent article, Ryan Higgins gives careful attention to the poetics of 2 Samuel 13.1–22, focusing on Tamar's speech. Higgins's analysis builds 'on the work of literary and feminist biblical critics in performing a close reading of direct discourse in 2 Sam 13:1–22', paying 'particular attention to the form and function of Tamar's speech' (Higgins, 2020, p. 26). 'Her words', he says, 'devolve through levels of dramatic mimesis, from the poetic (v. 12) to the prosaic (v. 13) to the inarticulate (v. 16) to the unintelligible (v. 19) to the nonexistent (v. 20)' (Higgins, 2020, p. 26). With Tamar's speeches as the fulcrum of his analysis, Higgins argues that 'the writer's use of speech' in 2 Samuel generally (including vv. 23–33) 'has compounded Tamar's victimization, exposed the failings of patriarchy, indicted men in positions of power, and had far-reaching effects as a critique on biblical gender ideology' (Higgins, 2020, p. 26).

This is an important argument, supplementing similar analysis in previous biblical scholarship. However, my purpose in this chapter in using Higgins's suggestive analysis is to get behind 'the writer' Higgins invokes, for my argument is that there are layers of redaction-driven 'writers', behind which we may find various renderings of Tamar's voice in the poetry of her speech. There is more than one 'Tamar' and more than one narration of rape.

My argument, in brief here and more fully later, is that the poetry re-members the voices of ordinary, subaltern women, lamenting their abuse at the hands of econo-patriarchy, and that their voices have been taken up – co-opted – within the account of the rape of an elite woman, the 'Tamar' of the final form of this story.

Drawing on Higgins's careful analysis of the poetry of Tamar's speech, I offer the following preliminary reconfiguration of Tamar's subaltern voice with 'She' starting in 2 Samuel 13.12, 13a, 14a:

ותאמר לו	And she said to him:
אל־אחי	Do not, my brother,
אל־תעניני	Do not debase me;
כי	for
אל־יעשה	it is not done,
כן	thus
בישראל	in Israel.
אל־תעשה	Do not do,
את־הנבלה הזאת	this vileness.

ואני	And I,
אנה אוליך	where will I walk,
את־חרפתי	with my disgrace?
ואתה	And you,
תהיה	you will be/become,
כאחד הנבלים	as one of the vile men,
בישראל	in Israel.
לא אבה	But he was not willing
לשמע	to hear
בקולה	her voice.

My translation and line arrangement of 2 Samuel 13.12–13a borrows from Higgins but is slightly different (see Higgins, 2020, p. 27), drawing also on the many years of CBS work on this text, where the pivotal CBS question ('What does Tamar say?') invites participants to hear the cadence of Tamar's speech in vv. 12–13. We have rephrased this CBS question over the years, attempting to slow down the reading and reception of this verse, drawing attention to each of the poetic elements in Tamar's speech (see, for example, West, 2019, pp. 161, 163).

As Higgins notes, 2 Samuel 13.12–13a evidence clear forms of parallelism (Higgins, 2020, pp. 28–9). Furthermore, there is a clear metrical cadence in the Hebrew text (for the characteristics of Hebrew poetry, see Naudé and Miller-Naudé, 2018, p. 305). This reconstructed anonymous speech of subaltern women is a remarkable poetic dialogical monologue. Unlike Higgins (2020, p. 29), I do not include v. 13b as part of the poetry of resistance. In our CBS work, we retain the final redacted version, of course, for it is canonical and so the given story we have in ordinary African Bibles. We always begin with the Bibles we have. The reception by participants in CBS's small groups of v. 13b, 'Now, speak now to the king, for he will not withhold me from you', leads to productive debate, echoed by Higgins (2020, p. 30), with some lamenting that Tamar is subdued by patriarchy and others insisting that she is using trickster tactics, trying to distract Amnon. However, I argue here that v. 13b is one of the narrative devices that co-opt the resisting rape poetry of both subaltern women and elite women into patriarchal discourse.

My tentative reconstruction of these Tamars' resisting poetry imagines v. 14a as a choral response by a group of women, her sisters, to the speaker, the anonymous 'she'. Her combined voices (in the singular) in v. 14a, I suggest, have later been co-opted and given to the narrator.

Higgins's analysis has offered me a textual clue in my delimitation of the resisting poetry (vv. 12, 13a, 14a). He notes that Tamar's 'long speech' is framed by the same verb of violence – חזק in vv. 11 and 14. He then goes on to say, 'its repetition here gives the impression that her long speech had not occurred at all' (Higgins, 2020, p. 31). I take Higgins's observation further. What if, I argue, her long speech had not occurred at all? What if this is textual evidence of a co-optation, whereby the lament of women who have survived sexual violence is included in a narrative account of the violence (חזק) done to a royal princess, Tamar?

Another 'writer', sympathetic to the plight of victims of rape, incorporates the poetic lament of ordinary women survivors of sexual violence as the speech of a particular woman, an elite woman, whose rape is narrated in order to critique Davidic leadership in general and the succession struggle in particular. How else do you infiltrate econo-patriarchy? Ordinary organized women, having performed this corporate chanted poem of resistance to rape in hidden sites, find in Tamar's royal story an infrapolitical site within which to insert their disguised voices. A story about the rape of Tamar the daughter of David is given voice/s.

Patriarchal co-optation

Characterization and direct speech drive the plot of the literary unit 2 Samuel 13.1–22. According to Higgins (2020, p. 26), '[D]ialogue plays a central role in the narrative. The action is framed by characters who manipulate speech, and the narrative advances through speech that manipulates characters.' The anonymous poem I reconstruct has been co-opted by authors/writers and reassigned to named characters. The resistance poetry of ordinary women is populated by royal characters and royal speech. What was a hidden poem of resistance became a public dialogue.

The narrative unit, as Higgins compellingly explains, has an eloquent coherence, with Tamar's speech acts at its pivotal centre. Her speech, as CBS women testify to, follows a trajectory in which Tamar's poetry 'devolves into prose, becomes unintelligible and then inarticulate, and ends in silence' (Higgins, 2020, p. 25); 'Tamar's speech devolves as the offense grows, from the impassioned plea of something like poetry to the rational rhetoric of something like prose to inarticulate desperation to unintelligible screams' (Higgins, 2020, p. 32). 'The writer' – who is my second writer – 'provides her with one of the most eloquent voices in biblical narrative.' Again, the many CBS women participants would concur. The reason, I suggest, is that 'she', Tamar the literary character, speaks with the actual voices of many nameless women. Higgins continues, 'Though other biblical writers may deny their women a voice or make them speak against their own interests, the writer of 2 Samuel 13 uses speech to focus our attention on Tamar's degradation, to connect silence and violence, and to lay the blame for fractured families and nations on those who would not hear her voice' (Higgins, 2020, p. 42). Her voice is audible and credible, I suggest, because it is the poetry of real presence, the actual choral voices of many absent women. Given this voicing, it is no wonder that 2 Samuel 13.1–22 constructs, says Higgins, 'a revolution around the refusal to listen to a woman' (Higgins, 2020, p. 42), which, as Higgins goes on to elaborate, impacts on David's house specifically and patriarchy more generally.

The emphasis in Higgins's analysis is on the use of this poetry of voice to critique monarchy and patriarchy. The emphasis in this chapter, in contrast, is on recognition of real compounded presences of actual absent women's voices, forging an alliance across ancient (and contemporary) social class to speak out against violence against women, all women.

Ekaterina Kozlova draws on Higgins's work in making a related argument about the centrality of this text in a critique of David's reign. Kozlova uses architectural images from 2 Samuel 13.1–20 and 2 Samuel 18.33—19.4 as 'structural "actors"' 'to create a "topography" of lawlessness in David's rule' (Kozlova, 2022, p. 24). Kozlova's argument is compelling in its detail, as she situates architectural space as a key component of the setting in each of these narrative units. In the case of the Tamar story, Kozlova locates Tamar's two speeches – two 'laments' – on either side of Amnon's bolted door: 'While on the inside Tamar petitions with words; while on the outside, she uses ritual gestures ... Separating these elocutionary acts of the princess, the barred door itself stands as a pregnant rhetorical symbol, and thus is "vocal" as well' (Kozlova, 2022, p. 7). The significance of architectural rhetorical symbols, like this door, is the focus of Kozlova's careful argument as she situates 2 Samuel 13.1–20 within the 'ancient genre known as *paraklausithyron*, "a lament beside a (closed) door"', within ANE sources, classical literature and the Hebrew Bible (Kozlova, 2022, p. 4).

Kozlova provides a plausible array of ancient literary devices which have been used to redact and so co-opt Tamar's voices, both the voices of the ordinary women she co-opts and her own royal story of rape. In Kozlova's analysis, Tamar's story is about David: 'Linked to the material before and after it, 2 Samuel 13 emerges as a pivotal chapter, retrospectively and prospectively looking at David's reign marked by corruption in all its varied forms' (Kozlova, 2022, p. 12). What Kozlova's analysis offers to my chapter is a delineation of the techniques of later co-optation. The purpose may be to critique a particular aspect of patriarchy, but it is patriarchal co-optation nevertheless, marginalizing and exploiting women's voices.

Higgins's and Kozlova's analysis is helpful for my argument, as both underscore the array of literary-narrative techniques informing patriarchal agendas at play in the co-optation of the anonymous Tamars' poetry. There is more than one 'writer' and more than one rape story. We can discern, I suggest, (1) the voices of subaltern women mourning and resisting male violence, (2) whose voices are adopted and adapted to articulate the royal Tamar's rape resisting lament, (3) whose voice is appropriated to provide comment on both the immediate narrative context in which David's sons contend violently for the dynastic throne and the larger narrative context of the defects of the Davidic monarchy. Contemporary kin eyes hear each of these voices of Tamar. Mosala recognizes the capacity of ordinary African readers and hearers of the Bible to see glimpses of almost absent kindred political and economic struggles in and behind ancient biblical texts; I invoke Mosala's image but adapt it to recognize the capacity of the many ordinary African women with whom we have read this text to hear the partially present voices of lamenting and resisting women in and behind Tamar.

Kin eyes hearing

Mosala argues, and the Ujamaa Centre concurs, that the poetry of absence may be partially recovered through contemporary kin eyes. Enough traces remain, argues Mosala, in the final form of biblical text 'to enable eyes that are hermeneutically trained in the struggle for liberation today to observe the kin struggles of the oppressed and exploited of the biblical communities in the very absences of those struggles in the text' (Mosala, 1986, p. 196). Kin struggles, as Scott's work demonstrates, assist us in recognizing how the hidden transcript disguises its presence within dominant discourse. Form-critical biblical studies' methodology reminds us too of the residual presence of oral discourses within and behind the biblical text.

My argument in this chapter is that there is poetic evidence of the voices of women survivors of sexual violence in 2 Samuel 13.1–22. While Trible and Higgins and Kozlova (and others) remind us that the entire literary unit (and its larger literary context) demonstrates remarkable literary-narrative qualities, we should not forget that this historically and sociologically composite narrative tells different rape stories.

What the analysis of this chapter offers to ongoing Tamar CBS work is the addition of an overt invitation to participants to stand in continuity and solidarity with these multiple-layered voices of Tamar. In many of our CBS we invite participants to report back from their small groups using drawing or drama or song. In one of our CBS, on Job 3 in the context of HIV, we invite participants to offer their own poetic renderings of the poetry of Job 3 (West, 2008). We might do something similar with our Tamar CBS. We have been reluctant to change the shape of our Tamar CBS. Its simple set of questions has enabled facilitation, allowing the facilitator to focus on other factors, such as the embodied responses of participants. A few short questions have also been an advantage when it comes to the translation of the CBS into other languages. However, the plausible recovery of resisting poetic lament within this story may offer a significant resource to our Tamar CBS. Our current version of the Tamar CBS is as follows:

> [2 Samuel 13.1–22 is read aloud, preferably dramatically. After the text has been read a series of questions follow.]
>
> 1 Read 2 Samuel 13.1–22 together again in small groups. Share with each other what you think the text is about.
>
> [Each small group is then asked to report back to the larger group. Each and every response to question one is summarized on newsprint. After the report-back, the participants return to their small groups to discuss the following questions.]
>
> 2 Who are the main characters in this story and what do we know about them?
> 3 What is the role of each of the male characters in the rape of Tamar?
> 4 What does Tamar say and what does Tamar do? Focus carefully on each element of what Tamar says and does.
>
> [When the small groups have finished their discussion, each group is invited to present a summary of their discussion. After this report-back, the smaller groups reconvene and discuss the following questions.]
>
> 5 Are there women like Tamar in your church and/or community? Tell their story.
> 6 What resources are there in your area for survivors of rape?

[Once again, the small groups present their report-back to the plenary group. Creativity is particularly vital here, as often women find it difficult or are unable to articulate their responses. A drama or a drawing may be the only way in which some groups can report.
Finally, each small group comes together to formulate an action plan.]

7 What will you now do in response to this Bible study?

[The action plan is either reported to the plenary or presented on newsprint for other participants to study after the Bible study.]

My suggestion to Ujamaa Centre colleagues would be to introduce a further question after the current Question 7. We do not encourage an immediate report-back after Question 5. It is important that each small group (divided by age and gender) feels safe, and when we facilitate we encourage each small group to be cautious about what they report when they return to the plenary gathering. The Tamar CBS requires the presence of trained counsellors who are available during and after the CBS. We assume, and the embodied engagements with Question 5 confirm, that much of what is shared remains in the small group as a hidden transcript. What is reported to the plenary is a public transcript version. By aligning Questions 5 and 6 we also connect the reality of violence against women with potential local resources to support survivors and to address violence against women. Question 7 then invites each small group and/ or the plenary group as a whole to formulate particular forms of action they will undertake, in the immediate, medium and long-term. We might envisage, I suggest, a liturgical form of action to follow, given shape by the reconstructed voices of Tamar.

Participants in the Tamar CBS always lament the reality of the churches as unsafe places for women. Indeed, when we were invited to use the Tamar CBS as part of the Anglican Communion's Lambeth Conference in 2008, on the day in which bishops and their spouses held joint sessions, the spouses group (consisting almost entirely of women) insisted that we change Question 5 to 'In what ways does the church abuse its power?', and Question 6 to 'In what way can we as leaders in the church respond to abuses of power?' (Sison, 2008; De Santis, 2008). Given the lived reality of the Church as an unsafe place for women and the reluctance of the Church to address violence against women, and given the excising of 2 Samuel 13.1–22 from most church lectionaries on a Sunday, concluding the Tamar CBS with a liturgical resource might be useful. I suggest we might offer the following final question:

8 How might we enable our own local churches to recognize this biblical story and our voices as women who have experienced sexual abuse? We can identify a poetic core to the speeches of Tamar which may come from the experience of ordinary women survivors of sexual violence. We can reconstruct their poetic voices as follows:

> And she said to him:
> Do not, my brother,
> Do not debase me;
> for
> it is not done,
> thus
> in Israel.
>
> Do not do,
> this vileness.
>
> And I,
> where will I walk,
> with my disgrace?
> And you,
> you will be/become,
> as one of the vile men,
> in Israel.
>
> But he was not willing
> to hear
> her voice.

How would you express this poetry in your own language? Write a related psalm of resistance and lament that could be used as a resource within the liturgical life of your church.

Though somewhat cumbersome, we could work with it and discern how we might adapt it further. What this reconstructed poem offers is further access for participants to the absences in the text, widening the text's capacity for appropriation by specifically connecting contemporary kin women with ancient ordinary women, and so offering further possibilities for '[w]hat comes after sexual violence' (Graybill, 2021, p. 3). Such an ending to the Tamar CBS enables Tamar's story to be read both as a prophetic voice of resistance in its own (canonical) right and to be read as a prophetic collection of different yet related voices, including the choral voices of ordinary subaltern women.

Conclusion

The experience of ordinary women identifying with Tamar has prompted my analysis in this chapter, intersecting as it does with the recognition within South African biblical hermeneutics that biblical texts are socio-historical composite sites of production and contestation. This confluence has led to an analysis of the poetry of Tamar's voice/s.

My chapter uses both the engagements of contemporary women with this biblical text and the details gleaned through socially engaged biblical scholarship of the text itself in order to discern a hidden poetic transcript of the voices of ancient subaltern women. Their marginal voices have found a public presence by being co-opted and re-used to tell the story of the rape of Tamar, David's daughter, adding their voices to hers. These voices of Tamar have been preserved for contemporary Bible hearers and readers because they have been re-used in later patriarchal debates about Davidic kingship. Through these layers of production and reception, Tamar's voices may yet be recognized, heard and appropriated by contemporary kin eyes.

Bibliography

Collective, Combahee River, 1977, 'The Combahee River Collective Statement', *Women's Studies Quarterly* 42 (3/4), pp. 271–80.

De Santis, Solange, 2008, 'Bishops, Spouses Discuss Power Abuses in Joint Session', *Episcopal Press and News*, available at https://episcopalarchives.org/cgi-bin/ENS/ENSpress_release.pl?pr_number=072908-04 (accessed 4.12.2023).

FECCLAHA, 2017, *Tamar Campaign: Contextual Bible Study Manual and Sermon Outlines on Gender based Violence and Peace*, Nairobi: The Fellowship of Christian Councils and Churches in the Great Lakes and the Horn of Africa (FECCLAHA).

Graybill, Rhiannon, 2021, *Texts after Terror: Rape, Sexual Violence, and the Hebrew Bible*, New York: Oxford University Press.

Higgins, Ryan S., 2020, '"He would not hear her voice": From Skilled Speech to Silence in 2 Samuel 13:1–22', *Journal of Feminist Studies in Religion* 36/2, pp. 25–42.

Horsley, Richard A., 2004, *Hidden Transcripts and the Arts of Resistance: Applying the Work of James C. Scott to Jesus and Paul*, Semeia Studies 48, Atlanta, GA: SBL Press.

Kalmanofsky, Amy, 2017, 'How Feminist Biblical Scholarship Can Heal Victims of Sexual Violation' in Amy Kalmanofsky (ed.), *Sexual Violence and Sacred Texts*, Cambridge: Feminist Studies in Religion Books, pp. 9–30.

Kozlova, Ekaterina E., 2022, '2 Samuel and the Architecture of Poetic Justice', *The Journal of Hebrew Scriptures* 22, pp. 1–24.

Meyers, Carol, 1988, *Discovering Eve: Ancient Israelite Women in Context*, Oxford: Oxford University Press.

Míguez, Néstor O., 2006, 'Latin American Reading of the Bible: Experiences, Challenges and its Practice', *Expository Times* 118/3, pp. 120–9.

Mosala, Itumeleng J., 1986, 'The Use of the Bible in Black Theology' in Itumeleng J. Mosala and Buti Tlhagale (eds), *The Unquestionable Right to be Free: Essays in Black Theology*, Johannesburg: Skotaville Publishers, pp. 175–99.

Mosala, Itumeleng J., 1989, *Biblical Hermeneutics and Black Theology in South Africa*, Grand Rapids, MI: Eerdmans.

Naudé, Jacobus A., and Cynthia L. Miller-Naudé, 2018, 'Alterity, Orality and Performance in Bible Translation' in K. Malmkjaer, A. Serban and F. Louwagie (eds), *Key Cultural Texts in Translation*, Amsterdam: John Benjamins Publishing, pp. 299–313.

Schüssler Fiorenza, Elisabeth, 1983, *In Memory of Her: A Feminist Theological Reconstruction of Christian Origins*, London: SCM Press.

Scott, James C., 1990, *Domination and the Arts of Resistance: Hidden Transcripts*, New Haven, CT and London: Yale University Press.

Sebidi, Lebamang, 1986, 'The Dynamics of the Black Struggle and its Implications for Black Theology' in Itumeleng J. Mosala and Buti Tlhagale (eds), *The Unquestionable Right to be Free: Essays in Black Theology*, Johannesburg: Skotaville Publishers, pp. 1–36.

Sison, Marites N., 2008, 'Bishops, Spouses Hold Joint Session: Lambeth Looks at Violence Against Women', *Anglican Journal*, available at https://anglicanjournal.com/bishops-spouses-hold-joint-session-lambeth-looks-at-violence-against-women-8003/ (accessed 4.12.2023).

Trible, Phyllis, 1984, *Texts of Terror: Literary-Feminist Readings of Biblical Narratives*, Philadelphia, PA: Fortress Press.

West, Gerald O., 2008, 'The Poetry of Job as a Resource for the Articulation of Embodied Lament in the Context of HIV and AIDS in South Africa' in Nancy C. Lee and Carleen Mandolfo (eds), *Lamentations in Ancient and Contemporary Cultural Contexts*, Atlanta, GA: SBL Press, pp. 195–214.

West, Gerald O., 2013, 'Deploying the Literary Detail of a Biblical Text (2 Samuel 13:1–22) in Search of Redemptive Masculinities' in James K. Aitken, Jeremy M. S. Clines and Christl M. Maier (eds), *Interested Readers: Essays on the Hebrew Bible in Honor of David J. A. Clines*, Atlanta, GA: SBL Press, pp. 297–312.

West, Gerald O., 2019, 'Recovering the Biblical Story of Tamar: Training for Transformation, Doing Development' in Robert Odén and Tore Samuelsson (eds), *For Better, for Worse: The Role of Religion in Development Cooperation*, Halmstad: Swedish Mission Council, pp. 153–65.

West, Gerald O., 2021a, 'Interrogating Ahithophel: Intersecting Gender and Class in Biblical Text and South African Context' in Monica Jyotsna Melanchthon and Robyn J. Whitaker (eds), *Terror in the Bible: Rhetoric, Gender, and Violence*, International Voices in Biblical Studies, Atlanta, GA: SBL Press, pp. 177–99.

West, Gerald O., 2021b, 'Jesus, Joseph, and Tamar Stripped: Trans-textual and Intertextual Resources for Engaging Sexual Violence Against Men' in Jayme Reaves, David Tombs and Rocío Figueroa (eds), *When Did We See You Naked? Jesus as a Victim of Sexual Abuse*, London: SCM Press, pp. 110–28.

West, Gerald O., 2021c, 'Tamar Summons Jesus: A Trans-textual (2 Sam 13:1–22, Mark 5:22–43, Matt 20:17–34) Search for Sectorial Solidarity with Respect to Gender and Masculinity' in L. Juliana Claassens, Christl M. Maier and Funlola O. Olojede (eds), *Transgression and Transformation: Feminist, Postcolonial and Queer Biblical Interpretation as Creative Interventions*, London: T&T Clark, pp. 184–203.

West, Gerald O., and Phumzile Zondi-Mabizela, 2004, 'The Bible Story that Became a Campaign: The Tamar Campaign in South Africa (and Beyond)', *Ministerial Formation* 103, pp. 4–12.

13

Under Rug Swept: Creating Space to Engage the Reality of Homophobic Hate Crimes in the South African Faith Landscape

CHARLENE VAN DER WALT

Introduction

The South African Queer poet and theatre maker Koleka Putuma articulates her experiences of navigating different suburbs in the city of Cape Town as a Black Queer womxn in her poem 'No Easter Sunday for Queers' (Putuma, 2021, pp. 25–30).[1] She explores the multiplicity of her embodied identities as she reflects on what it means to be the daughter of a pastor who navigates the world as an authoritative healer, on her creative process as a contemporary Queer theatre maker, as a Black womxn, and as womxn who loves womxn. She describes her movements between the Northern suburbs of Cape Town where she is the daughter of a pastor in her family home built on religious and cultural foundations and the Southern suburbs where she is a Black Queer theatre maker in the context of a diversity of university students at the University of Cape Town. Putuma (2017, p. 26) captures the complexities and the contestations of this process of identity navigation in a poetic liturgy when she writes:

> In the North, my hands are raised in worship
> In the South, my hands are raised in protest
> Either way, I am always surrendering
> The North says my body belongs in hell
> The South says my body belongs in a dump
> In both spaces, my body is at the mercy of men

The poem delves deeper into the contradictions and the complexities of these navigations as she brings into sharper focus the intersection of religion, faith and culture and the violence inflicted on the bodies of womxn and Queer people who do not fit in the culturally informed and religiously sanctioned norm prescribed by econo-heteropatriarchy (West, 2020).[2] Putuma (2017, p. 30) ends the poem with a harrowing reflection when stating:

I wonder,
• Should I be murdered tomorrow,
• Would he, my father, preach about me with the same passion he preaches about the death of a white man he has never met raised?
• Would he Google the other deaths?
• I want to ask him in the car after the service
• I wonder if he can tell how my body language has changed when we arrive in Rondebosch
• You should come to Bellville more often
• By Bellville, he means church
• Ok, I will
• I don't mean it
• What I really want to say
• or ask
• or talk about
• or ask is:

Daddy,
• If I were crucified
• And dumped in a tomb for three days
• And rose again as a headline
• Would you preach about me?
• Would you tell the congregation that it was my sin that made them do it?
• Would you call my murderers Pharisees or cowards or servants of God?
• Would you call yourself Judas?
• How would you roll my stone away?
• Would you preach about me?
• And what would you say?
• My daughter was murdered yesterday
• Or a lesbian was murdered yesterday?

Daddy,
• Would you even preach at all?

Putuma poignantly articulates intimate and important questions. Questions speaking to the complexity faced by Queer people in the Southern African context who, amid constitutional protection, navigate violence or the threat of violence (Eslen-Ziya et al., 2015). Reported cases of homophobic hate crimes saw a sharp increase in 2021 with 24 known victims of LGBTIQA+ murders that took place in South Africa between 12 February and 30 December 2021 (Iqual, 2022).

Conservative right-wing religious and cultural discourses are often employed to incite LGBTIQA+ condemnation, exclusion and violence (Van der Walt, 2022b). In popular engagements with the lives of LGBTIQA+ people in the South African context, there is often an understanding that the discourse informed by cultural and faith values is simple, black-and-white, predictable, and one-directional (Gevisser, 2017). According to this understanding, it is held that the Bible is clear on LGBTIQA+ realities. This positionality holds that there is no possibility for the inclusion of LGBTIQA+ people, that they are an abomination, and that their 'lifestyle' should be avoided, repented from, and corrected. It further holds that LGBTIQA+ people are immoral and only found on the fringes of society and could therefore in no way form part of any vibrant community, especially not faith communities. Faith and sexuality, according to this position, are not matters that can be discussed in the same context. Matters of sexuality and intimacy should best be engaged in a private setting, if at all. Queer people and their lives can as a result only be discussed and engaged in the context of violence. Violence, as commented on by Putuma, becomes the only conceptual frame for the discussion of Queer lives.

Within this context, a central question to the change-making work that we do at the Ujamaa Centre is how we change these underlying assumptions that inform so many matter-of-fact conversations about the lived realities of African LGBTIQA+ people.[3] How do we centre Queer lives in faith settings to enable and enhance complex contextual and embodied conversations? Foundational to the attempt to change the nature and style of the conversation is an ideological commitment to a particular positionality. The epistemological privilege in the 'Body Theology' work that we do at the Ujamaa Centre focuses on the embodied lived realities of African LGBTIQA+ people of faith.[4] Although the Centre does develop resources to assist faith communities to grapple with sexuality and sexual diversity in general, there has in recent years been an intentional shift to develop resources to specifically capacitate African LGBTIQA+ people to read the text for themselves and to reclaim the Bible as a source for liberation (West, Van der Walt and Kaoma, 2016).

The LGBTIQA+-centred work that the Ujamaa Centre is engaged with in collaboration with civil society partners such as the Uthingo Network, Inclusive and Affirming Ministries, and the Global Interfaith Network, is ongoing, developing, incomplete, and explorative.[5] The praxis reflections offered in this contribution do not only aim to offer best practice examples but also try to reflect on the ongoing and unfolding nature of the work and the challenges and 'failures' along the way. I draw great inspiration from the work of Jack Halberstam in their reflection offered in *The Queer Art of Failure*:

> Rather than searching for ways around death and disappointment, the queer art of failure involves the acceptance of the finite, the embrace, of the absurd, the silly, and the hopelessly goofy. Rather than resisting endings and limits, let us instead revel in and cleave to all of our own inevitable fantastic failures. (Halberstam, 2020, p. 187)

They argue along the same lines for the important imperative for Queer theory:

> Queerness offers the promise of failure as a way of life ... but it is up to us whether we choose to make good on that promise in a way that makes a detour around the usual markers of accomplishment and satisfaction. (Halberstam, 2020, p. 186)

Therefore, in the process of sharing this work and insights gained from it, I am trying to move away from the idea that it should be perfect, that it should cover all the bases, and that it should succeed in every way. I think of it, rather, as an invitation to ongoing conversation and collective reflection. At the Ujamaa Centre, we are also trying to move away from the idea of ownership, and therefore all the work that we do at the Centre is made available, however imperfect, through open-access publications and media platforms. Further, this contribution is deliberate in taking time for praxis reflection and evaluation. The aim is to slow down or interrupt the continuous cycle of implementation and roll-out that is so often dictated by funding agreements and prevalent in the NGO landscape and to make time to reflect more deeply how to engage with greater impact and intentionality.

Homophobic hate crimes and violence in the South African context

Before offering praxis reflections on two change-making initiatives developed by the Ujamaa Centre aimed at creating space for collective discussion, reflection and critical engagement within South African faith communities when engaging LGBTIQA+ lived realities, I hope to offer some contextual reflections speaking to the gender-based violence (GBV) realities faced in South Africa.

GBV is a pervasive global reality that impacts not only the embodied lives of many individuals but also has a far-reaching impact on communities. This is particularly true in the South African context where rape statistics have led to GBV being dubbed the 'second pandemic', second only to Covid-19 (Human Rights Watch, 2022). Understanding and constructing rape as a savage act committed by a brutal stranger has been undermined and undone by the overwhelming reality of GBV prevalent in intimate spaces (Moffett, 2006). Rape and the threat of rape as a reality playing out on deserted street corners and dark alleyways have been refuted by numerous reports of inhuman cruelty and annihilating violence committed in bedrooms and family homes and classrooms and meeting rooms and churches (Phiri, 2001; Du Toit, 2005). Although GBV is hugely underreported and often cloaked in shame and silence, no community goes unaffected by the embodied lived realities brought about by this form of violence (Palermo, Bleck and Peterman, 2014). As stated elsewhere (Terblanche and Van der Walt, 2022, p. 199), 'Although the vulnerability of the streets cannot be denied in the South African context, it is often the sheets that witness the most brutal acts of violence.'

When critically engaging the GBV landscape in South Africa, scholars have traced causality to a complex constellation of factors that include socioeconomic status, level of education, prevalence of alcohol misuse, and past experiences of GBV in families of origin (Jewkes and Abrahams, 2002). They argue that there is not one simple reason for GBV, but that a diversity of factors intersect with one another to create an environment that contributes to the reality of GBV. Important, however, for our discussion are the insights developed in GBV scholarship speaking to the ideological underpinnings of GBV. Scholars argue that the constellation of factors is ideologically underpinned by 'a culture of violence and the ideology of male superiority' (Jewkes, 2002, p. 1426). These two interconnected issues lie at the heart of GBV prevalence.

Patriarchy as a systemic reality that upholds male superiority and subsequent gender inequality is commonly informed and bolstered by religion and culture in the African context. Religious core beliefs and foundational narratives that are steeped in patriarchy are habitually uncritically transferred across generations and become seemingly unquestionable norms and values that inform and enable gender inequality and subsequently GBV (Dlamini, 2023). The role of faith in relation to gender equality is contested. Although faith can function as a barrier to gender equality, faith actors and faith communities could also potentially function as communities of care to those affected by GBV and communities of prophetic witness resisting injustice.

To sharpen the focus, South Africa is also considered the birthplace of a very specific form of GBV – namely, homophobic hate crime or so-called 'corrective rape'. Although the term is highly contested, it aims to name an act of violence against LGBTIQA+ people and women, committed by men ostensibly to 'cure' lesbians and Queer people of their non-conforming sexual orientation, or 'correct' them from it, 'disciplining' them to be 'proper' heterosexual women (Di Silvio, 2010; Mwambene and Wheal, 2015). Breen, Lynch, Nel and Matthews (2016) explore the reality of hate crimes in South Africa against the challenging and transitional societal realities as the task of nation-building and the establishment of a national identity remains ongoing work. In a landscape dominated by the systemic dehumanization of people of colour during the Apartheid regime, it is important to trace the systemic roots that underlie homophobic hate crimes. Following the foundational insights about the causality of GBV highlighted above, econo-heteropatriarchy as a systemic ideology informs the violence inflicted on Queer bodies and racialized bodies. The term articulates the systematic and institutionalized implications when dominant ideologies such as patriarchy, heteronormativity and capitalism align to inform dominant constructions and lived realities pertaining to gender and sexuality (Van der Walt, 2021, p. 149).

Foundational to the systemic ideology of econo-heteropatriarchy is a biological essentialist understating of sex that finds expression in the pervasive binary classification of sex in terms of male and female, resulting in a further insistence on the alignment of biological sex, understood in a binary way, in addition to gender identity and sexual orientation. Men are not only constructed as the polar opposite of women but also as of superior status and higher value. What it means to be a man in a hetero-patriarchal system finds expressions in hegemonic constructions of masculinity that frame men primarily as powerful providers, protectors and penetrators. Decision-making power pertaining to issues of sexuality and reproduction is reserved for men in a hetero-patriarchal system. Within this frame, reproduction is understood as a moral imperative, and this in turn leads to apparently stable notions of what constitutes a 'natural family'. The econo-heteropatriarchal norm portrayed in the media and reinforced in stable conceptual notions of love, marriage, family and success is so pervasive and dominant that alternative expressions of gender and sexuality are often erased, ignored or, at worst, exposed to violent correction.

In her 2002 article entitled 'Gender Violence and HIV/AIDS: A Deadly Silence in the Church', Beverley Haddad boldly called out the pervasive silence within African faith communities on lived realities relating to HIV/Aids and GBV. Sadly, amid numerous interventions since the publication of this important article, the pervasive silence remains within faith spaces when it comes to engaging GBV, and even more so in relation to homophobic hate crimes and violence as it remains a reality that is often 'under rug swept' (Morissette, 2002).

Discomforting interventions to spark conversation

Considering the often-pervasive silence within faith communities when it comes to GBV in general and homophobic hate crimes in particular, I now turn my attention to two interventions aimed at the disruption of the norm and the creation of space for collective discussion, reflection and critical engagement within South African faith communities. I draw inspiration for this work from the three imperatives for Global Citizenship Education as articulated by Yusef Wagid in an interview with Emiliano Bosio (2021) when he encourages educators to: (1) create discomfort with Deliberative Pedagogical intervention; (2) create awareness of belonging to a community and the responsibility that it holds; (3) become responsive to social justice interventions. Drawing from these imperatives as identified by Wagid, both of the interventions discussed below offer examples of how space can be created through implementing intentionally discomforting interventions to engage the reality of homophobic hate crimes in South African faith spaces and to unmask, destabilize and disrupt the norms of econo-heteropatriarchy:

The first intervention I would like to highlight is the annual Eudy Simelane memorial lecture hosted by the Ujamaa Centre, and the second intervention is the Ujamaa Centre's Contextual Bible Study on Genesis 37. In particular, the first part of the Joseph story in Genesis 37 forms the basis for the development of a Bible study that stands in a rich tradition of CBS examples that have been developed by the Centre to enable difficult conversations pertaining to gender and sexuality (West and Van der Walt, 2019).

The Eudy Simelane Memorial Lecture

The annual memorial lecture aims to reflect on the life of Eudy Simelane, a young lesbian Banyana-Banyana football player, and the tragic way in which she died, during a brutal homophobic hate crime in her hometown of KwaThema in Gauteng, South Africa.[6] The lecture offers an energy point every year to reflect on Queer lived realities situated in the intersection of sexuality, culture and religion in the South African faith landscape.

Eudy's death on 28 April 2008 sparked a widespread reaction, not only because she was a well-known football star or even because of the brutality of her gang-rape murder, but maybe most poignantly because of the intimacy of the crime. In the 2021 version of the Eudy Simelane Memorial Lecture, zethu Matebeni harrowingly shares some of the intimate details as the assailants recalled some of the final words of recognition spoken by Eudy before she died as she recognized the men who were violating her.[7] Her death, which was the first to be called a 'corrective rape', happened within the intimate landscape of her hometown, a short distance from her home, the police station, the school, and the church where her family worshipped (Doan-Minh, 2020). The murder site has subsequently been developed into a public park that gets tidied once a year for a media event. Visiting the murder site and walking across the little footbridge that activists have built as a symbolic tribute to Eudy, one question has always haunted me: What kind of neighbourhoods or cities are we living in, or have we been part of co-constructing, where this type of brutality can take place within such intimate proximity?

Such questions are of course not only limited to Eudy's death or to the community where this brutal attack occurred, especially if one considers the violence, brutality and dehumanization that take place in our homes, churches and intimate spaces every day in South Africa. This reality came into even sharper focus as GBV and homophobic hate crimes only escalated and became more brutal during the Covid-19 pandemic (Dekel and Abrahams, 2021). Further, the Covid-19 pandemic contributed to the increase in insecurity and vulnerability that LGBTIQA+ people experience. LGBTIQA+ people are vulnerable to intersecting oppressions because of sex, race, class and gender, and as refugees and asylum seekers they were denied access to healthcare. The national government instituted lockdown regulations that placed limitations on the movement of citizens and had major implications for LGBTIQA+ people (Van der Walt and Davids, 2022).

As alluded to earlier, LGBTIQA+ people are often engaged in discourse exclusively focused on violence. Although the dehumanization and brutality often faced by our community are undeniable, in the process of developing the work associated with the Eudy Simelane Memorial Lecture we have aimed to shift the conversation from violent representations of death to remembering in order to inspire reflections on community, agency and life. This finds clear expression in the trajectory of lectures that have taken place since 2016 and that have formed the basis of ongoing reflection (West, Zwane and Van der Walt, 2021).

The first Eudy Simelane Memorial Lecture and Workshop was delivered by former Constitutional Court Judge Edwin Camaron, a person who has been instrumental in the protection of LGBTIQA+ rights in and through the South African Constitution. The convening took place in Pietermaritzburg in April 2016 and was hosted by the Ujamaa Centre, together with The Other Foundation, the Pietermaritzburg Gay & Lesbian Network, the KwaZulu-Natal Christian Council, and the Humanities College of the UKZN. The co-ordinating theme for the lecture and workshop was 'Homophobia & the Churches in Africa: A Dialogue'.

The second Eudy Simelane Memorial Lecture and Workshop took place in Pietermaritzburg in October 2017 and placed more emphasis on working with church leaders. The Revd Smadz Matsepe, who served as the Methodist Minister in KwaThema during Eudy's death and who conducted her funeral, delivered the lecture. Though each lecture and workshop were structured by our See-Judge-Act praxiological process at the Ujamaa Centre, we also structured the Eudy Simelane Memorial Lecture and Workshop series itself using the See-Judge-Act process: 2016 (See), 2017 (Judge), and 2019 (Act). The focus of the first Eudy Simelane Memorial Lecture and Workshop was on 'seeing' the reality of Black lesbians and the focus of the second was on discerning and constructing theological resources with which to 'judge' this reality, building biblical and theological pastoral capacity. The 2019 lecture shifted location from Pietermaritzburg to KwaThema and was set to be delivered by Mama Malley Simelane, Eudy's mother, who had become a brave ally to the LGBTIQA+ community. The thematic focus of the 2019 lecture intended to create space for reflections by parents, families and friends of LGBTIQA+ people and the possibility of accompaniment and care. One week before the lecture, Mama Simelane sadly passed away, and our reflections pertaining to pastoral care, support and accompaniment became tangible as we mourned her passing together at the memorial service arranged in her memory.

Besides the process and knowledge production dimensions of the lectures that have been highlighted above, the lecture convenings annually created space for movement building, networking, support and accompaniment. In 2020, due to the Covid-19 pandemic and the resulting limitations of movement, we were challenged to find an alternative way to create a sense of community and to offer support to so many who were isolated and vulnerable. In 2020 we approached the South African Queer poet and theatre maker Koleka Putuma, quoted in the opening of this chapter, to deliver a digital lecture. The conversation-style lecture was pre-recorded and released during the 16 Days of Activism Campaign engaging GBV in South Africa to focus specific attention on the reality of homophobic hate crimes in the South African context. The 2020 lecture used memory as an entry point to enable reflections on Queer agency, community and life. The lecture reflected not only on Eudy's death but also on her life and asked questions about how this memory of Eudy informs our collective sense of identity and agency. The lecture offered an exploration of counter or alternative narratives to create a balance of stories and memories and, in so doing, illustrated the importance of not only engaging stories of violence or extraordinary stories of triumph, but ordinary stories of the everyday. To capture some of these stories we used the hashtag #RememberEudy for the lecture, and we asked African Queer folk to share their own stories of agency and life on social media if it was safe for them to do so. We produced a T-shirt for the lecture and mailed it to key NGO/civil society partners to distribute among stakeholders. Amid our physical isolation, it was remarkable to see so many #RememberEudy posts or familiar faces wearing the lecture T-shirt in photos posted by LGBTIQA+ people and allies.

Considering the reach, impact and significance of the 2020 digital lecture, we approached Professor zethu Matebeni, the first SARCHI Chair in Sexualities, Genders, and Queer Studies based at the University of Fort Hare in South Africa, to deliver the 2021 digital lecture. The theme for the 2021 lecture was 'Men, Masculinities, and Homophobic Hate Crimes', and aimed to create space to address the under-explored intersection when it comes to addressing homophobic hate crimes.[8] The memory of Eudy's life and death served as an entry point to cultivate greater awareness and understanding, and also to enhance a collective sense of community and to spark an imagination of the possibility of working towards a Queer South Africa.

Since the release, the lectures have taken on a life of their own, and have been used by the Ujamaa Centre and other civil society partners in various change-making initiatives and also as part of the pedagogical offerings within the Gender and Religion Program within the School of Religion, Philosophy and Classics at UKZN. We have found both the provocative digital lectures to be important examples of how one can queer and disrupt normative discourse, understandings and even styles of engagement to create and enhance space to have difficult or uncomfortable conversations pertaining to sexuality and violence.

Where the digital lecture finds its way into private viewing spaces, classrooms, small groups, or even family settings, I now turn my attention to a second conversation-starter intervention aimed at faith communities and those who gather to read the Bible together.

Contextual Bible study on Genesis 37

Rather than shying away from faith leaders and conversations about Sacred Scriptures, which is so often the case among civil society organizations engaging SRHR realities, the Ujamaa Centre develops Contextual Bible Study (CBS) resources in order to enable difficult conversations pertaining to embodiment, gender and sexuality as part of the Body Theology work that we do. Although the back-and-forth quoting of source texts might seem like a dead end in contemporary ethical discussions, the Ujamaa Centre offers a method of engagement that uses the Bible as a dynamic entry point for critical engagements. I will offer some learnings developed from praxis reflection in the process of drawing on the Genesis 37 narrative as a reflective surface in the context of homophobic hate crimes when reading the Joseph story with African LGBTIQA+ people. The story of Joseph in Genesis 37 has become a dynamic spark to enable African LGBTIQA+ people to read the text for themselves. In line with the ideological commitments outlined above we are committed to doing work with and alongside African LGBTIQA+ people (Van der Walt, 2022a). The Genesis 37 CBS, among others, centres on the experiences and interpretative resources of those for whom so-called issues of gender and sexuality are embodied and lived realities every day.

The Genesis 37 CBS process starts with a dynamic embodied engagement with the story as it is acted out by the participants in the reading process. Joseph is singled out by his father Jacob who gives him a coat of many colours. The coat is not the only thing that makes him stand out, as he shares his dreams of greatness with his – less than amused – brothers. Joseph and his embodied difference are the problem in the plot and violence becomes the answer in the narratives unfolding. The nuances and complexities of the narratives become tangible as participants get the opportunity to perform the story and to experience something of the temporal and spatial elements of the plot's unfolding. Joseph's embodied difference and the emotions and corrective behaviour that it invokes are used as entry points to offer a dynamic reflective surface for those who are often excluded and violated because of the difference that is written on the body. The Genesis 37 CBS has become a dynamic tool to encourage and capacitate African LGBTIQA+ people to trust their interpretative resources and challenge normative ideas about who has authority over the text and who gets to say what it means.

The story has become a helpful tool to think about violence aimed at keeping the norm intact and how normative family structures and traditional practices are often co-opted in these normalizing violent technologies. The Genesis 37 CBS follows a sequence of three rounds of questions reflecting on embodied difference, violence and impulses for hope. I will limit my reflections to the first two sets of questions. After a dramatic reading of the text and a basic character and family structure analysis, the first set of questions sets up the conversation by reflecting on how Joseph is set apart in the story. The questions read as follows:

1. Do a dramatic reading of the story. What is this story about?
2. After reading the story together, identify the main characters. Describe the relationship between the different characters. What do we know about the characters mentioned in the story from previous episodes?
3. How is Joseph portrayed in this story?
   (a) How is the relationship between Joseph and his brothers described?
   (b) How is the relationship between Joseph and his father described?
   (c) How would you describe the family dynamic?
4. Joseph is clearly set apart in this story. What contributes to his otherness?
5. Joseph is given a coat of many colours by his father Jacob. The only other biblical reference, in the original Hebrew, to this type of garment is found in 2 Samuel 13.18b and is described in the translation as a coat fit for a princess. How is the coat described in this story and what is the significance of the garment? What feelings does it evoke among the brothers?
6. Read verses 5–10 again. Besides being set apart because of his dress, Joseph is also described in the story as a dreamer. What is the effect of his dreams on his family?

The obvious ways in which Joseph stands out in the story – namely, his dress and dreams – become a clue for exploring more subtle systemic realities that further inform his outsider status. Just like his father, Jacob, who dwelled among the tents, Joseph also does not live up to the masculine ideal. The way in which his brothers respond to him through violent acts often functions as prompts to stimulate contemporary discussions about how boys are treated to 'make men' out of them.

After spending some time reflecting on the ways in which Joseph is set apart in the story, we slow down the reading process to examine the ways in which those closest to Joseph respond to his embodied difference and the systems and tools used to keep the norm intact. It is especially Genesis 37.18–24 that offers a rich and complex reflective surface to enable these conversations. The complexity of the scene is explored by using the following questions:

7 Jacob sends Joseph to his brothers where they are tending the flock in the field. What emotions are evoked when they see him coming from afar and why?
8 Read verses 18–24 together. How do Joseph's brothers respond to his embodied difference?
9 Read verses 10–13 again. What do you think informed Jacob's decision to send Joseph to his brothers in the field?
10 In light of the discussion above, think about your own lived experience.
11 Have you experienced situations where your otherness made you vulnerable or where your identity has been questioned?

Through the implementation of the Genesis 37 Bible study, it has become clear that embodied experiences of difference for LGBTIQA+ people, and the violence that it often evokes, offer a unique interpretative entry point for collective engagement. LGBTIQA+ people recognize themselves, their families and their trauma in the story of Joseph. Just like Joseph is seen from afar, LGBTIQA+ people often experience standing out from the expected norm when difference is written on the body. Joseph is called by a mocking name and violently stripped of his ornate garment, which functions as an identity marker, and banished to an empty cistern separated from his family and community. This depiction of violence is poignantly reminiscent of the experiences of contemporary LGBTIQA+ people in African settings. The most shocking moment of the story is arguably when the brothers sit together to have a meal, an intimate act of community and care, just after violently separating Joseph from themselves. These depictions of violence, however shocking, crack open space for us to think about how acts of normative policing and violence continue to uphold the norm in the communities, churches, schools and families that we belong to, or sometimes only belong to for as long as we toe the line and 'pass' according to the ideals underpinned by the ideology of econo-heteropatriarchy.

Conclusion: Breaking the silence

Amid the #MeToo movement, activist interventions, law-making strategies, enhanced reporting structures and numerous attempts at awareness raising, there is still often a deafening silence when it comes to GBV, a tendency to sweep homophobic hate crimes under the rug. This is, of course, not surprising if one considers the shame, guilt, blame and power imbalances that are so often pervasive when it comes to these realities. However, the only way to talk about these realities is by talking about it, by finding words for the unspeakable, by naming that which remains stuck in our throat. Eudy's death and the stripping of Joseph's personhood because of their embodied difference give us narrative entry points: may we find communities brave enough to risk uncomfortable conversations so that the silence can be broken.

Bibliography

Bosio, Emiliano, 2021, 'Prof. *Yusef Waghid Global Citizenship Education Interview Series with Dr. Emiliano Bosio*', *YouTube*, available at https://youtu.be/jyeMBeKtzCc (accessed 15.12.2023).

Breen, Duncan et al., 2016, 'Hate Crime in Transitional Societies: The Case of South Africa' in Jennifer Schweppe and Mark Austin Walters (eds), *The Globalization of Hate: Internationalizing Hate Crime?*, Oxford: Oxford University Press, pp. 126–41.

Dekel, Bianca, and Naeemah Abrahams, 2021, '"I Will Rather be Killed by Corona than by Him…": Experiences of Abused Women Seeking Shelter during South Africa's COVID-19 lockdown', *PLOS One* 16/10, e0259275, available at https://journals.plos.org/plosone/article?id=10.1371/journal.pone.0259275 (accessed 16.1.2024)

Di Silvio, Lorenzo, 2010, 'Correcting Corrective Rape: Carmichele and Developing South Africa's Affirmative Obligations to Prevent Violence Against Women', *Georgetown Law Journal* 99, pp. 1469–500.

Dlamini, Zamantshali, 2023, 'Buried Alive in the Dungeon – Examining the Patriarchal Language of Religion and how Acts of Faith Inform GBV in Sacred Spaces', *Stellenbosch Theological Journal* 9, 1, pp. 1–22.

Doan-Minh, Sarah, 2019, 'Corrective Rape: An Extreme Manifestation of Discrimination and the State's Complicity in Sexual Violence', *Hastings Women's Law Journal* 30, pp. 167–96.

Du Toit, Louise, 2005, 'A Phenomenology of Rape: Forging a New Vocabulary for Action' in Amanda Gouws (ed.), *(Un)thinking Citizenship: Feminist Debates in Contemporary South Africa*, Lansdowne: University of Cape Town Press, pp. 253–74.

Eslen-Ziya, Hande et al., 2015, 'Equal but Separate? LGBTI Rights in Contemporary South Africa' in Umut Korkut et al. (eds), *Discursive Governance in Politics, Policy, and the Public Sphere*, New York: Palgrave Macmillan, pp. 179–89.

Gevisser, Mark, 2017, *Canaries in the Coal Mines: An Analysis of Spaces for LGBTI Activism in Southern Africa*, Johannesburg: The Other Foundation.

Haddad, Beverley, 2002, 'Gender Violence and HIV/AIDS: A Deadly Silence in the Church', *Journal of Theology for Southern Africa* 114, pp. 93–106.

Halberstam, Jack, 2020, *The Queer Art of Failure*, Durham, NC: Duke University Press.

Human Rights Watch, 2022, 'South Africa: Broken Promises to Aid Gender-Based Violence Survivors', available at https://www.hrw.org/news/2021/11/24/south-africa-broken-promises-aid-gender-based-violence-survivors (accessed 14.02.2022).

Iqual, Roberto, 'Human Rights Watch Asks SA Govt what it's Doing to Stop LGBTIQ Murders', available at https://www.mambaonline.com/2022/01/27/hrw-asks-sa-govt-what-its-doing-to-stop-lgbtiq-murders/ (accessed 27.12.2022).

Jewkes, Rachel, 2002, 'Intimate Partner Violence: Causes and Prevention', *The Lancet* 359 (9315), pp. 1423–9.

Jewkes, Rachel, and Naeema Abrahams, 2002, 'The Epidemiology of Rape and Sexual Coercion in South Africa: An Overview', *Social Science & Medicine* 55/7, pp. 1231–44.

Matebeni, zethu, 2021, Eudy Simelane Memorial Lecture, *YouTube*, available at https://www.youtube.com/watch?v=eh3k6fPwkf8 (accessed 15.12.2023).

Moffett, Helen, 2006, '"These Women, they Force Us to Rape Them": Rape as Narrative of Social Control in Post-Apartheid South Africa', *Journal of Southern African Studies* 32/1, pp. 129–44.

Morissette, Alanis, 2002, *Under Rug Swept*, California: Maverick Recording Company.

Mwambene, Lea, and Maudri Wheal, 2015, 'Realisation or Oversight of a Constitutional Mandate? Corrective Rape of Black African Lesbians in South Africa', *African Human Rights Law Journal* 15/1, pp. 58–88.

Palermo, Tia, Jennifer Bleck and Amber Peterman, 2014, 'Tip of the Iceberg: Reporting and Gender-based Violence in Developing Countries', *American Journal of Epidemiology* 179/5, pp. 602–12.

Phiri, Isabel Apawo, 2001, 'Domestic Violence in Christian Homes: A Durban Case Study', *Journal for the Study of Religion* 14/2, pp. 85–101.

Putuma, Koleka, 2017, *Collective Amnesia*, Cape Town: uHlanga Press.

Putuma, Koleka, 2020, 'Eudy Simelane Memorial Lecture', *YouTube*, available at https://www.youtube.com/watch?v=iuteht-DahA (accessed 15.12.2023).

Putuma, Koleka, 2021, *No Easter Sunday for Queers*, Cape Town: Manyano Media.

Terblanche, Judith, and Charlene van der Walt, 2022, 'Towards Global Citizenship Education in South Africa: Cultivating Deliberative Encounters in the Context of Gender-based Violence' in Emiliano Bosio and Yusef Waghid (eds), *Global Citizenship Education in the Global South*, Amsterdam: Brill, pp. 198–220.

Van der Walt, Charlene, 2021, 'Come On, Come Out, Come Here, Come Here … Queer Expressions of Desire in Genesis 28–31' in L. Juliana Claassens, Christl M. Maier and Funlola O. Olojede (eds), *Transgression and Transformation: Feminist, Postcolonial and Queer Biblical Interpretation as Creative Interventions*, London: Bloomsbury, pp. 145–60.

Van der Walt, Charlene, 2022a, '"The Bra Is Wearing a Skirt!" Queering Joseph in the Quest to Enhance Contextual Ethical Gender and Sexuality Engagements' in Manitza Kotzé, Nadia Marais and Nina Müller van Velden (eds), *Sexual Reformation? Theological and Ethical Reflections on Human Sexuality*, Eugene, OR: Wipf & Stock, pp. 94–109.

Van der Walt, Charlene, 2022b, 'I Won't Behave Myself. I Won't Hate Myself. Harnessing the Multi-coloured Butterfly in Genesis 37 as an *Izitabane* Icon' in Peter-Ben Smit et al. (eds), *Building Bridges Towards a More Humane Society: Explorations in Contextual Biblical Interpretation on the Occasion of the 25th Anniversary of the Bridging Gaps Exchange*, Geneva: Globethics.net Co-Publications & Others, pp. 31–50.

Van der Walt, Charlene, and Hanzline R. Davids, 2022, 'Heteropatriarchy's Blame Game: Reading Genesis 37 with Izitabane during COVID 19', *Old Testament Essays* 35/1, pp. 32–50.

West, Gerald O., 2020, 'A Trans-textual and Trans-sectoral Gender-economic Reading of the Rape of Tamar (2 Sam 13) and the Expropriation of Naboth's Land (1 Kgs 21)' in Jin Young Choi and Joerg Rieger (eds), *Faith, Class, and Labor: Intersectional Approaches in a Global Context*, Eugene, OR: Wipf & Stock, pp. 105–21.

West, Gerald O., and Charlene Van der Walt, 2019, 'A Queer (Beginning to the) Bible', *Concilium* 5, pp. 584–93.

West, Gerald O., Charlene Van der Walt and Kapya John Kaoma, 2016, 'When Faith Does Violence: Reimagining Engagement Between Churches and LGBTI Groups on Homophobia in Africa', *Hervormde Teologiese Studies* 72, pp. 1–8.

West, Gerald O., Zwane Sithembiso and Charlene Van der Walt, 2021, 'From Homosexuality to Hospitality: From Exclusion to Inclusion: From Genesis 19 to Genesis 18', *Journal of Theology for Southern Africa* 168, pp. 5–23.

Notes

1 I thank Koleka Putuma for the permission to cite the poem; it has subsequently been developed into a play; see Koleka Putuma, 2021, *No Easter Sunday for Queers*, Cape Town: Manyano Media.

2 For a definition and more comprehensive engagement with the term, see below.

3 The Ujamaa Centre for Biblical and Theological Community Development and Research is based within the School of Religion, Philosophy and Classics at the University of KwaZulu-Natal (UKZN).

4 The Ujamaa Centre has five key focus areas: (1) Body Theology, which explores issues related to embodiment; (2) Bread Theology, which reflects on socioeconomic issues; (3) Earth Theology, which focuses on environmental justice; (4) People's Theology, which engages community activism; and (5) Public Theology, which reflects on the public role of faith and religion. While Body, Bread and Earth Theology develop work exploring thematic focus areas, People and Public Theology are primarily concerned with methodological issues. The praxis reflections offered in this chapter aim to contribute to ongoing work in the area of Body Theology.

5 The Ujamaa Centre has ongoing partnership relationships with several NGOs or civil society organizations that work towards the protection, inclusion and affirmation of African LGBTIQA+ people in South Africa, but also regionally in

Africa. For more on the Uthingo Network, see https://www.uthingonetwork.org.za/ (accessed 15.12.2023). For more on Inclusive and Affirming Ministries, see https://iam.org.za/. For more on the Global Interfaith Network, see https://gin-ssogie.org/ (accessed 15.12.2023).

6 KwaThema is a township southwest of Springs in the district of Ekurhuleni, Gauteng, South Africa. It was established in 1951 when Africans were forcibly removed from Payneville because it was considered by the apartheid government to be too close to a white town.

7 The 2020 and 2021 versions of the Eudy Simelane Memorial Lecture are available for download and livestreaming at https://www.youtube.com/watch?v=iuteht-DahA and https://www.youtube.com/watch?v=eh3k6fPwkf8 (accessed 15.12.2023).

8 The lecture was again launched during the 16 Days of Activism Campaign and because of a greater possibility for gathering we hosted two watch parties. The first took place in Pietermaritzburg and was co-hosted with Uthingo Network and the second was hosted in Cape Town at the landmark Labia Theatre. The digital lecture and watch parties sparked lively debate and critical conversation.

Index of Scriptures and Other Ancient Sources

Old Testament

Genesis

9	3
12	3
16.30–31	3
17.6–8	38
19	3–4
19.30–38	3–4, 38
19.31–36	38
31.15–18	38
34	3, 54
34.7	88
37	10, 231, 235–7
37.5–10	236
37.10–13	237
37.18–24	237
38	3
39	3

Exodus

1.15—2.10	199
20.14	50

Leviticus

15.19–25	55
18.19	55
18.20	50
20.10	50

Numbers

5.11–31	4
25	7, 29–31, 33–9, 41–3
25.1–3	29
25.4–5	29
25.6	36
25.6–9	30
25.8	30
25.11–13	30
25.12	36
25.14–15	30, 37
25.18	36, 38
31	38
31.15–18	38

Deuteronomy

21.10–13	3
22.22	4
22.25–27	4
22.28–29	4

Judges

10.13	179
10.16	179
19	4, 64, 73, 165
19.23	88
19—21	3, 34

20	64	11.2	50, 55
20.8–10	64	11.3	30
20.48	77	11.4	51-1, 55, 58
20—21	3, 65	11.5	57
21	64–5, 67, 73–7, 114	11.8	55
		11.16	58
21.1	64	11.27	58
21.6	64, 88	11—12	51
21.8	64	12.7–12	50
21.12–15	64	12.20	55
21.19–21	65	12.25	51
21.22	65, 73, 113	13	3, 24, 54
21.23–24	65	13.1–22	208–9, 214, 216–20

1 Samuel

		13.11	216
12.13–14	49	13.12	88, 214–16
16	50	13.13	214–17
16.12	49	13.14	214, 216
16.13	49	13.16	57, 214
16.18	49	13.18	236
16.21	50	13.18–19	21
17.41–51	49	13.19	57, 214
18.1	50	13.20	18, 214
18.6–7	50	13.23–33	214
18.7	49	16.20–23	3
18.20	50	18.33—19.4	217
18.27	49	23.34	50
24.10–15	49		
25	49	*1 Kings*	
27	49	1	52
27.3	49	1.4	52
27.5–6	49	1.13	52
31	39	1.15–21	52
		1.17	52

2 Samuel

		1—2	48, 52, 58
1.26	50	2	52
5.1–5	50	2.22	52
11	3, 48, 52		
11.1	51	*1 Chronicles*	
11.1–5	54	22.9	51

INDEX OF SCRIPTURES AND OTHER ANCIENT SOURCES

Esther
1.1	104
1.3	104
1.4	104
1.5	104
1.9	104
1.10–12	107
1.11	105–6
1.19	109
1.20	113
1–2	104, 106
2.2	106
2.3	106, 116
2.8	116
2.9	117
2.10	108, 117
2.14	110
2.15	117
2.18	117
2.21	117
3.2	108
4.10	117
4.11	108
4.12–14	108
4.16	117
5.2	108
5.3	106
5.6	106

Job
3	219

Psalms
2.11	179
99.2	180
101.23	180

Isaiah
40.3–4	20
44.3–4	20
47.3	3
49.13	20
51.3	20
51.10	24
51.12	20
51.17	22, 24
51.17—52.2	7, 16, 18–22, 24–5
51.18	24
51.18–19	19
51.19	18, 20
51.21	18
51.22	24
51.23	18
52.1	20, 22
52.2	21
54.1	18
54.1–3	20
54.7–8	20
54.8	24
55.12	20

Jeremiah
13.20–27	3
13.26	21
14.12	18
23.9–29	3
24.10	18
29.18	18
31	199, 201
31.15	196, 199, 201
31.31	201
50.41–46	3

Lamentations
1	19
1.21	18
1.6	23
1.14	21
1—2	19, 21

2.1	23	2	92
2.4	23	2.4	89
2.8	23	2.5	88
2.10	21, 23	2.7	21, 88–9
2.13	23	2.8–9	92
4.22	23	2.12	3, 88–9, 92
51.21	18	2.14	88, 93
		2.15	89
Ezekiel		2.16	88, 93
16.37	21	2.16–27	94–5
16.36–42	3	2.18	93
23.9–29	3	2.21–22	93
		11.1	199
Hosea			
1—3	3, 83–5, 91–6	*Nahum*	
1.2	85	3.5–7	3

New Testament

Matthew		6	9, 173
2	195, 197, 200	6.6	178
2.18	10, 192, 196, 199	6.22	178
26.28	201	*1 Corinthians*	
27.26–31	157, 163, 165	4.1	178
27.27	167–8	6.9–10	4
		7	9, 173
Mark		7.22	179
15.15–20	157, 165		
		2 Corinthians	
John		11.23–33	178
8	177		
8.1–11	5	*Galatians*	
		4.19	179
Acts			
12.20–23	158	*Ephesians*	
		6.5–8	182
Romans		6.5–9	176
1.1	178		

Philippians
1.1   178

Colossians
3.22   182
3.22—4.1   176

1 Thessalonians
2.7   179
2.11–12   179

1 Timothy
6.1–2   176

Philemon
1   178
10   179

1 Peter
2.18–21   177
2.18–25   182

Revelations
1.13   177
2   132
2.19–24   4
2.22   4, 177
2.22–23   127
17   133
17.2   177
17.4   177
17.16–17   128, 132
17—18   4, 177
18.3   177

Ancient Texts

Appian
Bella civilia (Civil wars)
1.13   189n18

Historia romana
(Roman history)
7.7.9   189n18

Chariton
Chaereas and Callirhoe 175

Chrysologus 197

Cicero
In Verrem
2.5.169   190n27

Diodorus Siculus
Historical Library
13.58.1–2   189n18
17.35.7   189n18

Herodas
Mimes 5.6   175

Herodotus 165, 177
Histories
8.32–33 189n18

Horace
Satires
1.2.119   175
1.3.80–83   190n26

Josephus 157–61, 163–4, 166, 168–9
Jewish Antiquities
18.129   157

19.343–52	158
19.353–59	159
19.354	160
19.358	158
19.366	169

Juvenal
Satires
6.223	190n26

Livy (Titus Livius) 177, 189n19
History of Rome
(Ab urbe condita)
21.13	189n18
21.57	189n18
22.33.2	190n26
26.13	189n18
29.17	189n18
33.36.3	190n26

Lucian (of Samosata) 162, 179

Amores (Pseudo-Lucian)
11	162
11–19	162
13	162
14	162
15	162
16	162
25	179
27	179

Petronius
Satyricon
53.3	190n26
75.11	175

Photios 164
Codex 238	164

Plutarch
Mulierum virtutes
259–60	189n18

Polybius
Histories
21.38	189n18

Seneca (the Elder)
Controversies	4, 175
Praefatio	10, 175

Sumerian Texts
Enki and Ninḫursaĝa 143–5, 150
Enlil and Ninlil 147–50
Inana and Šukaletuda 145–7, 150

Tacitus
Agricola
15	189n18
31	189n18
Histories	
2.72.1–2	190n27
4.14	189n18

Index of Names and Subjects

Abasili, Alexander 54–5
abduction 65, 194
absence 1, 10, 68, 181, 203, 208, 210–11, 218, 221
abuse 65, 67, 72, 75, 94–5, 158–9, 164–5, 174, 178–9, 214
  domestic 91
  male 24
  of power 56, 78, 94, 198, 220
  of prisoner 158–9, 164
  religious 67, 220
  sexual 3, 9, 53, 67, 164, 174, 180, 182, 221
Adelman, Rachel 23–4
adultery 4–5, 30–1, 34, 48, 50–1, 54, 57–8, 86, 88, 127, 133, 177
  Sotah ritual 4
agency 8, 57–8, 66, 76, 83, 91, 95, 133, 233
  female 16, 75, 94
  Pauline 179
  personal 87
  queer 234
aggression 51, 124, 196, 203, 213
Agrippa, *see* Herod Agrippa
AIDS, *see* HIV/AIDS
Alexander, Jeffrey 95
#AmINext 193
Amnon 21, 24, 57, 211–12, 215, 217
Apartheid 196, 203, 230
  post-apartheid 1

apocalypse 121–4
Arafat, Karim 126, 133
Areias, Anne 105, 109, 114, 118
  The Bachelorette 105, 114, 116
assault 2, 3, 16, 51, 53, 59, 89
  post-assault 132
  physical 176
  sexual 57–8, 87–8, 121–2, 125, 127–8, 131, 133–4, 173, 176–7, 181
Attinger, P. 144–5
  Sumerian tales 144
Atwood, Margaret 87
authority 52, 93, 97, 127, 168, 178–9, 181, 198, 236
autonomy 67, 91, 103, 107, 109, 111, 119, 121

Baal of Peor 29, 34, 36, 38
Babylon 3, 4, 23, 127–8, 132–3, 141, 200
Bach, Alice 74–5
The Bachelor (television) 8, 114, 102, 103, 107–11, 115–18
Bailey, Randall 55, 101, 111, 117–18
Bathsheba 3, 7–8, 48, 50–60, 84
Bat Tzion, *see* Daughter Zion
Beal, Timothy 109
Beard, Mary
  on Aphrodite of Knidos 161, 162
Bell, Stephanie 87

INDEX OF NAMES AND SUBJECTS

betrayal 34, 88, 182
Bird, Phyllis 86
blame 51, 56, 88, 93, 129, 146, 161, 217, 238
  self-blame 23–4, 93, 95, 149
  of victim 63, 78, 89
body
  enslaved 176
  female 4, 34–5, 37, 42, 54–5, 144, 225
  integrity of 36, 90, 197
  male 36, 42
  naked 21, 54–5, 88, 128, 132–3, 161, 164–5
  purity of 43
  social 35, 36
  queer 226, 237
Bosio, Emiliano 231
boundaries 35, 43, 74, 110, 128
  racial 71
Bowins, B. 148, 149
bride 76
  bride-price 73–4
  bride-wealth 74
  captured 77
Brown, Raymond 163
Brueggemann, Walter 193, 203
Burke, Tarana 53, 137n6

Camaron, Judge Edwin 233
Canova, Paola 71
captive 3, 4, 20–1
Care Work: Dreaming Disability Justice (Piepzna-Samarasinha) 22
Caruth, Cathy 90
Cera, Michael
  This Is the End (film) 122–4
chastity 30–1, 114
  unchastity 175
Chilton, Bruce 160–1, 163, 172n6

church 71–2, 96, 164, 192, 200, 219–21, 226, 229, 231–2, 237
  leaders of 233
Ciocca, G. 149

Claassens, L. Juliana 7, 15, 39
class 6, 49, 177–9, 197, 203, 232
  elite 180
  exploitation 39
  marginalized 210
  social 217
  underclass 210
Clines, David 49, 84, 92
Cobb, Kirsi 7–8
coercion 87, 108, 109, 110, 111, 114
Coetzee, J. M. 1–2, 11, 15–17, 19, 27n2, 39
colonization 174, 198, 203
  colonial power 127
  colonized 182
  colonizer 119
  postcolonial 182
complementarianism 70
compliance 87
Connell, Raewyn 8, 48–50, 54, 59, 62n1–2, 195
consent 34, 55–6, 73–4, 76, 101, 103, 112–13, 115, 117–18, 121, 141–2, 144–5, 147, 162, 173, 181
  ambiguous 116
  given 102
  informed 110
  legal 108
  male 114
  negotiating 119
  sexual 8, 54, 101, 107, 111
  women's 107–9
conquest 105, 118, 124–5, 134, 167

INDEX OF NAMES AND SUBJECTS

male 103
military 126
sexual 114, 116, 118–19
contamination 36, 42, 203
Contextual Bible Study (CBS) 10, 209–21, 231, 235–6
control 4–5, 16, 91, 93, 94, 103, 107–9, 111, 114, 118, 124, 134, 174, 197–8, 204
  male 113
  patriarchal 58
  social 173
  uncontrolled 95, 146, 162
Cooper, J. S. 147–8, 154n24
Cozbi 7, 29, 31, 34–5, 37–8, 41–3
Critical Fabulation 8, 76
crucifixion 5, 158, 166, 177–8

Daughter Zion 3, 7, 15–16, 18–25
David 7, 24, 48–59, 213, 217, 222
  adultery with Bathsheba 3, 7–8, 50–1, 55, 57
  daughter, Tamar 3, 23
  Jonathan and 34, 50
Davidson, James 126
Davidson, Steed 6, 7, 8
  'Will You Accept This Rose?' 8, 101–19
death 4, 9, 35–7, 52, 57, 77, 85, 87, 90, 122, 145–6, 157–8, 167, 180, 193, 197–8, 202, 226, 228, 232–4, 238
  heroic 51
  mourning of 51
  shameful 178
  social 174
depression 149
desire 20, 37, 65, 76, 88, 117, 146, 205–6
  desired 91–2, 196, 204

masculine 42
  psychological 149
  sexual 30, 35, 51, 55, 126, 162
Dickson, K. 145
Dinah 3, 24, 88
disability 22, 194, 202–3
domestic violence 94, 198, 203
Douglas, Mary 35
dreams 17, 19, 40, 77, 94, 101, 132, 148, 235–6
Dubrofsky, Rachel 106
Dunbar, Ericka 102, 105
Dworkin, Andrea 7, 32, 35, 37, 39–41, 43, 47n17–18

Emanuel, Sarah 127–8, 134
embodied 198, 220, 227, 229, 235–8
  identities 225
  responses 219
empathy 33, 53
empower 9, 53, 90, 92, 94, 134, 137
  disempower 90, 95
Enki and Ninḫursaĝa 141, 150
Enlil and Ninlil 141, 143, 147–50
#EnoughisEnough 195
Esther 8, 101, 102–19
ethnicity 6, 73, 117
Eudy Simelane Memorial Lecture 10, 231–3
Evans, C. A. 197, 199–200
evil 68, 123, 127, 181, 197
exploitation 194, 210–11, 218
Exum, Cheryl 2, 54–5, 84–5

faith 64, 67–8, 70–1, 76–7, 96, 225–6, 230
  Christian 31
  communities of 10, 227, 229, 231–2

INDEX OF NAMES AND SUBJECTS

faithless 92
 interfaith 228
 leaders of 235
fantasy 35, 103, 115, 117
Farrow, Ronan 53
Faulkner, William 29
fear 4, 19, 57, 71, 77, 90, 115,
 149, 166, 178, 204, 213
feminism 40, 75
feminist 3, 4, 11, 16, 32, 33, 64,
 133, 208
 anti-feminist 131
 challenges 2
 critique 24, 31, 41–2, 214
 interpreters 41, 66
 literature 41
 Midrash 41
 narratives 131
 non-feminist 40
 radical 7
 rewriting 1, 39
 scholars 2, 25, 39, 43, 65
 wisdom 43
Field, Samantha 86–7
Flaubert, Gustave 40
Fontanesi, L. 148, 149
foreignness 4, 124–6, 178–9, 189
forgiveness 71–2, 75, 84
Fox, Michael 104, 106
France, Richard 198–201
Frechette, Christopher 23, 96,
 100n6
Friedman-Rudovsky, Jean 63,
 71–3
Frilingos, Christopher 179
Fricker, Miranda 33–4
Fry, Alexiana 8, 94

Gadotti, A. 142, 153n8, n13,
 154n25, n27, 155n38
Gay, Roxane 123–4

gaze 69
 male 50, 55–6, 106
 reader's 54
gender 3, 5, 6, 8, 32, 60, 71,
 118–19, 127, 141, 174, 176–7,
 191, 198, 200, 203, 220,
 231–2, 234–5
 Christian notions of 122
 equality 230
 gender-play 117
 identity 230
 ideology 214
 imbalance 108
 inequality 196, 229–30
 hierarchy 56–7, 59, 78
 norms 86
 opposite-gender 106
 patterns 180
 practice 49
 relations 56, 59
 theory 193
gender-based violence (GBV) 5–6,
 10, 17–18, 24–5, 192–4, 203,
 205, 229
Global Citizenship Education 231
Global Interfaith Network 228
Goldberg, Evan 121–2, 129, 131,
 132
Goldner, L. 146
Goodwin, Megan 67, 75–6
Graaff, Karen 196
Graves, Robert 157
Graybill, Rhiannon 7, 15, 22–3,
 28n3, 65–6, 76, 103, 108, 121,
 137n4, 189n21
grief 10, 21–2, 24, 66, 78, 194,
 199, 202, 204
guilt 4, 31, 56, 58, 63, 73, 76, 81,
 89, 95–6, 113, 116, 149, 202,
 238

Haag, Pamela 111, 112
Haddad, Beverley 231
Halberstam, Jack 228
Hartman, Saidiya 76, 82n20
hate crime 10, 89, 225, 227, 229–35
healing 16, 20, 22, 25, 91, 94, 203
health 2, 23, 150, 203–4
hegemonic masculinity
  lamenting 204–6
  'not all men' 203–4
  power to build and destroy 198
Heinecken, Lindy 196
Herman, Judith 20, 28n5, 81n14, 90–1, 94–5, 100n5
Herod Agrippa 9, 157–61, 163–4, 166–70
  Berenice, Mariamme and Drusilla 160
  daughters abused after his death 158–61
  mockery 163–6
  threat of Messiah 192, 198–9
  violent acts of 201
Herod the Great 157, 167, 192, 193, 196–7, 204
Hertzberg, H. W. 54
heterosexual 103, 178, 201, 203, 230
Hewitt, Heather 57–8
hierarchical 33, 56, 59–60, 134, 201
  power 69
Higgins, Ryan 214–18
himpathy 33–4, 42
HIV/AIDS 219, 231
Holland, Mary 57–8
Holt, Else 106, 111, 117
homophobia 10, 225, 227, 229–30, 234–5, 238

hooks, bell 204
Hosea and Gomer 199–200
  husband/God metaphor 92
  marriage metaphor 8
  rape of Gomer and 88–9
  Rivers's Redeeming Love and 83–96
  story of 85
  submission to male authority 93–5
Huber, Lynn 128
Huizinga, Johan 102–3, 115–16
Hultin, Jeremy 165
humiliation 18, 20, 159, 177
  private 166
  public 161
  sexual 4, 92, 127
hypersexuality 148–50

identity 75, 86, 95–6, 122, 125, 169, 195, 213, 225, 234, 237
  Gender identity 230
imagination 5, 84, 159, 234
  Apocalyptic 134
  wild female 63–5, 67, 73, 76
indecency 9, 157–69
inequality 33, 35, 196, 229–30
infants 197–8, 201–2
intercourse (sexual) 3–4, 29, 36, 39, 40, 48, 50–1, 55, 57, 112–13, 142, 144–5, 148
  forbidden 4, 36
integrity 203
  bodily 36, 90, 197
intertextuality 11, 22, 178
Israel 34, 50, 58, 64, 86, 95–6, 211, 214–15, 221
  feminized 4
  Israelites 29, 30, 35–6, 38, 49, 74–5, 92, 199–200

INDEX OF NAMES AND SUBJECTS

Jabesh-Gilead 8, 34, 64–5, 75
Jacobs, Dewald 6, 10
Jacobsen, T. 154n22
Jesus 5, 9, 122, 127, 129, 131, 157–9, 163–70, 174, 177, 179–80, 198–202
Jezebel 4, 127–8, 133, 177
Jones, Logan 193, 195, 201, 202, 204
Judea 50, 124, 126–7, 134, 157, 167–8, 197–8
justice 22, 25, 141, 145–7, 202, 231
injustice 33–4, 58, 202, 230

Kantor, Jodi 8, 53–4, 56–7, 59–60
Kelle, Brad 88, 92
Kessel, Alisa 5–6
kidnapping 3, 73
Kirk-Duggan, Cheryl 111
Klangwisan, Yael 41–2
Klassen, Pamela 69, 73, 81n10–11
Klein, Lilian 54, 55
Koenig, Sara 84
Kozlova, Ekaterina 217–18
Kramer, Elise 124
Kreutzer Sonata, The (Lev Nikolaevich Tolstoy) 7, 29–39, 40, 41–3

labour, birth 8, 17
Lacuna (Fiona Snyckers) 1–2, 7, 9–11, 15–17, 19–25, 39, 48, 54, 57, 59, 65, 75, 78, 144, 158, 164, 170, 210
lament 10, 20, 192–6, 199, 200–5, 210, 214–21
Lawrence, D. H. 40
Leick, G. 142, 153n12, 154n23, 155n37

Lenkievicz, Rebecca 53
lesbian 10, 226, 230, 232–3
black 233
Levite 88, 165
Levite's concubine 3, 4, 34, 64, 73
Lev-Wiesel, R. 146
Levy, M. S. 149
Lewis Hall, Elizabeth 159, 193, 195–6, 199, 202, 204–5
LGBTQIA+ 10, 192, 194, 201–2, 227–30, 232–7
Lloyiso, Gijana 192–4, 202, 205
Lopez, Davina 126
Lot 3, 4, 38
love 8, 30, 33, 38–41, 43, 50–1, 68, 78, 90, 114–15, 162, 205, 225, 231
of Christ 83, 91
mutual 93–4
self-sacrificing 91
loyalty 33, 36, 50, 197–8
Luz, Ulrich 163–4, 168, 169

Macchi, Jean-Daniel 104
'*Madoda Sabelani*' (song) 10, 192, 194–6, 199–203, 205
Magic Circle 8, 101–3, 115–17
Maier, Christl 7–8, 18, 23
Maluleke, Tinyiko 196, 200
Mandolfo, Carleen 16, 21, 23, 25
Manne, Kate 33, 46n4, n8
Mans, M. J. 197, 201
Marbury, Herbert 173, 181, 191n46
marriage 30–2, 34, 38, 49, 50, 52, 71, 76, 83, 85, 91–2, 95, 102–3, 106, 111–18, 142
forced 3
marriage-by-capture 73–4
metaphor 4, 8

INDEX OF NAMES AND SUBJECTS

patriarchal 94, 119
  renewal of 93
  traditional 107
Marshall, J. W. 127–8
masculinity 7, 10, 32, 34–5, 48–9, 180, 193, 203, 230
  hegemonic 7, 10, 48–50, 54, 57–9, 192–3, 195–9, 201–5, 230
  toxic 203
  White 106
Masenya, Madipoane 196, 198
Matebeni, zethu 232, 234
Matsepe, Smadz 233
McKenzie, Steven 54
Mead, Rebecca 70
memory 21–6, 28, 48
men see also masculinity; patriarchy
  complementarianism 70
  enslaved 121
  female virginity and 73, 74
  gaze of 55–6
  humiliation 4
  perks and privileges 33
  rape of 75, 131–2
  sexual violence against 4
#Menaretrash 203
Mennonite colony 70–1
Messerschmidt, James 62n1, 195
metaphor 92–3, 127
  bodies 4
  marriage 4, 8
  rape 124
  slave 9, 178–80
  victory 126
  woman 2, 18, 128
#MeToo 48, 53, 57, 59, 123, 238
Mhlangulana, Aphiwe 194
Middleton, Kim 17–18, 27n2
Midianite 7, 29–30, 36–8
Minister, M. Cooper 35

misogyny 31, 33–4, 39, 43
  cultural 40
  literary 41
Moabite 34, 36–8
mocking 9, 157, 165, 237
  of Agrippa 166, 168, 170
  of Jesus 158, 163, 168
Mordechai
  access to king 116
  control of Esther 108, 111, 116–17
  Haman and 117
  owns Esther's sexuality 118–19
  refusal to bow down 108
  trades Esther for power 102
Morrow, W. 143
Mosala, Itumeleng 210–13, 218
Moses 29, 37–8, 199, 200
Mukherjee, Sreyashi 103, 106, 108, 111, 114–15

Nadar, Sarojini 196, 200
narrating 60
  hope 25
  recovery 16, 20, 23, 25
  sexual violence 6, 32, 43, 76
  trauma 16, 20, 29
narrator 20, 22–3, 25, 30, 50–1, 54–6, 58–9, 64, 68–9, 211–12, 215
  unreliable 19, 21
Neely, Winfred 50, 55–6
Neshat, Shirin 166
Nicol, George 55
nudity 55–6, 165

obedience 174
  disobedience 76
O'Brien, Julia 28n7, 94
O'Collins, Gerald 178
O'Connor, Kathleen 23, 95

255

Onstad, Katrina 63, 68, 76
oppression 41, 112, 181–2, 210–11, 218
  oppressive power 48, 213
  oppressor 148

pain 17, 22, 60, 66, 69–70, 90, 143–5, 150, 158, 195, 199, 204
Pajé, Dacia 103, 106, 108, 111, 114–15
Pasqua, Christina 69, 73, 81n10–11
patriarchy 24, 49, 67, 101, 173, 180, 195, 204, 213, 215–17, 229–30
  econo-heteropatriarchy 226, 230–1, 237
  White heteropatriarchy 5
Paul
  Philemon and Onesimus 177
  sexual charged rhetoric 4
  slavery metaphors 173, 178–9, 181–2
Phinehas 29, 30–7, 41–2
Piepzna-Samarasinha, Leah Lakshmi 22
Pilate, Pontius, soldiers of 168
Plaatjies van Huffel, Mary-Anne 192
poetry 6, 10, 210–19, 221
Polley, Sarah 64, 69–70, 72, 76
Poser, Ruth 18, 96
Post Traumatic Stress Disorder (PTSD) 143, 146, 148–9
power 16, 33–5, 39, 43, 48, 50–4, 56–7, 59, 77–8, 84, 91, 94, 102, 104–5, 108, 110, 112, 114, 117, 124, 127–8, 134, 144, 160, 173–5, 178, 195–7, 199, 200, 213–14, 230, 238
  abuse of 198, 220
  colonial 127
  hierarchical 69
  male 103, 117–18, 126, 204
  patriarchal 92
  powerless 87, 95, 180, 211–12
  public 107
  sexual 113, 118
  structures 2, 48, 49
prostitution 85, 86
  Hong Kong sex workers 93
Punt, Jeremy 5, 9
purity 32, 35, 42–3, 71
  culture 89
  ideological 37
  impurity 36
  ritual 56
  sexual 36
Putuma, Koleka 225–7, 234

queer 16, 226–7, 230, 232, 235
  studies 234
  theatre 222
  theory 228

race 6, 106, 109, 197, 203, 210, 232
rape 1–3, 5, 7–8, 15–18, 20–1, 23–4, 31–2, 34, 36, 40–1, 48, 53–4, 57, 59–60, 63, 68–74, 76, 78, 88–9, 108, 121, 123–4, 141–50, 160, 162, 173, 176–7, 182, 192–4, 203, 208, 211–18, 222, 229
  aftermath of 7, 16, 19, 22–3, 25
  biblical 11, 89
  collective (mass) 8, 34, 64, 70–3, 76
  corrective 230, 232
  culture 5–10, 38, 58, 95–6, 121–2, 128, 131, 173–4, 177, 179, 181–2

INDEX OF NAMES AND SUBJECTS

economic 74
gang rape 64, 73, 88, 232
language of 20
jokes 9, 121–4, 132–4
male 4
memory 17, 19
myths 89
narrating 1, 2, 6, 8–11, 15, 18, 25, 32, 43, 51, 58, 101, 141, 143, 150, 210, 214, 216
normalize 5
Rape Awareness South Africa (RASA) 18
scripts 24
stories 2, 7, 16, 22, 76, 121, 209, 217–19
trauma 19, 22, 147
victim of 3, 4, 19, 63, 89, 116, 133, 145–50, 216
reality TV 6, 101–2, 108–10, 114–16, 118–19
 The Bachelor 8, 101, 103–19
 The Bachelorette 105, 114–16
#RememberEudy 234
Richlin, Amy 124, 133, 173, 189n14
Rivers, Francine 8, 83–8, 90–4, 96
Rogen, Seth (*This is the End*) 121–2, 129, 131, 132, 134
Rubin, Gayle 102–3, 112–14

Saint Augustine 68
scapegoat 46n6, 67
Scarry, Elaine 39
Schauenburg, K. 125
Schrader, Maria 8, 53
 She Said (film) 8, 48
Schüssler Fiorenza, Elisabeth 2, 121, 188n13, 208
Scott, James 212–13, 218

Scurlock, J. 142, 154n23, 155n46
sex, *see* intercourse
sexuality 3, 4, 67, 71, 75, 92, 103, 105, 107–8, 111, 113–14, 118–19, 173–4, 176, 203, 227, 230–2, 235
 female 4, 71, 74
 male 105–6, 203, 230
 marital 56
shame 23, 58, 71–2, 74–5, 77, 110, 149, 162, 165–6, 178, 229, 238
Shaner, Katherine 175, 179, 180, 188n11
Sherwood, Yvonne 86, 89, 92, 93
Shore, Emily 89, 91, 94, 96
silence 11, 18, 22, 24, 39, 56–60, 65–6, 68, 73, 75–6, 88, 164, 166, 170, 196, 200, 202–3, 205, 211, 216–17, 229, 231, 238
Simon, G. 146
slavery 121, 173–82, 198
 metaphor 9, 178–9
Smith, Amy 125
Smith-Christopher, Daniel 95–6, 100n3
Snyckers, Fiona (*Lacuna*) 1–2, 7, 10–11, 16–24, 27n2, 39
social media 115–16
Song, Angeline 119
South Africa
 Covid-19 pandemic 232, 234
 gender-based violence 10, 192–206, 202
 historical legacies 203
 homophobic hate crimes 227–38
 'No Easter Sunday for Queers' (Putuma) 225–7
 resistance against violence 193

INDEX OF NAMES AND SUBJECTS

Southwood, Katherine 73–5, 81n17, 82n18
Sternberg, Meir 84
Stiebert, Johanna 89
Stoker, Bram 40
stories and retellings 65, 84, 85–6, 141–50, 175
  critical fabulation 76
  fictional retelling 72–3
  speaking up 57–8
survivor 8, 16, 18–19, 25, 36, 53, 58, 65–6, 69, 71–2, 76, 89–91, 95, 216, 218–21
sympathy 33, 40, 66

Tamar 3, 10, 18, 21, 24, 57, 88, 208–22
This is the End (film) 9, 121, 129, 132, 134
  rape jokes 128–34, 131, 133
Tjemolane, Leballo 194
Toews, Miriam 8, 63–4, 67–70, 72, 75–6
Tolstaya, Alexandra Lvovna 47n16
Tolstaya, Sofiya Andreevna 7, 31–2, 38–43
Tolstoy, Lev Nikolaevich (*The Kreutzer Sonata*) 7, 29, 30–2, 35, 37–41, 43
Tombs, David 5, 9, 128, 177
Townsend, Julie 17–18, 27n2
trauma 1, 10, 18, 37, 41, 57, 66, 75, 83, 87, 90–1, 94–6, 141–3, 146–7, 150, 182, 237
  cultural 23, 95, 96
  generational 203
  narratives 23–5, 30
  recovery from 19, 24, 35, 86
  re-narration of 37–9
  sexual 49, 50, 55, 148, 149

  symptoms of 75, 143, 146, 148, 150, 153n15
  theory 91, 143, 182, 191n45
  traumatic memory 16, 18, 20–2
Trible, Phyllis 2, 10, 12, 65–6, 208–9, 211–13, 218
Twohey, Megan 8, 53–7, 59–60

Ujamaa Centre for Biblical and Theological Community Development and Research, UKZN 10, 208–9, 211, 218, 220, 227–9, 231, 233–5
United Kingdom
  definition of rape 141
United States Department of Justice
  definition of rape 141
Uthingo Network 229

van der Kolk, Bessel 143
van der Walt, Charlene 6, 10
van Dijk-Coombes, Renate Marian 9
Venarchik, Anna 90
Vickroy, Laurie 87
victim *see also* rape
  blaming of 23, 96, 133, 161
  female 43, 56, 89
  male 4, 9, 169
  virgin 65, 147, 148
  non-virgin 38
virginity 64, 65, 73–5, 147, 148
voice 39, 40, 57, 60, 124, 192, 195, 196, 200, 202, 210, 211, 212, 213, 214, 215, 216, 217, 218, 221, 222
  absence of 210–11
  of Daughter Zion's 19
  lamenting 193, 214, 218
  male 175

poetic 10, 209, 221
subaltern 10, 211
women's 217–18

Wagid, Yusef 231
warfare 3, 4, 18, 146
Warren, Meredith 8–9, 173, 177, 180, 189n22–3
Weems, Renita, J. 2, 138
Weinstein, Harvey 8
  complicit assistance 58, 59
  #MeToo movement 53
  implied consent 54–5
  She Said 48
  silence broken 59
  women speaking up 56–8
West, Gerald 6, 10, 226
Westermann, Claus 192–3, 196, 200–1
Wilkinson, Alissa 68, 70

witness 24, 39, 58, 64, 229
  female 38
  prophetic 230
  unreliable 19
women 5–6, 30, 63, 65, 70, 71, 76–8, 109, 127–8, 129–31, 202
  'belong' to men 4
  enslaved 3
  feminine coded good 33
  as gifts 112
  mutual support 76–7
  'provoking' 34–5
  subaltern hearing 210–22
  virginity 73, 74–5
Woolf, Virginia 39

Zeichmann, Christopher 167, 172n14
Zimri 30, 31, 34–7, 41–2

www.ingramcontent.com/pod-product-compliance
Lightning Source LLC
Chambersburg PA
CBHW022044290426
44109CB00014B/974